THE
INSIDERS' GUIDE ®
TO
Greater
Lexington
and the Kentucky Bluegrass

9 780912 367477

TO
Greater
Lexington
and the Kentucky Bluegrass

by
Jeff Walter
and
Ruthie Maslin

The Insiders' Guides, Inc.

Co-published and marketed by:
Lexington Herald-Leader
100 Midland Avenue
Lexington, KY 40508
(606) 231-3100

Co-published and distributed by:
The Insiders' Guides, Inc.
P.O. Box 2057 • Highway 64
Manteo, NC 27954
(919) 473-6100

•

FIRST EDITION
1st printing

•

Copyright ©1994
by the *Lexington Herald-Leader*.

•

Printed in the United States
of America

•

ISBN 0-912367-47-4

Lexington Herald-Leader
Specialty Publications

Manager
Bill Bass

Coordinator
Genie Graf

Assistant Coordinator
Dianna Moyer

•

Independent
Advertising Representative
Glenn Goldstein

•

The Insiders' Guides®, Inc.

Publisher/Managing Editor
Beth P. Storie

President/General Manager
Michael McOwen

Creative Services Director
Mike Lay

Partnership Services Director
Giles Bissonnette

Fulfillment Coordination
Gina Twiford

Distribution Manager
Julie Ross

Controller
Claudette Forney

The University of Kentucky Wildcats play their home games in downtown's Rupp Arena. The arena and adjoining facilities are used for concerts, trade shows and other events.

WHO'S #1 IN LEXINGTON REAL ESTATE?

Bill Skelton thinks **you** *are.*

It's this philosophy that has put Bill Skelton where he is today -- one of Lexington's most successful real estate professionals. By placing the needs of his clients first, Bill works hard to meet those needs.

Isn't that what you hire a Realtor to do?

Bill Skelton

Serious choices demand serious help.

Call Bill today at
(606) 321-SOLD.

Or call toll-free at
1-800-860-7468.

RE/MAX® *Creative Realty*

Table of Contents

Photo: Lexington Herald-Leader

Quilts are popular items at many Central Kentucky antique stores.

Preface

*B*etween them, the authors have lived in the greater Lexington area for more than 20 years. In this time, they have dined in many restaurants; been members of various organizations; attended untold athletic and cultural events; participated in who knows how many activities; traveled the highways, city streets and back roads of this region; interacted with thousands upon thousands of people.

In other words, we have basically done what most people do wherever they might live: We have *lived* here. And, as is the case with so many of us, we have often done these things without giving them a whole lot of thought. You might say we have tended to take it all for granted.

A project such as *The Insiders' Guide to Greater Lexington* is designed to illuminate the reader, to present him or her with information, insight and perhaps a few words of wisdom. We hope that everyone who reads this book will gain a better understanding of the Lexington area and all it has to offer. The pleasant surprise is that this project has also illuminated its writers. Forced to take stock of our own experiences, and do a fair amount of research to supplement our acquired knowledge, we gained a new appreciation for this place we call home.

But a book, however well intentioned and however well researched, cannot do justice to a city such as this. Use it as a guide for further exploration, not as the sole source of your Lexington knowledge. Experience the city and the region for yourself. While we have made every attempt to provide you with accurate and useful information, we cannot pretend to be objective. As an insiders' guide, this book is inherently subjective, filled with our personal observations, tastes and opinions. As a result, you may disagree with parts of it, and that is certainly your right. We welcome your feedback: If you think we've really missed the boat on something, let us know; on the other hand, we're open to fawning praise, too.

Happy reading.

About the Authors

Jeff Walter, a University of Kentucky graduate, has lived in Lexington since 1983. He is a former sportswriter for *The Daily Independent* in Ashland, Kentucky, and was a copy editor for the *Lexington Herald-Leader*. Walter started his own communications business, Vital Communications, in 1991 after seven years with the *Herald-Leader*.

Walter provides advertising, marketing and public relations services for a variety of Central Kentucky companies in fields ranging from construction to manufacturing to retailing. His writing has been honored by the International Association of Business Communicators.

The Insiders' Guide to Greater Lexington is Walter's first book as a credited author, although he has ghostwritten two books and a five-hour audio script on personal and professional development.

In his spare time, he spends time with family and friends, helps coach his son's T-ball team, plays basketball, conducts culinary research on the backyard grill and writes songs.

Walter and his wife, Roberta, an artist and schoolteacher, have rediscovered Lexington from a child's perspective with their son, Reece, who provided key consulting services during the writing of *The Insiders' Guide to Greater Lexington* and is demanding a share of the profits.

A Navy "brat" who has spent the better part of her life on the move, *Ruthie Maslin* adopted Kentucky as her "home state" after living here for the past 12 years. She maintains there is something in the air in Kentucky that makes the state a hard place to leave once you've gotten settled in.

A graduate of the University of Kentucky School of Journalism, Ruthie has worked in a variety of media jobs — everything from editing a local magazine and writing press releases, to writing weekend TV news and editing the "Lifestyles" section of a small daily newspaper.

Since she could never really make up her mind what area of journalism she liked the best, she became a publications and design consultant and now writes whatever anyone will pay her to write. She also works with several local literary programs and is trying to get her first novel published while she is working on her Ph.D.

She figures the more roads you try, the more likely you are to finally find one that actually goes somewhere.

In her spare time, Ruthie likes attending poetry readings, sitting around coffee shops and discussing issues of great societal and philosophical magnitude, cooking, spending time with her family, and traveling the width and breadth of America.

Finding a ticket to see the Wildcats is next to impossible unless you are a student, will pay scalpers' prices or have a great aunt who left her season tickets to you in her will.

Acknowledgments

*I*n addition to his eternally understanding wife, Roberta, and inspiring son, Reece, Jeff Walter would like to thank:

Dr. Thomas D. Clark, Melvin Boyd Cunningham, Toby Kavanaugh and Sonny Wigginton for their gracious cooperation in providing oral histories;

Beth Storie, Genie Graf, Bill Bass and Dianna Moyer for their motivational work as coordinators, editors, fact questioners and paycheck signers;

Jim Niemi and Linda Smith-Niemi for their friendship, emotional support and research assistance;

Adra Brandt for career guidance;

John Bobel, Rob Bolton, Mary Breeding, John Campbell, Marsha Caton, Audrey Companion, Doug Crutcher, Karen Edelstein, Carolyn Edwards, Don Edwards, LuAnn Farrar, Mike Fields, Doug Gibson, Eric Gregory, Tim Haymaker, Al Isaac, Jim Jordan, Eleanor Leonard, Louie Mack, Andy Mead, Ed Moores, Tina Moorhead, Kent Pearson, Georgia Ringo, Dale Sexton, Howard Snyder, Jan Swauger, Martin Taylor, Fred Trogdon, Walter Tunis, Grady Walter, Ted Walter, Vicki Weesner, Linette Wheeler, Deborah Winograd, Dave Winters, the Lexington Public Library, the Greater Lexington Chamber of Commerce and WRFL for assorted insights and factual contributions; Sharon Thompson for sharing her recipes;

And co-author Ruthie Maslin, without whom *The Insiders' Guide to Greater Lexington* would be half the book it is now.

*L*exington has a temperate climate. We usually have mild winters — a few days of snow, a couple of months of freezing temperatures, and then it's spring. But every once in awhile Mother Nature throws us a curve ball, and that's what happened during the final few weeks of finishing this book.

So far, 1994 has brought us lots of snow, freezing rain, and a week or so of sub-zero temperatures. At one point, the Governor of Kentucky closed down all the major highways and interstates for several days.

While this is atypical weather for Central Kentucky, it did serve as a reminder of what being a part of this community really means. Many folks stayed home and enjoyed a little time off with their families. There were also thousands of people stranded on the highways or in area towns. And there were those folks who absolutely had to go out to work or for emergencies, and many of these found themselves stuck on slick roads and in major traffic jams.

It was a tense time, but somehow,

people in Lexington and the surrounding area managed to keep calm and keep a good sense of humor about the situation. Everywhere you looked, cars were being pushed off slick spots in the road, or hauled out of ditches by the friendly folks with four-wheel drives. People donated food and blankets to make-shift shelters for the homeless, as well as for stranded travelers. In the midst of this emergency, a sense of camaraderie and community could be felt throughout Central Kentucky.

In a way, that same kind of effort went into producing this book. A project of this magnitude requires the cooperation of a great many people. While I won't even attempt to list every single person who helped me with my part of this project, there are a few folks I'd like to mention.

First and foremost, I want to thank my family for their patience, prayers, support and help during my harried moments (and there were a few).

There were also many people who gave me information or suggestions for the book, but a few in particular went well beyond the call of duty in this respect, often taking me on tours or doing research on their own about a particular area I was writing about. These include Dean Cornett, Linda Caldwell, Carolyn Bell, Scott Mandl, Randy Patrick, Crystal Wilkinson, Patti DeYoung, Melanie Morguson, Jon Adland (he gets double thanks for help and humor), Tom House and Julian Aurelius.

Finally, I'd like to thank my editors Genie Graf and Beth Storie for their professionalism, good vocabularies, and eye for detail.

Lexington

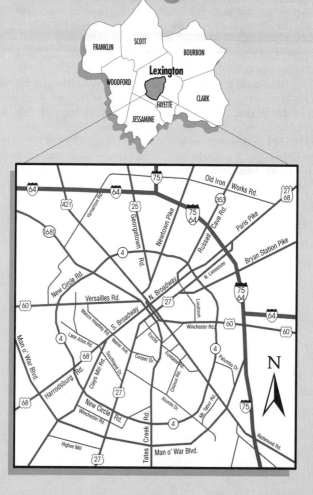

Greater Lexington

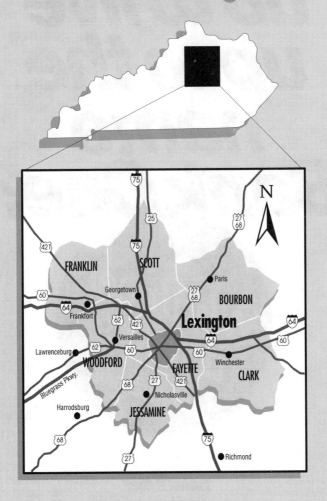

What'll we do to live up to the name Bank One?

Whatever it takes.
Bank One, Lexington, NA
Member FDIC

Inside
Lexington

*L*exington, the county seat of Fayette County in Central Kentucky, lies in the center of the Bluegrass region, a scenic area widely known as the best place in the world to raise thoroughbred horses. And it also happens to be a fine place to raise *families.*

The 1990 U.S. Census showed 225,366 residents of the consolidated Lexington-Fayette Urban County, which covers 280 square miles. The Lexington metropolitan area, which includes the six bordering counties of Bourbon, Clark, Jessamine, Madison, Scott and Woodford, has a total population of 412,019. That makes it the 87th-largest metropolitan area in the nation, according to the U.S. Commerce Department.

Quality, of course, is more important than quantity, and the Lexington area has earned a national reputation for its quality of life. It was no surprise to area residents when a recent book, Lee and Saralee Rosenbergs' *50 Fabulous Places To Raise Your Family*, included Lexington.

The Rosenbergs based their decision on such criteria as accessibility, affordability, climate, crime rates, education quality, ethnic and religious diversity and scenic beauty.

With Louisville to the west and Cincinnati to the north, both of which are roughly 75 miles away, Lexington forms a "Golden Triangle" containing more than one-third of Kentucky's population and more than half of its manufacturing jobs. In recent years, this area has proved attractive to new, expanding and relocating businesses.

The Toyota Camry plant in Georgetown near Lexington is the crown jewel of this Golden Triangle, and it has brought a number of satellite automotive plants to the area.

But just what kind of a place *is* Lexington, really?

Well, the Lexington area is the kind of place a queen might choose to take a vacation from the rigors of royal life. In fact, Queen Elizabeth II has visited the Bluegrass on a number of occasions, and her visits had nothing to do with the castle on U.S. 60. (For more information on the castle, see our chapter on Kid Stuff.)

The area is also fit for a sheik; just ask the four Maktoum brothers, who fly in annually from the independent Arab state of Dubai to buy Kentucky horses and who own several horse farms and horse-related businesses in the Bluegrass. Former President George Bush has frequently visited his close friend Will Farish, a horseman in nearby Woodford County.

Lexington is the kind of place where 18-year-olds from inside and outside the state's borders flock for their college education and then never go home. Instead they stay, find jobs and start new Lexington families. It's where a number of people within large national and multinational corporations reportedly have turned down better-paying transfers because they didn't want to leave their Kentucky homes. People who are born here are likely to grow old here.

Lexington is also the kind of place an outsider can come and quickly have a number of personal stereotypes dispelled. There's no point in trying to hide the fact that a number of incorrect perceptions — some romantic, others demeaning — exist about our fair state. Spend some time in Lexington, Kentucky's second-largest city, and you're likely to make some startling discoveries. For example, we *do* wear shoes, a large number of us are very well educated and most of us in Lexington don't live on farms.

To outsiders, the widespread perception of the Bluegrass region may be one of green, rolling farmland populated with thoroughbreds and surrounded by white plank fences: the postcard version of Lexington. You'll find that scene here, to be sure, although development in recent years has converted large amounts of "green space" into strip malls, office complexes, apartments and townhouses. Lexington still boasts nearly 100 neighborhood and community parks in addition to the beautiful, nearby 1,032-acre Kentucky Horse Park.

But geographically, socially, culturally and economically, Lexington is a lot more diverse than many newcomers expect, and its diversity continues to increase, as a result of both choice and necessity.

Perhaps as a result of Lexington's diversity, some marketing types have gotten the idea that the city is, well, sort of "typical." A 1992 article in *American Demographics* magazine ranked Lexington as the fifth most typical city in the country, after Tulsa, Okla.; Charleston, W.Va.; Midland, Texas; and Springfield, Ill.

This ranking, the article said, was based on Lexington's age and racial makeup and its housing value. According to figures from the 1990 Census, 67.6 percent of Lexington's population is between the ages of 18 and 64, and 84.5 percent is white. The average house was valued at $91,840.

From a marketing standpoint, what these figures basically mean is that Lexington is a good place to test new products. As a marketing executive for Lexington-based Long John Silver's told a *Herald-Leader* reporter, the community "covers the blend from rural to urban. It's not small townish and not big cityish." Lexington "is exceptionally like the United States as a whole," added the editor of *American Demographics*.

We choose to interpret that as meaning we have our fingers on the pulse of America, that we're on the cutting edge. After all, insiders know that, in many other ways, the Lexington area is *anything* but typical. It has its own distinct character — and it has given birth to some distinct characters.

You put us on the map!

You demand easy access to your money. That's why National City Bank has fourteen conveniently located branch offices, plus five additional ATM locations, to serve you. Day or night, rain or shine, look for our bright green signs all around Lexington. Now your money and you can be at the same place at the same time!

National City
Bank

(606) 281-5100

Lexington's skyline is dominated by the blue-haloed Lexington Financial Center.

Lexingtonians have enriched the world in countless ways, including important contributions to the worlds of politics, business and industry, education, medicine, aerospace, art, literature, music and sports.

Probably Lexington's most famous citizen was Henry Clay, the eloquent and passionate statesman who became known as "the Great Compromiser" in the early 1800s and who once told the Senate he would "rather be right than be President." Being right is important to us, and we tend to be passionate in defending our deepest beliefs.

Henry Clay was hardly the only notable personality to emerge from the Lexington area. Another pair of Clays, Cassius Marcellus Clay (Henry's cousin) and his daughter Laura Clay, became widely known for their fiery support of slave emancipation and women's rights, respectively.

Mary Todd, who became Mrs. Abraham Lincoln, was born and reared in Lexington. John Hunt Morgan, whose family moved to Lexington from Alabama when he was five or six, became a Confederate general and the devil-may-care leader of a band of guerrillas known as Morgan's Raiders. Morgan's nephew, Thomas Hunt Morgan, born in Lexington in 1866, won the 1933 Nobel Prize in physiology or medicine for his groundbreaking heredity research.

Many other famous people have been born or reared in Lexington, attended school here or achieved some measure of their fame while living in the area. We are proud — in most cases — to call them sons and daughters of Lexington.

They include James Lane Allen, a best-selling novelist of the late 19th and early 20th centuries; John C. Breckinridge, who served as vice president under Buchanan; brothel owner Belle Brezing, who reportedly was the inspiration for Belle Watling in *Gone With the Wind;* businessman and former governor John Y. Brown Jr. and his wife Phyllis George, a former Miss America and television sportscaster; historian Thomas D. Clark; bluegrass banjo legend J.D. Crowe; painter Henry Faulkner; and Harlan Howard, songwriter of such country hits as "Heartaches by the Number" and "I Fall to Pieces."

Wait! There's more, including Preston and Anita Madden, noted horse farm owners and party hosts; jazz musician Les McCann; author Ed McClanahan; surrealist photographer Ralph Eugene Meatyard; rising young country star John Michael Montgomery; three-time Kentucky Derby winner Isaac Murphy; astronaut Story Musgrave; NBA coach Pat Riley; actor Harry Dean Stanton; novelist Walter Tevis, whose novels *The Hustler* and *The Color of Money* became hit movies; and Jim Varney, a gifted actor (seriously) who nevertheless is best known as the notoriously stupid Ernest P. "Hey Vern!" Worrell of movies and commercials.

Without a doubt, there are others whom we have either mentioned elsewhere in this book or overlooked entirely. And someone is sure to let us know about them.

In many ways, Lexington and its surrounding regions comprise a land rife with contradictions. Perhaps that is to be expected in a border state that couldn't decide, as a whole, which side to fight on during the Civil War.

The state's ambivalence is understandable when you realize that the presidents of both the Union and the Confederacy are native sons, born less than one year and 100 miles apart. Abraham Lincoln was born February 12, 1809, near Hodgenville, about 80 miles southwest of Lexington. During his presidency, he would periodically return with wife Mary to visit his in-laws. Jefferson Davis, Lincoln's adversary during the war, was born June 3, 1808, in Fairview in Todd County, a little farther southwest. Before beginning his military career, Davis spent two years as a student at Lexington's Transylvania University.

Although Union soldiers from Kentucky outnumbered Confederates by a three-to-two margin, downtown Lexington features a statue of John Hunt Morgan atop a stallion. (Over the years, there has been some controversy over the stallion, because Morgan's best-known horse was a mare named Black Bess. Perhaps because of this, a somewhat warped local tradition involves painting bright red a most un-Bess-like portion of the statue stallion's anatomy.)

There are many other examples of Lexington's dual nature:

• While the entire state is generally considered to be in the heart of the Bible Belt, Kentucky has long achieved its reputation in the international marketplace with what some view as vices: bourbon, tobacco and gambling on horses. According to many accounts, bourbon whiskey was invented by a Baptist minister, the Rev. Elijah Craig of nearby Georgetown.

• While Lexington has many of the conveniences and cultural opportunities of a larger metropolitan area — and is within a little more than an hour's drive from both Louisville, west on I-64, and Cincinnati, north on I-75 — you don't have to travel far to "get away from it all" on a quiet country road, nature trail or scenic waterway.

• While the economy was built on agriculture and related fields, the area is home to a number of thriving manufacturing industries that provide everything from automobiles and automotive accessories, air conditioning, computers and textiles to peanut butter and Dixie Cups. Construction, both commercial and residential, also makes a significant contribution to the economy.

• While you can find plenty of eateries serving home-style Kentucky cookin' served up with cheerful Southern hospitality, if you're in a hurry you can also find virtually any kind of fast food you'd want. In fact, Lexington is one of the top fast-food markets in the United States, and several of the nation's leading fast-food chains have headquarters in the state. The city also has its share of upscale gourmet dining establishments.

• And while country and bluegrass are the styles of music most associated with Kentucky, there's also room for alternative, blues, classical, funk, heavy metal, jazz, reggae and rock 'n' roll. A thriving local music scene, supported in large part by college students, complements a fairly steady supply of national acts that appear in local nightclubs as well as in the 23,000-seat Rupp Arena. Lexington also has opera, ballet and a philharmonic orchestra. The other arts are well represented also, with Actors' Guild and several other performing and visual arts organizations.

Lexington's climate is also diverse, sometimes to an extreme. There are definitely four distinct seasons. Summers tend to be hot and humid, and winters can be snowy and numbingly cold (Just ask anyone about the winter of 1993-94). Spring and fall are more moderate, although some springs can be quite rainy.

Through any type of weather, however, the natural beauty of the Bluegrass rises to the forefront. If you've ever seen the first dogwood blooms at the start of a Kentucky spring, driven south on I-75 on a fall weekend when the leaves are turning glorious shades of gold and orange, or stopped along a quiet country road to savor the Christmas-card-like timelessness of a snow-covered horse pasture, you'll understand what we're talking about.

Every winter, regardless of what is happening outside, temperatures around the state rise with the start of basketball season. To thousands of University of Kentucky basketball fans throughout the state, Lexington is the site of Mecca, otherwise known as Rupp Arena, home of the "Big Blue" Wildcats.

Lexington's skyline is dominated by another "Big Blue," the Lexington Financial Center. If you're ever out driving in the area and lose your bearings, simply locate the blue light in the sky; like a beacon, this neon piping along the top of Lexington's tallest building will lead you right back downtown.

As has been the case in many cities across the country, as Lexington has grown outward, and malls and strip shopping centers have proliferated, downtown has suffered. Lexington has taken a number of steps to reverse this trend, with mixed results.

Victorian Square and the Market Place were expensive renovations of

old downtown buildings into modern shopping and restaurant complexes. Although some tenants, including the Lexington Children's Museum in Victorian Square, continue to thrive, others have struggled and closed. A number of downtown storefronts also have remained vacant for years. In October 1993 the historic but decrepit "Ben Snyder block" on Main Street was razed after a prolonged debate. To many Lexingtonians, the buildings had come to symbolize a painful choice — preservation or practicality?— with consequences extending far beyond that one block.

On the other hand, downtown Lexington has Rupp Arena and the adjoining Civic Center complex; three top-quality hotels in the Hyatt Regency, the Radisson Plaza Hotel and the Gratz Park Inn; an elegantly restored 1887 Opera House; a beautiful new five-story library; a new bus station; and three small but scenic parks. It is also the site of the Kentucky

World Trade Center, a relatively new addition created to help in-state businesses grow in the global marketplace.

Tomorrow's business and political leaders can build a solid foundation for successful careers through education in Lexington's public schools, which are among the finest in the state. There are also more than a dozen private schools available, both parochial and independent, in Lexington.

Lexington's public schools, like those elsewhere in the state, are working hard to meet new requirements set forth in the Kentucky Education Reform Act of 1990, a landmark bill intended to balance inequities among the state's richer and poorer school districts. The act, while controversial, has gained national praise and has been called a model for other states.

The University of Kentucky, the state's largest institution of higher learning, has its main campus here. Lexington is the home of

Transylvania University, a small but nationally respected liberal arts college whose precursor was the first institution of higher learning west of the Alleghenies. There are also several business, technical and trade schools within the city.

This brief overview should give you at least an idea of the possibilities that exist for you in Lexington, regardless of how long you plan to stay. The rest of this book will provide more details.

Mark Twain has been quoted as saying something like, "When it's time for me to die, I'm going to move to Kentucky. Everything there happens 20 years later."

Oh, well. That's just one opinion. Only the most thin-skinned of natives could take offense at such a humorous remark. And there is indeed some truth in those words.

Although we have had our share of innovators in fields ranging from diplomacy to the arts to technology (as you'll discover in the course of reading this book), no one is about to confuse Lexington or any other Kentucky town with L.A. or the Big Apple as a leading trend-setter. On the other hand, life is a great deal less hectic here than in those coastal hotbeds. We like it that way.

Photo: Lexington Herald-Leader

After nearly four years of repairs for fire damage, the Kentucky Theatre downtown reopened to a sell-out crowd in 1992.

Whether you're just passing through Lexington, planning a vacation visit here or moving to the area — or even if you're a longtime resident who has purchased this book to find out whether you've been missing anything — just relax, take some time to get to know the people and, above all, enjoy yourself. Lexington will be here for a long, long time.

What we mean when we say 'bluegrass'

Let's talk about bluegrass — all of it.

We realized, in the course of writing this book, that you might be confused about the meaning of the term "bluegrass." That's only natural because, as we are willing to admit, we have been woefully inconsistent in our use of the term. What do we mean when we say "bluegrass"? Well, that just depends.

Throughout this book, we have used the word to denote no fewer than four different meanings. Perhaps these explanations will help put things in context.

Bluegrass, the Grass (poa pratensis)

When you live in Kentucky, there's a good chance that someday, out of the blue, someone from Connecticut or Wyoming or Louisiana will ask you: "Do you really have blue grass in Kentucky?" How you choose to answer this question will depend on your personality, as well as your mood at the time.

If you're not really up to a botanical conversation, you might take the terse-and-true-though-slightly-misleading route and say, "Yes, we do have bluegrass in Kentucky."

If you're a stickler for accuracy, you'll probably give a brief but fact-filled discourse like: "We do have a plant called bluegrass, scientifically known as poa pratensis, but it's really dark green. It does, however, appear to have a bluish tint at certain times, especially in the early morning when the dew is still on the ground. Incidentally, this plant — which thrives on the limestone in Kentucky's soil and has played such a key role in the development of our fine horses and livestock — originated overseas and was brought to North America by English settlers in the first half of the 17th century. It was previously known by such names as 'smooth-stalked meadow grass" and 'white man's foot-grass.'

Or, if you're a sports-minded person (and a smart aleck), you might choose to say: "Yes, which proves that God is a Kentucky Wildcat fan."

"The Bluegrass State"

Because bluegrass adapted so well to Kentucky and so heavily influenced the development of the state's signature animals, the nickname "The Bluegrass State" was almost inevitable. But it's not the only nickname. At various times, Kentucky has also been known as "Land of Tomorrow," "Meadowland" and "Dark and Bloody Ground," all of which have been put forth as possible translations of the Cherokee word that gave the state its name.

Bluegrass, the Region

The term "The Bluegrass," as used to denote one of Kentucky's five primary geographic regions, generally refers to the state's north-central portion, an area of more than 8,000 miles bordered by the Ohio River on the north and west and, on the east and south, by a hilly, rocky, semicircular area known as the Knobs.

The Bluegrass Region, which contains the state's highest concentration of *poa pratensis,* has been the site of much of the early settlement in Kentucky. It includes Louisville and Lexington, the state's two largest cities, as well as the Northern Kentucky area near Cincinnati, and is home to more than one-half of Kentucky's total population.

Kentucky's other regions are the Eastern Coal Field (also known as the Appalachian Plateau or the Cumberland Plateau); the Pennyroyal Region (or "Pennyrile," as many Kentuckians pronounce it); the Western Coal Field; and the Jackson Purchase Region. In addition, the Knobs are considered by some geographers to be a separate region.

At the heart of the Bluegrass Region is the area referred to throughout this book as Greater Lexington.

Bluegrass, the Music

Bluegrass music is a form of country music generally performed on acoustic stringed instruments including the guitar, banjo, upright bass, mandolin, fiddle and dobro. It usually features high-pitched tenor lead vocals and harmonies. This form of music, also sometimes called mountain music or hillbilly music, evolved from a wealth of diverse influences, including folk, Irish and Scottish ballads and reels, blues, jazz and gospel.

Kentucky has given birth to some of the best-known bluegrass musicians in the world, most notably Bill Monroe, whose band the Blue Grass Boys popularized the style in the 1940s.

(For more information on Kentucky musicians, see Music: Past, Present and Future.)

This statue of Confederate Gen. John Hunt Morgan stands in front of the Fayette County Courthouse.

Photo: University of Kentucky Photo Archives

Lexington's Main Street, circa 1915-1920.

Inside
Lexington History

Whiskey, racehorses, and burley tobacco. That's what comes to mind for most folks today when they think about Lexington and the Central Kentucky region.

But Lexington's history is a veritable extravaganza of colorful people, exciting events and bitter controversy.

It all starts about 500 million years ago, when what is now Lexington and the surrounding Bluegrass region were at the bottom of a large, shallow sea. Today, remnants of that ancient ocean survive in the limestone foundation that underlies most of the region.

Some of the area's earliest inhabitants were the Paleoindians. Arrowheads used by this group of people some 10,000 years ago have been found in the Lexington area.

The Adena people inhabited the area from about 1000 B.C. to 1000 A.D. However, by the time European settlers first arrived in the area, there were no longer any permanent Indian settlements. The region was used primarily as a hunting ground for numerous tribes including the Iroquois, Cherokee, Wyandot, Kaskaskia, Chippewa and Shawnee.

The first pioneers to view the area as they trekked inexorably westward were awed by the beauty of the countryside, proclaiming it another Eden. The gently rolling hills and lush vegetation seemed to make it an ideal site for settlement.

In fact, the famous frontiersman Daniel Boone (remember the old TV show?) paved the way for the establishment of the first two permanent settlements in Kentucky just a short distance from Lexington at Harrodsburg to the southwest, and Boonesboro to the southeast. Both of these forts have been reconstructed and thousands of people from across the country visit them each year.

Originally called Masterson's Station, the area was renamed Lexington in 1775 in celebration of the Massachusetts site of the famous Revolutionary War battle. In 1779, Col. Robert Patterson led a group of settlers from Harrodsburg to the Lexington area. They built Fort Lexington to protect themselves from attacks by both the Indians and the British during the Revolutionary War. Fayette County (in which Lexington is located) was formed the following November. In the early 1770s, what is now Kentucky was actually part of Fincastle County, Virginia. It was later divided into Kentucky County, Virginia, out of which Fayette County was formed. The county was named for the famous French General Lafayette. Lexington became an official city in 1782.

During those early years, Lexington was the site for many "firsts" in American history. In 1780, Transylvania Seminary (now Transylvania University) became the first college chartered west of the Alleghenies. 1787 saw the establishment of the first newspaper west of the Alleghenies — *The Kentucky Gazette,* published by Lexingtonian John Bradford. And the first performance in America of a Beethoven symphony took place right here in Lexington in 1817.

The late 18th and early 19th centuries saw Lexington transformed from a crude pioneer settlement into a cultivated center of business, agriculture and the arts. One of the leading agricultural mainstays of that time was the cultivation of hemp and its manufacture into rope and bagging for cotton bales. As recently as World War II, hemp used for rope, twine, burlap and cotton bagging has played a major role in Bluegrass farming. And while it is now illegal to grow or possess hemp (marijuana), it is still widely cultivated in the area.

Among Lexington's preeminent citizens around the turn of the 18th century were the nationally famous portrait painter Matthew Jouett (who did portraits of such famous men as Henry Clay and Gen. Lafayette), noted physician Dr. Samuel Brown (who introduced smallpox vaccination into the region), and the renowned statesman and orator Henry Clay ("The Great Compromiser"), who moved to Lexington in 1797 from his home state of Virginia. Clay's Lexington estate, Ashland, is open to the public for tours.

Lexington was known in those days as "the Athens of the West." It quickly became the state's largest community, as well as a thriving center of commerce and politics. Kentucky's first governor was elected here, and it was also the site of the meeting of the first legislature.

Part of the success and early rapid growth of the city can be attributed to the fact that Lexington was at a sort of crossroads for explorers and travelers. Most Kentucky trails and roads passed near or through the city and, therefore, so did most of the commerce. Lexington's elevated position among Kentucky cities rapidly changed, however, with the invention of the steam engine and the subsequent increase in importance of riverboat commerce with the South. Through the 1820s and 1830s, river cities Louisville and Cincinnati gradually replaced Lexington as the premier regional town.

Although it was no longer the queen city of the frontier, Lexington continued to grow and expand its holdings in the Bluegrass region. Eastern Lunatic Asylum, built in 1824 in Lexington, was one of the first mental hospitals in the country. The 1820s also saw the rise in stature of Lexington's Transylvania University to one of the preeminent universities in the nation with its emphasis on law and medicine. However, public education fell by the wayside during the early years, and the first public schools weren't opened until the 1830s. In 1833, Thomas Barlow and Joseph Burien built the second steam locomotive constructed in the U.S. in Lexington.

It was in 1833 that Lexington suffered a major blow in a cholera epidemic that wiped out nearly 10 percent of the city's population of 6,000. One of the city's greatest unsung heroes emerged during this epidemic. An indentured servant, William "King" Solomon, repeatedly risked his own life and health by burying the numerous dead left by the epidemic.

In the years leading up to the Civil War, Lexington focused its efforts on the building of roads and, later, a railroad to connect the city with Frankfort and Louisville, all in an attempt to maintain its economic competitiveness with the river cities.

Throughout the middle of the 19th century, as in the rest of the country, political tension began building in Lexington, half of whose population was made up of slaves. By the 1850s, Lexington had grown into one of the major slave markets for the region. Some of the most vehement opposition to this mass commerce in human flesh came in the voice of ardent abolitionist Cassius Marcellus Clay, a distant cousin of Henry Clay. Cassius Clay published an antislavery newspaper on Mill Street in Lexington — the *True American* — until it was shut down by local slavery proponents. Clay's paper was surrounded by bitter controversy from the very start. By the time the first issue rolled off the presses in June 1845, Clay was prepared for the worst. The *True American* offices were fortified on the outside with sheet iron, and there were two small brass cannon, as well as an array of other armaments including shotguns and swords, at the ready inside. Clay also rigged an emer-

gency escape route through a trapdoor in the roof and strategically placed powder kegs throughout the establishment so that he could blow up the office if the need arose.

The end of the *True American* did not come violently, however. A vociferous proslavery group of citizens finally succeeded in getting the Lexington Police Court to issue an injunction against Clay and his newspaper, and the offices were shut down just a few months after they opened.

This clash between pro- and antislavery factions was just the beginning of a long and tragic struggle between ideologies that changed the face of Kentucky — and the nation — irrevocably. As a border state, Kentucky was ripped apart, not so much from actual Civil War battles as from the philosophical and political rifts that divided families, friends and business partners. Hundreds of Lexington citizens joined the armies of both the Confederacy and the Union.

While Lexington's most significant military figures were Confederate soldiers — John C. Breckinridge and the famous cavalry raider John Hunt Morgan — the city was occupied by Union troops for much of the war. Many buildings on the Transylvania University campus were used as hospitals for Union troops injured in the fighting.

The issue of slavery and the strong adherence to vastly differing political ideologies factionalized the city during the years surrounding the Civil War. The late 19th century found Lexington, along with the rest of the nation, struggling to heal the rifts that cut deep into the lives of nearly every American.

But time passed, and Lexington continued to grow. The federal land grant provisioned by the Morrill Act enabled the state to found the Agricultural and Mechanical College of Kentucky in 1865. This college would grow into the University of Kentucky.

During this time, the local media experienced a spurt of growth as well. The *Thoroughbred Record Weekly* appeared for the first time in Lexington in 1875. In 1888, the first issue of the *Kentucky Leader* (later the *Lexington Leader*) was published as a Republican newspaper. The *Morning Herald* (later the *Lexington Herald)* was first published in 1896. These two newspapers would combine some 80 years later into the present *Lexington Herald-Leader,* which is owned by the Knight-Ridder Co.

In 1889, the horse- and mule-drawn streetcars that had been used in Lexington since 1882 were replaced by electric streetcars. The 1890s saw tobacco edge out hemp as Kentucky's main cash crop, and Lexington would later become the world's largest burley tobacco market. The Lexington Opera House, still in operation today in its restored state, was built in 1886.

In 1905, Andrew Carnegie donated money to construct an impressive public library in historic Gratz Park. The old library was recently renovated and is now home to the Carnegie Center for Literacy & Learning, which houses such programs as Operation Read and The Writer's Voice of the YMCA of Central Kentucky. It was also around the turn of the century that Lexington's own James Lane Allen became one of the nation's premier novelists.

The late 1800s and early 1900s produced some of Lexington's most colorful and progressive women. In 1881, the famous madam, Belle Brezing, started her first "bawdy house" across the street from the Transylvania University campus. Brezing would continue to operate her "red light" establishments in Lexington until she was forced out of business during World War I. Brezing was the inspiration for the character of Belle Watling in Margaret Mitchell's novel *Gone with the Wind.*

This was also the era of reform, and Lexington women quickly moved to the forefront of the suffragist movement and played important roles in improving conditions for the poor and immigrants. Among these was Laura Clay, daughter of Cassius Clay, who became a national leader on the issue of women's rights. She served as president of the Kentucky Equal Rights Association for 24 years and was also a supporter of the temperance movement.

Sophonisba Preston Breckinridge became the first woman to be admitted to the Kentucky bar, and after practicing law in Lexington, she attended the University of Chicago and became the first woman to earn a Ph.D. in political science. She also served as president of the American Association of Social Work.

Madeline McDowell Breckinridge, the great-granddaughter of Lucretia Hart and Henry Clay, as well as a descendent of Dr. Ephraim McDowell, used her powerful family's position and her natural leadership abilities to force political change. She achieved needed changes in child labor laws, a state juvenile court system, a tuber-

Daniel Boone established one of the first two permanent settlements in Kentucky. Both are near Lexington.

culosis sanitarium, a park system for Lexington, and a playground and model school for poor children.

Despite intense segregation and oppression by such groups as the Ku Klux Klan, Lexington's black community produced many notable artists, doctors and other professionals during the early part of the 20th century. Among these were the sculptor Scott Hathaway, doctors T.T. Wendell and John E. Hunter, and jockey Isaac Murphy. However, lynchings were not uncommon during this period, and a Lexington lynch mob created a national stir in 1920 when it tried to storm the Fayette County Courthouse to lynch Will Lockett, a black man accused of murdering a white girl. Gov. Edwin Morrow sent in state troops to control the mob, and during the ensuing confrontation, the troops fired on the crowd, killing six people and injuring many others.

It was during this time that Lucy Harth Smith was growing up. She would become one of Kentucky's most prominent black leaders. After holding the position of principal of the Booker T. Washington Elementary School, in 1955, she became the only woman ever to serve as president of the Kentucky Negro Education Association.

The economic havoc that the Great Depression wreaked on much of America during the early years of the 20th century left Lexington fairly unscathed. It was during the first decades of the 1900s that the new racetrack was built at Keeneland and the Blue Grass Airport began operations (1942).

Following World War II, Lexington experienced a surge of economic growth in the rapid increase in the number of large companies that moved to the area, including such major firms as Square D, Dixie Cup, and the typewriter division of IBM. Between 1954 and 1963, Lexington's employment grew 260 percent.

Today, Lexington is continually ranked among the best places to live in the United States. It is big enough to provide many of the opportunities and conveniences of major cities, yet is small enough to avoid many of the hassles of big-city living. Because it is situated on I-75, the major north-south interstate corridor in the eastern United States, Lexington always has a lot of interesting activities going on, from big-name rock 'n' roll acts to major sporting events (especially in terms of college basketball and football, as well as PGA tournaments and international equestrian events).

The local thoroughbred industry adds a swash of excitement and elegance to the community, especially around Derby time in May and during the Keeneland sales, when everyone from British royalty to soap opera stars converges on Central Kentucky.

A strong local arts community, a wealth of service, professional, social and civic organizations, and a commitment to preservation of historic structures all add depth to life in Lexington, where the challenge — today as in the past — remains to temper a cultural environment richly steeped in tradition with a strong sense and awareness of the issues facing us as we head into a new century. The challenge is to maintain our historical vision as we peer into a rapidly changing future.

215 Laurel

Insiders' tip from the new Insiders' Guide to Greater Lexington:

Insiders know how to buy their Kentucky Lottery tickets by 11 PM for that night's drawing.

This informative, 500-page guide will give an insider's insight into:

- Lexington and the Bluegrass
- Area history
- Horse industry
- Schools and universities
- Restaurants
- Accommodations   *Insiders Guide*
- Arts   *Lex. Her. Leader*
- Retirement   *100 Midland*
- Kid stuff   *Lex. Hy*
      40508 - 1999
- Shopping   *(606) 231 - 1688 or*
- Day trips   *(800) 274 - 7355*
- and much more!

ordered 4/18/93   CCU check

The Insiders' Guide to Greater Lexington is available at the Herald-Leader, 100 Midland Avenue. You can order by phone or mail in the coupon below.

Dr. Thomas D. Clark: Reflections from Kentucky's historian laureate

*T*hroughout Kentucky and the South — and, indeed, throughout much of the country — the name Thomas D. Clark is synonymous with history. His numerous books have painted affectionate, yet objective, portraits of the South and its institutions.

Dr. Clark, Kentucky's historian laureate, was born in Mississippi in 1903. Lexington has been his permanent home since 1928, although he has taken frequent leaves to study, teach and lecture around the country as well as overseas. He is a graduate of the University of Mississippi with a master's degree in history from the University of Kentucky and a doctorate from Duke. In addition to UK, where he was chairman of the history department and a major force in the establishment of the library's Special Collections, Clark has taught at a number of American universities, including Harvard, Duke, Stanford, North Carolina, Indiana, Tennessee and Rochester. He also has lectured overseas in several countries and at Oxford University.

Insiders' Guide author Jeff Walter spent a little more than an hour visiting with Dr. Clark at his home, which lies on a quiet, well-shaded street in an established and gracious south Lexington neighborhood. The noted historian spoke of Lexington with the intellectual authority of one who has spent his life studying an area, combined with the warmth and conviction of one whose heart belongs to the area.

The first question was, of all the places he might have lived, why did he choose Lexington, Kentucky? For Dr. Thomas D. Clark, it was not a difficult choice.

"I came to Lexington in September 1928 as a graduate student at the University of Kentucky. I came fresh out of the University of Virginia, where I completed my last quarter of course work for my A.B. degree, but really out of Ole Miss, the University of Mississippi. That was quite a contrast, coming in from Charlottesville in Virginia or from the lower South.

"I was impressed by three or four things in this community, which have ever impressed me. One was the fact that this was an old, settled community with two or three layers of distinct history. First it was a major pioneering town, and my primary academic interest was in the

Photo: Lexington Herald-Leader

Dr. Thomas D. Clark, Kentucky's historian laureate, is shown here during a visit to Shakertown.

Western movement. There are not many places any better than Lexington, Kentucky, to launch a study of the Western movement because you're right in the middle of the old pioneer movement and you're right on the edge leading out to the expanded Western front.

"I like the people here. It took me some time to get used to them, but once I did become acquainted with them, I developed a real fondness for both the Central and Eastern Kentuckians. And by that, I don't mean to slight the Western Kentuckian, either, but they are three different breeds. And the reason I mentioned the Bluegrass and Eastern Kentucky is that so much of Eastern Kentucky has fed into this community and given it a distinct flavor. And given it a leadership quality, in many cases.

"I liked the fact that the institutions had some age on them. Take Transylvania University, for instance, or the Lexington Public Library. The main street of the town itself. In my early days of living in Lexington, Main Street was a very fascinating place to be. You could walk down Main Street in those days and see people all along that you knew. You got acquainted with business people. It was really a rural courthouse town with a lot of sophistication about it, because of its institutions, because of its tremendously prestigious legal bar and because of its educational centering in the state. All of those things attracted me to this region.

"The economy has ever been a fascinating fact. I still get a real deep nostalgic tingle when tobacco turns that golden color and you cut tobacco. You know you're really going from one season to the other. And whatever may be the harmful effects of tobacco, a field of golden burley is a very attractive thing indeed.

"I didn't know very much about the horse industry, almost nothing. But there was a world that lent a certain amount of glamour to the region, in two forms. First in the sporting nature of a lot of the people here, and the fact that the horse farmers preserved islands of beauty. Those things were very attractive.

"I'd have to say that, in my long years here in Lexington, my association with the University of Kentucky was a warm and affectionate affair. It still is, although I've been retired from that faculty over 20 years. The University of Kentucky was a warm, family community when I joined the faculty here. It was a place where you developed a lot of close friends on the faculty. You had a lot of social intercourse with them. We knew a lot about one another's families and the faculty children. And we obviously knew a lot about the fortunes and travails of the university itself.

"Thank goodness I've lived long enough to see the development of a very fine library with a wonderful facility — Special Collections — in the university. It's a thing that's very attractive to a scholar, and it's very necessary to him, and it's a thing that ties you very tightly to the university.

"It's hard for me to define, but there was an air of independence here, which I found very attractive. But no matter how independent these Central Kentuckians may appear, there's always, back of it, a warm, human spirit.

Lexington's busy Main Street, circa 1938

"I had opportunities to leave this community on three or four different occasions — very attractive offers from other universities. And I remained here because I did like the community. My children grew up here and went to school here. They later went to college elsewhere, for the simple reason that I wanted to get them away from simply living their whole life in one groove. My daughter lives in Bowling Green now, but my son and my grandchildren still live here in Lexington.

"This is a good home town for people to grow up in. I couldn't think of a more attractive place to live anywhere if you want a quiet, secure, family place.

"I also admire this community for the many cultural advantages that it's offered. I'm not a musician, but over the years it has brought here a lot of musical talent. It has developed a lot of writing talent. And these Kentucky authors have made major contributions, and still are, to the culture and life of this region. For instance, you have writers who, although they don't live in this community, have at the same time been an integral part of it.

"Wendell Berry, for instance, whose father- and mother-in-law live here in town, and who's taught at the University of Kentucky. Wendell is about as much a part of this community as he is over in Henry County. There's Bobbie Ann Mason, over in Anderson County. But she's here all the time. She's a graduate of the university; Wendell's a graduate of the university. They're centered here.

"Looking back, the most precious thing to me about this community in my experience has been the students I had. I have great affection for those students. I see them now, and they're grown into gray-haired men and women. There's a lot of attachment there, and that's a very precious thing to have.

"This has never been a community for the average individual to get rich in," Clark said with a laugh. "It's been a hometown community where you've made a living but there was no real means for most people to accumulate wealth. I never desired to do that. But it's been a town where, in the early days, you could go to the bank and they knew who you were, and if you wanted to borrow some money, they didn't have to ask any questions about you. They already knew about you. It's a town where, in the early days, you'd go to see your doctor and he most likely was a good friend of yours. Even if he wasn't, you saw him at a great many social affairs.

"I want to emphasize my service in the university, which is the very heart of this community. Whatever may come here and whatever may develop, the university is the throbbing heart of this community and for its students. Not only has the university generated within the community a very rich cultural dynamics, but think of the people who have come here to the university and have remained in the community and given it leadership. The community has fed heavily on the university.

"Lexington, going all the way back in its history to Dr. Sam Brown and the Transylvania University medical faculty, has been an important medical center. You can feel pretty secure health-wise and medical service-wise because of the very ample medical facilities here. Hospitals, doctors, a very good sprinkling of specialists in many areas. You can find about any medical service here that you would need, outside of some very major things for which they might send you to some specialist outside. That is added security to a community.

"Despite the history of segregation and the troubles that the community is having right now racially, I've always found a lot of harmony here among the races. In the field of religion, this is a highly 'church' community. But it sometimes can be pretty casual about its religion. You will have a rushing through the Sunday morning service so that the congregation can get to a basketball game," Clark said with a laugh. "I'm not a basketball fan; I couldn't care less about basketball. But, lord oh lord, it's a religion!

"I come from a rural, agrarian background, and I've always appreciated the rich mix of urban agrarianism that has prevailed in this community. I can't think of any place in the United States where the country immediately surrounding the urban area is so attractive as here. That's not only on the face of the land itself, but it's in the folk mores of the people and, really, in the setting down of roots in the region. It has been a very rich rooting experience throughout all of its history, a very intimate association between people and the land, whether they own any of the land or not. I like the agrarian *flavor* of the region.

"I can't say much for the climate. The climate is unpredictable. There are some very delightful months in the year here in Kentucky. For instance, there's a letter in the door there to a brother of mine down in Texas in which I told him that I'm sure we're going to have a wonderful color this fall because of the heavy foliage that we have. That adds to the attraction, the changing seasons here. Once you get used to it, they don't bother you.

"When I look back at the friends I've had here, I cannot think of any place where one could have a better heartwarming friendship with people. In the past, I've known the newspaper people here. Living next door to me was Bud Guthrie, who wrote the Pulitzer Prize-

Photo: Lexington Herald-Leader

Dr. Thomas D. Clark holds an American Indian ceremonial ax presented to him by the Board of Directors of the Henry Clay Memorial Foundation. Clark was the first recipient of the award. The ax was found in the attic of Ashland, Clay's home, during its renovation and dates to 2,000 B.C.-5,000 B.C.

winning novel *The Way West* and wrote *The Big Sky*. And my association with authors in this community and in this state has been a real heartthrob for me.

"And finally, Lexington is centrally located to Kentucky, and it's also centrally located to much of the nation itself. The rest of the country is easily accessible to this community.

"That's why I like living here."

Yet, despite his deep love for the Bluegrass, Clark has written frankly and extensively about the past and present problems of the city and the state. He has never felt the urge to sugarcoat those aspects — such as slavery, Appalachian poverty and the narrow-mindedness of some people — that might cast an unfavorable light on the region.

"I am a historian, and I try to be objective," he said. "This community doesn't *need* sugarcoating. It's mature enough, old enough, settled enough that it can take objective facts about Kentucky and the Lexington community. Lexington has a lot of warts, always has had, and the warts come along with the jewels. I've tried always to be objective. I've never had any impulse to be otherwise. A historian shouldn't get into the business of subjectivity.

"I've enjoyed writing about Kentucky. I've gotten a big thrill out of it. This last book of mine, *The Voice of the Frontier*, which was an editing job — I relished every moment that I worked on that. And *Kentucky: Land of Contrast*, my history of *Kentucky; Bluegrass Cavalcade; Rampaging Frontier* — those books I thoroughly enjoyed doing, but I also profited from the availability of rich materials here in this community."

A moment later, Clark returned to the subject of Lexington's rich heritage: "jewels," "warts" and all.

"I've known people — lawyers, doctors, sons of bitches, the whole crowd. When I walk down Main Street now, I try to visualize, for instance, the days when slaves were sold on the courthouse square, or when Abraham Lincoln might have walked up that main street, certainly when Henry Clay drove up and down that street, or when John C. Breckinridge or Cassius M. Clay or Isaac Shelby came here to organize the state government. You can just go on and on endlessly. When James Lane Allen was writing about this region. . . .

"Just think of going over the crossing of Limestone and Main streets. There was a great flow of people who came here, pioneers who came into this region. Just think, up and down that main street, how many people of prominence have traveled. There have been few towns in the United States of this size visited by as many prominent people as this town. And you try to visualize all that pageantry of human beings. And then think of all of the less-important folks who, for the first time, had come to something approaching a city, and they walked up and down that main street. It's been a mecca for a world of people and for young men and young women setting out on careers.

"They come through the universities — Transylvania and the University of Kentucky. I try to think of men like Dr. Frank L. McVey riding down Main Street. He was a tremendously important man in this town. . . . There was Charlie Staples, who loved this town as few people have ever loved it, who wrote the book called *Pioneer Lexington* and who made that card index in the Lexington Public Library. And then just imagine the authors James Lane Allen and John Fox Jr. Later on there were other authors who traveled this way, including Bud Guthrie, who worked in the heart of the town.

"And then think of the characters like Eddie Young, a bum who frequented the heartland of the city. Or the old character called Long John, who walked around here in a stovepipe hat. Or that little dog, Smiley Pete, that hung around the corner. Or Sweet Evening Breeze, who breezed through Main Street. Think of all the visitors who came to the Phoenix Hotel and the Lafayette Hotel, that wonderful dining room at the Lafayette Hotel. All of those things added to the richness of life in this community."

While Clark still sees evidence of the pioneer spirit in some areas of modern-day Lexington, he thinks more of it is needed.

"There's one area in which we need it very much right now, and that's in the field of education. The Kentucky Education Reform Act must not fail. It must not fail. . . .

"This pioneering challenge is here in the area of finding new economic missions. This is what we're doing, I think, to a very large extent. This community is becoming rapidly industrialized, and it's on a new frontier of service. A lot of service areas, like hospitals and educational institutions. A lot of this manufacturing area is service industry. It's on the cutting edge of environmental improvement. It must do some pioneering in diversifying its agriculture, with the tobacco business sagging as it has.

"And it has some challenges in the racial field and in the field of planning. What this community is going to be about in the next couple of decades — is it going to be just an old frontier community scattering itself all over creation without planning and regulation? Or is it going to make up for some past mistakes by careful planning and careful determination where the community is going?

"At the same time, I think the community is pioneering in a good many aspects of its life. This is a much more cultivated community than it once was. It's more sophisticated, and certainly it has become more cosmopolitan, with Toyota and other industries coming here. IBM brought a tremendous influx of new blood to the community.

"Geographically, historically, sociologically, financially — you can measure it by any criteria you want to measure it by — this is a central nerve center for not only Kentucky but for most of this Ohio Valley region. Just think what happens here. You've got two major highways, I-64 and I-75, going through, plus some secondary roads. But one of the biggest assets and one of the biggest liabilities this community has is I-75.

"The asset is it puts this community in direct communication with the Great Lakes frontier and with the rising industrial South. I-64 does it to a lesser extent (east-west). The liability is that an awful lot of undesirable elements drift into this community — the drug trade, for instance. And I-75 is a highway lined with wreckage. The other day I drove my farm truck up to some land I have in Eastern Kentucky. I think I saw two wrecks between here and Richmond. That's a liability. But, nevertheless, it puts you in easy touch with the nation itself."

Asked to offer his views of Lexington's future, Clark did so after expressing some reluctance. "I'm a historian, not a prophet. . . . I simply don't know, obviously. I wouldn't be sitting here," he said with a laugh.

"I'm just going to make a guess. I'd say its future lies more in the service and industrial areas. Its future is going to depend less and less on tobacco. I think that's pretty obvious. Its future is going to depend more and more upon effective, efficient transportation.

"How well it protects its environment and, tremendously important, how well it's able to protect its water resource. This is a town that could face a disaster readily if this river in any way failed. I saw that happen in 1931 . . . it's had periods in the past, too. Water has ever been a problem here in this Bluegrass country. And the Kentucky River at the moment is as vital as a main artery in the human system. If they ever tap the Ohio River, that will lessen the strain, but they haven't tapped the Ohio River. That's going to be important in the future. Does it have the water capacity to grow?

"I think the future of this town will depend on how well this merged county-city government operates. If it shows the same dynamic development it has in the past, then it's going to do well.

"And, above all, this community must harmonize its racial relations.

"I'm sure I should be guessing about other things, but those seem to be all right off the top of my mind."

Inside
Lexington's Neighbors

Lexington has good neighbors, and these communities continue to grow closer together into an area that is increasingly recognized for its productivity as well as its natural beauty, friendly hospitality and all-around livability. Residents of Lexington's neighboring communities enjoy the benefits of city life along with a small-town atmosphere.

"Greater Lexington," or the Lexington metropolitan statistical area, consists of Fayette County and six adjoining counties: Bourbon, Clark and Madison to the east and, to the west, Scott, Woodford and Jessamine. Most of Scott County is actually north of Fayette County, while most of Madison is south of Fayette.

We have also included Franklin County, which includes the capital city of Frankfort, in this chapter because of its proximity and because, after all, it is the capital. Just be aware that Franklin County's population is not included in the figures for the Lexington metropolitan statistical area, or "MSA," as certain bureaucratic types are prone to say.

The sequence of the county overviews in this chapter is as follows: Madison, Jessamine, Woodford, Franklin, Scott, Bourbon and Clark. We arrived at this order by starting with Madison County, the largest of the six, and then proceeding clockwise around Fayette County, which lies at the center.

Fayette County and its six neighbors share similar histories, cultures and economies. In general, what's good for one community is good for the others through a positive domino effect. A new manufacturing plant in Winchester, for example, will employ a number of Lexingtonians. Thousands of people commute to work from one county to another in the Bluegrass. Many Lexington workers even live outside the metropolitan area and drive an hour or more one way to get to and from their jobs. Those who do so insist that it's not nearly as tiresome as it might seem. In a big city like New York or Chicago, it can take an hour just to get from one side of town to another. In the Bluegrass, you're at least going to see some pretty scenery during your commute.

Making phone calls within the metropolitan area can be tricky if you're not sure which calls are local and which are long distance. In listing phone numbers, we have taken a "Lexocentric" approach toward phone numbers, listing them the way you would dial them if calling from Lexington. A number listed with a (502) area code is a long-distance call from Lexington; a number listed with a 1- preceding it is in the (606) area code but is still long distance. Confused? For a more detailed explanation, see Getting Around.

This chapter features some of the places and events of interest in each county. Other more prominent ones may be found in our chapter on Central Kentucky Annual Events and Festivals.

Madison County — Richmond and Berea

OK, time for a quiz. What do all of the following have in common: one of the nation's first pioneer settlements, the country mansion of an explosive and outspoken 19th-century abolitionist, the site of a famous Civil War battle, and the oldest working pottery west of the Alleghenies?

If you don't know the answer, you should take a half-hour drive south from Lexington on I-75 to Madison County (the location of all the above-mentioned points of interest) where you can find the historic and picturesque towns of Richmond (in the northern part of the county) and Berea (in the southern part).

As Lexington's most immediate south-east neighbors, Richmond and Berea are a pleasant mix of the excitement of the city and the peacefulness and beauty of the foothills of the Appalachian Mountains. While much of the county is agricultural, Richmond and Berea are both college towns with thriving business and industrial bases.

Madison County has about 56,000

residents. It is home to two major institutions of higher learning — Eastern Kentucky University in Richmond, and Berea College. Madison County farmers produce some 11 million pounds of tobacco and raise about 64,000 head of cattle each year on the more than 245,000 acres of farmland in the county.

While agriculture service industry forms the backbone of much of the local economy, an increasing industrial base is transforming the Madison County work force. More than a dozen industries with over 100 employees now call Madison County home.

The growing industrial base includes several automotive products manufacturers, such as Motor Wheel (semi-truck hubs and brake drums), Sherwin Williams Co. (automotive coatings), Irvin Automotive Products (metal stamping), and Tokiko Manufacturing (shock absorbers for the Ford Motor Co.), which aligns nicely with the Toyota plant just outside of Lexington to the north.

Other major Madison County industries include Ajax Magnathermic Corp. (induction heating and melting equipment, industrial and gas dryers), Alcan Aluminum (recycling), Dresser Industries Inc. (pressure gauges), Electronic Assembly Inc. (electronic subassemblies), Exide Industrial (industrial batteries), Gibson Greeting Card Inc., Hyster Co. (forklifts), Continental Metal Stamping (metal stamping assemblies, tool & dies), Philips Lighting Co. (miniature, halogen and automotive lamps), Parker Seal Co. (O-ring and shaped seal parts), and Yuasa Exide Inc. (electrical insulated underground wire and cable).

Photo: Lexington Herald-Leader

Visitors to Fort Boonesborough can watch a blacksmith at work.

Madison County and its two main cities of Richmond and Berea really offer the best of both worlds. With Lexington just a half-hour to the north, Knoxville two hours to the south, and Cincinnati and Louisville within a couple hours' drive, Madison Countians can take advantage of all the best parts of big city living and still be able to return to the quiet beauty of home.

Madison Countians take a great pride in their rich history and tradition. Indigenous arts and crafts produced and marketed in Berea, preserving the fine old traditions of mountain handiwork, are a big drawing card for the nearly 250,000 visitors who come each year to the quiet, rustic town located in the foothills of the Appalachian Mountains.

Founded in the mid-1800s by Rev. John G. Fee and named after the New Testament town where people "received the Word with all readiness of mind," Berea is home to more than 46 arts and crafts galleries, studios and workshops. It is designated the "Folk Arts & Crafts Capital of Kentucky," and many of the finest regional and national artists and craftspeople display their works at three major arts and crafts fairs held at Berea's Indian Fort Theatre in May, July and October. Berea College, which was founded in 1855 as the first interracial college in the South, is also located here.

Madison County is filled with many well-preserved examples of period architecture, not to mention a reconstructed fort of frontiersman Daniel Boone. In addition, one of the major battles fought in Kentucky during the Civil War — the Battle of Richmond — is re-enacted in Richmond every August.

Established by the Virginia Legislature in 1785 (before Kentucky became a state), Madison County is Kentucky's seventh oldest county and the largest county in Central Kentucky (446 square miles). It was named after James Madison, the fourth president of the U.S.

Throughout its 200-year history, Madison County has been home to both the famous and the infamous.

Perhaps the area's most famous resident was also one of its earliest — Daniel Boone.

Boone and his company of pioneers reached the Kentucky River on April 1, 1775, and began building Kentucky's second settlement, Fort Boonesborough, located in what is now the northeastern corner of Madison County. Boone's fort has been reconstructed as a working fort open to the public, featuring blockhouses, cabins, and period furnishings. Resident artists offer pioneer craft demonstrations using antique tools from the 18th century.

A little over a quarter of a century after Boone established his frontier settlements in Kentucky, Madison County received a unique Christmas gift in the form of Christopher "Kit" Carson who would grow up to become one of the nation's most famous hunters, pathfinders and soldiers. Kit Carson was born Dec. 24, 1809, on Tates Creek Pike just three miles from Richmond.

In the northern part of Madison County you can still tour the mansion of famous abolitionist and Kentucky statesman Cassius Marcellus Clay, cousin of Lexington's Henry

Clay, "The Great Compromiser." Cassius Clay was one of Kentucky's most colorful historical figures. Known as "The Lion of White Hall" (White Hall is the name of his mansion), Clay was a noted abolitionist, politician, publisher, U.S. minister to Russia, and friend to Abraham Lincoln. He was also instrumental in the founding of Berea College.

In more recent history, baseball Hall of Famer Earle Combs attended Eastern Kentucky University in Richmond before going on to play alongside Babe Ruth for the New York Yankees where he led the American League in at-bats (648), hits (231), and in triples in 1927, 1928 and 1930. A debilitating car wreck in 1934 cut short his career as a player, but Combs went on to coach the Yankees, St. Louis Browns, Boston Red Sox, and the Philadelphia Phillies. After retiring to a small community in southern Madison County — Paint Lick — he died in 1976 and was buried in the Richmond Cemetery.

As the largest county in the Bluegrass, Madison County is, needless to say, chock full of great and interesting places to visit. It's impossible to detail them all, but the following are some of the high points. When visiting the area, be sure to check out Richmond's historic downtown walking tour which showcases some of the most beautiful historic architecture in the area. Information on this is available by calling the Richmond Tourism Commission at 1-623-1000, ext. 210.

You will also want to spend at least a day in Berea checking the numerous arts and crafts studios and shops as well as the dozens of great antique shops, which are filled with lots of great stuff.

Places of Interest

FORT BOONESBOROUGH STATE PARK
Ky 627   *1-527-3131*

In addition to its historical significance as Kentucky's second settlement, built by Daniel Boone and his company of explorers in 1775, Fort Boonesborough is a popular recreational tourist spot, attracting thousands of visitors each year in its role as part of the Kentucky State Parks system.

A new public swimming pool is the latest addition to the park's camping and visitor facilities, which include 167 camping sites with electricity and water hook-ups (as well as primitive sites), tours of the reconstructed fort and museum, boating and fishing on the adjacent Kentucky River, an 18-hole miniature golf course, picnic areas and playgrounds.

To get to Fort Boonesborough, take the Winchester exit off I-64 or exit 95 off I-75.

BYBEE POTTERY

Ky 52 (Irvine Road)   *1-369-5350*

The Cornelison family has been making pottery at this site, which is the oldest existing pottery west of the Alleghenies, since 1845. Bybee Pottery, located nine miles east of Richmond, is one of those don't-miss-it-or-you'll-really-regret-it experiences that even native Madison Countians never seem to tire of. And it's hard to explain exactly why. The building itself is a place you would likely overlook just driving by. And it's not a big operation.

But, there's just something incredibly appealing about the approximately 125,000 pieces of primitive pottery produced from native clay at Bybee Pottery each year that keeps collectors flocking back for more. Admission to the pottery, which is open Monday through Friday from 8 AM-noon and 12:30-4 PM, is free. But unless you get there long before the doors open at 8 AM on Monday, Wednesday and Friday, don't count on getting much pottery. Those are the days the family stocks the shelves, and die-hard Bybee buffs gather before dawn, rain, snow or sleet, to stake out a place in the lines that form at the front and back doors of the pottery. When the doors open, it's every person for herself, with the showroom usually cleared in 10-15 minutes.

To get to Bybee Pottery, take Exit 87 off I-75 into Richmond. Follow the road you are on when you get off the interstate until it intersects Ky 52 (Irvine Road). Turn right. The Bybee Pottery turn-off is about 9 miles from town on the left.

BEREA COLLEGE
APPALACHIAN MUSEUM

Jackson Street   *1-986-9341, ext. 6078*

For anyone even remotely interested in the history of the Appalachian Mountain region, the Berea College Appalachian Museum is a gem of a small museum. Featuring exhibits depicting Appalachian life as far back as the 1800s, the Appalachian Museum also has many audiovisual displays showing traditional crafts being made by contemporary mountain artists. Area folk artists and craftspeople are featured in special exhibits throughout the year.

Located just behind Boone Tavern on historic Berea Ridge, the Berea College Appalachian Museum is open February through December, Monday through Saturday, 9 AM-6 PM, and Sunday, 1-6 PM.

BATTLE OF RICHMOND
DRIVING TOUR

Info at Richmond City Hall,
Main Street   *1-623-1000, ext. 210*

Follow the paths of Union and Confederate troops during one of the earliest and bloodiest military engagements of the Civil War in Kentucky. The self-guided driving tour of the Battle of Richmond offers the opportunity to visit the high points of this battle that spelled a rousing victory for Confederate troops.

Maps of the tour route, as well as audiocassettes detailing the history of the stations along the tour, are available at the Richmond Tourism office in City Hall. The tour takes about two hours.

CHURCHILL WEAVERS

Lorraine Court, Berea   *1-986-3126*

Founded in 1922 by former missionaries Eleanor and Carroll Churchill, Churchill Weavers became Berea's first non-college industry. Today, it is one of the nation's premier handweaving studios, and signature Churchill Weavers ties, baby throws and blankets are sold throughout the world.

Tours of the loomhouse, where you'll see everything from warping to weaving and finishing, are offered free Monday through Friday, 9 AM-noon and 1-4 PM, although hours may vary seasonally. Call ahead to be sure the loomhouse is open. A gift shop at the studio is open Monday through Saturday, 9 AM-6 PM, and Sunday, noon-6 PM.

To get to Churchill Weavers, take exit 76 or 77 off I-75 into Berea and follow US 25N to KY 1016. It's not as complicated as it sounds. There are lots of signs and very friendly people around if you have any trouble finding it.

BEREA COLLEGE CRAFTS

Log House Craft Gallery   1-986-9341, ext. 5225
800-347-3892

Since 1893, Berea College students and master craftspeople from the Appalachian region have collaborated in the production of fine traditional art and crafts. Today, more than 150 students work and learn through the Berea College Crafts program.

In addition to showrooms in the Log House Craft Gallery and other locations around the state, including the Civic Center Shops on Main Street in Lexington, the Berea College Crafts program has several working studios around the Berea College campus where visitors can see fine, indigenous woodcraft, weaving, ceramics, broom-making and wrought-iron work in the process of being made. Call one of the above numbers for a "Guide to College Crafts" for more details.

WHITE HALL STATE HISTORIC SITE

500 White Hall Shrine Road   1-623-9178

Visiting the beautiful Italianate mansion of outspoken abolitionist Cassius Marcellus Clay in the northern part of Madison County is a true aesthetic and historical delight. The extensive grounds are well-maintained, and the restored home is filled with many gorgeous examples of period furnishings, many of which are from the original home itself.

White Hall is open daily, April through Labor Day, 9 AM-5 PM, and is closed Mondays and Tuesdays through October. A small admission is charged for tours, but there is a discount offered when buying admission tickets for both White Hall and Fort Boonesborough at the same time. To get to White Hall, take exit 95 off I-75 and follow the signs.

HUMMEL PLANETARIUM & SPACE THEATRE
Kit Carson Drive, EKU campus 1-622-1547

Located on the campus of Eastern Kentucky University in Richmond, the Hummel Planetarium is the 11th largest planetarium in the nation. State-of-the-art star show equipment takes you billions of miles out into space on a journey of science and fantasy. The Hummel Planetarium and Space Theatre also features large-format films and a unique gift shop.

A nominal admission is charged for the star shows and films, which are shown Thursday through Sunday at 7:30 PM and Saturday and Sunday at 3:30 PM. To get there, take exit 87 off I-75. Kit Carson Drive turns off the main road from the exit (the Eastern By-Pass).

GIBSON BAY GOLF COURSE AND LAKE REBA RECREATIONAL COMPLEX
2000 Gibson Bay Drive, Richmond   1-623-0225

The crown jewel of Richmond's newest recreational complex is the beautiful but challenging 18-hole championship public golf course designed by internationally renowned Michael Hurzdan. The Gibson Bay Golf Course features 33 bunkers, plenty of water, lush rolling greens, and four to five tee boxes at each hole.

Lake Reba Recreational Complex features some 450 acres of nature trails and sports areas, including 14 baseball fields, four soccer fields, archery range, lakeside picnic pavilion, driving range, horseshoes, basketball and volleyball, as well as fishing.

For more information on Richmond, contact the Richmond Tourism Commission at 1-623-1000, ext. 210. For more information about Berea, contact the Berea Visitors Center at (800) 598-5263.

How to Get There

You have three basic routes to get to Madison County, and one involves a ferry. The quickest and easiest route, barring a major accident or construction, is to take I-75 south from Lexington. There are six exits off the interstate in Madison County, two north of Richmond, two Richmond exits and two Berea exits.

You could also take U.S. 25 south from Lexington. You pick this highway up off of Richmond Road across from Jacobson Park (which is where U.S. 25 cuts off). This is a picturesque ride through the country on a two-lane road. It has entry onto I-75 before and after the Clays Ferry Bridge across the Kentucky River (which is the county line), as well as at several places in Madison County. Staying on U.S. 25 will take you through Richmond south to Berea where you can again join I-75.

The third option for going to Madison County is much more round-about, but also more fun if you have the time to do it. Take Tates Creek Road out of Lexington until you come to the Valley View

Ferry across the Kentucky River leading into Madison County.

Jessamine County — Nicholasville and Wilmore

Jessamine County, like the fragrant jessamine flower, is a creation of great natural beauty. Some of the most awe-inspiring scenery in the Bluegrass can be found in this county formed from Fayette in 1798.

Nicholasville, the county seat, is 12 miles south of Lexington. Because of continuing development on U.S. 27, the main Nicholasville-Lexington corridor, the two cities seem to be growing steadily closer to each other. Idle talk of eventual annexation by Lexington has never been taken seriously, however, because Jessamine Countians are proud of their unique heritage and identity. After all, this is a place where, each September, about 200 locals band together to put on an outdoor drama called *Jessamine*. Although it's nice to be so close to Lexington, where many Jessamine Countians commute to work each day, most of them — believe it or not — probably wouldn't want to live there.

The county, which covers 177 square miles, was apparently named in recognition of the abundance of jessamine growing along the banks of woodland creeks in the area. It might also have been named for Jessamine Douglas, a beautiful settler's daughter who, according to legend, was killed by Indians. Since the young girl was surely named for the flowers, both of these theories may be true.

As for the name of the county seat, we know that it was named for Col. George Nicholas, who served in the Revolutionary War and later played a key role in drafting the Kentucky Constitution. It was the Rev. John Metcalfe who named and planned the town. The town received its charter in 1812 and was incorporated 25 years later.

More than 90 percent of the county's land is occupied by farms that produce such crops as tobacco, corn, fruit and vegetables and that raise livestock and poultry. The fertile Kentucky River valley in which the county lies helped attract early settlers, who in the late 18th century made hemp a major crop that persisted for three-quarters of a century. At one point, Jessamine County was the largest hemp producer in the state. Proximity to the river was also an advantage in the establishment of whiskey distilleries.

The river also made the area an important site to both armies during the Civil War. Union and Confederate troops occupied Nicholasville during the war, and Camp Nelson was established on the river in 1863 as

Insiders' Tips

Central Kentuckians enjoy the crystal-clear taste of Highbridge Spring water from Jessamine County.

a Union recruitment center and sanctuary for escaped slave families. Despite the Union presence, however, the area was not safe from Gen. John Hunt Morgan, who stormed into Nicholasville with his cavalry on September 3, 1862, and within a few hours recruited 1,000 rebels. Today, Camp Nelson National Cemetery serves as the final resting place for not only Civil War soldiers but also dead from World War I and II, Korea and Vietnam.

The 1990 U.S. Census listed a population of 30,508 in Jessamine County; there were 13,603 residents in Nicholasville. Wilmore, established by the Cincinnati Southern Railroad in 1876, is the county's only other incorporated town, the home of Asbury College and Theological Seminary and a favorite spot for antique lovers.

Although Nicholasville has in the past been considered a "bedroom community" of Lexington, Jessamine County has a strong manufacturing base of its own to complement its agriculture. Nearly 2,000 people are employed by about 30 Jessamine County manufacturers, several of which are located in an industrial park at the south edge of town.

Some of the larger companies are Sargent & Greenleaf Inc., maker of high-security locking devices; Gulf States Paper Corporation, paperboard folding cartons; Hospitality Specialty Company, sanitary napkins and disposable diapers; Donaldson Company Inc., which makes mufflers, air cleaners and other equipment for the construction, industrial, agricultural and mining industries; Thompson International, automobile wheel trim; Trim Masters Inc., automobile seating; and Alltech Inc. Biotechnology Center.

Other products manufactured within the county include carbon wire, wood cabinets and other furniture, electrical equipment, tools and dies, packaging film, paint, plastic bottles and clothing.

It is nature, however, that has provided this community with its greatest resources (other than its *people*, that is). In addition to sheer splendor of the palisades area, Jessamine County also has its share of timelessly beautiful horse farms, as is evident during a drive through the countryside. At Keene, a small community four miles northwest of Nicholasville, the remains of a late-19th-century Greek Revival-style health spa are on display.

As the county's five antique malls will attest, reminders of the past are a constant here. Downtown Nicholasville itself is a historic district. The Jessamine County Courthouse lawn holds monuments to Revolutionary War soldiers and to Confederates. The oldest recorded business in Kentucky, the Valley View Ferry (see Kid Stuff) crosses the Kentucky River between Jessamine County and Madison County, its neighbor to the east. The locals also claim that the first celebration of American independence west of the Allegheny Mountains was held in the county. Incidentally, they still like to celebrate with annual fairs, festivals and parades.

Today Nicholasville revels in its history, even as the clock in the tower of its majestic 19th-century courthouse reminds us all that time marches on. County residents seem to realize that it is possible to pay tribute to the past while living in the present and preparing for the future. They have adapted as necessary, preserving the things that are worth preserving.

Need more proof? Consider the tale of Asbury College. It was founded by the Rev. John Wesley Hughes, once-illiterate farm-boy-turned-minister who received a heavenly vision of a school. Finding the right location was essential. He turned down one Kentucky site before being invited by a Methodist minister to consider Wilmore. Although the community was then just a railroad "whistle stop" with a few houses, Hughes evidently found it sufficiently divine. He established his college in 1890, naming it in honor of Francis Asbury, a circuit rider who became the first Methodist bishop in the American colonies. A prosperous little town grew around the college, but then in 1909 much of the campus burned. Wilmore residents, fearful of losing their beloved college, pitched in and raised $15,000 to rebuild it on the same site.

Today, the Rev. Hughes' impression of Wilmore still holds true, not only for Wilmore but also for Jessamine County as a whole. He called it "a model place . . . a good country,

fine citizenship, healthful, easily accessible, a quiet place."

Places of Interest

KENTUCKY RIVER PALISADES
Scenic stops on U.S. 68, U.S. 27 and Ky. 29

For a breathtaking view of the river, try looking down from sheer limestone cliffs towering 300 feet above the banks. These rugged gray cliffs, which stretch for 75 miles, were cut by the river as it stubbornly plotted its course millions of years ago. Watch for signs to the scenic stops along the highway. Hikers at nearby Raven Run Nature Sanctuary — see The Great Outdoors chapter — can trek to the palisades, sit on a big rock and marvel. About 350 acres of the palisades area in Jessamine and Garrard counties are being converted into a nature preserve.

JESSAMINE CREEK GORGE PRESERVE
Privately owned land in southwestern Jessamine County
Info: The Nature Conservancy   259-9655

This may be the closest thing to a virgin forest you can find in this part of the country. The international Nature Conservancy has identified more than 350 species of plants and 25 species of animals in the gorge, which also contains, among its cliffs and crevices, two caves with rare bat populations. The gorge is also largely inaccessible and on private land; to visit it, you'll have to arrange a private guided tour by calling the Nature Conservancy. Only three or four tours are offered each year, at a cost of $10 a person.

HIGH BRIDGE
Ky. 29, Wilmore

At 275 feet above the Kentucky River, this is the nation's highest railroad bridge over a navigable stream. The original High Bridge, built near Wilmore in 1877 for the Cincinnati Southern Railroad and dedicated by President Rutherford B. Hayes, was also the first cantilever bridge in North America. It was replaced in 1911.

HIGHBRIDGE SPRING
WATER COMPANY
Ky. 29, Wilmore   *858-4407*

This bottler of fresh, clear, sweet spring water drawn from a limestone quarry 160 feet underground has demonstrated convincingly that Jessamine County nature also has good taste. The company sells $2,000,000-3,000,000 worth of the stuff in bottles each year.

How To Get There

The most direct route from Lexington to Nicholasville is by U.S. 27 (Nicholasville Road). But if you prefer to travel on winding, two-lane country roads dotted with plank-fenced horse farms — and who doesn't? — you should go by way of U.S. 68 south (Harrodsburg Road). From Harrodsburg Road, you can head east toward your destination by taking either Ky. 169 or, a few miles farther, Ky. 29.

For more information on opportunities available in Jessamine County, call or visit the Jessamine County Chamber of Commerce, 102 North Main Street in Nicholasville, 887-4351.

Woodford County — Versailles and Midway

One sure way to identify yourself as an outsider in Woodford County is to walk into the county seat speaking French. In other words, when you're in Versailles, Kentucky, the correct pronunciation is "Ver-SALES," not "Vare-SIGH," even though the town was named after the French city where Revolutionary War hero Lafayette attended school. (The county's name also has its basis in the war; it was named in honor of Gen. William Woodford, a Virginia officer who died a prisoner of the British.)

Versailles, which lies about 12 miles west of Lexington on U.S. 60, is closely linked historically and economically to its neighbor. Robert Patterson, who led the expedition that originally settled in Lexington, was also involved in the settling of Versailles. The Virginia legislature created Woodford County from Fayette County in 1788, four years before Kentucky was to become its own state. Versailles was incorporated in 1837.

The Civil War deeply affected Woodford County, as it did much of Kentucky. Confederate forces, aided by the cunning strategies of the omnipresent John Hunt Morgan, briefly occupied Versailles in 1862 after destroying the railroad line and confusing Union troops with bogus telegraph dispatches. Union troops controlled the town both before and after the rebel occupation, at one point guarding every street corner and forbidding the assembly of more than two people. In and near Midway there were also some significant events, most notably the burning of the train station and looting of the town by Confederate guerrillas led by the notorious Marcellus Jerome "Sue Mundy" Clarke, and the execution by Union troops of four guerrillas.

The 1990 U.S. Census listed 192-square-mile Woodford County with a population of 19,955, of which 7,269 lived in Versailles. Midway is the county's other incorporated town; unincorporated communities include Duckers, Faywood, Nonesuch, Pisgah, Troy and Zion Hill.

Today, many Woodford County residents commute to work in Lexington. On the other hand, many people from Lexington and surrounding areas commute to Woodford County, which regularly has the state's lowest rate of unemployment. Major employers within the county include the Sylvania fluorescent lighting plant, which GTE sold in 1993 to Osram; Rand McNally & Co., which produces books and maps; and the Texas Instruments thermostat and switch plant.

Woodford County has a rich agricultural history that continues today. The limestone-rich soil and the rolling nature of the land make the area ideal for corn, tobacco, horses,

livestock and poultry, and the county is one of the state's leading agricultural money-makers. It also has a number of horse farms, including such heavyweights as Airdrie Stud, Lane's End, Pin Oak and Three Chimneys. Elizabeth II, the queen and thoroughbred breeder, has often visited Lane's End Farm. Its owner, William S. Farish III, is a close friend of former President George Bush, who also been a frequent visitor to the farm.

Like its French namesake, which is famous for its beautiful Palace of Versailles, the Versailles in Central Kentucky is noted for its architecture, particularly in many of the homes that were built in the early 1800s.

The railroad has played, and continues to play, an important role in the daily life of Woodford County, which like most of the state is not embarrassed by nostalgia. From Versailles to charming Midway, where Main Street is divided by train tracks and lined with antique and crafts shops, to its rural county roads, a jaunt through Woodford County is a trip into the past.

Midway, so named because of its location "midway" between Lexington and the capital city of Frankfort, was the first town in Kentucky to be developed by a railroad company, and its streets were named for members of the Louisville & Nashville Railroad's board of directors. In addition to 176 buildings on the National Register of Historic Places and plenty of quaint shops where you can buy antiques, crafts and other gifts, Midway is also home to Midway College, the only women's college in Kentucky.

Adding to the county's historical charm are its bed-and-breakfast inns, which are great places to stay for those who want to experience real Southern hospitality in an old-fashioned household setting.

Famous residents of Woodford County have included John J. Crittenden, who served as Kentucky's governor from 1948 to 1950, and Lt. Gen. Field Harris, who commanded the U.S. Marines during World War II and the Korean War.

But the county's most beloved and most controversial son has undoubtedly been Albert B. "Happy" Chandler, who was governor in 1935-39 and 1955-59, and who also served as commissioner of baseball from 1945 to 1951, the period in which Jackie Robinson broke the color barrier and blacks began playing in the major leagues. The Chandler Medical Center, part of the University of Kentucky, is named for Chandler. Unfortunately, the former governor became increasingly controversial in his later years as a member of the University board of trustees. After he allegedly made racial slurs at a couple of board meetings, many Kentuckians called for his resignation or forced removal from the board. He died in 1991 at his Versailles home.

The Chandler family, which publishes *The Woodford Sun* weekly newspaper, remains prominent in the county and the state. Ben Chandler, grandson of the former governor, is now Kentucky auditor as well as the newspaper publisher. And Happy Chandler remains a colorful figure in Kentucky history.

Curiously, despite all the "significant" events in Happy Chandler's life — the good, the bad and the ugly — this author's most vivid memory of the former governor is of his singing, in a quaveringly emotional voice, "My Old Kentucky Home" before the start of a UK basketball game.

Places of Interest

PISGAH CHURCH
710 Pisgah Pike   *873-4161*

In the Bible, Pisgah was the mountain from which Moses' eyes first beheld the Promised Land. In Woodford County, it's a beautiful little stone country church in the "wildwood," and it's almost equally capable of evoking a spiritual experience. In 1784 a group of Presbyterians settled in the area, founding the first Presbyterian church west of the Alleghenies. They built a log church in 1794, which was renovated in the Gothic style in 1868. The church, which still has an active congregation of about 120, has magnificent stained-glass windows with scenes of native wildflowers.

Pisgah Church lies at the heart of the picturesque Pisgah Historic District. This area, truly a "must-see," has roads lined with 200-year-old osage orange trees and dozens of old farms with stone fences. The small building behind the church, opened by the Presbyterians in 1794 as the Kentucky Academy, was used for other church functions after the school merged with Transylvania University in 1798. Tennis courts on the church grounds are the site of the weeklong Pisgah Invitational Tournament held each August.

Take Pisgah Pike (Ky. 1967 north), the first road past the castle as you head out Versailles Road from Lexington. The church is less than 3/4 of a mile up the road on your right. Happy Chandler is buried in the church cemetery.

JOUETT HOUSE
255 Craigs Creek Road, 5 1/2 miles west of Versailles   *873-7902*

This is the former residence of Jack Jouett, a Virginia-born Revolutionary War captain who became known as "the Paul Revere of the South." In June 1781, he made a heroic ride through the Virginia backwoods to warn Gov. Thomas Jefferson, Patrick Henry and other members of the Virginia General Assembly of an impending British attack. Jouett was also the father of antebellum portrait artist Matthew Jouett. The house is open for tours from April 1 to October 31.

BLUEGRASS SCENIC RAILROAD & BLUEGRASS RAILROAD MUSEUM
U.S. 62 west at Beasley Road   *873-2476*

The Bluegrass Scenic Railroad takes passengers on a 90-minute old-fashioned train ride through pastoral Woodford County farmland, with an optional side trip by foot to Young's High Bridge, a circa 1888 railroad trestle spanning 1,658 feet across and 280 feet above the Kentucky River. Special events are held throughout the year, including re-enacted train robberies, a Halloween "ghost train" ride and the Santa Claus Special.

The Bluegrass Railroad Museum,

a nonprofit volunteer organization devoted to railroad restoration, displays a variety of railroad artifacts, including a 1960s caboose used by the Louisville & Nashville Railroad and a restored steam engine. The museum is open weekends from mid-May through October. Train rides are offered at 10:30 AM, 1:30 PM and 3:30 PM Saturday and at 1:30 PM and 3:30 PM Sunday in season. Standard prices are $6 for adults, $5 for seniors (62 and older) and $4 for children ages 3 through 12. Group discounts are available for groups of 20 or more with advance purchase.

NOSTALGIA STATION TOY & TRAIN MUSEUM
279 Depot Street   *873-2497*

This former L&N depot is stocked with a number of working electric trains, along with other toys and railroad memorabilia. Nostalgia Station is open from 10 AM to 5 PM Wednesday through Saturday and from 1 PM to 5 PM Sunday. Admission is $3 for adults, $2.50 for seniors, $1.50 for children and free for those 5 and younger.

How To Get There

The most direct route from Lexington to Versailles, by way of U.S. 60 (Versailles Road), is lined with landmarks. A few miles outside the city limits, you'll go by Calumet Farm on your right and, immediately after that, you'll simultaneously pass Blue Grass Airport on your left and Keeneland on your right. A little farther ahead on your right looms the mysterious castle (see Kid Stuff), which will continue to keep us all guessing until somebody finally buys it and opens it to the public.

For more information on opportunities available in Woodford County, call or visit the Woodford County Chamber of Commerce, 279 Depot Street in Versailles, 873-5122.

Franklin County — Frankfort

Frankfort, a hilly city nestled on both sides of an S-shaped curve of the Kentucky River, is the site of the creation of Kentucky's laws and a fair amount of its whiskey. (Feel free to insert your own punch line here.) The city has a storied and colorful history, much of which remains in evidence today. And it's safe to say that history will continue to be made here.

Frankfort, which lies 26 miles northwest of Lexington and has a population of 25,968, is the state capital as well as the seat of Franklin County, population 43,781. The county, formed from Mercer, Shelby and Woodford counties in 1794, was named for Benjamin Franklin; we'll discuss the origin of the city's name later.

Whatever one might say about today's political maneuverings, they fall short of the drama that marked those of the late 18th and early 19th centuries. Even the manner of deciding the location of Kentucky's capital would seem to say something — at least to the cynic in all of us — about the state of politics in general. In effect, Frankfort became Kentucky's capital in 1792 because its citizens outbid Lexington and several other towns. Then, as now, money (and real estate) talked.

So did firearms. In January 1809, Lexington's fiery native son Henry Clay became embroiled in a heated debate with Humphrey Marshall, his nemesis in the state House of Representatives, on the subject of British imports. The argument on the House floor degenerated into name-calling and, eventually, a duel on the banks of the Ohio River across from Louisville. Both were wounded, neither seriously. Modern-day political duels are fought with mud, not guns.

It is perhaps unfair to characterize Frankfort only in terms of politics, even though state government has been the leading employer for as long as anyone can remember. Rich farmland constitutes nearly three-quarters of the 212-square-mile county, which also benefits from the manufacture of such products as underwear and automotive parts as well as bourbon (for more information on the latter, see our chapter on Distilleries and Breweries).

In 1751, surveyor Christopher Gist became one of the first pioneers in the area, which was a popular Indian hunting ground, by following an ancient buffalo trace to the Kentucky River. Gist was followed in subsequent years by some of the legends of the pioneer era: John Finley, Daniel Boone, George Rogers Clark. The first settlement, one mile south of present-day Frankfort, was established in 1775 by brothers Hancock and Willis Lee — which is why today there's a Leestown Road from Lexington to Frankfort. The city of Leestown thrived for more than 100 years before being absorbed by Frankfort.

The name of Frankfort stemmed from a 1780 Indian attack that killed a pioneer named Stephen Frank. The site of the attack was dubbed Frank's Ford, which eventually was transformed into Frankfort.

In the early 19th century, Frankfort's population was second only to Lexington's among Kentucky towns. Its river location made it a desirable site for manufacturing and shipping a variety of products such as rope, clothing, glass and tools. Its location also made it a prime target of Confederate and Union forces during the Civil War. The rebels occupied the town for about a month in September and October 1862, and on June 10-11, 1864, Frankfort fought off an attack by John Hunt Morgan.

Frankfort's history since then has been marked by adversity as well as by hope. On the negative side are such racially and politically charged events as postwar Ku Klux Klan violence, the 1900 assassination of Democratic gubernatorial candidate William Goebel and continuing revelations of corruption by elected officials. On the plus side are the 1882 opening of the Clinton Street School, an educational landmark for black children, and the founding five years later of the State Normal School for Colored Persons, the teacher-training school that became Kentucky State University. The verdict is still out on the Kentucky Education Reform Act, the complex 1990 legislation that, in the name of equity, has fundamentally changed the way the state's school systems operate.

These and other developments ensure that when Kentuckians think about their future, it will be hard for them to avoid thinking about Frankfort.

The Kentucky Vietnam Veterans Memorial is one of the nation's most unusual, with a sundial that casts a shadow on the anniversary of each veteran's death.

Places of Interest

KENTUCKY STATE CAPITOL
Capital Avenue   (502) 564-3449

Today's Capitol building, Kentucky's fifth, is a beautiful, domed, French Renaissance-style building that invites many comparisons to the U.S. Capitol. The imposing structure was begun in 1905 and completed in 1910 at a cost of $1.75 million. The Capitol Annex, a near replica of the statehouse without a dome, was finished in 1952. The ground floor of the Capitol features a variety of changing historical and cultural exhibits.

The highlight of the Capitol grounds is the Floral Clock, a working timepiece 34 feet in diameter with thousands of colorful flowers covering its face.

Free Capitol tours are offered from 8 AM to 4:30 PM Monday through Friday, 8:30 AM to 4:30 PM Saturday and 1 PM to 4:30 PM Sunday. Reservations are suggested for groups.

EXECUTIVE MANSION
Just east of the Capitol   (502) 564-3449

This mansion, the official governor's residence since 1914, overlooks the Kentucky River. It was built of Kentucky limestone and reportedly was modeled after Marie Antoinette's summer villa. Free guided tours, which include the state dining room, ballroom, reception room and formal salon, are offered Tuesday and Thursday from 9 AM to 11 AM.

LIEUTENANT GOVERNOR'S MANSION
420 High Street   (502) 564-3449

Here's where the Kentucky governor lived until 1914, when he got new digs and the lieutenant governor moved into the old. This federal mansion is the oldest official executive residence still in use in the United States. Free tours are available from 1:30 PM to 3:30 PM Tuesday and Thursday.

OLD STATE CAPITOL AND KENTUCKY HISTORY MUSEUM
Broadway at St. Clair Mall (502) 564-3016

The Kentucky Historical Society moved into this 1831 Greek Revival structure in 1920. Fifteen years earlier the building — the fourth capitol — and its site had been deemed too small for a fifth statehouse. Take note of the self-supporting staircase. Next door, the Kentucky History Museum, also maintained by the Historical Society, highlights the state's social history from early settlement to the 1900s. Free tours are offered from 9 AM to 4 PM Monday through Saturday, noon to 4 PM Sunday.

FRANKFORT CEMETERY

215 East Main Street   (502) 227-2403

The highlight of this peaceful, well-shaded cemetery is the grave site of Daniel and Rebecca Boone. Although the Boones were originally buried in Missouri, where they had lived the last years of their lives, their remains were moved to Kentucky in 1845; a monument was placed over their graves in 1862. From the grave site, perched on the edge of a hill, visitors can gaze down upon the Kentucky River and the state Capitol.

Native artist Paul Sawyier is also buried here, as are sculptor Joel Tanner Hart, whose poem "The Bivouac of the Dead" is inscribed in part at the gate to Arlington National Cemetery; and Richard M. Johnson, vice president under Martin Van Buren. Frankfort Cemetery is open from 7 AM to 8:30 PM during the summer and 8 AM to 5:30 PM during the winter.

KENTUCKY VIETNAM VETERANS MEMORIAL

Coffee Tree Road

This strikingly unusual memorial, honoring those Kentucky natives who died in Vietnam, resulted from a push by surviving veterans. A looming sundial is designed so that the point of its shadow touches the name of each veteran, etched on the ground in granite, on the anniversary of his death. The memorial, on the grounds of the State Library and Archives, is open until dusk.

KENTUCKY MILITARY HISTORY MUSEUM

East Main Street at
Capital Avenue   (502) 564-3265

The Kentucky Historical Society operates this museum, appropriately located in the Old State Arsenal building. The state's military history is traced through photographs and displays of weapons, flags and other artifacts. The Kentucky National Guard and militia and the Civil War are especially emphasized. The tour is free, but large groups should make reservations. The museum is open from 9 AM to 4 PM Monday through Friday.

FLYNN'S

Frankfort Plaza   (502) 875-5815

For a glimpse of how Kentucky laws are made, you can go to the Capitol and watch the General Assembly in session — or go get a beer and some behind-the-scenes insight at Flynn's, a noted watering hole for state senators, representatives and lobbyists. How noted? During one of his many disputes with the legislature, former Gov. Wallace Wilkinson wondered aloud: "What are they putting in the bourbon at Flynn's these days?" Food is offered, too, but the real attraction lies in the dark and smoky tavern atmosphere with campaign posters and other memorabilia covering the walls.

REBECCA-RUTH CANDIES

112 East Second Street   (502) 223-7475
(800) 444-3766

Combine pecans, powdered sugar and 100-proof bourbon, then dip the whole concoction in rich chocolate, and what do you get? You

If traffic is backed up on I-75, U.S. 25 is a good alternate north-south route. It cuts off from Richmond Road across from Jacobson Park and runs south past Berea. There are opportunities to re-join I-75 at the Madison-Fayette county. border, twice before you get to Richmond, and then again in Berea.

get an intoxicating treat that before 1986 was technically a federal offense to mail beyond Kentucky's borders — and you get the biggest claim to fame for this candy-maker founded in 1919. Schoolteachers Rebecca Gooch and Ruth Hanly are credited with inventing "bourbon balls," whose popularity has spread far beyond Kentucky's borders. Rebecca-Ruth Candies also makes "Blue Monday" cream candy, peanut brittle and many other delicacies that your dentist really doesn't need to know about.

The sales room is open from 8 AM to 5:30 PM Monday through Friday and from 9 AM to 5:30 PM Saturday. Free factory tours are offered from 9 AM to 4:30 PM Monday through Thursday, January through October. No tours are available in November and December because everyone is too busy filling holiday orders.

ZEIGLER HOUSE
509 Shelby Street   (502) 227-7164

The Zeigler House, built in 1910, is the state's only building designed by Frank Lloyd Wright. Its design, created in Wright's famous prairie style, was advertised in 1907 in *Ladies Home Journal* as the "$5,000 fireproof house." A few modifications were made for the Frankfort version, originally owned by the Rev. Jesse R. Zeigler and his family.

Wright fanatics Jim and Jane Brockman, who had visited 300 Wright structures and dreamed of owning one, moved from Western Kentucky in 1991 to buy and restore Zeigler House. Now the house, which is on the National Register of Historic Places, looks much as it did in 1910. Its lighted stained-glass case over the fireplace and other features are in museum quality. The Brockmans live here and offer tours — by appointment only, please — for $4. Since tours began in 1992, the house has had more than 2,000 visitors from all over.

LIBERTY HALL HISTORIC SITE
218 Wilkinson Street   (502) 227-2560

Liberty Hall, begun in 1796 and completed in 1801 by John Brown, Kentucky's first U.S. senator, also served as the site of the first Sunday School west of the Alleghenies. According to some accounts (including that of the caretakers), Liberty Hall is haunted by at least two ghosts: a relative of John Brown's wife and a Spanish opera singer. The Orlando Brown House, home of the senator's son, is also included on the tour, as are the landscaped grounds and a formal garden. Four daily tours are offered Monday through Saturday at 10:30 AM, noon, 1:30 PM and 3 PM. There's a Sunday tour at 2:30 PM. Cost is $4.50 for adults, $4 for seniors and $1 for ages 6 through 16. Group and AAA discounts are also available. Groups must call in advance. Liberty Hall and the Orlando Brown House are closed in January and February.

BUCKLEY WILDLIFE SANCTUARY
1305 Germany Road,
6 miles off U.S. 60   (606) 873-5711

This 275-acre sanctuary, operated by the National Audubon Society, is a sanctuary to deer, birds, possum (Kentuckians say it without the "o") and the occasional skunk. Hard telling what you'll see on a given visit, but you'll always find nature trails and a nature center, and sometimes workshops and other special events are scheduled. Buckley Wildlife Sanctuary is open from 9 AM to 5 PM Wednesday through Friday, 9 AM to 6 PM Saturday and Sunday. Admission is $2 for adults, $1 for children.

SWITZER BRIDGE
Highway 1262, Switzer

This 1855 covered bridge, which spans Elkhorn Creek in rural Franklin County, is one of only 13 still remaining in Kentucky. It was restored once in 1906, then underwent a complete restoration a few years ago.

In addition to the attractions listed above, Frankfort has numerous other historical buildings, many of which can be seen on a downtown walking tour.

How To Get There

To get to Frankfort from Lexington, take U.S. 60 (Versailles Road)

east. At the red light on the outskirts of Versailles, where you see a shopping center on your right and a number of fast-food restaurants on both sides of the road, U.S. 60 turns right and heads north. You're about halfway there: It's about 13 more miles to the capital city.

If you'd like a pleasant alternate route, take Leestown Road (U.S. 421) from Lexington. It's two lanes all the way, but you won't mind as you wind past miles of farms bounded by stone and plank fences beneath a shady canopy of old trees. If you're driving, try to remember to keep your eyes on the road. You can take Ky. 1681 (Old Frankfort Pike), which will eventually get you to the capital after lazily winding past Midway and some prime Bluegrass green space.

For more information on opportunities available in Franklin County, call or visit the Frankfort/Franklin County Tourist and Convention Commission, 100 Capitol Avenue, (502) 875-8687.

Scott County — Georgetown, Stamping Ground and Sadieville

Indians. Settlers. A Baptist minister. Bourbon whiskey. George Washington. Buffalo. Railroads. A college. A Japanese auto plant.

Throw these disparate elements together, stir, mix in a couple of obligatory visits by our old friend John Hunt Morgan and, finally, add

MEREDITH CRISP CAN GIVE YOU THE INSIDE STORY ON TOYOTA IN KENTUCKY.

Want to find out why Toyota Motor Manufacturing, U.S.A., Inc. in Georgetown, Kentucky received the prestigious J.D. Power 1993 "Gold Plant Award" as top auto manufacturing plant in North America?

Then come to Georgetown and meet Meredith Crisp. This Georgetown College biology major is one of a team of bright, personable tour guides who show visitors around the plant every week.

If you'd like to take a tour (given Tuesdays and Thursdays for ages 8 and older), call (502) 868-3027 for reservations. We think you'll enjoy seeing the great things that are going on. And meeting Meredith and our other guides. After all, who better to tell our inside story than an outstanding young Kentuckian?

TOYOTA

TOYOTA MOTOR MANUFACTURING, U.S.A., INC.

the likelihood of a happy ending. You've got the makings for one heck of an epic novel — or the true story of Scott County, Kentucky.

Georgetown, the seat of the 286-square-mile county, lies seven miles north of Lexington, little more than the proverbial stone's throw away on Interstate 75. In fact, Scott County is descended from Fayette County. It was created from Woodford County, an offspring of Fayette County, on June 1, 1792, one of two counties established by Kentucky's first legislature. The county was named for Gen. Charles Scott, governor from 1802 to 1812; the city was named in honor of the first president of the United States.

The county population, according to the 1990 U.S. Census, is 23,867. Georgetown's population is 11,414. Tiny Stamping Ground and Sadieville, with just a few hundred people between them, are also incorporated towns in the county.

Since the opening in late 1987 of the Toyota Motor Manufacturing Company's Camry plant, Scott County's contributions to Greater Lexington's economy, and to that of the entire state, have increased exponentially. The original $800 million manufacturing-facility investment has grown to $2 billion through an expansion plant and the addition of plants to produce power trains and V-6 engines. Toyota employs about 4,500 people — 96 percent of them Kentuckians — and has an annual payroll of more than $185 million.

Although controversy was generated by the generous package of tax breaks, industrial development bonds funding and other incentives that the state offered to land Toyota, the decision appears to be paying off. Toyota's arrival has helped lure more than 50 automotive-related plants to the state, and the company has made significant contributions to public schools, colleges, universities and charities in the area. Meanwhile, the cars made in Georgetown have twice earned J.D. Power Quality Awards as the best-built cars in the nation.

Scott County's industrial base also includes Johnson Controls' automotive seating plant; The GCA Group, which produces wiring harnesses; Hoover Group, wire products; and The Molding Company, injection molders. The Scott County School System, Georgetown College, Winn-Dixie, city and county government, Scott General Hospital, Kroger and Kmart are also major community employers.

But let's flash back for a moment to earlier times, more than 200 years ago when the area was truly a wild place where buffalo roamed—hence the name Stamping Ground for one of the county's towns — and there was not a sushi bar to be found anywhere. The main characteristic of the area then was its untamed beauty: rich and verdant forests, gracefully rolling hillsides, springs. These features were to set the tone for Georgetown's early economy, which remained almost exclusively agricultural until just before the Civil War.

The area's recorded history began in 1774 when a surveyor named John Floyd, a member of a party that was locating land warrants for French and Indian War veterans, discovered a spring near present-day Elkhorn Creek. He named it Royal Spring and claimed 1,000 acres but did not settle there. The probable first settlers in the area were the John McClelland family from Pennsylvania, who built a cabin at the site in October 1775. In July 1776, as democracy was being born on the East Coast, a group of soldiers and explorers that included Daniel Boone's contemporary Simon Kenton built a fort on the spring bluff. But after an Indian attack on the fort just four days after Christmas in 1776, the settlers took the hint and left.

It wasn't until 1782 that any further settlement was attempted. The Rev. Elijah Craig arrived with some members of his Baptist congregation, intent on founding a settlement called Lebanon. The Virginia legislature incorporated the town in 1784 and six years later renamed it George Town. It officially became Georgetown in 1846.

The Rev. Craig was an enterprising sort who held a variety of skills in addition to preaching. He grew hemp for rope, made paper, established a "fulling" mill for the treatment of cloth and, according to some accounts, invented bourbon whiskey. He also established a school that was a precursor to Georgetown College, the first Baptist college west of the Alleghenies.

The county's farms produced large quantities of livestock as well as corn, flax, fruits and vegetables and hemp, which soon was supplanted by tobacco as the major crop. Later, manufacturing facilities turned the wealth of raw materials into such goods as whiskey, rope, lumber, paper, flour, meal and cloth.

Scott County's sympathies during the Civil War ran almost 10-to-1 in favor of the Confederacy, and Scott Countian George W. Johnson was even elected Kentucky's provisional Confederate governor in 1861. Nevertheless, John Hunt Morgan and his men made two uninvited visits to Georgetown in 1862 and 1864, wreaking their usual havoc and, on the first occasion, camping for two days on the courthouse lawn.

These raids set back progress a little, but the resilient county quickly recovered with help from the railroads, which provided connections with Louisville, Frankfort, Versailles, Paris, Cincinnati and more distant destinations like Nashville and New Orleans. Sadieville was formed in the late 1870s as a shipping connection on the Cincinnati Southern line. Industrialization began to take off in the years after World War II, and in recent years, Scott County's accessibility via railroads and Interstates 64 and 75 has continued to be instrumental in its industrial development.

Famous Scott Countians, in addition to the ones mentioned earlier in this section, include James Campbell Cantrill, a former state and U.S. representative who in the first part of the century helped bring about more equitable market prices for farmers; and James Fisher Robinson, who served as Kentucky governor during 1862-63, the midst of the Civil War.

Places of Interest

Today, Georgetown has a variety of attractions to satisfy interests ranging from historical to automotive to shopping. Main Street has numerous historical buildings dating back to 1869, and also contains five antique shops and malls featuring more than 25,000 square feet of old stuff. More antique shops can be found during a drive through the surrounding countryside. Georgetown also holds an annual Festival of the Horse (see the chapters on Horses and Annual Events).

ROYAL SPRING PARK
South Water Street   863-2547

The site of Georgetown's birth, and possibly bourbon's birth as well, Royal Spring Park features a small local history museum and an 1874 cabin built by a freed slave. The park, which also contains a deck, benches and picnic area, is open year round; the cabin is open April through September.

CARDOME
U.S. 25   863-1575

This property, where James Fisher Robinson lived before becoming governor in 1862, also served as a monastery and academy for the Roman Catholic Sisters of the Visitation. The name, coined by Robinson, comes from the Latin *carus domus*, or "dear home." Now the site holds a community center with the Scott County Museum for Local History. Free tours are available.

GEORGETOWN COLLEGE
400 East College   863-8011

The picturesque campus of this small college is a great place to take a leisurely walk and see examples of classical Greek Revival and other styles of architecture.

Photo: Lexington Herald-Leader

The Cane Ridge Shrine superstructure houses the old Cane Ridge meeting house, which was built in 1791.

NEW ZION

Newtown Pike

New Zion is said to be Kentucky's oldest black settlement. The community of about 75 people is on the Scott-Fayette County line on Newtown Pike.

TOYOTA CAMRY PLANT

Cherry Blossom Way
(I-75, exit 26)   868-3027

The Toyota Camry plant, the Japanese company's first wholly owned U.S. manufacturing facility, offers free tours at 8:30 AM, 10 AM, noon and 2 PM Tuesdays and Thursdays, and also at 6 PM Thursdays. Reservations are required, so call in advance.

CAROLINA POTTERY OUTLET MALL

I-75, exit 26 at U.S. 62   863-3660

Designed for the modern shopper, this mall has about 20 outlet shops offering discount prices on name-brand wares including shoes, cookware, jeans, books and power tools.

How To Get There

From Lexington, take I-75 north. That's the quick and easy way. For added enjoyment, however, take U.S. 25 (Georgetown Road).

For more information on opportunities available in Scott County, call or visit the Georgetown-Scott County Tourism Commission, 160 East Main Street in Georgetown, 863-2547.

Bourbon County - Paris

It may seem strange to some for a county in the heart of the Bible Belt to share its name with an alcoholic beverage. Especially a dry county where you can't even buy alcoholic beverages. But such is the case with Bourbon County, Lexington's closest neighbor to the northeast.

In fact, the alcoholic beverage was named after the county, since many claim it was there that it was first produced. Part of the distinctive flavor of the whiskey came from the limestone water from local springs. The question, however, of where Kentucky Bourbon originated has never quite been resolved to everyone's satisfaction, and there are a number of towns that claim the origination of the drink.

Paris, the county seat of Bourbon County, is located about 15 miles northeast of Lexington in one of the most beautiful regions of the Bluegrass. In fact, Paris and the surrounding countryside seem to typify what people picture in their mind's eye when they think of Bluegrass horse country. Some of the most famous Kentucky horse farms are located here, including Claiborne Farm, Stone Farm, and Stoner Creek Stud.

While it had some pioneer residents as early as 1776, the town was officially established in 1789 by the Virginia legislature.

It was originally called Hopewell after the New Jersey hometown of Lawrence Protzman, who donated 250 acres for the establishment of a county seat in the mid 1780s. The official name was changed to Paris in 1790 to correspond with the naming of the county (Bourbon) after the French royal house of Bourbon in appreciation of its help during the Revolutionary War.

Bourbon County was the fifth of

nine counties formed by the Virginia Assembly before Kentucky became a state. In fact, Bourbon County was formed from part of Fayette County, of which Lexington is the county seat.

Paris has had its share of famous residents and visitors over the years. Historic Duncan Tavern, built in 1788, hosted pioneer explorers Daniel Boone and Simon Kenton.

The Kentucky legislature established the Bourbon Academy in Paris on 6,000 acres of land in 1798. Lyle's Female Academy opened for classes in 1806. Just 20 years later, Paris served as a temporary home to a famous American educator — William H. McGuffey, author of the *McGuffey Reader* — while he was on a break from Washington College.

Paris has another permanent famous inhabitant. John Fox Jr., Bourbon County native and author of such famous local color novels as *The Little Shepherd of Kingdom Come*, is buried in the Paris Cemetery.

Not to be overlooked are Bourbon County's famous animal residents. Among the great thoroughbred racehorses associated with this county are Secretariat (who in 1973 became the first winner of the Triple Crown since Citation in 1948), Riva Ridge and Swale.

Places of Interest

While visiting picturesque Paris and Bourbon County, there are several points of interest you want to be sure not to miss.

CANE RIDGE MEETINGHOUSE
KY 537   *1-987-5350*

Cane Ridge Meetinghouse, built in 1791, is the site of the origination of the Christian Church and Christian Church (Disciples of Christ) denominations during the "Great Revival" of 1801. That summer, more than 20 Presbyterian, Baptist, and Methodist preachers met at the Cane Ridge Presbyterian meeting house, preaching throughout the days and nights from wagon beds and tree stumps to congregations of more than 20,000 people who came to the revival.

Thought to be the largest one-room log structure in the country, Cane Ridge Meetinghouse is open daily free to the public April through October, 9 AM-5:30 PM. To get to the Meetinghouse (which is seven miles east of Paris), take US-460 to Ky. 537.

DUNCAN TAVERN
323 High Street   *1-987-1788*

Historic Duncan Tavern, built by Maj. Joseph Duncan in 1788, is the Kentucky headquarters for the Daughters of the American Revolution. It has been host to such famous historic figures as Simon Kenton and Daniel Boone. Located in downtown Paris, Duncan Tavern is open to the public Tuesday through Saturday, 10 AM-noon and 1-4 PM. John Fox, Jr.'s library is located in one of the Tavern's 20 rooms. The library contains original manuscripts of several of his novels dealing with life in the mountains of eastern Kentucky. Admission is $1.50 for adults, 75 cents for ages 1-11.

COLVILLE COVERED BRIDGE

Colville Road, 3 miles south of Ky. 32 near the Bourbon-Harrison county line

The Colville Covered Bridge, located four miles northwest of Millersburg on Hinkston Creek, is one of a handful of functioning covered bridges in Kentucky. Built in 1877, Colville Covered Bridge is 124 feet long and 18 feet wide. It is a single span bridge of Burr truss construction, and is on the National Historic Register.

STONER CREEK DOCK

Located at the end of Chambers Street   1-987-3625

For outdoor recreation, consider taking a canoe trip on Stoner Creek, a wide, gentle stream that runs past several famous Bluegrass horse farms, including Claiborne, Stone and Brave Brook. Canoes, paddle boats, fishing boats and pontoons can be rented from the Stoner Creek Dock for a modest fee (about $20 per boat for a half-day rental, about $30 per boat for a full day).

Reservations are recommended but not required.

CLAIBORNE FARM

Winchester Road

Over the years, Bourbon County's Claiborne Farm has been home to some of the finest horses in the world, including Kelso, Buckpasser, Bold Ruler, Swale, Danzig, Forty Niner, and Mr. Prospector.

Probably its most famous horse resident, however, was Secretariat, who retired to stud at the farm in 1974, and died and was buried there in 1989. Claiborne Farm is open to visitors by appointment only. Call the Paris-Bourbon County Chamber of Commerce at 1-987-3205 for more information about horse farm tours.

STONE FARM

1873 Winchester Road

Another famous Bourbon County horse farm, Stone Farm has been home to such racing greats as Halo, Bold Forbes, and Gato del Sol. It is also the birthplace of Sunday Silence.

As with Claiborne Farm, Stone Farm is open to visitors by appointment only. Call the Paris-Bourbon County Chamber of Commerce at 1-987-3205 for more information.

How To Get There

To get to historic Paris and Bourbon County, take U.S. 68/27 northeast out of Lexington. Also known as Paris Pike, this road meanders through some of the most beautiful horse farm country in the Bluegrass. Famous horse farms you will pass on the way from Lexington include Gainesway, Greentree Stud, Walmac,

Insiders Like:
Beer cheese at Hall's on the River in Clark County (Winchester).

Insiders' Tips

C.V. Whitney, Duntreath, and Manderly. In total, there are more than a dozen horse farms along Paris Pike.

An added sightseeing bonus is the miles of old hand-laid stone fences that line Paris Pike between Paris and Lexington.

Clark County — Winchester

When you visit Winchester in Clark County, Lexington's closest eastern neighbor (just 16 miles on I-64), don't be surprised to see folks everywhere walking around drinking something out of bright green bottles. The soft drink is Ale-8-One, and it is produced right in Winchester.

Ale-8-One got its name from a name-the-soft-drink-contest held in the 1920s by G.L. Wainscott, who developed the formula for the drink. The winning entry was Ale-8-One — "A Late One." The name — and the popularity of the drink — stuck.

Ask Clark Countians why they like Ale-8-One more than other soft drinks, and they'll be hard-pressed to pinpoint just what it is that makes this drink so unusual. It has a taste reminiscent of ginger ale, but it's less fizzy and less gingery. Actually, it doesn't taste that much like ginger ale at all. Yet it doesn't taste like 7-UP or Sprite, either. The taste is subtle, understated. It grows on you, but you can't say exactly why.

The best idea is to buy one — Winchester Insiders say the version in the ice-cold 12-ounce returnable bottles taste best — and drink it. And then try to figure out why everyone is raving about it.

You might also want to visit the Ale-8-One bottling plant. The drink has been bottled in Winchester since 1926. Tours of the plant are offered Monday-Thursday, 8:30 AM-4:30 PM, and visitors are asked to call in advance (800-736-2538) if they want to tour the plant. The Ale-8-One boutique is open Monday through Friday, 8:30 AM-4:30 PM. To get there, take the Van Meter Road exit off I-64 to Carol Road.

However, there is more to Winchester than its soft drinks.

The city and county have a long and rich history as one of the state's oldest settlements. Clark County was established in December 1792, as Kentucky's ninth county, the same year Kentucky became a state. John Baker named the city after his hometown of Winchester, Virginia, which was named for the city in England that is home to the beautiful Winchester Cathedral. The county itself was named for one of America's most well-known heroes of the American Revolution in the West, Gen. George Rogers Clark.

Some of the earliest inhabitants of the area were the Shawnee, who farmed and hunted on about 3,500 acres in the southeastern part of the county. Archaeologists are still looking for the exact location of the Shawnee village named Eskippakithiki, which means "blue lick." It was named thus because of the salt-sulphur springs that attracted game to the area.

Famed Kentucky statesman Henry Clay, "The Great Compromiser," gave his first and last Ken-

Photo: Lexington Herald-Leader

Carl Scheider, an Ale-8-One vice president, said most customers want the beverage in the green, returnable bottles.

tucky speeches in Winchester. Clay also practiced law in the Clark County Courthouse.

Clark County also gave birth to one of Kentucky's most famous sculptors, Joel Tanner Hart, born here in 1810. Hart's first experience with sculpting was as a headstone engraver for a local marble company. He later studied in Europe and went on to create some of the state's greatest sculptures, including famous busts of Cassius Marcellus Clay, Andrew Jackson and John Jordan Crittenden, as well as a full statue of Henry Clay that took more than a decade to complete. You can find a historical marker commemorating Hart's birthplace on Mount Sterling Road.

One of Winchester's more recent claims to fame is that much of the movie *The Flim-Flam Man* was filmed in Clark County.

Today, Winchester has about 15,800 residents. While Clark County has a primarily agricultural economy, several major manufacturing plants in Winchester—including Ale-8-One, Sylvania, Leggett & Platt, and Winchester Farm Dairy — provide an industrial base for the local economy. Many people living in the area work in Lexington. They say the short commute is worth the benefits of small-town living.

Places of Interest

The quiet beauty of Winchester and Clark County makes it an ideal spot for unhurried sightseeing and leisurely shopping. Downtown on Main Street, you'll be treated to the sight and experience of numerous historic buildings, unique places to eat (such as the Phantom Tea Room

Horse-drawn sleigh rides take visitors to the Kentucky Horse Park on a wintry tour of the grounds.

and the Engine House Deli, both located on Lexington Avenue), and lots of fun and unusual places to shop for antiques and specialty items.

Information on the Historic Main Street Walking Tour is available at 2 South Maple Street, Monday through Friday from 8 AM-5 PM, 1-744-0556. Among the highlights you'll want to be sure to see are the Art-Deco Leeds Theatre and the Winchester Opera House, built in 1887, which has been converted into an antique mall.

If history is your interest, you should check out College Park, located in the heart of Winchester. The park is on the site of the former Southeastern Christian College, some of the original buildings of which are still around the park. College Park also features an old statue of Daniel Boone carved by A.D.

Fisher, which was moved to the park from its previous site near Fort Boonesborough overlooking the Kentucky River. The statue is inscribed in honor of Daniel Boone: Hunter — Surveyor — Soldier, "An Instrument ordained to Settle the Wilderness."

HOLLY ROOD MANSION
Burns & Becker streets   1-744-6623
1-744-6616

Holly Rood mansion, home of Kentucky's 12th governor, James Clark, was built in 1813-14. The historic home was renovated and furnished with period pieces by the Winchester-Clark County Heritage Commission in 1976.

It is open for public tours and special events by appointment only. Admission is only $1, so it's a great value for your money.

OLD STONE MEETINGHOUSE
Boonesboro Road

Built in 1792, Old Stone Meetinghouse is the oldest established church west of the Alleghenies. Daniel and Rebecca Boone attended services here.

PIONEER TELEPHONE MUSEUM
203 Forest Avenue   *1-745-5400*
1-745-5131

This one-room museum features switchboards, booths and phones from as early as 1877. It is open free to the public on Mondays, 1-4 PM.

LEEDS THEATRE
37 N. Main Street   *1-744-6437*

This Art-Deco theatre, built in 1925, quickly became one of Winchester's most popular entertainment sites. It was closed in 1986 and was later purchased and renovated by the Winchester Council for the Arts. It opened as the Leeds Theatre and Performing Arts Center in 1990, and is now used for local arts productions.

How to Get There

Getting to Winchester from Lexington is fairly easy and straightforward. Your two basic options are either to take Winchester Road (U.S. 60) out of Lexington, which is the more scenic route, or to take I-64 west off I-75 as it goes past Lexington. This is the more direct route. There are two main Winchester exits off I-64.

Inside
Getting Around

*I*f you're reading this, you're probably either A) trying to figure out how to get here, or B) you're already here, and you're trying to figure out how the heck to get to all the great places we'll be telling you about in the rest of this book. Well, you've come to the right chapter.

On the following pages you will find information on everything from how to drive around Lexington yourself (or how to have someone else drive you around in a bus, taxi, limo, or horse-drawn carriage), to how to fly in, call anywhere in the surrounding region, or ship yourself out (if you are a package).

If you get to the end of the chapter and you're still lost, just remember that you're in the friendly and ultra-hospitable South, and most anyone around would be glad to tell you where to go (no, not like that) or at least point you in the right direction. Plus, except for the usual rush-hour traffic and a few pesky one-way streets downtown, Lexington is very accessible and easy to navigate.

Driving

Ah yes. The Great American Adventure. Give me a full tank of gas and an open highway, and I'll be one happy camper (if you *are* a happy camper, check out Campgrounds elsewhere in this book). In this section, we'll approach driving in Lexington from the outside in.

Lexington is conveniently situated on the eastern United States' major north-south interstate highway corridor — I-75. This makes it easy to get here from Detroit to Miami. There is almost always a heavy flow of traffic on I-75, and it often increases to problem proportions around holidays, especially the Fourth of July, Labor Day and Thanksgiving. However, work is under way to make the interstate more accommodating to the large volume of traffic it carries each day. I-75 is currently being widened to six lanes from Georgetown north of Lexington to past Berea south of Lexington.

There are five Lexington exits off I-75. All but one eventually cross New Circle Road, the four-lane road ringing much of Lexington (more about that later). Starting from the south is Exit 104, locally known as the Athens-Boonesboro exit — Athens is pronounced "A-thens" unlike the traditional pronunciation of the Greek city. Going into Lexington, this road eventually becomes four-lane Richmond Road, which eventually becomes Main Street and takes

Taking a carriage ride is a great way to enjoy downtown.

Photo: Lexington Herald-Leader

you right downtown. Depending on the traffic flow, it takes about 15-25 minutes to get downtown from I-75. The speed limit decreases from 55 to 45 to 35 the closer you get to downtown.

Next is Exit 108, or Man o' War Boulevard, named, like many of Lexington's streets, after a famous thoroughbred race horse. This is the only exit that doesn't hit New Circle, primarily because Man o' War is itself an arc (outside the ring of New Circle) around much of Lexington — about 16 miles long. It does, however, cross Richmond Road. Man o' War services most of the fast-growing southern section of Lexington, including many of the new subdivisions and apartment complexes, from I-75 to Versailles Road in the west. There are about a dozen stoplights along its route, and the speed limit is 45 mph (compared to 55 on New Circle), but you can get, for

instance, from the interstate to Blue Grass Airport without ever getting into the downtown traffic.

Exit 110 — Winchester Road — is next in line. This is this author's personal favorite route to downtown Lexington, mainly because while it is busy, the traffic seems to move along fairly well, and one usually can get downtown in about 10 minutes. Speed limits on this four-lane road drop from 55 to 45 around the intersection with New Circle, and then to 35 as you approach downtown. A center turning lane prevents folks making left turns from slowing traffic at intersections. Winchester Road eventually ends at Main Street.

Three miles farther north is Exit 113. This exit leads out of Lexington on Paris Pike or into Lexington on Broadway. Broadway leads into downtown from the northeast past some of the city's most historic buildings, including Transylvania University, the first college west of the

Insiders know that the neon light atop "Big Blue," the Lexington Financial Center, will lead you right into the center of town. If lost, find Big Blue and follow it.

Alleghenies, and the Lexington Opera House. If you are heading toward an event at Rupp Arena, this is the route to take. Once Broadway crosses Main Street and starts heading out of town to the west, it becomes Harrodsburg Road.

The final exit — 115 — is Newtown Pike. Newtown Pike is not as congested as some of the other feeder routes, but it crosses Main Street northwest of downtown, so you have to backtrack a short distance if you want to go downtown. Newtown Pike takes you past the famous Marriott's Griffin Gate Resort and golf course complex, as well as past Lexmark International, one of Lexington's major manufacturers, producing IBM laserprinters, typewriters, office supply equipment and keyboards.

East-west interstate travelers are serviced by I-64 which runs from Huntington, West Virginia, in the east to Louisville in the west. I-64 and I-75 join for about a 7-mile stretch around the northern part of Lexington, splitting off into separate roads just north of exit 115 and between exits 110 and 113.

Once you're in Lexington, the key navigational feature is New Circle Road. New Circle is like the sun — you can always tell which way you're going in relation to it. Roughly, Lexington is laid out like a giant bicycle wheel with downtown at its hub and

"spokes" running out in the form of nine major feeder roads — clockwise from the south, Tates Creek, Nicholasville, Harrodsburg, Versailles, Leestown, Newtown, Broadway, Winchester and Richmond. Many of these roads are named for the surrounding towns they link with Lexington.

Lexington's three major malls are on Nicholasville Road (Fayette Mall), Harrodsburg Road (Turfland Mall), and Richmond Road (Lexington Mall). Blue Grass Airport is on Versailles Road.

Nicholasville Road is a little tricky, because Monday through Friday its lanes change. That means that from 7 to 9 AM traffic going into downtown from New Circle gets an extra lane (making three total inbound lanes plus a center turning lane), reducing the traffic going out of town to one lane. This process is reversed from 4 to 6 PM.

Lights across the road at regular intervals indicate which lanes are in use by whom. Green arrows over a lane indicate you can drive in that lane, a yellow "X" means the lane is for turning only, and a red "X" means the lane is for use by traffic going the opposite direction. It sounds confusing, but it doesn't seem to cause many problems, so don't worry about it too much. If you end up in the wrong lane, plenty of people will honk at you to make you aware of your mistake.

Now to downtown and its one-way streets. Most streets are divided into "North" and "South" segments at Main Street, and "East" and "West" segments at Limestone Street. Street numbers start at 100 at these intersections and increase in both directions.

Main Street is one way (westbound) from Vine Street to the Civic Center (just past Broadway). Two flanking streets, Short Street to the north and Vine Street to the south, are one-way the other direction. Streets crossing Main Street alternate one-way directions, with the exception of Rose Street, Martin Luther King Boulevard and Broadway, which are two way north-south roads.

Traveling to the south of Main Street (the general direction of the University of Kentucky campus), streets running parallel to Main Street — Vine, High, and Maxwell — alternate one way directions until Euclid Avenue, which is two-way. To the north of Main Street (toward I-75), generally, the streets are "numbered," like Second Street, etc., and run in alternating one-way directions.

Again, it sounds confusing, but actually, the layout of downtown is fairly logical and straightforward. A special, politically incorrect note to male drivers: If you get lost, for heaven's sake, please stop and ask directions!

If you don't want to try to navigate on your own, you can check out one of the following options.

Public Transportation

About 175,000 people use the Lexington public transportation (LexTran) system each month. The Transit Authority of Lexington offers 17 main bus routes throughout the city, including two trolley routes downtown and connecting bus routes to the UK campus that run on 25-minute intervals in circular routes.

To get a bus schedule or to have one of the LexTran information clerks help you find which bus to take to get where you want to go, call 253-INFO, Monday-Friday, 7:30 AM-4:30 PM. Schedules are also available at the following locations: the Transit Center, 220 Vine Street; Transit Authority office, 109 West Loudoun; Central Library or any public library branch; Fayette County Health Department, 650 Newtown Pike; Lexington-Fayette Urban County Government Center, 200 East Main Street; Turfland Mall information desk, Harrodsburg Road; Central Bank (Kincaid Towers); or on the route's bus.

LexTran bus fares are 80 cents

Insiders know that, according to Kentucky state law, drivers must stay in the right lane except when passing on the highway.

Insiders' Tips

for adults, 40 cents for disabled and people older than 65, and 60 cents for youth ages 6-18. Children younger than 6 ride free. To get the reduced rates, you must present your LexTran ID card, available at the transit Center or the Transit Authority office Monday through Friday, 8:30 AM-4:30 PM. Exact change is required, and once you pay the fare, you can get a free transfer to another bus or trolley.

If you ride the bus a lot, you can save money by purchasing a LexTran pass. Adult monthly passes (unlimited rides) are $30. Elderly/Disabled monthly passes are $15. Twenty-ride adult passes are $15, and 20-ride youth passes are $10.

Trolley rates are 25 cents for adults and 10 cents for disabled and senior citizens.

One note: LexTran does not offer regular bus service on Sundays, and Saturday schedules are more limited than the weekdays. For more information about weekend service, see the "LexDart" section below.

LexTran's "Wheels" service, provided in conjunction with the American Red Cross, meets the requirements of the Americans with Disabilities Act by providing door-to-door transportation for the disabled. Call 253-INFO to see if you qualify for this service. The Wheels fare is $1.60 one way.

LexTran offers free ride service on the University of Kentucky campus through its Blue and White routes. Trolley service connects the campus to downtown. The UK trolley stop is on Euclid Avenue.

Many people working in Lexington live outside the main metropolitan area and commute to work each day. In connection with Bluegrass Area Ridesharing, LexTran offers two commuter options. LexVan is a commuter vanpool leasing service with 15 passenger vans, and it is recommended for people living at least 15 miles from the same general employment area. For instance, a group of people living in Richmond (about 25 miles south of Lexington) who all work downtown might get a LexVan group together. This saves money on individual gas and car wear and tear and parking, while at the same time helping the environment by reducing the amount of hydrofluorocarbons being pumped into the ozone layer from automobile exhaust. LexTran will help you get your vanpool together.

Another commuter service is 233-POOL, an office that helps people set up commuter carpools.

For those Lexingtonians living outside the main LexTran bus routes, those who no longer get bus service because of route changes, and those who don't get Saturday or night bus service, LexDart often saves the day. There are three main types of LexDart service. Limited LexDart, for passengers who received bus service before route changes but no longer do, or for those who have regular bus service but no night or Saturday service, takes passengers from their door to the nearest LexTran transfer point for regular bus fares.

Sunday LexDart service is door-to-door transportation within the Lexington service area, and costs $1.10 per mile.

Rural LexDart service is for those living outside the LexTran service

Photo: Lexington Herald-Leader

Blue Grass Airport, across Versailles Road (U.S. 60) from Keeneland, connects Lexington and Central Kentucky to the world.

area. Transportation from your door to the nearest LexTran transfer point is offered Monday-Friday from 6 AM to 7 PM. The cost is $1.10 per mile.

Remember: All LexDart services have to be scheduled in advance. Call 254-DART to schedule your service or for more information.

Taxis and Limousines

If you want to have someone else drive you around, Lexington has several taxi and limousine options available.

HOLIDAY CAB, LEXINGTON YELLOW CAB, AND UNITED TRANSPORTATION INC.
708 W. Third Street   *231-8294*

With a fleet of 24 propane-powered Chevrolet Caprices, this consolidated taxi company provides ser-

vice to Lexingtonians 24 hours a day, 365 days a year. Rates are $1.90 flat rate for any call, plus $1.60 a mile for up to four people. Discount coupons offering a 20 percent discount for senior citizens and the disabled are available at the main office on West Third Street.

GOLD SHIELD LIMOUSINE INC.
2623 Regency Road   *255-6388*

With stretch limousines accommodating up to eight passengers, Gold Shield Limousine Inc. offers hourly and daily limousine, van and luxury sedan rental. Limousine rates for six-passenger vehicles are $45/hour (two-hour minimum), and $550/day. Rates for eight-passenger limousines are $65/hour (two-hour minimum), and $650/day.

Gold Shield also has available (for

travel in Kentucky only) a "luxuriously appointed" executive coach that seats 23 passengers. This vehicle is equipped with a galley and bar, restroom, TVs, stereo and CD player.

LIMOUSINE'S INC. LAND TRANSPORT
Bluegrass Field   255-4981

Limousine's Inc. offers shuttle service to and from Blue Grass Airport, with fares ranging from $5 to $25 in the Lexington area. Stretch limousine service is available throughout Kentucky for $45/hour with a two-hour minimum.

HAPPY'S LIMO SERVICE
1167 Commercial Drive   252-1541

Happy's Limo Service, with its fleet of one charcoal-grey and two white stretch limousines, services all of Kentucky at a rate of $45/hour, two-hour minimum. Happy's has a special one-way rate of $100 from Lexington to either the Cincinnati or Louisville airports.

Carriage Rides

What could be more romantic than a ride with that special someone in an elegant horse-drawn carriage through some of downtown Lexington's most beautiful areas?

Lexington Livery gives you and up to three other people at a time a chance to experience Lexington in the mode

of days gone by. Carriage rides are offered nearly every night from 7:30 to 10:30 PM during most of the year. Exceptions are nights when there is bad weather January through March.

Carriage rides depart from the Vine Street entrance of the Radisson Hotel and ride through historic Gratz Park and beautiful Triangle Park during the 25-minute tour. The cost is $25 for up to four people. Reservations are not usually necessary, except for peak times at Christmas and New Year's Eve. To make reservations or for more information, call 259-0000.

Airline and Bus Travel

If you want to come by air or by land, Lexington has several options to offer at Blue Grass Airport through Delta, USAir, United Express, Comair, Atlantic Southeast Airlines, American Eagle and TWA, or through Greyhound bus service.

BLUE GRASS AIRPORT
4000 Versailles Road   254-9336

Located five miles west of Lexington in some of the region's lushest horse country, Blue Grass Airport was transferred to the city of Lexington from the U.S. Army Air Corps in 1945. Located on a 1,000-acre site, Blue Grass Airport houses 10 regional and national carriers with 61 depar-

Insiders' Tips

Whenever possible, insiders avoid Nicholasville and Richmond roads during peak traffic times.

tures daily to major cities around the country. Connections to international airline service as well as an in-house U.S. Customs department make international travel to and from Lexington convenient as well.

GREYHOUND

477 New Circle Road NW   299-8804

About eight buses a day go through the Lexington Greyhound bus line station, which is open daily 7:30 AM to 11 PM. Typical one-way rates include $50 from Lexington to Chicago, $99 to New York City, and $110 to Tampa. There is a no-smoking policy in effect for the buses.

Greyhound also has a package express service (call 299-0428 for more information) that offers, for instance, same-day delivery to Chicago for $25 for up to ten pounds, and $15 for overnight delivery.

Telephone Service

It may seem strange to have a section on local phone service and how to use it, but as Lexington and its surrounding cities (for more details on these, see Lexington's Neighbors) continue to expand toward each other, their phone service needs are changing. It wasn't too long ago that it was long distance to call any of the surrounding towns from Lexington or vice versa. Now that has changed for some of the towns.

So here's the low-down. Calls between Lexington (basically, all the exchanges starting with a "2") and Georgetown (863, 867, and 868 exchanges), Wilmore (858 exchanges), Versailles (873 and 879 exchanges), Midway (846 exchanges) and Nicholasville (885 and 887 exchanges) are all local calls. However, long-distance rates apply when calling between each other, such as a call between Wilmore and Versailles. The exception to this is calls between Georgetown and Midway, which are local calls.

One note about phone numbers listed in the *Insiders' Guide® to Greater Lexington*: Numbers are listed as they would be used if called from Lexington. That is, Lexington is in the "606" area code, so other numbers in that area code that are long-distance calls from Lexington have a "1" before the exchange. If you are calling from another area code, you need to add the "606" when dialing.

Phone numbers in the state's other area code — "502" which includes most of the western half of the state — have the area code listed in front of the number. If a phone number has nothing in front of the exchange, that means it is a local call from Lexington. It may not, however, be a local call from everywhere in the Bluegrass area.

Photo: Lexington Herald-Leader

Pam Miller is Lexington's mayor.

Inside
Government

Fayette County Government

Most newcomers to Lexington soon become acquainted with the initials LFUCG. While you're better off not trying to pronounce these letters as a word, you'll probably find yourself writing them on checks for things like city taxes and sewer user fees.

LFUCG stands for Lexington-Fayette Urban County Government, the voter-approved entity that took effect January 1, 1974. The new charter created a merged city-county government made up of a mayor and a 15-member Urban County Council. The council — which has authority to pass local ordinances, establish budgets and levy certain taxes — consists of one representative for each of the county's 12 districts plus three at-large members. District representatives are elected to two-year terms; at-large council members serve for four years.

(The map in this chapter shows Fayette County's 12 council districts.)

In addition to giving Lexington a larger population, the merger of city and county governments also eliminated duplication in services and allowed more coordinated efforts in such areas as planning, law enforcement and public safety, public educa-

tion and parks and recreation.

Lexington's mayor is Pam Miller, a 15-year veteran of the Urban County Council. Miller, who was vice mayor when Mayor Scotty Baesler was elected to the U.S. House of Representatives in November 1992, took over Baesler's position in January 1993 and served the remainder of his term. In November 1993, she was elected to her first term as mayor.

Teresa Isaac is vice mayor, a position given to the top vote-getter among the at-large council candidates.

It's a good idea to get to know the council member representing your district. He or she was elected to serve you and other people who live in your neighborhood and should be willing to talk with you about any matters that you think the council should address.

The phone number for the Urban County Council office is 258-3200; most council members also have their home numbers listed in the phone book. The mayor's office number is 258-3100. The Public Information office is at 258-3010. For other LFUCG information, call 258-3000.

In addition to the 12 council districts, Fayette County is divided into five school board districts, seven state legislative (representatives) districts, and four state senatorial districts. District determinations are based on population.

When you register to vote as a new Lexington resident, the county clerk's office will be able to tell you which districts your address is in. The office number is 253-3344; ask for Voter Registration. You might also be interested in picking up a copy of the Blue Sheet, published annually by the local League of Women Voters, a non-partisan group. Call 266-2847 to get on the list to receive a Blue Sheet, which lists your government officials from the U.S. president on down. The public library also has copies.

All of Fayette County is contained in the sixth U.S. Congressional district, the fifth Supreme Court district, the fifth Court of Appeals district, and the 22nd Circuit Court and District Court districts.

Urban County Council Members

At-large — Teresa Isaac
              Charles W. Ellinger
              David Stevens
District 1 — George A. Brown Jr.
District 2 — Robert R. Jefferson
District 3 — Kathy Pratt
District 4 — Isabel Yates
District 5 — Fernita Wallace
District 6 — Bobby Flynn
District 7 — Willy Fogle
District 8 — Fred V. Brown
District 9 — Roy Durbin
District 10 — Sandra Shafer
District 11 — Jack Hillard
District 12 — Gloria Martin

Photo: Lexington Herald-Leader

Brereton C. Jones is governor of Kentucky.

State Government

Brereton Jones is the governor of Kentucky. Paul Patton is the lieutenant governor. Bob Babbage is secretary of state. Chris Gorman is the attorney general. All are Democrats.

The Kentucky General Assembly is made up of 38 state senators serving four-year terms and 100 state representatives serving two-year terms. We have listed the names, addresses and phone numbers of legislators representing all or parts of Fayette, Bourbon, Clark, Franklin, Jessamine, Madison, Scott and Woodford counties.

STATE SENATORS

Tim Philpot (R)
12th District (Fayette)
3060 Harrodsburg Road,
    Suite 205
Lexington, KY 40507
224-4999 office, 224-3093 home

Michael R. Moloney (D)
13th District (Fayette)
259 West Short Street
Lexington, KY 40507
255-7946 office, 268-1784 home

Fred Bradley (D)
20th District (includes Franklin)
Indian Ridge Farm
Franklin, KY 40601
(502) 564-2294 office,
(502) 227-4443 home

Tom Buford (R)
22nd District (includes Jessamine)
708 Richmond Avenue
Nicholasville, KY 40356
885-1867 home

John A. "Eck" Rose (D)
28th District (includes Clark)
P.O. Box 511
Winchester, KY 40391
1-744-4338 home

Ed Ford (D)
30th District (includes Bourbon,
   Fayette, Scott and Woodford)
Route 2, Box 419
Cynthiana, KY 41031
1-224-2850 office, 1-234-1164 home

At publication, the 34th District
seat was vacant after the resignation
of Landon C. Sexton. By the time
you read this, however, a replace-
ment will probably have been
elected.

State Representatives

Lonnie Napier (R)
36th District (includes Madison)
302 Danville Street

Lancaster, KY 40444
1-792-4289 office, 1-792-4860 home

Robert R. Damron (D)
39th District (includes Jessamine)
231 Fairway Drive West
Nicholasville, KY 40356
263-7009 office, 887-1744 home

Stan Cave (R)
45th District (includes Fayette)
1100 Mount Rushmore Way
Lexington, KY 40515
255-9500 office, 273-7106 home

Joe Barrows (D)
56th District (Franklin, Jessamine and Woodford)
152 Stout Avenue
Versailles, KY 40383
873-9768 home

C.M. "Hank" Hancock (D)
57th District (Franklin)
514 Murray Street
Frankfort, KY 40601
(502) 227-2666 office,
(502) 223-3662 home

Mark Farrow (D)
62nd District (includes Scott)
2785 Stamping Ground Road
Stamping Ground, KY 40379
863-6288 office, 535-6104 home

Jim LeMaster (D)
72nd District (includes Fayette,
   Bourbon)
127 Duncan Avenue
Paris, KY 40361
231-8500 office, 1-987-7873 home

Drew Graham (D)
73rd District (includes Clark)

10984 Iron Works Road
Winchester, KY 40391
1-842-3020 home

Ernesto Scorsone (D)
75th District (Fayette)
167 West Main Street
Lexington, KY 40507
254-5766 office, 254-3681 home

Ruth Ann Palumbo (D)
76th District (Fayette)
10 Deepwood Drive
Lexington, KY 40505
299-2597 office, 299-2598 home

Jesse Crenshaw (D)
77th District (Fayette)
117 Constitution
Lexington, KY 40507
252-6967 office, 259-1402 home

Leslie Trapp (D)
78th District (Fayette)
1045 Lane Allen Road
Lexington, KY 40504
277-6868 office, 277-7728 home

Bill Lear (D)
79th District (Fayette)
732 Lakeshore Drive
Lexington, KY 40502
231-3000 office, 269-4852 home

Harry Moberly, Jr. (D)
81st District (Madison)
P.O. Box 721
Richmond, KY 40475
1-622-1501 office, 1-624-2781 home

U.S. Congress

In Washington, Kentucky has two U.S. senators and six representatives. (There were previously seven congressional districts, but districts were redrawn in 1991 based on figures from the 1990 census.) Every county in the Lexington metropolitan statistical area is contained within the 6th District, which is represented by Scotty Baesler, the former mayor of Lexington.

U.S. SENATORS
Wendell H. Ford (D)
Room 173-A Russell Senate
    Office Building
Washington, D.C. 20510,
    (202) 224-4343
or 343 Waller Avenue, Lexington,
    KY 40504, 233-2484

Mitch McConnell (R)
Suite 120 Russell Senate Office
    Building
Washington, D.C. 20510,
    (202) 224-2541
or 155 East Main Street, Suite
    210, Lexington, KY 40507,
    252-1781

U.S. REPRESENTATIVE
Scotty Baesler (D)
6th District, 508 Cannon
    House Office Building
Washington, D.C. 20515,
    (202) 225-4706
or 444 East Main Street, Suite
    103, Lexington, KY 40507,
    253-1124

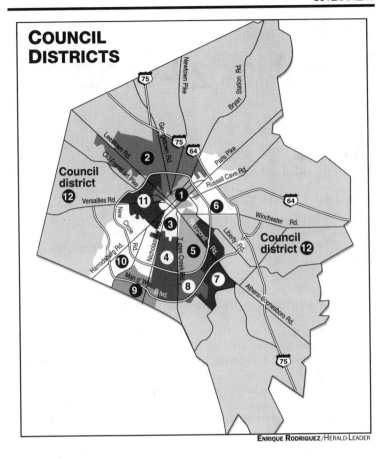

COUNCIL DISTRICTS

ENRIQUE RODRIGUEZ/HERALD-LEADER

Political Parties and Organizations

Democratic Party of Fayette County
820 Lane Allen Road, 225-5269

Republican Party of Fayette County
861 Corporate Drive, 223-4120

Bluegrass Chapter of the National
Organization for Women
P.O. Box 22151, Lexington, KY,
40522, 277-1140

League of Women Voters of
Lexington, Inc.
P.O. Box 22045, Lexington, KY,
40522, 266-2847

Inside
Law-abiding Lexington

Here's a warning to all manure collectors, fortune-tellers and masked men and women: You may be subject to penalty under the law.

According to the Lexington-Fayette County Code:

• The accumulation of manure is prohibited, unless it is stored in a properly constructed pit or receptacle.

• It is illegal to charge money for foretelling the future or conducting a seance.

• Unless it's Halloween and you're 12 years old or younger, you are breaking the law if you wear a mask or disguise on a public street. Another law, which may or may not be related, requires hotel guests to register under their "true names" in writing, giving their permanent address and place of employment.

Chances are, of course, that none of these laws affects you. You may want to know, however, about the laws covering more mundane, day-to-day issues like licenses, traffic laws, pets and taxes. And that's why we've written this chapter.

On the Road

Gotta have a driver's license. New residents who drive must get their Kentucky driver's license within 30 days of moving to the state. With a valid current license from another state, in most cases all you'll need to do is pass a written test and eye exam and pay the $8 fee — cash only, please. Driver's licenses are valid for four years from date of issue and must be renewed by the end of your birth month. A combination driver's license and motorcycle license, also good for four years, is $18.

To get your license, visit Room 206 of the county clerk's office downtown at 162 East Main Street, 254-9861, between 8:30 AM and 4 PM.

If you don't have a license from anywhere, you'll need a learner's permit first. It costs $2, and you must pass an eye test and a written test. Spend the next month practicing your road skills, then arrange to take the road test, which, if passed, enables you to get your license. The minimum driving age in Kentucky is 16.

If you're in high school, there's something else to keep in mind if you don't want to rely on Mom to be your prom chauffeur: Fayette County schools enforce a 1990 state law that denies driver's licenses to students who drop out, make poor grades or play too much hooky.

School districts are required to notify the state Transportation Cabinet when a 16- or 17-year-old quits school, fails to pass at least four

Lexington has a seat-belt law. Should you be pulled over for another traffic violation and be seen not wearing your seat belt, you could be fined $25, in addition to getting in trouble for whatever reason got you pulled over in the first place.

Insiders' Tips

classes or has nine unexcused absences in a semester. The Division of Driver's Licensing then revokes the licenses of those students. Students who apply for licenses or learner's permits must produce a school form verifying that they are in school and passing.

To regain their licenses, students or dropouts must successfully complete a semester of school. Or they can turn 18, calendar permitting.

Blue-plate special. Automobiles of permanent residents must be licensed in Kentucky. Upon moving to Lexington from out of state, you are required to obtain a Kentucky license plate within 15 days. To pick up your blue-and-white Kentucky plate, complete with the twin spires of Churchill Downs, visit Room 102 of the county clerk's office, 162 East Main Street, 253-3344. Bring the original certificate of title, proof of insurance, $14 and proof that you paid sales tax when you bought the vehicle. The license plate must be renewed each year.

If you have not paid sales tax on your vehicle, you'll also have to pay a six percent tax on its retail value, with a 10 percent discount on the tax if the car is new.

Under the influence. When it comes to drunken driving, there is

no such thing as benefit of the doubt in Kentucky. Prosecutors are not required to prove that a suspect is impaired; an "illegal per se" provision assumes that anyone with a blood alcohol content of 0.10 or higher is intoxicated. And the penalties can be very steep.

Drunken driving is a serious offense anywhere. It is taken very seriously in Lexington, where unmarked Ford Crown Victorias and other cars patrol the streets to stop intoxicated motorists before they can hurt anyone.

Throughout the state, which toughened its drunken driving law in 1991, a first offense is punishable by a fine of $500 plus court costs, as much as 30 days in jail and a 90-day driver's license suspension.

A fourth offense in a five-year period is a Class D felony punishable by up to five years in prison.

Buckling the trend. There is no statewide seat-belt law, but Lexington and Louisville, among others, have enacted their own ordinances making seat-belt use mandatory. Lexington's ordinance is a secondary law, which means a police officer can issue a citation only after stopping a motorist for another traffic violation.

Once stopped, however, you

could be fined $25 plus court costs for not wearing your seat belt. Pleading ignorance won't help: The law is posted at all entrances to Fayette County.

After the law became effective in July 1990, surveys found that more than 75 percent of local drivers and passengers were wearing their seat belts. This was the highest percentage ever for an entire community, according to the National Highway Traffic Safety Administration, which awarded Lexington its first national "70-plus" award.

Strapping in the kids is even more important. Failure to buckle a child less than 40 inches tall — in general, a child younger than 4 — can result in a $50 fine. Drivers of pickup trucks are exempt from the law if the cab is filled with adults in addition to the child.

Turning on red. Unless a sign indicates otherwise, right turns on red are permitted after the driver has come to a complete stop. Left turns on red are permitted when turning from a one-way street onto another one-way street. Again, you should stop first.

Arrows and X's. A green arrow on a traffic light indicates an appropriate lane for driving, a yellow "X" indicates a left turning lane and a red "X" indicates lanes in use by oncoming traffic. Understanding these signals is especially important when traveling on Nicholasville Road, where some lanes' directions change throughout the day.

Passing school buses. A motorist who illegally passes a school bus can be fined $100 to $500, jailed 30 days to six months or penalized six points on his or her driver's license, depending on whether it is the first, second or third offense. On a four-lane road, passing is illegal on the same side of the road as the bus but allowed for traffic going in the opposite direction.

The fast lane. The left lane of a limited-access, four-lane highway is for passing. Slow drivers in the left lane are considered just as potentially hazardous as speeders, and they can be fined $20 to $100.

Radar detectors. There is no local or state law prohibiting the use of radar detectors. That doesn't mean, of course, that we are condoning the excessive use of speed by people who know where the cops are and aren't.

Window tinting. A state law restricts the amount of tint permitted on vehicle windows. Front side windows must allow 35 percent of sunlight to get through. Rear side windows must allow 18 percent of sunlight to get through. A tint allowing 5 percent sun transmission is allowed on the rear window if the vehicle has two side view mirrors. Failure to comply is a misdemeanor equipment violation.

Parking. You could be fined if you park on a sidewalk or other pedestrian travel area, leave your vehicle parked on the street for more than 24 hours or block a driveway. Vehicles more than seven feet wide, 20 feet long or seven-and-a-half feet high cannot be parked on residential streets for more than two hours in most cases. Out-of-town visitors can get a permit from the Division of Police that will let them park a recreational vehicle on a residential street for 24 hours.

If you get a parking ticket in Lexington, you may want to gamble on the chance that police are too busy chasing criminals to come after you. You're better off, however, paying the fine, which doubles if not paid within 30 days. An expired meter will cost you $4 initially, while illegal parking carries an $8 fine if paid on time. Eventually, ignored parking tickets could land you in circuit court, and wouldn't that be a hassle?

Saturday is free parking day at all city parking meters, most of which are found in the downtown business district.

Animals

Gotta have a pet license. Within Fayette County's Urban Services Area, every dog owner must buy a $1.50 state license as well as a local license, which is $1.50 for spayed or neutered dogs and $8.50 for unaltered dogs. State licenses are not required for cats, but each cat owner in the Urban Services Area must buy a local license, which is $3 for spayed or neutered cats and $10 for unaltered cats. Licenses must be renewed each July. Violators face a $50 fine.

The requirements apply to all dogs and cats, whether they stay inside or outside the house, with a couple of exceptions. Dog or cat owners older than 65 and those who own service animals, such as lead animals for the blind, can buy a lifetime license, which is $3 if the animal is spayed or neutered and $10 if not. Animals kept 30 days or less for the purpose of breeding or showing do not require a license as long as the owner has current proof of rabies vaccination.

Licenses are available through the Lexington Humane Society, 1600 Old Frankfort Pike, 233-0044, and through a number of veterinary offices. To get a license, take a rabies certificate and any proof of spaying or neutering, but leave the animal at home.

Animal control. Dogs must be kept on a leash at all times; pets that roam the streets or create nuisances can earn fines for their owners. Dogs and cats must be vaccinated for rabies between four months and six months of age. Animals are also subject to Lexington's noise-control ordinance (details below).

The big scoop. It may be a dirty job, but somebody has to do it. And that somebody is the pet owner. When your dog or cat — or, presumably, your horse or monkey — does its business on a city sidewalk or street or in a park or someone else's yard, it's your business to clean it up. The "pooper scooper" law carries a $50 fine for violators.

Sound Law

Lexington has an ordinance prohibiting "noise disturbances," which are loosely defined as "any sound which annoys a reasonable person of normal sensitivities" — a definition that could surely make for some intriguing courtroom debate — across public places or right-of-ways.

There are some time restrictions for certain activities when they cross "dwelling unit boundaries":

• No lawn mowers, power tools, loudspeakers, public address systems, powered model vehicles or "miscellaneous noises" between 11 PM and 7 AM weekdays, or before 9 AM on weekends.

• No musical disturbances or barking dogs at any time.

Any person who makes one of these noises that goes beyond his or her property line can be given a warning citation or a fine. On the surface, this seems strict. But police seem more interested in enforcing the spirit of the law than the exact letter, and they generally investigate only when they receive a complaint.

Incidentally, wearing loud clothing while not on a golf course may earn you some strange looks, but there's no law against it.

Other Laws

"Good Neighbor" ordinances. Lexington has a number of ordinances — including the ones on animal and noise control and parking — designed to promote neighborhood peace and protect property and people. A couple of others:

• Property owners or occupants must maintain public sidewalks adjoining their property and keep them free of obstructions.

• Tall weeds, trash and debris, junked vehicles and other such items are considered nuisances and can result in fines.

"How to Be a Better Neighbor," a free booklet detailing these and other "Good Neighbor" ordinances, is available from the Lexington-Fayette Urban County Government. Call 258-3010.

Gotta have a marriage license. A marriage license will cost you $22 in cash, and it's good for life, at least theoretically. You can get it at the county clerk's office, 162 East Main Street, from 8:30 AM to 4 PM Monday through Friday. No waiting period, physical or blood test is required. Limit one to a customer, please.

Alcoholic beverage sales. The minimum drinking age in Kentucky is 21. Restaurants, bars and other licensed establishments can sell alcoholic beverages from 6 AM to 1

AM Monday through Saturday and from 1 PM to 11 PM Sunday. "Package stores," as state authorities refer to stores that sell beer, wine and liquor, are allowed to be open from 7 AM to 1 AM Monday through Saturday. No package alcohol sales are permitted on Sunday or before polls close on election days. You'll have plenty of time to drink *after* you find out whom you've just elected.

Some Taxing Subjects

Kentucky retail sales tax, paid by the consumer, is 6 percent. Some products, including most groceries, are exempt.

Property tax must be assessed at 100 percent of its fair cash value. The first $16,000 of a homestead owned by people 65 and older is exempt if they live on the property. A mobile home may qualify for the homestead exemption if it is on a permanent foundation.

School tax is 3 percent of your utility bills (electric, natural gas, water, telephone and cable television).

In addition to these taxes, Kentucky levies an individual income tax, and the Lexington-Fayette Urban County Government an occupational license tax on all wages, salaries and commissions earned in the county.

Photo: Lexington Herald-Leader

Kentucky leads the nation in the production of burley tobacco and is second to North Carolina in overall tobacco production. This farmer is cutting tobacco stalks and spearing them, a practice usually done in August.

Inside
Agriculture, Business and Industry

*L*exington's economy today is built on a healthy mixture of manufacturing, retailing, services and, of course, agriculture. This latter category is the one most associated with the Bluegrass, probably because the fertile land has given rise to the state's best-known exports: horses, burley tobacco and bourbon whiskey, which is made with corn, wheat, rye and barley.

For years, Kentucky was one of the nation's top producers of corn, and the endlessly versatile grain is still an important crop, as are hay and soybeans. But among agricultural products, tobacco still rules, with Kentucky leading the nation in the production of burley and trailing only North Carolina in overall tobacco production. Lexington is home to a large tobacco auction market as well as the Burley Tobacco Growers Cooperative Association.

Cattle and livestock have long contributed heavily to the economy of Central Kentucky and the rest of the state. In 1987, Kentucky cattle and calf sales totaled $1.51 billion, more than tobacco and second only to horse sales.

Hemp has also played an important role, especially during Lexington's early years and during World War II, when farmers were encouraged to grow the crop for rope. Some Kentuckians claim the plant continues to be the state's top cash crop, albeit an illegal one. No longer needed for rope, the *Cannabis sativa* plant, also known as marijuana, owed its resurgence to its popularity as a mind-altering substance. Gatewood Galbraith, a Lexington lawyer, based his 1991 gubernatorial campaign on the legalization of hemp to boost the state economy. Although he received 5 percent of the vote, more than most people expected, today's hemp growers still must maintain a low profile.

But, despite all the agricultural images that persist, Lexington and Central Kentucky have long proven that the area is also fertile for the growth of virtually any other type of business. In fact, Lexington's ability to weather the Great Depression better than a lot of other American cities has been attributed to the diversity of its economy. Today you'll find a variety of manufacturing operations — there are more than 50 plants in Fayette County alone — along with a wealth of employment opportunities in areas ranging from retail, tourism, hospitality and banking to government, education, medicine and communications. As might be expected, the equine industry is also a major employer, directly providing more than 20,000 jobs throughout the state.

According to a report in the July 1993 issue of *Governing* magazine, the Lexington-Fayette County area is among the ten cities with the lowest unemployment in the nation. Those who are looking for jobs may be able to find work through more than a dozen temporary agencies and employment services.

More than half the state's manufacturing jobs are contained within the Lexington-Louisville-Cincinnati triangle. New manufacturing operations continue to view Lexington and surrounding counties as a viable option for new plants or relocations. Advantages include railroad access and proximity to two major east-west and north-south highways, Interstates 64 and 75, which put Lexington within 500 miles of two-thirds of the U.S. population. In addition, surrounding counties provide a sizable work force for hiring, and the state has shown a willingness to provide attractive tax breaks and other incentives to attract new businesses.

Greater Lexington's largest employer is the **University of Kentucky**, the state's largest institution of higher learning, with 10,000 people on its payroll, including employees of the school's **Chandler Medical Center**. **Toyota Motor Manufacturing USA**, which opened its billion-dollar Camry plant in Georgetown in December 1987, employs 4,500. The **Fayette County Public School System** employs more than 3,600. **Lexmark International**, which manufactures color computer laser printers, typewriters and related products, has 3,000 employees, and the **Lexington-Fayette Urban County Government** has 2,950.

The **Veterans Administration Medical Center** employs 2,000, **Central Baptist Hospital** 1,600, **Saint Joseph Hospital** 1,500. **Square D Company**, which makes circuit breakers and other electrical equipment, employs 1,200. **Ashland Oil**, the largest corporation in the state, has 1,100 office workers in Lexington. Companies with 1,000 employees are **Kentucky Utilities**, which provides electricity to thousands of Bluegrass homes; **IBM Corporation**, including its **ISSC** subsidiary; **The Trane Company**, manufacturer of commercial air-handling units; **McAlpin's** clothing retailer; and map and book manufacturer **Rand McNally & Co.**

Other major employers include **GTE South** with 980, **Bank One,** 970; **Good Samaritan Hospital,** 826; **Lexington Clinic,** 800; **United**

Photo: Lexington Herald-Leader

Thiel Audio Products in Lexington makes speakers that range in price from $1,100 to $11,000 a pair. Pop singer Janet Jackson is one of the company's customers.

States Post Office, 900; and **Texas Instruments;** 700. **James N. Gray Construction Co.**, Kentucky's largest general contractor, has 400 employees. (Employment figures are courtesy of the Greater Lexington Chamber of Commerce.)

In addition to the Toyota Camry, Lexington-area companies also produce such mainstays of American culture as Dixie Cups (**James River-Dixie Northern Company**), Jif peanut butter

Chock-full o' nuts

There are 1,218 peanuts in every 28-ounce jar of Jif.

(**Procter & Gamble**), and Speedo swimsuits (**Kentucky Textiles** of Paris). Fast-seafood giant **Long John Silver's** has its headquarters in Lexington, as does **Fazoli's,** a rapidly growing, quick-serve Italian restaurant chain.

Gall's Inc. is the top supplier of police, fire and safety equipment in the country. And **Hunter Manufacturing Group** is the nation's largest producer of licensed Major League Baseball, NBA, NFL and other sports ceramic and glassware products.

In recent years, Lexington has also begun to make a name for itself as a hotbed for the development and manufacturing of innovative technologies, as well as for other products.

Lee T. Todd, Jr., an electrical engineer who graduated from the University of Kentucky and later taught there, founded two companies in Lexington to make de-

Photo: Lexington Herald-Leader

Although the assembly line is high-tech, bicycles are used at Toyota Motor Manufacturing in Georgetown for transporting parts and getting around.

vices he patented while at the Massachusetts Institute of Technology. One, **DataBeam**, was a pioneer in the production of teleconferencing systems. The other company, **Projectron**, manufactures cathode-ray projection tubes for uses including military and civilian flight-simulation training. In 1990 Projectron became a part of Hughes Aircraft and now operates in a gleaming high-tech structure on Newtown Pike.

Lexington is also the home of **Thiel Audio Products**, a maker of top-quality Thiel loudspeakers. The components were created by James Thiel and his brother, Tom, who attended the University of Kentucky. The speakers have been highly acclaimed by audiophile magazines and have received prestigious awards from stereo magazines in the United States and Japan.

Mas-Hamilton Group, a Lexington company that manufac-

tures and markets high-security locks, received *R&D Magazine's* 1993 "R&D 100 Award" for its Model X-07 self-powered electronic combination lock. **Multi-Link Inc.**, which recently moved from Lexington to larger quarters in Nicholasville, has come up with several "intelligent call routing" devices for telephones.

Businesses, especially smaller ones, in Lexington and throughout the state have some valuable allies in finding creative approaches to marketing, financing and other areas.

• The **Kentucky World Trade Center**, 410 East Vine Street, 258-3139 or (800) 233-5982, is a private, nonprofit corporation founded in 1988 to help find international markets for Kentucky products. Assistance provided by the center includes product counseling, assistance in understanding the export process and trade leads on agents and distributors in other countries.

• The **Kentucky Small Business Development Center**, with an office on the University of Kentucky campus, provides one-on-one counseling, continuing education programs and management and technical assistance to existing and potential small businesses. There are 14 regional service centers around the state. Call 257-7666 for counseling or 257-7667 for general information.

• The federal **SCORE Small Business Administration** program, 1460 Newtown Pike, 231-9902, has 20 volunteer counselors with varied business backgrounds who help small businesses and would-be businesses find solutions to their operating and start-up problems. (SCORE stands for Service Corps of Retired Executives) Services are free of charge.

One fortunate aspect of Lexington's industrialization is that it hasn't acquired an "industrial stink." Unlike many American cities with large manufacturing bases, Lexington has been able to attract primarily "clean" industries that do not cause large amounts of pollution. As a result, Lexingtonians are far more likely to breathe in the pleasant aroma of roasted peanuts from the Procter & Gamble plant than they are any malodorous chemicals.

Just call it the sweet smell of success.

"All in the Family: Five Generations of Hillenmeyer Nurseries"

Folks always warn, "If you're going to go into business, don't work with your family!"

The five generations of the Hillenmeyer family who have run a large Lexington nursery for the past 152 years are proof that it can be done. You can build and run a successful long-term business with your family members as partners.

The second oldest business in Lexington still in the same family, Hillenmeyer's Nursery was started by a French immigrant — Francis Xavier Hillenmeyer — in 1841, making it one of the oldest nurseries in the country.

In those days, as in the present, Hillenmeyer's numbered among its customers some of the most prominent Lexingtonians of the day. Perhaps the most famous was John C. Breckinridge, who was the youngest vice president of the United States. Breckinridge was particularly interested in grape roots (to start vines) and peach trees. Other early customers included the Clays, Warfields, Hunts, Morgans, Pattersons, Scotts and Buckners.

Francis' youngest son, Hector Francis Hillenmeyer, took over the management of the business around 1876. Some of the nursery's most interesting customers during this period and into the early 20th century were the Shakers of Pleasant Hill. (See Daytrips for more history on this utopian religious community.)

"According to stories told in the family for years, the Shakers would come to Lexington in horse and buggies, of course, and load up on fruit trees to put on their farm down at Shakertown," recalled Robert Hillenmeyer, a member of the fourth generation of Hillenmeyer nurserymen. "They would spend the night because of the length of the trip, and my grandmother would feed them early in the morning, and they'd take off to go back home."

Hector (Robert's grandfather) was an interesting and intelligent man who enjoyed writing and weather watching in addition to his work with the nursery. His daily weather records, kept from 1879 till his death in 1923, predate a Lexington weather record bureau. Hector also wrote a column for the newspaper, and shortly before his death published a pamphlet titled "Synoptic History of the American Grape" in 1922.

In 1910, Hector's two youngest children — Louis E. and Walter W. Hillenmeyer — took over the nursery business. In 1915 they acquired the site of the present nursery office on Sandersville Road in northern Fayette County.

This site has an unusual and interesting history dating back to the early part of the 19th century when Lexington was one of the major manufacturing cities of the west. Col. Lewis Sanders built a cotton factory on the present Sandersville Road site, and the factory was eventually sold to the Oldham Todd Company in the early 1820s. Robert Todd, the father of Mary Todd Lincoln, was one of the owners of the factory. Shortly after Mary Todd married Abraham Lincoln, the future United States president visited the factory on several occasions during his monthlong stay in Lexington before going to Congress in 1847.

Following several more decades as a cotton mill, the site was sold to Stoll and Company, who produced Old Elk bourbon whiskey there with water from a nearby spring. The warehouse used for aging the whiskey is still in use today as nursery storage and operations space. The site was again sold in 1900 to the Kentucky Distillers and Warehouse Co. from whom the Hillenmeyers purchased it fifteen years later.

Walter W. and Louis E. (Robert's father) ran the business together until Walter's death in 1935. Louis' sons, Louis Jr. and Robert, along with Walter's son, Walter Jr., ran the nursery together until Louis and his sons bought out the business in 1964.

Robert, who is now retired, started his full-time work with the nursery shortly after World War II when he returned to Lexington to open Hillenmeyer's first garden center, the second in the Midwest and a revolutionary concept for its time. What made it so revolutionary, Robert explained, was the idea that people could actually drive to the nursery, pick out what they wanted and take it home with them. Prior to the garden center, people would actually go out into the fields and pick out what trees and shrubs they wanted. The nursery staff would then dig up the plants and deliver them the next day.

Today, Robert's nephews, Stephen and Christopher, are the fifth generation of Hillenmeyers to run the nursery. This concept of keeping the business in the family permeates every level of the business, Robert said. To date among Hillenmeyer's employees, there have been 34 families in which sons have followed their fathers in working at the nursery.

"I think that says something about the quality of people we have and hopefully the job we offer," Robert said.

Robert noted two longtime former employees, "Uncle Billy" Jones, who worked with four generations of the Hillenmeyer family from 1887 to 1941, and Syl Stanley, who worked with three generations of the family.

Robert also recalled some of the amusing nicknames the employees often had. "Hucker," "Vinegar" and "Ouki" were among the more unusual. Then there was "Jack and Bill," so named because he was always telling everyone he had two brothers named Jack and two named Bill. He actually did, since his mother and father each had sons named Jack and Bill from former marriages.

As children, Robert remembered, he and other children in the family and area would be delightedly frightened of "Uncle Jim" Stringer who would pull out his pocketknife and threaten to cut their ears off when they would beg coal biscuits out of his lunch pail at noon.

The enjoyment and pride the Hillenmeyer family and employees have had from their work is evident by the success of the business. Hillenmeyer Nursery work can be seen throughout Lexington. The company has done all the planting at Keeneland Race Track and Triangle Park downtown, and much of the planting at IBM (now Lexmark), the Lexington Opera House, and at many area horse farms.

On three occasions Hillenmeyer's has won top beautification awards from the national nurserymen's association — one for downtown beautification in Maysville, one for a courtyard for a new IBM building, and one for work at North Ridge Horse Farm.

Hillenmeyer's has grown a great deal in the 20th century. In addition to the garden center added in 1951, a branch center was opened on Nicholasville Road in 1956. This center later closed, and a full service Garden Center was opened at a new Nicholasville Road location in the early 1980s. One of the largest nurseries in the region, Hillenmeyer's divides up its business among wholesale, landscaping and garden sales.

As Robert looks back on his many years in the family nursery business, he says the true enjoyment he has derived from his experience is from doing something he loves with people he loves.

"Just the opportunity to deal with nature and all its wonders would make it a pleasant, wonderful kind of occupation," he adds. "It has given me a lifetime of fulfillment that was pleasurable in every respect."

Inside
Commercial Real Estate

*T*he rest of the country is waking up to the benefits of Lexington as a center for distribution. Because of the city's enviable position at the juncture of Interstate 64, a major east-west artery, and Interstate 75, a major north-south artery, products shipped from Lexington can reach about three-quarters of the U.S. population within a day. That's one reason, local real estate brokers say, that the commercial real estate market in Lexington is doing quite nicely, thank you.

"Companies all over the United States, especially on the East Coast and West Coast, see Lexington as a convenient and economical location from which to distribute products to the rest of the country," said Doug Gibson of The Gibson Company, a Lexington real estate firm. "So the business growth of our community is being enhanced by an accident of geography." This trend affects the residential real estate picture as well, because large numbers of people are coming to Central Kentucky to work in distribution centers, and many of them are buying houses.

Al Isaac, president of Isaac Commercial Properties, quoted statistics compiled by his company as convincing evidence of a healthy retail market. His figures showed a retail vacancy rate of just 6.82 percent as of June 1993. Industrial/warehouse vacancies as of October 1993 were estimated at 7 percent. Office vacancies were higher but still respectable by nationwide standards.

At this writing, Lexington had more new land available for industrial space than for retail space, brokers say. Part of this is due to peculiarities of zoning regulations, and speculative building may help reduce the oversupply. The undeveloped Coldstream Farm, most of which is zoned for use as a research park, is considered by many to be a prime area that could greatly enhance Lexington's growing corporate reputation. With the recent addition of sewers clearing the way for development, the Coldstream research park could become a home to pharmaceutical, biotechnology, mining research and other companies that would create hundreds of new jobs. In the words of Gibson, "Just as Atlanta is the hub of airports, in the next decade, Lexington is going to be the hub of distribution centers in mid-America."

KENTUCKY INDUSTRIAL DEVELOPMENT COUNCIL
100 Capital Avenue,
Frankfort   (502) 227-9653

This statewide nonprofit group, funded by its members, is similar in some ways to a chamber of commerce. It helps communities prepare for industrial and economic development by providing a forum for them to network and hold training seminars and conferences four times a year.

LEXINGTON UNITED

Blue Grass Airport, Suite 38   225-5005

Lexington United Inc., operating from a building called the Bluegrass Business Location Center, is an umbrella marketing group that markets the Greater Lexington area as a location for manufacturing, warehousing and distribution, regional and corporate offices, research and development. About 65 percent of its funding is from the private sector and the remainder from local government. The corporation, which has advertising and public relations programs as well as a direct-call program, maintains extensive databases on the area as a business location. It also assists in site selection, with an inventory of available sites and buildings available in the seven-county area.

Industrial Parks and Areas

While the Coldstream Research Campus appears to hold a world of potential for Lexington, other prime sites are available.

Perhaps the busiest corridor for growth at the moment is that on and near Leestown Road. The Leestown Distribution Center is a multiple-occupant building that is home to Philip Morris, Jerry's Restaurants, Xerox Service Center, Bearing Dis-

tributors, Digital Equipment Corp. and others.

About half a mile on out Leestown Road is the Trade Street/Merchant Street/Over Drive area, with McAlpin's Distribution Center, Grayhawk, Clark Manufacturing and Distributing Plant, GTE, Hammond Productions, Kentucky Utilities, Dolly Madison Bakery and others.

Straight across from that area is developing Westhampton Corners, bordered on three sides by Leestown, Mercer and Greendale roads. A Toyota Industrial Equipment forklift facility, Toledo Scales and Van Dyne Crotty are among the occupants of these buildings.

After crossing Greendale, Mercer Road gets really busy, with Rexroth Pneumatics Division, James River Corp.'s Dixie Cup plant, Square D, UPS and The Trane Company. Federal Express, an expanding W.T. Young Storage facility and a new Columbia Gas building are on Greendale.

Nearby, off Georgetown Road, are the main post office and several other assorted shipping and distribution centers.

The Blue Sky development just past the Interstate 75 interchange at Athens-Boonesboro Road, is another large industrial site.

Available sites elsewhere in the Bluegrass include the 242-acre industrial park off Interstate 64 at Winchester, a 170-acre park on Georgetown Road in Paris and a 166-acre site in Richmond.

Office Parks and Buildings

From an office standpoint, businesses can choose from a number of

Insiders know that those "BGT" plaques on the front of buildings downtown stand for the Blue Grass Trust for Historic Preservation.

excellent facilities either downtown or in suburban settings.

Downtown

LEXINGTON FINANCIAL CENTER

The gleaming black, 30-story structure at 250 West Main Street is the closest thing Lexington has to a skyscraper. Often referred to as "Big Blue" because of the blue neon lights at the top, it is widely considered the premier office building in the community. Prominent tenants include The Webb Companies; Liberty National Bank of Lexington; United Bancorp of Kentucky; IBM; James N. Gray Construction Co.; Sherman-Carter-Barnhart architects; Prudential Securities; KPMG Peat Marwick CPAs; and several legal firms, including Stites and Harbison, Brown Todd & Heyburn, and Newberry Hargrove & Rambicure.

VINE CENTER

This complex, which covers the city block bordered by Broadway, Vine, Mill and Main streets, includes the Radisson Plaza Hotel. Among the office tenants are Bank One, Clark Material Handling, Dupree Mutual Funds, CSX Transportation's Coal Development division, Thomas Clark Bloodstock Ltd., National Mines Corporation, the Council of

State Governments and the legal firms of Greenbaum Doll & McDonald and Frost & Jacobs.

FIFTH THIRD CENTER

Fifth Third Bank and the Lane real estate and communications companies are the primary occupants of this nine-story building at 26 West Main Street.

Southwest

CORPORATE CENTER

Corporate Center, a circle of nearly 20 buildings off Harrodsburg Road near New Circle Road, is probably the most desirable office park in Lexington. Among its dozens of tenants are Toyota, Unisys, Wang Laboratories, GTE Service Corp., Bloodstock Research Inc., several U.S. Department of Agriculture agencies, the Council for Burley Tobacco, Price Waterhouse, GMAC Financial Services, King and Schickli patent and copyright attorneys, the Fayette County Republican Party and several insurance companies and temporary employment agencies.

PARAGON CENTRE

Paragon Centre, on Alexandria Drive near Harrodsburg Road, consists of the One Paragon and Two Paragon buildings, with a third building in the middle occupied by American States Insurance. Paragon tenants include Breeders' Cup Limited, Eastman Kodak, McGraw-Hill Information Systems, AT&T, ARDIS national headquarters, Metropolitan Life and Transamerica Financial.

SOUTHCREEK PARK

This office development on Harrodsburg Road is home to the Lexington division of the ClinTrials pharmaceutical testing company and the Ohio Casualty and Massachusetts Mutual insurance companies, among others.

South

LEXINGTON GREEN

Two buildings behind the Mall at Lexington Green contain some of the top office space in the city. Among the tenants are DataBeam Corp., the IDS Financial Services division of American Express, RE/MAX Creative Realty, Bank One Mortgage, New York Life, Lambuth Financial and Square D employee services.

REGENCY OFFICE COURT

This 47,238-square-foot development at 2201 Regency Road comprises seven single-story buildings. All tenants have their own outside entrances and first-floor offices, most with views of a garden or courtyard. Tenants include the Kentucky League of Cities, State Auto, Liberty Life Insurance, Washington National Life Insurance, Roche Biomedical Laboratories and five mortgage companies. The project was designed for smaller-office users who

want control of their environment.

The "south corridor" also is home to Tates Creek Office Centre, at 4701 Tates Creek Road, and a number of office buildings on Waller Avenue.

Southeast

PERIMETER OFFICE PARK

The six-story, 67,600-square-foot Perimeter Centre, at the heart of this office park off Alumni Drive, includes GTE Directories, MCI Telecommunications, Blue Cross & Blue Shield of Kentucky, Republic Savings Bank, Nationwide Insurance and Weatherly Consumer Products. Six additional buildings in the park are home to Kentucky Sports Medicine, Bluegrass ADD, Nationwide, Manpower, CM Personnel Services, Prudential A.S. de Movellan Real Estate and others.

EAGLE CREEK OFFICE PARK

This still-developing park next to Humana Hospital off Richmond Road is the former site of the Bluegrass Sportsmen's Club. Lots are still being sold in the 48-acre park, which at this writing is home to Allstate Insurance, Lovejoy Medical, Central Brace Shop and a branch of the Lexington Public Library. Eagle Creek Dental Group's facility will soon be completed if it isn't by the time you read this, and Ashland Oil, which has its corporate headquarters on nearby Dabney Drive, has additional offices planned for 20 acres it has bought.

Northeast

EXECUTIVE PARK

Executive Park, a multi-use office and research park at Winchester Road and Interstate 75, consists of five single-owner buildings in addition to Executive Place, a multitenant building with space for rental and a shared conference room. Corporations with buildings or offices in Executive Park include SmithKline Bioscience, Whitaker Banks, McCoy & McCoy environmental engineers, Mountain Enterprises highway contractors, the Wilderness Road Girl Scouts Council and the Kentucky High School Athletic Association. Executive Park is managed by The Wilkinson Group, which also has its offices here.

North

GRIFFIN GATE PLAZA

This retail, restaurant and office complex on Newtown Pike contains such tenants as The Future Now computer education company, American HomePatient medical equipment, SpectraCare home health agency, the Kentucky Board of Bar Examiners, Dictaphone Corp., Office Equipment Co., Griffin Gate Realty and Radnor Homes.

Commercial Real Estate Companies

ISAAC COMMERCIAL PROPERTIES, INC.
870 Corporate Drive, Suite 402   224-2000

Isaac Commercial Properties, founded in 1986 by Al Isaac Jr., specializes in the leasing, sales and management of retail, office and industrial/warehouse properties and raw land in Central Kentucky. The company also provides site selection services, property valuation and market and feasibility studies.

THE GIBSON COMPANY
340 South Broadway   233-3038

This commercial real estate brokerage and management firm, in business since 1964, manages and sells shopping centers, office buildings and industrial buildings. Doug Gibson, who was director of economic development for six years under Mayor Scotty Baesler, and Billy V. Smith are the principal owners.

HAYMAKER COMMERCIAL REAL ESTATE
Regency Business Center,
191 West Lowry Lane   278-9000

Tim Haymaker's five-year-old company specializes in commercial real estate, property management and maintenance, as well as commercial and residential land devel-

---

Insiders know to avoid any social situations revolving around Lake Lexington, at least until further notice. This legendary body of water, which might be an 11-acre lake near Rupp Arena if it existed, alas does not exist. Yet.

Insiders' Tips

opment. Haymaker has a management contract for the Beaumont project on Harrodsburg Road, which will be the largest mixed-use development in Lexington, and several prominent office properties.

LANE CONSULTANTS
269 West Main Street   233-3003

Lane Consultants handles sales and leasing, tenant representation, consulting, appraisals and other services. The company maintains a high profile through its omnipresent green-and-white signs around town, television advertising during sports events, and *The Lane Report* magazine.

Commercial Developers, Builders, Architects and Engineers

CALLER & ROSENSTEIN
343 Waller Avenue   255-5180

Steve Caller and Irving Rosenstein started their development business in 1967; both have since been joined by a son. Caller and Rosenstein are primarily commercial developers of shopping centers, with about 15 centers in the area, including the huge new Randall's grocery on the north side, Crossroads Shopping Center off Nicholasville Road, and other strip centers in Richmond, Winchester, Nicholasville and Frankfort. Enterprise Park on Old Frankfort Pike was also developed by the company, which owns and operates the Liquor Barns on Southland Drive and Richmond Road.

CMW ARCHITECTS AND ENGINEERS
326 South Broadway   254-6623

CMW, also known as Chrisman

Miller Woodford Inc., started in 1962 with three employees and has grown to 40 employees. CMW, which also has a Richmond office, provides a full range of services, including architecture; civil, electrical and mechanical engineering; and interior decorating and design. It has a strong criminal justice division specializing in jails and courthouses and has also done extensive work with medical facilities and schools. CMW's design work includes the Kentucky Horse Park, Gainsborough Farm and Saint Joseph Office Park.

EKHOFF OCHENKOSKI POLK ARCHITECTS
201 West Short Street   231-7538

This diverse architectural firm, founded in 1981 by Paul Ochenkoski and Rick Ekhoff as EO Associates, added Richard Polk as a partner a few years ago. The firm's work includes renovation and certified historic rehabilitation as well as new commercial office buildings, hospitals and medical facilities, laboratory buildings, jails, horse farms and exclusive residences. The firm designed French Quarter Suites, Applebee's Restaurants, Chevy Chase Plaza, One Plaza East and the University of Kentucky baseball stadium, as well as the new Kroger on New Circle Road. Court Square Building and Gratz Park Inn downtown were historic rehabilitation projects.

JAMES N. GRAY CONSTRUCTION CO.
2500 Lexington Financial Center   281-5000

Gray Construction, Kentucky's largest general contractor, got its start with a barn-building project in the '50s and was incorporated in 1960 in

Glasgow, Kentucky. Now the company, which specializes in industrial design/building and process engineering, is involved in projects across the country, including a soy sauce plant in Salem, Oregon. Gray's ability to work with Japanese companies in the United States has earned it contracts with such heavyweights as Toyota, Toshiba and Hitachi. Major projects in Central Kentucky have included Hughes Display Products on Newtown Pike, Hitachi Automotive Products in Harrodsburg, the Kentucky Chamber of Commerce in Frankfort and the Children's Learning Center in the Danville industrial park.

JOHNSON/ROMANOWITZ ARCHITECTS & PLANNERS
301 East Vine Street   252-6781

Johnson/Romanowitz, founded in 1946 in Lexington, now has a second office in Louisville. The firm specializes in commercial institutional architecture, particularly for area schools and colleges. For the University of Kentucky, the firm designed the Singletary Center for the Arts, Patterson Office Tower and the Mines and Minerals building. Other high-profile projects have included Lexington Financial Center, the Kentucky Veterans Center in Wilmore and the last major expansion of Blue Grass Airport. Johnson/Romanowitz also served as associate architect for Rupp Arena.

MASON & HANGER ENGINEERING
2355 Harrodsburg Road   223-4773

In 1920, Mason & Hanger Engineering built the Lafayette Hotel, a former Lexington landmark. Since then it has provided a wide spectrum of design, construction and technical services, including architectural, planning, industrial and environmental. The company — a subsidiary of Mason & Hanger-Silas Mason Company — has been involved in the Applied Science and Technology Center, the Robotics & Automated Manufacturing Center and Commonwealth Stadium at the University of Kentucky. Other local projects include the IBM/Lexmark complex, Lexington Civic Center and Thoroughbred Park.

OMNI ARCHITECTS
212 North Upper Street   252-6664

Omni was founded in 1975 and merged in 1981 with another prominent local architectural firm, McLoney and Tune Architects. Today almost half of its work is in health care. The firm has designed several buildings at the expanded University of Kentucky Medical Center, including the Markey Cancer Center, as well as Kentucky Clinic on Nicholasville Road and the new Kentucky Clinic South on Harrodsburg Road. Omni — which has done work for universities and secondary and elementary schools, a number of office parks and public housing projects — also designed Manhattan on Main and Southland Christian and Centenary United Methodist churches.

ROSS/FELDMAN ARCHITECTURE INC.
206 West Main Street   254-4018

Ross/Feldman is a full-service interior design/architectural firm with about 20 employees. Since its founding in May 1970, the firm has been involved in extensive historical restoration work in Lexington and elsewhere. Lexington restoration projects include the refurbished and expanded Lexington Opera House, Spindletop Hall and the McAdams & Morford Building, which houses Ross/Feldman's offices. The firm has been involved with other performing arts theaters, more than 100 schools and educational facilities, and 200 federal housing projects.

THE ROUSE COMPANIES
2201 Regency Road   275-5000

Since founding The Rouse Companies in 1978, W.L. "Bill" Rouse III has built hundreds of homes and two office condominium projects. The company, which was formerly involved in the United Building Systems lumber and manufacturing plant with Cutter Homes and Barlow Homes, owns and manages about 100,000 feet of local office space, a small shopping center, several office warehouse buildings and a number of residential rental units. It is also involved in three current residential land development projects.

SHERMAN-CARTER-BARNHART ARCHITECTS
1900 Lexington Financial Center   254-1351

Sherman-Carter-Barnhart Architects, formed in 1979, is the largest architectural firm in Kentucky. It provides services in a variety of related disciplines, including interior design, facility surveys and studies, site planning and development and master planning. Among the more prominent local projects designed by this award-winning company are the main Lexington Public Library building, Lexington Financial Center, The Market Place, the Victorian Square renovation and various local government projects including urban revitalization and new public housing. Sherman-Carter-Barnhart has also designed a number of projects across the country.

THE SOUTHCREEK COMPANY
175 East Main Street   255-1500

This 20-year-old corporation, an equal partnership with J. Pat Williams, Ted W. Hahn and Harold H. Mullis, is primarily involved in building office parks, including Saint Joseph Office Park and 200,000 square feet of doctors' offices in three buildings. The Southcreek Company also built the nearby Picadome Center, Southcreek Park on Harrodsburg Road and the Meyers Building downtown. Other developments include a shopping center in Woodford County and land development for subdivisions in Versailles and Nicholasville.

THE WEBB COMPANIES
3000 Lexington Financial Center   253-0000

The Webb Companies is a full-service real estate management, commercial development and property management company. Webb developments have contributed significantly to the character of downtown Lexington with such landmarks as Lexington Financial Center, Vine Center and the Radisson Plaza Hotel, Merrill Lynch Plaza, the Chamber of Commerce building, Victorian Square, The Market Place and The Woodlands.

Inside
Neighborhoods and Homes

*O*nce you've found a place to live in Lexington, there's a little game you should try. (If you haven't found a place, bear with us, and we'll discuss your situation presently.) First you need to find a long-time resident. It could be one of your new neighbors, or someone you meet at church or the grocery. Who the person is doesn't matter as much as whether he or she has lived in Lexington long enough to remember the "good ol' days." Casually steer the conversation toward the subject of your new neighborhood. Then wait to find out whether your new friend says, "I remember when it used to be out in the boonies."

Unless you live downtown, there's a fairly good chance that you will get such a response. ("Boonies" is a Kentucky colloquialism meaning "where Daniel Boone once walked.") In recent years, Lexington has grown quickly, spreading subdivisions and shopping centers into the once-virgin countryside. And the entire metropolitan area has grown with it.

Understandably, many of us get concerned about the pace of growth. The Bluegrass is a place widely known for its countryside, not for its subdivisions and shop-

ping centers, although some of those are very nice. The challenge is finding a balance: nice home, nice stores and restaurants, nice view. In the last year, the powers-that-be have strengthened Kentucky's commitment to its resources. More than $7 million a year in federal money, plus matching local and state money, will be allocated to maintain scenic and historic sites, including the picturesque horse farms so closely associated with the state. In 1993, a $1 million grant was announced to help preserve what Gov. Brereton Jones referred to as "the rich cultural heritage" of the Lexington area.

Which brings us back to the underlying theme of this book: Lexington is a great place to live. The fact that you're reading this book would seem to indicate that you 1) live in Lexington, 2) are thinking about living in Lexington or, 3) are visiting Lexington.

Lexington has a variety of neighborhoods to suit your lifestyle, aesthetic preferences and budget. We have established "old money" areas with elegant 19th-century homes on shady, tree-lined streets; luxurious condominiums with a wealth of amenities; "starter home" neighborhoods filled with young families; a number of well-landscaped new "executive" communities characterized by large estate homes; and more.

Obviously, we can't come close to mentioning every Lexington neighborhood. What we have tried to do is come up with a cross-section that is representative in terms of location, style, age and price of home. In trying to come up with a representative sampling, we have sought the opinions of local Realtors and other experts.

According to data from the Lexington Chamber of Commerce, the average sale price of a new 1,800-square-foot, detached home in one of Lexington's urban areas was $111,287 in 1992. The average monthly rent for an unfurnished two-bedroom apartment with 1 1/2 bathrooms was $528.88.

In looking for a home, you may come across the phrase "urban service area." Fayette County's urban service area is, in a nutshell, land that is developable, meaning it has access to sanitary sewers. The concept of the urban service area was designed to help preserve horse farms and other rural areas. Other factors that enter into the equation are topography, watersheds and such; if you really want to know the minute details, you can contact the Division of Planning at 258-3160.

When the city and county governments merged in 1974, those areas that received certain urban services such as sewer service, garbage collection, street sweeping and street lights maintained those services. Fayette County neighborhoods are taxed at varying rates depending on the level of services they receive. All new developments are required to be connected to sanitary sewers and have street lights and city garbage collection. Some older areas do not have all these services; for example, residents of certain neighborhoods have to contract with a private company for garbage collection.

To reach a different level of service, which means an increase in the tax on the district, a neighborhood must go through a petition process and obtain a certain percentage of signatures. Realtors should be able to provide that information about any neighborhoods you're considering, or call Public Works at 258-3400.

Lexington has nearly 150 active neighborhood associations. If you visit the Division of Planning at the Lexington-Fayette Urban County Government building, on the 10th floor at 200 East Main Street, you can pick up a directory of neighborhood associations as well as a 34"x42" neighborhood associations map. Call 258-3160 first, however, to make sure these items are still available.

Numerous houses and other buildings in Lexington's downtown areas fall under the auspices of local zoning laws designed to protect the area's historic districts. Properties in historic zones require approval by a design review board before any exterior changes can be made. For more information, call the Historic Preservation Office at 258-3265. The Blue Grass Trust for Historic Preservation is a society with a similar goal: preserving and protecting the area's cultural history and monuments. These buildings are distinguished by the "BGT" plaques that grace their fronts.

Neighborhoods

A cautionary note: If you want a house sitting on a big lot, you'll have to either buy an older house or pay a lot of money. Because land today is costing developers more, they are compensating by putting more houses on the same amount of space.

Of course, buying an older house isn't necessarily a bad thing, by any means. Greater Lexington has thousands of older houses that are elegant, fascinating and beautiful. Tradition can be a wonderful thing.

During most parts of the year — with the general exception of the Thanksgiving-to-New-Year's season — you can find whatever type of property you want. Buy now before the interest rates go up. We'd love to have you as a neighbor.

Downtown and Central Lexington

GRATZ PARK

Gratz Park is tiny, with only about 15 residences. But this downtown neighborhood might well contain more history per square foot than anywhere else in Lexington. Its development dates to 1793, when it became home to the forerunner of Transylvania University; it became Gratz Park in 1884. In 1955 it became the first organized historic district in Lexington when citizens determined to save the Hunt-Morgan House banded together and formed a society that later grew into the Blue Grass Trust for Historic Preservation.

The park is named for Benjamin Gratz, a lawyer, hemp manufacturer and Transy trustee who played an important role in Lexington's 19th-century development. Throughout the 1800s some of the city's most influential doctors, lawyers, educators, publishers, generals and statesmen lived in this area of just over an acre. Today it retains much of its historic flavor with the Hunt-Morgan House, Bodley-Bullock House, the Carnegie Center for Literacy and Learning (former site of the Lexington Public Library) and other landmarks. The wide variety of architectural styles — including neoclassical, Greek Revival, Italianate, Queen Anne and Federal — makes it possible for students of architecture to trace the development of the city.

In the mid-'80s, residents of homes around the park sold bricks for 50 cents each and raised $28,000 to put brick walkways in the park. Strangely enough, in recent years there has been a fair amount of turnover, which has been a source of some consternation to those who have lived in Gratz Park for 30 years or more. Because the park represents many periods of architecture, the prices of these homes, when available, may vary from $250,000 or less to more than $750,000. Obviously, not everyone will get a chance to buy a one. If you ever do, you'll truly own a piece of Lexington's history.

CHEVY CHASE

We're talking about neither the comedian nor the D.C. suburb. Lexington's Chevy Chase is its own entity, a prestigious one that seems to evoke something of a mystique. It's a large but relatively stable neighborhood — even considering the fair amount of rental property lying within its borders — that was started in the '40s. Before that, it was farmland, but close enough to town that the Ringling Brothers and Barnum & Bailey Circus would pitch a tent in the area each year to put on the greatest show on earth for Lexingtonians.

Today Chevy Chase is blessed with access to several good restaurants and any number of specialty shops, as well as to downtown and the University of Kentucky. Tates Creek Road, Euclid Avenue/ Fontaine Drive, Chinoe Road and Cooper Drive are the approximate boundaries. The residential areas reflect a diversity of styles, from charming brick and fieldstone houses to four-plexes. Always middle- to upper-middle-class, in the last decade or so Chevy Chase has steadily acquired more of a yuppie sheen.

Difficult as the neighborhood's character might be to define, Chevy Chasers are determined to preserve it. The neighborhood association showed it could unite with some clout when it challenged the developers of Chevy Chase Plaza on Euclid Avenue, claiming the planned nine-story restaurant, retail and office development would irrevocably damage the area's character. Ultimately the plaza was built at five stories, with the upper ones recessed from the road. And everyone seems to be at least reasonably happy with the result.

ASHLAND PARK

The Ashland Park neighborhood was developed around the turn of the century from the original Woodland Horse Farm, which was then on the outskirts of town. With its houses built between 1880 and 1910, it has been placed on the National Register of Historic Places. The neighborhood provides a splendid array of Colonial Revival, Tudor Revival, American Foursquare and Victorian residential architecture among large trees, green lawns and medians. These houses, which generally sell in the $150,000 range, have traditionally provided homes for community business and government leaders, professionals and educators from the University of Kentucky.

The nearby Ashland neighborhood, which includes the estate of Henry Clay, was designed by the architectural firm of Frederick Law Olmsted, which also designed New York's Central Park and many Louisville parks in the early 20th century. Both of these neighborhoods, while conducive to gracious and quiet residential living, are close to downtown, UK, major transportation routes and neighborhood specialty shops and services.

West and Southwest Lexington

GARDENSIDE AND GARDEN SPRINGS

These two neighborhoods, once on the edge of town, now have the convenience of being near (within easy walking distance for most people) Turfland Mall, two major groceries and various shops and neighborhood parks. The elementary, middle and high schools that serve Gardenside and Garden Springs are widely considered to be among the best in town. This author must admit a positive bias toward these two neighborhoods, because he has lived in one or the other since moving to Lexington in 1983.

Gardenside, developed in the early to middle '50s, contains a variety of ranch, story-and-a-half and two-story homes, mostly brick or stone, selling from $65,000 to $100,000 and up. Unlike most newer neighborhoods, these homes are distinguished by comfortably sized lots. Garden Springs, about 15 years younger than neighboring Gardenside, was built on land that was once part of a horse farm. Its streets are named after trees or flowering plants — Azalea, Larkspur, Honeysuckle and Pinebloom, for example. Houses average around $80,000. Both of these neighborhoods are home to a primarily middle-class neighborhood populated with lots of families, children, dogs and cats.

FIREBROOK

Firebrook, a little over a mile south of Man o' War Boulevard off Harrodsburg Road, not far from the Jessamine County line, is one of Lexington's newest and most prestigious neighborhoods. Although the neighborhood is only about three years old, its history can be traced back to its original land grant in 1793. An elegant mansion and guest house from those early days are still standing.

At present there are about 150 occupied homes in Firebrook; 400 are projected. These houses, all custom built by some of the top developers in the city, range from $170,000 to $750,000, with most falling in the $200,000 to $300,000 range. Amenities include tennis courts, swimming pool and cabana, jogging trail, club house with fitness room and kitchen, and two stocked lakes.

HARRODS HILL

Development of Harrods Hill began in the late '70s, and the neighborhood now comprises a variety of ranch, two-story, brick traditional and contemporary houses, priced from $100,000 to more than $200,000. It is also well landscaped with nice lots. But Harrods Hill, while containing some beautiful homes, may be even more notable for its "neighborly" aspects. The neighborhood association is active and publishes an annual directory to foster interaction among its residents. There is a city park with a soccer field, playground and basketball court; residents can also become members of a recreational complex with tennis courts, pool and sundeck.

The population of the neighborhood is diverse, with retired people, singles, executives and families with teens and younger children. A recently constructed shopping center, with several restaurants, a large grocery and various other shops, has added greatly to the convenience of Harrods Hill.

Our Homes Have Been Known to Move People.
Over 1,400 to be Exact!

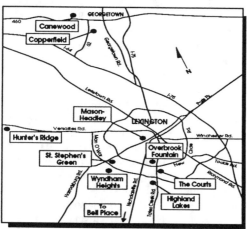

Barlow Homes has built over 1,400 homes throughout the region since 1979. Visit one of our models today. It may be a moving experience!

Barlow Homes
Building for Generations

3130 Custer Dr., Lexington, KY 40517 Phone: (606) 272-3423

STONEWALL COMMUNITY

Stonewall Community, built in about four phases in the '60s, is a quiet, largely working-class neighborhood characterized by huge lots, many of which are a half-acre or larger; a variety of styles; and a lot of shared neighborhood pride. The primary developer was Stoll Meyers, which also developed the Dixie subdivision in northeast Lexington's Eastland Parkway neighborhood (see below). Houses range from $90,000 to $175,000.

Stonewall, like many of Lexington's well-established neighborhoods, is a place filled with retirees who have spent most of their lives in the same house. But it's also a place where many children grow up, leave and then return to live with their own families. The pride that residents take in their neighborhood is evident in the $10,000 that they raised, spurred by a promise of matching funds from the city, to develop a nature park on a seven-acre wooded area that was left undeveloped. Stonewallers will also tell you it's a great walking neighborhood.

DOGWOOD TRACE, COPPERFIELD AND CLEMENS HEIGHTS

These three attached neighborhoods near the Jessamine County line are primarily professional, upper-middle-class. Dogwood Trace, built in the mid-'80s, consists mainly of two-story houses, with a few larger one-stories, selling for $130,000 to $220,000. A large field separates Dogwood Trace from nearby Copperfield, a similar development that is several years younger and a little less expensive. Clemens Heights, which also lies partially between Dogwood Trace and Copperfield, is distinguished by attractive split-foyer homes and Mark Twain-inspired street names.

South Lexington

BELLEAU WOOD AND WALDEN GROVE

Many families who have been moved to Lexington because of corporate transfers settle initially in the Belleau Wood/Walden Grove area, which is composed mainly of modern-style homes ranging from $65,000 to $110,000 in Belleau Wood and up to $150,000 in Walden Grove, which lies on the opposite side of Wilson Downing Road. The relocation aspect has lent a certain "transient" flavor to the neighborhood, because many people live here for three to five years before moving to another part of town. The population consists largely of young professionals in the early 30s to mid-40s, many with young children. Prime selling points of the neighborhood are its relatively affordable homes, its convenience to Fayette Mall and Tates Creek Centre, a park with a city-run program and a neighborhood association that holds an annual Easter egg hunt and a family picnic.

HARTLAND

Hartland, a fully planned, all-residential community, is 500 acres of single-family homes ranging from $150,000 to significantly higher. It is characterized by beautifully landscaped boulevards, decorative streetlights and grand entryways. When the development is complete, there will be 1,000 single-family homes; at this writing, it was 70 percent-80 percent complete.

A private membership amenity package provides access to a Junior Olympic-size swimming pool, six tennis courts and a clubhouse building. Two areas within Hartland — the estate and executive areas — are contained within the main sections and offer varying levels of additional amenities.

North and Northwest Lexington

There's a fairly widespread perception that all the good places to live are on the south side of Lexington. Boy, does this ever tee northsiders off! They point out, correctly, that there's simply more available land on the south side for new developments. Then they add that not that much old real estate is available because "people in this area don't move . . . so if you want to buy a classy old house on the north end, you may have to wait for someone to die." Talk to several long-time residents of the north side, and you're likely to encounter a rather fierce sense of pride in what this part of Lexington has to offer.

MEADOWTHORPE

Meadowthorpe, a subdivision planned in 1949 on property owned by distillery owner James E. Pepper, is an old-fashioned neighborhood filled with traditional homes and plenty of history. For example, the land once contained an airport known as Halley Field; Charles Lindbergh landed here in 1928 and stayed in the "old mansion" nearby. Today there are about 500 single-family homes in Meadowthorpe, with the average house priced at $80,000 to $87,000. These homes don't often come on the market, however, because people are inclined to stay there. Many residents have lived in their homes for 30 to 40 years, and in recent years numbers of young people who grew up in the neighborhood are moving back to raise their families.

ELKHORN PARK AND DEEPWOOD

These neighborhoods, which were "county" before the merger in 1974, lie on opposite sides of North Broadway. Elkhorn Park is a traditional neighborhood that was developed slowly around the middle of the century; as such, it exhibits much individuality. Houses, if you can find an available one, generally range from $80,000 to $135,000. Mature trees line the streets, and there are six triangular traffic islands. In 1993, the neighborhood got a city grant to beautify the islands and went about the task with vigor. Deepwood is smaller, more elite and more expensive. Both neighborhoods are among that category of neighborhoods where people come home to live. And two fine new groceries in the vicinity — a Randall's and a Kroger — have made things even better.

East Lexington

EASTLAND PARKWAY

Eastland Parkway is a road that leads northeast from New Circle Road toward Interstate 75, then makes a U-turn and heads back southwest until it hits Winchester Road. Eastland Parkway is also a neighborhood that comprises two subdivisions — Dixie and Eastland — where development began 30 to 35 years ago. Eastland Parkway, the road, is the main feeder street for the neighborhood. Dixie came first; although a few families bought lots and then had homes built, most of the homes were already built, then put up for sale under the slogan "Dixie in '60."

Most of the residences are brick or partly brick single-family. There is a mix of people, from young professionals to retirees, and there is a range of homes and prices suitable for first-time buyers on up. The neighborhood also contains duplexes and apartment complexes.

The Eastland subdivision, which has some larger and higher-priced homes, is split from Dixie by a little creek. It was developed by Stoll Meyers, the company that did Stonewall Community (see above). Eastland was built when IBM was expanding rapidly, and many IBM people bought homes here. Prices in this diverse neighborhood range from $60,000 up to much more for the finer, custom-built homes.

IDLE HOUR

Idle Hour is bounded by Richmond Road, New Circle Road, a small industrial warehousing area

and the Idle Hour Country Club. Lexington Mall and an assortment of Richmond Road restaurants are within spitting distance. Most of the streets are named for saints: St. Margaret, St. Ann, Sts. Michael and Mathilda and so on. It's a largely middle-class neighborhood built during the '50s — one of the city's last big new neighborhoods before Eastland Parkway came along — and it's aging gracefully. Most of the houses are ranches or Cape Cods of brick or fieldstone, and they generally sell for between $60,000 and $80,000.

ANDOVER

Andover Golf & Country Club is a focal point of this fast-growing, upscale subdivision, which was started about 1990. Todds Road divides the golf course (there's an access tunnel beneath the road) and splits the neighborhood into two sections: Andover Hills and Andover Forest. Both sections have a healthy supply of doctors, lawyers and other professionals. Most of the 400 or so homes, many of which line the golf course, are custom-built, two-story, brick traditional homes with prices ranging up to $500,000. Exceptions are Andover Park, a new area within Andover Hills built by Cutter Homes with houses starting around $120,000, and Golf Villas, a small section of about 30 condominiums occupied primarily by retirees.

Real Estate Agents

Real estate agents are seemingly everywhere, in case you haven't noticed. But that fact shouldn't keep you from looking for one. Although there are plenty of agents out there, not all of them are right for you. So you should take steps to ensure that you and your agent are a good match.

If you're coming from somewhere else and you have a home to sell in that particular area, then you probably have a real estate agent

It's the sign that brings you home.

As soon as you notice one RE/MAX sign, it seems you just can't help but spot another. RE/MAX signs are everywhere because RE/MAX associates across North America lead the real estate industry in sales per agent. There really isn't any doubt that RE/MAX is the sign of success.

So when you're moving to Lexington, look for the sign that brings you home.

Look for RE/MAX. Out in Front.

In 1993, Lexington received the deed to McConnell Springs, a 20-acre site in western Fayette County surrounding a sinkhole and continually bubbling underground spring. Frontiersmen who were camping at the site in 1775, upon learning of the Battle of Lexington in Massachusetts, named their campsite Lexington. The town was founded four years later. A fund-raising campaign is under way to turn the area into a park.

there. Find out if that agent has a contact with any companies in this area. Realtors do a lot of networking at national conventions, handing out cards and saying things like, "If you ever have anybody coming this way, call us."

The first step in a Realtor search is to make a phone contact, talk to the person and try to get a feel for whether you would like to work with him or her. Give your impressions to your Realtor. "We often get calls from Realtors in other towns saying, 'Jane and John are moving to Lexington,'" said Carolyn Edwards, a Fister associate who is immediate past president of the Lexington Board of Realtors. "I give them a call immediately and tell them: 'We got this information from your Realtor there. Can I send you a packet of what I can do for you, or a homes magazine or corporation RELO packet?'"

Regardless of your impression of your first contact, it's a good idea to interview at least two or three other Realtors from different companies. Ultimately, you need to choose whoever makes you feel most comfortable. "This is the largest investment you're going to make," Edwards said. "You need to be represented. You need someone you feel comfortable with, someone you can share your innermost thoughts with, someone you can tell, 'Hey, you're way off track. This isn't what we want at all.'"

In a similar vein, if you are the seller, you should keep in mind that you are selling what very well may be your most prized possession. So you want someone who is going to work hard to market your property, someone who will stay in touch with you and keep you informed of any progress.

With the advent of buyer brokerage, the Bluegrass real estate picture is changing. Traditionally, agents have held contracts with sellers of properties, which means that, while duty-bound to be honest and fair, their loyalties and legal responsibilities have been to the seller. Under the practice of buyer brokerage, which has been big for years out West but is just catching on in this part of the country, an agent signs a contracts with a buyer and exclusively represents him or her for the duration of the contract. "That's the way it should be," one Realtor said. "Buyers have just as much right to representation as sellers do."

Nowadays, sellers are providing disclosure statements that reveal virtually anything they know about the properties being sold: histories, what might be wrong, what has been fixed and so on. If you're buying a house, you should seriously consider finding an agent who will sign you on as an exclusive client and will do what he or she can to get you in the house you want. "Cooperation in compensation" has turned upside-down the traditional guide-lines for paying a Realtor. Sometimes the seller, eager to sell, continues to pay the full commission. In other cases the buyer is willing to pay part of the cost.

One result of such changes, it appears, is a more open market on an even playing field. It's not a buyers' market or a sellers' market but rather one in which a win-win situation is likely.

In general, the real estate firms listed in this chapter are the ones with the biggest market shares. Keep in mind, however, that bigger doesn't necessarily mean better. You have specific needs, and only you can accurately determine who can best fulfill those needs. There are numerous one- and two-person firms in the area, and you may well find someone at one of those companies who does the job for you. On the other hand, there is often a clear cause-and-effect relationship between those agents and companies that are most successful and the level of service they provide. Those listed here have developed good reputations over the years. If you'd like information about other companies in the area, call the Lexington Board of Realtors at 276-3503.

RECTOR-HAYDEN REALTORS
Lexington office,
2100 Nicholasville Road   276-4811
    (800) 228-9025
Versailles office,
260 Crossfield Drive   873-1299
Georgetown office,
118 East Main Street   278-0005

With 100 full-time sales associates, locally owned Rector-Hayden is the Lexington area's number one real estate company. The firm, which has been serving the Bluegrass since 1969, provides services in all areas of residential real estate for Greater Lexington and surrounding areas such as Lawrenceburg, Cynthiana and Owenton. Through The Relocation Center, a specialized department within the company, Rector-Hayden helps make relocation less of a hassle for corporations as well as for transferring employees and their families.

PAUL SEMONIN REALTORS
3358 Tates Creek Road   269-7331
3580 Lyon Drive   224-0707
670 Perimeter Drive   268-1223
Relocation division   (800) 548-1650

Louisville-based Paul Semonin Realtors, the largest real estate agency statewide, is second only to Rector-Hayden in Lexington with more than 160 agents in the Bluegrass area. The company specializes in residential but also offers some commercial properties. The "Semonin Home Show," a half-hour paid advertisement at noon Sundays on Channel 18, highlights some of the best current listings.

RE/MAX ALL STAR REALTY
Relocation   (800) 859-8788
Two Paragon Centre   224-7711

RE/MAX CREATIVE REALTY
Lexington Green Office Building   273-7653
Relocation   (800) 860-7468

RE/MAX OF THE BLUEGRASS
501 Darby Creek Drive, No. 15   263-4663

Lexington has three full-service RE/MAX franchises dealing in residential, farm and commercial properties. The oldest, Creative, has some of Lexington's top producers and a large number of certified relocation professionals among its 40-plus associates. RE/MAX All Star Realty, which opened in October 1992, now has 16 associates. Broker/owner T.L. Wise has been in business in Lexington for 17 years. RE/MAX of the Bluegrass, the new kid on the block, has eight associates. In additional to residential properties, it offers buyer representation, property management, executive leases, help in securing optimum financing, new construction and historical properties.

FISTER & ASSOCIATES REALTY
1050 Chinoe Road   268-2533

Since its founding in 1982, this firm has rapidly grown into one of Central Kentucky's largest. While spe-

cializing in farms and residential properties, it also has a commercial division. Fister & Associates Realty, which maintains 35 to 50 agents throughout Greater Lexington, has an excellent relocation department and an extensive corporate packet. Agent Carolyn Edwards is immediate past president of the Lexington Board of Realtors.

TURF TOWN PROPERTIES, INC.
2560 Richmond Road   268-4663

Turf Town Properties maintains a high profile despite its size — five partners and 16 associate agents. This 15-year-old, locally owned company provides a full gamut of services, with residential properties ranging from $40,000 starter homes to fine Bluegrass estates. Its agents are known for their experience, market knowledge and high production. Turf Town is also a member of All Points Relocation Service.

BUYERS ONLY REALTY, INC.
293 South Ashland Avenue   268-4650

This four-associate firm, founded by Molly Hannifin in 1991 and operated out of her historic Ashland Park home, is notable for its practice of representing buyers exclusively. Although many firms are now beginning to offer buyer brokerage, Buyers Only is apparently the only one in Lexington that represents only buyers. It has earned its niche, and in the process has taken over the entire ground floor of the house.

CENTURY 21 DAMPIER REAL ESTATE

1910 Harrodsburg Road   278-2322
(800) 442-8909

Century 21 Dampier Real Estate is a full-service company that has been in business for 15 years. It provides expert relocation services for both incoming and outgoing residents. The company has 32 agents and deals in residential and commercial properties and investments. Century 21 Dampier Real Estate also has a property management department and its own auction company.

SMITH REALTY GROUP

Tates Creek Centre, 4071 Tates Creek Road,
Suite 101   271-2000
134 East Main Street,
Georgetown   863-1733
1845 Main Street,
Paris   1-987-6666

With three Bluegrass offices and 38 associates, Smith Realty serves the entire Greater Lexington area. Since Doug Smith founded the agency more than 20 years ago, it has grown into a full-service company. Services include residential, farm, commercial and multi-family properties, a relocation program, property management and maintenance, auctions and new construction. Smith works out of the Georgetown office; Carol Bryant is the managing broker for Lexington.

THE PRUDENTIAL
A.S. DE MOVELLAN REAL ESTATE

620 Perimeter Drive   266-0451
(800) 928-0451

Prudential A.S. de Movellan is a 28-year-old company that has been a Prudential franchise for four years. The Prudential affiliation gives the agency the ability to enter 5,000 markets all over the United States as well as in Canada and Europe. A.S. de Movellan, which has 45 full-time associates, deals in residential and commercial properties and also has a strong relocation department for incoming corporate transferees. Residentially, the company maintains the highest average sale price among Lexington agencies, says President Tony de Movellan, but it also handles moderately priced homes.

JUSTICE REAL ESTATE

518 East Main 255-6600, (800) 455-5580

COLDWELL BANKER
JUSTICE REAL ESTATE

518 East Main 255-3657, (800) 455-5580

Bill Justice, a 15-year veteran of the Lexington real estate market, founded his own agency in 1980. Today the company has two divisions. The residential division, Coldwell Banker Justice Real Estate, is part of the country's largest real estate franchise. The farm division, Justice Real Estate, specializes in horse farms and other rural properties. According to Justice, this division has sold more farm property than any other company in the region in the last decade.

REALTY WORLD —
MAYS & ASSOCIATES, INC.

296 Southland Drive   278-7501

Realty World's Lexington franchise is a medium-size, primarily residential company that has been in business since 1984. The 25 associates' commitment to quality rather than quantity is reflected in an annual list-to-sale ratio that has exceeded 90 percent since 1990. Bonnie Mays, a native Kentuckian and University of Kentucky graduate, is the principal broker.

WHITMAN AND ASSOCIATES, INC., REAL ESTATE

3198 Custer Drive   273-1666
                    (800) 326-5744

Harry Whitman's company, founded in 1975, has the resources to not only sell your house or help you find one, but also to build you one. An "in-house" construction and development company are among the added features of this company, whose owners have more than 40 years of management experience. In addition to residential, Whitman and Associates also offers services in such areas as farms, commercial and investment properties and business brokerage. The company is also a member of the RELO/Inter-City Relocation Network.

KAY LEDBETTER & ASSOCIATES

Corporate Center,
3070 Harrodsburg Road   223-8992

This small company, which maintains an average of about 10 agents, specializes in horse farms and estates. Kay Ledbetter, who has been involved in the sale of a number of prominent horse farms, is the exclusive Kentucky member of the Estates Club and Club Immobilier, which produce magazines that are distributed nationally and internationally. These memberships extend Ledbetter & Associates' coverage to Europe, South America, the Far East and Canada. The company

also handles residential and commercial properties.

Builders and Developers

As is the case with Realtors, the builders and developers in this chapter by no means form an exhaustive list. You can find dozens of talented builders in the Bluegrass; just drive around and look at the signs in the yards of homes under construction. These are simply a few of the biggest and best-known who have distinguished themselves in various areas of the Lexington market.

BALL HOMES, INC.
3399 Tates Creek Road   268-1191

Ball Homes, one of Lexington's largest and oldest builders, specializes in affordable housing in the $65,000-140,000 range. The 35-year-old company builds about 200 houses a year and expects to have six or seven subdivisions under way in 1994. Ball Homes is a family operation: Ray Ball Jr. is president, founder Don Ball is a vice president and three other family members are officers. About 30 floor plans are available, from ranches to two-story traditional homes with basements; square footage generally runs from 1,000 to 2,700.

BARLOW HOMES, INC.
3130 Custer Drive   272-3423

Founder James Barlow has been in the business for 34 years, and Barlow Homes, Inc., for 15. The company concentrates on upscale $70,000-110,000 homes for first-time buyers and "transitional" homes from $100,000 to $170,000.

Barlow homes are spread across south Lexington from Todd's Road to Harrodsburg Road. The company has two Georgetown neighborhoods, including a golf-course development, and one each in Versailles and Nicholasville. Barlow does limited custom building but will customize its 35 available floor plans.

MIKE CRAVENS BUILDER
705 Cooper Drive   268-7704

Since 1971, Cravens has built more than 400 houses in the Lexington area, as well as a few small office buildings. His work is almost all for-sale housing. Although Cravens likes to build in the $60,000-100,000 range, the lower interest rates of the last year or so have prompted him to build more homes priced from $125,000 to $170,000. He does his own designs, which have changed over the years from contemporary to more traditional. Cravens homes grace a number of Lexington subdivisions; there are about 40 in Walden Grove in south Lexington.

CUTTER HOMES
3131 Custer Drive   273-2006

In 1993, Cutter was one of five U.S. builders to win a national Award for Construction Excellence from the Home Owners Warranty Corp. Cutter, noted for its follow-up service after the sale, has 30-plus flexible floor plans ranging from $75,000 "patio homes" to country-club-type homes priced up to $170,000, like those in east Lexington's Andover Park subdivision. Cutter is a partner with Barlow

Photo: Lexington Convention and Visitors Bureau

Neighborhoods in Lexington range from historic to brand new.

Homes in United Building Systems, a lumber and manufacturing company that makes pre-engineered panels used in the homes.

HACKER-THOMPSON PARTNERS
153 Patchen Drive 269-0040

The Woods, Cumberland Hill and Andover Hill are among the prestigious neighborhoods developed by Joe Hacker and Troy Thompson. Hacker and Thompson, who have been in business as developers for 15 years, design the subdivisions and build the streets and amenities, then market the neighborhoods to builders and the general public.

KESSINGER BUILDERS
AND KESSINGER REALTY
408 Bristol Road 269-6963

Ted Kessinger, who has been in the development and building business since 1979, specializes in solidly built start-up homes in the $70,000-80,000 range. Most of the 30 or so homes he builds each year are two- and three-bedroom ranches with two baths and at least a one-car garage. Kessinger designs his own floor plans and markets the homes through his realty company. A recent development is Pleasant Point, a 115-house project off Richmond Road that is nearing completion.

FIRST LEXINGTON CO.
1999 Richmond Road 268-1085

First Lexington is a real estate development firm whose services run a broad range from development of single-family residential subdivisions to strip shopping center sites. Condominium development is one of the company's specialties. Among the prominent projects in which First Lexington has been involved are the luxurious Richmond East condominium and office complex and land development for the Eastwood subdivision built by Cutter Homes.

Custom Builders

ATCHISON CONSTRUCTION
COMPANY
2011 Rambler Road 275-4052

John G. Atchison III, president, has been in business since 1978. He is now building 15 to 25 custom contract homes a year, with an average price of $250,000 to $350,000. Atchison has built all around Lexington, with a number of homes in such popular and prestigious newer subdivisions as Firebrook, Andover Forest and Hartland.

MAC CRAWFORD BUILDER
107 Commerce Drive,
Nicholasville 885-7022

Mac Crawford and his team of full-service custom home builders have been in business since 1972. Crawford is a "scattered-sight" builder who will build wherever someone has an empty lot. He also does remodeling, renovation, restoration and insurance repair, as well as some light commercial work. The company creates some of its own exterior and interior designs. It's a small company, averaging six or seven new houses a year ranging from $150,000 on up, with a solid reputation for quality and service.

DALTON BUILT HOMES

2125 Rothbury Road   273-8016

Don Dalton has been building fine homes in Lexington and Louisville for about 18 years. He specializes in upper-end customer homes from $400,000 to $700,000. There are 70 to 80 Dalton homes in the Hartland area alone. Dalton also offers design services and draws most of the plans he builds; his favorite plans, which are about 5,500 square feet, are in the French Colonial style.

FIRST KENTUCKY HOMES, INC.

1365 Devonport Drive   255-9548

This family-owned business, headed by Jim Ball, works with developers, builders and subcontractors to produce custom-designed homes. First Kentucky, most known for the Palomar subdivision off Harrodsburg Road, also built Stone Creek and Fairhaven subdivisions in south Lexington. The company's capabilities are diverse, from two-stories, ranches or practically anything else a customer might want.

KEN HILER BUILDER, INC.

Four Pines Drive   268-1035

Hiler entered the business in 1970 and has been building a wide range of custom residential and commercial properties. Residences, which include townhomes and condominiums, typically start at $300,000; commercial properties range from $300,000 to $800,000. Recent developments include Four Pines in the Lansdowne Merrick area of south Lexington and Meadowthorpe Plantation in northwest Lexington.

PADGETT CONSTRUCTION, INC.
181 Southland Drive 276-1200, 268-9700

Tom Padgett's 15-year-old company specializes in custom-building projects from renovations to very large homes, from Colonial reproductions to European styles to contemporary. Padgett Construction is a small company that limits itself to a few projects at a time but with great attention to detail. The company builds primarily in Fayette County but does some work outside the county. One recent project is a collection of large "garden homes" in Castlegate subdivision in south Lexington's Chinoe Road-Alumni Drive area. Homes start at $225,000.

THE PHILLIPS GROUP, INC.
Leo and Jeannie Phillips 263-3430

The husband-and-wife duo of Leo and Jeannie Phillips, in business since 1960, has designed, built and sold numerous homes in the prestigious Andover Forest, Hartland and Firebrook neighborhoods. These superbly crafted luxury homes generally range from $200,000 to $400,000. Jeannie Phillips does most of the design work. The Phillipses, who build about 14 homes a year, won a number of awards during the Lexington Parade of Homes in June 1993. Both husband and wife are Realtors who belong to the multiple listing service.

Temporary Housing
STUDIO PLUS
2750 Gribbin Drive	266-4800
3575 Tates Creek Road	271-6160

Studio Plus leases new, furnished efficiency apartments with flexible terms. Rates run from $39 to $59 a night, depending on the length of stay. Amenities include all utilities, free cable TV, microwave, pool, exercise room and laundry facility. The Gribbin Drive apartments have 60 units; Tates Creek has 72. Studio Plus accepts most major credit cards.

Several Lexington hotels offer executive suites with short and extended terms available for corporate relocations and other temporary housing needs. Hotels with executive suites include the Campbell House, 1375 Harrodsburg Road, 255-4281; Courtyard By Marriott, 775 Newtown Court, 253-4646; and Hilton Suites of Lexington Green, 3195 Nicholasville Road, 271-4000. (For more information on accommodations, see Hotels and Motels.)

Apartment Complexes and Condominiums

There are several criteria to consider when searching for an apartment or condominium to rent. The weight you lend to each one depends upon your personal preferences, lifestyle and budget. For some people, price will be the dominant factor. Others might choose a property based on factors such as style, amenities, location, convenience or security considerations. Most complexes have laundry facilities and

an outdoor pool. Among the other amenities available are indoor pools, tennis and volleyball courts, whirlpools or saunas, fireplaces, washer and dryer connections, individual alarm systems, exercise and weight rooms, garages or covered parking and clubhouses for private parties. Some properties even have restaurants and bars on the premises.

At some complexes, the renter pays all utilities. Other properties include all or most of the utility charges in the flat monthly rate. If you hate paying bills, it may be worth your trouble to find a place where everything is included.

We have selected a cross-section of nice properties from the many available in Lexington. It may seem as if we have focused more on the south end than the north, but that's simply because more property tends to be available on the south end. If you need additional help, call the properties themselves, pick up one of the free guides available all over town, or call one of the location and referral services (see below). Only you know which characteristics matter most to you. It may seem a cliché to say Lexington has something for everyone, but it's essentially true. Although, in general, most properties maintain a low vacancy rate, with a little persistence you can find what you're looking for.

BISCAYNE APARTMENTS (NORTH)
150 Northland Drive   254-4502

These secluded apartments off North Broadway range from $335 for one bedroom to $385-405 for two bedrooms.

BRANDYWINE APARTMENTS (SOUTH)
1550 Trent Boulevard   272-7226

Prices range from $409 for one bedroom to $570 for two bedrooms at this attractive complex featuring an elegant clubhouse and pools with sundecks.

BRECKINRIDGE COURT (SOUTH)
420 Redding Road   271-1655

Rent is $395 to $480 for a one bedroom and $545 to $580 for two at this apartment complex with fireplaces, vaulted ceilings and private patios and balconies.

CLOISTERS ON THE GREEN (SOUTH)
3501 Pimlico Parkway   272-4561

One bedroom is $419 to $449, two bedrooms are $519 to $549 and three bedrooms are $719 to $749. There are two pools, and Tates Creek Golf Course is nearby.

THE GATE HOUSE (EAST)
1825 Liberty Road   252-4489

All utilities are included in the $345 for one bedroom and $425 for two. The indoor pool is surrounded by tropical plants.

THE GREENHOUSE (SOUTH)
3543 Tates Creek Road   272-7686

A one-bedroom apartment runs $475-590 and a two-bedroom $675-825 at this attractive complex overlooking a lake and featuring tennis courts, covered parking and an exercise room.

THE HERITAGE APARTMENTS I (EAST)
2150 Richmond Road   266-4011

These roomy apartments, minutes from UK and downtown, are $365 for one bedroom, $409 for two and $540 for three. Small pets are permitted.

MATADOR NORTH (NORTH)
1053 Winburn Drive   299-3118

Two-bedroom apartments are $300-350 and three-bedroom $425-450 at this complex featuring playground and picnic areas and 24-hour security.

MERRICK PLACE (SOUTH)
3380 Tates Creek Road   266-0714

Spacious one- to three-bedroom apartments and townhouses with fireplaces range from $415 to $965.

PARK PLACE APARTMENTS (SOUTH)
4030 Tates Creek Road   273-7464

Vaulted ceilings, sunrooms and other luxuries are found at these spacious two-bedroom apartments starting at $819. Corporate suites are available.

PARK PLAZA APARTMENTS (DOWNTOWN)
120 East Main Street   252-5559

One-bedroom apartments at this convenient downtown location by the library are $475 to $655, all utilities and basic cable included. Two bedrooms range from $625 to $865. Two-bedroom luxury penthouses are $825 to $1,300.

THE RACQUET CLUB (SOUTH)
3900 Crosby Drive   271-2582

The Racquet Club boasts of an "exclusive country-club atmosphere" with restaurant and bar, racquetball and volleyball, indoor and outdoor pools, marble fireplaces and more for $430-555 for one bedroom and $645-710 for two.

SADDLEBROOK APARTMENTS (SOUTHEAST)
151 Todds Road   266-1191

One-bedroom apartments are $380-410, two-bedroom $420-490 and three-bedroom $540-590. There are two pools, tennis, volleyball and a weight room.

SHILLITO PARK APARTMENTS (SOUTH)
3500 Beaver Place Road   223-9891

Fireplaces, screened patios and a variety of athletic opportunities are available here at $465 for one bedroom and $575 for two.

TURFLAND APARTMENTS (SOUTHWEST)
2070 Garden Springs Drive   278-6056

One bedroom is $365, two bedrooms $435, including utilities, with an indoor pool open year round.

Rental Assistance

These location and referral services are generally free to the users. The companies are paid out of the advertising budgets of the property owners.

APARTMENT & HOME LOCATING SERVICE
2891 Richmond Road, Suite 112 268-1022

LEXINGTON APARTMENT REFERRAL
694 New Circle Road Northeast 255-5450

Home Improvement Supplies

BUILDING MATERIALS

CENTRAL KENTUCKY SUPPLY CO. INC.
1077 Eastland Drive   254-9341

CONGLETON LUMBER CO. INC.
635 East Third Street   254-2371

84 LUMBER CO.
2345 Palumbo Drive   269-3384

FURROW BUILDING MATERIALS
1306 Versailles Road   253-2038

KENTUCKY-INDIANA LUMBER CO. INC.
2525 Palumbo Drive   268-0953

LEXINGTON BUILDING SUPPLY CO. INC.
1260 Industry Road   254-8834

LOWE'S
128 West Tiverton Way   273-5151
1209 New Circle Road Northeast 259-2880

WICKES LUMBER
1551 Mercer Road   233-4878

PAINT AND WALLCOVERINGS

PERSPECTIVES INC.
352 Longview Drive   277-0521

Perspectives, just off Southland Drive behind Big Valu, stocks more than 50,000 rolls of wallpaper and also carries Coronado paint. The store's helpful, no-pressure staff also keeps customers coming back. Before buying, you can take samples home to see how particular patterns will look in your house. Perspectives offers cash discounts.

COLOR & SUPPLY CO. INC.
Factory Store
909 National Avenue   254-3836
Warehouse Store
624 West Fourth Street   255-5557
242 Southland Drive   277-2777
Tates Creek Centre   271-2078

Color & Supply, manufacturers of Town & Ranch paints, offers more than 5,000 custom colors.

DEVOE PAINT
180 Moore Drive   278-9326

According to Devoe, the company was founded in 1754 and is the oldest paint company in America. Its paint, made in Louisville, are sold primarily to commercial users, but retail users are welcome. Devoe has custom matching.

PORTER PAINTS

199 Moore Drive	276-1447
354 East Main Street	254-3878
100 Patchen Drive	266-0422

Porter's prime market is professional painters and contractors. Porter has a wide range of paint grades and washabilities, more than 800 colors and custom matching.

SHERWIN-WILLIAMS CO.

341 Eastland Shopping Center	255-7736
2551 Regency Road	277-2570

Sherwin-Williams carries its popular paints as well as a complete line of accessories. Free decorating assistance is provided.

SUPERIOR PAINT & DECORATING

2551 Regency Road	276-5264

Superior features Benjamin Moore paints, wallpaper, fabrics, mini-blinds, window treatments and more.

CARPET AND RUGS

BAILEY'S CARPET BARN

4976 Old Versailles Road	254-4852

BUDDY'S CARPET

4013 Nicholasville Road	273-0333
477 New Circle Road	293-1828

CARPET WORKS

360 Longview Drive	277-4135

CARPET WORLD

390 New Circle Road NE	253-0004

DANA KELLY ORIENTAL RUGS INC.

870 East High Street	266-9274

DICKENS FLOOR COVERING

187 Moore Drive	277-1956

JACK & JAN'S CARPETS
1030 New Circle Road NE   233-7847

KINNAIRD & FRANCKE INTERIORS
163 North Patchen Drive   269-5371

PERSIAN RUG GALLERY
237 East Main Street   254-3669

**SUFF'S FURNITURE
& ORIENTAL RUGS**
228 East Main Street, Georgetown 233-9924

TV Shows and Publications

"THE REAL ESTATE PREVIEW"

This local-access cable TV show, produced by the Lexington Board of Realtors, provides a taste of what's currently on the market. It airs 12 times a week: Monday through Friday from 11 AM to noon and 5:30 PM to 6:30 PM, Saturday from noon to 1 PM and Sunday from 11 AM to noon.

"SEMONIN HOMES SHOW"

This half-hour paid commercial for Paul Semonin Realtors airs at noon Sundays on Channel 18.

HARMON HOMES MAGAZINE
2250 Regency Road   277-9067

The Bluegrass-area edition of this free national magazine is published every two weeks and can be found near the entrances of many groceries, drugstores and shopping centers.

THE REAL ESTATE BOOK
273-8200

This free publication is available at numerous locations around town.

BUILDER HOMES AND ACCESSORIES
NEW HOME BUYERS GUIDE
224-6795

Builder Homes, as this free publication is known, is sponsored by the Home Builders Association of Lexington.

LEXINGTON APARTMENT GUIDE
P.O. Box 4207, Lexington 40544 223-4085

Bob Culp founded this free publication, the largest apartment guide in the Bluegrass, more than 10 years ago. It consists of paid advertising by apartment communities and is distributed at 560 locations in a six-county area.

APARTMENT BLUE BOOK
4053-C Tates Creek Road, Suite 208

This publication is also distributed free.

Inside
Schools and Day Care

Some 33,000 youngsters were enrolled in the Fayette County Public School System's 56 schools (which includes 32 elementary schools, 10 middle schools for grades 6-8, six high schools, seven magnet schools or programs, and three alternative schools) in 1993. There are more than 2,000 teachers and 1,400 classified personnel working in the system. Some 1,200 of the teachers have their master's degrees and half that many have their Rank 1, which is 30 graduate hours beyond the master's degree. Fayette County's 13 independent and parochial schools enroll more than 4,000 students.

That's a lot of numbers. But if you attended the Fayette County schools, you'd probably not have much trouble dealing with a lot of numbers. Fayette County Public Schools students consistently score above state and national averages on the SAT and ACT, and over 72 percent of high school graduates continue on to college.

Before you enroll your child in a Lexington school, there are a few things you should know about. The first is the Kentucky Education Reform Act, or KERA as it is more fondly known. The Kentucky public school system was declared unconstitutional a few years back, basically because of inequities in financial resources between districts such as Lexington and Louisville that have a fairly good economic base from which to draw operating money, and smaller rural districts that do not.

Passed by the Kentucky General Assembly in 1990, KERA primarily establishes performance outcomes for all students and requires schools to ensure that all students successfully meet these outcomes. Major provisions of the reform act include school-based decision-making councils that allow parents and teachers to become more actively involved in determining how individual schools are run. Ungraded primary school replaces kindergarten through third grade and allows students to progress at individual rates.

Other KERA provisions include such things as incorporating technology and family resource and youth services centers into the school setting.

The reasons you should know at least a little about KERA is that it not only significantly affects your child's educational experience, both structurally and philosophically, but it is also being looked at nationally as a model for school reform. Plus, everyone's always talking about it.

FAYETTE COUNTY PUBLIC SCHOOLS
701 East Main Street
(Central Offices)   *281-0100*

The Fayette County public school system is governed by a five-member board of education. School board members are elected to four-year terms. Current school board members are Barth Pemberton, chair; Jim Gardner, vice chair; Joyce Gash; Robert Slone; and Nancy Stage. The school year runs from the end of August to the end of May.

Age Requirements

Age requirements for entering the public school system are as follows: a child who becomes 4 years old before October 1 of the year they are entering school is eligible for the preschool program, as are children ages 3-5 with special needs, who would benefit from an early intervention program. School attendance is compulsory in Kentucky for students ages 6-16. Children must be 5 years old on or before October 1 of the year they enroll to be eligible for the Primary Program. Any child who becomes 6 years old on or before October 1 must enroll for that school year.

Immunizations and Medical Exams

All children entering school are required by Kentucky state law to present a valid immunization certificate upon registration. Fayette County Public Schools require students to be immunized against polio, diphtheria, tetanus, rubella (German measles), and rubeola (red measles).

All students entering the sixth grade are required to have a second measles/mumps/rubella vaccination prior to the beginning of school. Additionally, each child enrolling in the school system for the first time must be tested for tuberculosis within one year prior to registration. Also, all first-time enrollees (including transfer students) must have a medical examination within six months prior to or one month following admission. Students entering the sixth grade must have another examination prior to the start of school.

Special Schools and Programs

In addition to regular programs, Fayette County has a number of magnet schools and programs that focus on at-risk students, students with special needs and special abilities, Spanish-speaking students, and students pursuing specialized technical and arts education.

The School for Creative and Performing Arts at Bluegrass, or SCAPA, provides students in grades 4-8 who are specially talented and/or specially interested in the fine arts an opportunity to pursue those interests while providing a solid academic foundation. The school day runs a little longer — 8:50 AM-4:10 PM — to make sure students are getting full exposure to the creative and basic educational process. Instruction in visual arts, music, dance, drama and creative writing complement the basic mandated curricu-

Sayre School

"The Independent Choice"

Montessori through Grade Twelve

Extended Day Program
Preschool through Grade Five

Established 1854

194 North Limestone   **(606) 254-1361**

lum. Students are admitted competitively based on an interview and audition, evaluations from former and current teachers, and parent interviews. There are currently about 230 students enrolled.

The Lexington Traditional Magnet School for students in grades 6-8 is a highly enriched and structured academic program focused on the development of intellectual skills and a high academic achievement. The 750 students at the Traditional Magnet School focus on a disciplined and rigorous educational program that includes consistent attendance, punctuality, adherence to a dress code, and required participation in at least one extracurricular activity.

There are 192 students currently enrolled in the Spanish Immersion Program, housed at Maxwell Elementary School. This program is open to incoming second-year primary students and is designed to help children develop proficiency in a second language, achieve cross-cultural understanding, and achieve English language arts skills comparable to or surpassing those of students in English-only programs. The school day is divided into two parts: the first half is spent in the target language (in this case, Spanish), and the second half is spent in English.

Other special programs include

Insiders' Tips

It may have been a merchandising masterstroke, but insiders know that the coonskin cap worn by Daniel Boone (a k a Fess Parker) on the TV show and in our minds was not authentic. Dan'l preferred a black felt hat.

The Lexington Public Library, founded in 1795, is the oldest circulating library west of the Allegheny Mountains.

the Math, Science and Technology Center at Paul Laurence Dunbar High School, a four-year program of study that offers students additional academic and hands-on opportunities in the scientific and technological fields. The Eastside and Southside Centers for Applied Technology offer comprehensive programs for secondary students in technology, graphic arts, electronics, health services, carpentry and horticulture. Central Alternative School, for students in grades seven through 12, gives students who do not function well in a regular classroom setting an individual instructional approach. Fayette School fo-

cuses on students with emotional or behavioral problems. And Fayette County High School targets students who have dropped out of school, potential dropouts, or students on academic probation.

We have included information about some of the bigger private and parochial schools in Lexington below.

Private and Parochial Schools

While there are many excellent educational opportunities available in the public school system, many parents choose to send their children to private or parochial schools,

which offer special programs or special emphases, such as Bible study or performing arts.

THE LEXINGTON SCHOOL
1050 Lane Allen Road   278-0501

Founded in 1959, The Lexington School is a private co-ed school for kids in preschool through the ninth grade. The school stresses a traditional curriculum with a fine and performing arts component. A 12,000-volume library, interscholastic soccer, basketball and tennis teams, and small classes are among the strong points of the school. In the upper school — for grades seven through nine — the course of study is college and high school preparatory, with lab-based science courses and sequential courses in art, music and drama. The school enrolls about 480 students, and some testing is required before admission. Call for information on tuition rates.

BLUEGRASS BAPTIST SCHOOL
1330 Red River Drive   272-1217

About 190 students attend Bluegrass Baptist, which was established in 1969 for preschool through 12th grade education. The school offers a traditional curriculum with a Christian emphasis. An interview is usually required prior to admission.

Tuition ranges from $780/year for preschool to $1,740/year for one child in grades one through 12. For families with more than one child attending, the rate per child drops.

LEXINGTON CATHOLIC HIGH SCHOOL
2250 Clays Mill Road   277-7183

With an enrollment of 525 stu-

dents, Lexington Catholic ranks among the largest of Lexington's private and parochial schools. Open to students in grades nine through twelve, the school stresses a pre-college curriculum. Freshmen are required to take a placement test. Interscholastic sports, such as basketball and soccer, and other extracurricular activities play a big role in students' lives. The school was established in 1951.

Tuition for parish students is $2,695 per year. For non-parish students, it is $3,495 per year.

MARY QUEEN OF THE HOLY ROSARY
2501 Clays Mill Road   277-3030

Established in the early 1960s, Mary Queen of the Holy Rosary serves students in kindergarten through the eighth grade. There are about 507 students enrolled, mainly from parish families.

Tuition for non-parish students is $2,300/year. For parish students, tuition ranges from $1,200/year for one child to $2,200/year for three or more students from the same family.

THE LEXINGTON CHRISTIAN ACADEMY
P.O. Box 23160, 40523   223-8502

Lexington Christian Academy stresses a strong academic curriculum combined with a spiritual perspective. Bible-based principles are incorporated into the entire academic experience for students in preschool through 12th grade. As for extracurricular activities, students can participate in basketball, baseball, soccer, tennis, golf and swimming. Students attend a weekly chapel service and follow a strict

dress code. (We give the post office box for the central contact here because different grades are housed in different locations.)

Tuition for preschool programs runs from $100 to $300 per month. For grades K-12, tuition ranges from $3,048/year to $3,276/year.

TRINITY CHRISTIAN ACADEMY
3900 Rapid Run   *271-0079*

Established in 1988, Trinity Christian Academy offers students in kindergarten through the eighth grade a Bible-based Christian education. About 100 students are enrolled in the school. An interview and testing are required prior to admission.

Tuition ranges from $720/year for the two-day preschool program to $2,835/year for the eighth grade.

SAYRE SCHOOL
194 North Limestone   *254-1361*

Established in Lexington in 1854, Sayre School is one of the oldest schools in the Southeast. Since that time, Sayre has continued to cement its reputation as one of the finest coeducational college preparatory schools in the area. About 500 students attend Sayre in programs from Montessori and pre-kindergarten to senior high school. Sayre operates on the self-contained classroom format, as opposed to the ungraded primary system now being used by public elementary schools in Kentucky.

Sayre students receive a well-rounded education that emphasizes college preparation but also includes athletics, fine arts and community service. Students are actively involved in community service projects, such as the middle school (grades 6-8)

students' commitment to spending one day a month volunteering in nursing homes, food banks and other service organizations.

Small class size, individual attention and an open athletic policy that ensures all children can participate in athletics, are just a few of the things that make Sayre special.

Before admission, students are screened developmentally at the preschool level, and academically in grades 1-12. Only students performing at or above grade level are admitted. Tuition costs range from $3,000 (for preschool) to $6,500 (for senior high school) annually.

One note to parents: Several of the state-mandated admission requirements listed in the section on the public schools also apply to private and parochial school students, including compulsory education for kids ages 6-16, and some of the immunization and medical examination requirements. Please refer to that section for details.

STANLEY H. KAPLAN EDUCATIONAL CENTER LTD.
2201 Regency Road   *276-5419*

The oldest and largest standardized test and licensure preparation service in the United States, Kaplan Educational can help you get ready to score well on a wide range of standard admission tests, from the ACT and SAT to the MCAT (medical school) and GRE (graduate school). Kaplan Educational can also help students prepare for the NCLEX (RN board review), LSAT (law school admission test) and GMAT (business school admission test).

Academic Excellence...

Lexington Catholic High School

2250 Clays Mill Road
Lexington, Kentucky 40503
Telephone: (606) 277-7183
Fax: (606) 277-4959

...with Lifetime Values

Kaplan offers both live and videotaped classes, with an average tuition of $600 for eight-to-12-week sessions. Last year, more than 800 area clients used Kaplan's test preparation services.

Child Care

The good news is, Lexington has about 140 licensed daycare centers and 33 certified day care homes. The bad news is, it's often difficult to get your child or children into one of these programs. In fact, if you have an infant or toddler, it will be close to impossible, since there is typically only a 1 percent vacancy rate in this age group.

There is, however, a nonprofit agency that can help. The Child Care Council of Kentucky can give referrals to parents for child-care facilities that best suit them and their situation. Carolyn Covington, director of the Child Care Council, said her agency answers 3,000 information calls per year. The majority of people who contact the council are new parents, parents of preschool-age children, and people who are just moving into the area.

When these parents call the council for help, staff members ask them for such information as their geographic location, their work location, and the ages of their children. The council staff person then searches through the referral database that contains all the licensed and certified facilities in a 17-county area. The parents are then given a list of facilities that best match their needs.

Covington added, however, that the Child Care Council does not make recommendations or referrals: It simply tries to help parents meet their day-care needs.

Kentucky recognizes four basic categories of day-care services. Non-regulated care facilities are usually private homes that care for three or fewer non-related children. Certified family day-care homes are for one to six children. Type 2 facilities are licensed family day-care homes that can accommodate seven to 12 children, and Type 1 licensed family day-care facilities are for 12 or more children.

Covington noted that, while on-site employer-sponsored daycare is not as widespread in Lexington as it is in many other cities, several large employers, such as Toyota Manufacturing in Georgetown and the University of Kentucky, have highly rated on-site facilities.

A number of Lexington churches, and several local hospitals including Saint Joseph and Cen-

tral Baptist, have state-of-the-art on- or near-site day-care centers. Additionally, the YMCA of Central Kentucky holds after-school programs in area schools for older children.

The Child Care Council is also an excellent resource for child-care providers. Each year, it provides training and technical assistance to 2,000 such caregivers in Central Kentucky. A resource library containing many of the most up-to-date child-care books and resources is available for use by the public.

For more help in finding the right child-care facilities for your kids, call the Child Care Council at 254-9176, Monday-Friday, 8 AM-5 PM.

Lexington Public Library

*I*f Andrew M. Calla were alive to visit the main Lexington Public Library today, he would surely find himself at a loss for words. Fortunately, he'd be in just the place to do a little research and find them.

Calla, a pharmacist by trade, was the first librarian of the Lexington Library Co., which ultimately grew into a great source of civic pride for anyone who lives in the Bluegrass. The Lexington Public Library, often called the oldest library west of the Allegheny Mountains, today has its main location in a visually breathtaking $9.4 million building at 140 East Main Street. In addition, there are four branches, bookmobiles and dozens of free programs.

The journey from these humble beginnings to today was not an easy one. It was filled with obstacles involving finances and fires as well as public opinion. Through the years, small groups of determined Lexingtonians have persevered in their belief that such a city is deserving of a fine, well-stocked edifice for the intellectual and spiritual edification of its residents.

Anyone who is inclined to take for granted the benefits of a "free" public library should bear in mind that the Lexington Public Library's predecessor was a subscription library. What that means is that users of the library were required to become shareholders and pay an annual fee for the right to use its books and other materials. Even then, there were deadbeats whose names periodically were purged from the membership rolls because of their failure to pay up. The cost of maintaining a library was, and still is, considerable. There have been dark periods in Lexington history when, much to the chagrin of book lovers, the library was forced to cease operations.

The Lexington Library Co. was formed January 1, 1795, to serve Transylvania University students and the rest of the growing community. The library founders, who met at the Old State House, included a number of Lexington's most distinguished early civic leaders, including Transylvania President Harry Toulmin. Calla, the pharmacist, must have taken the position of librarian because of a deep love for books. There was no great financial reward in it for him — he was paid a grand total of $50 a year for his services and rental space, for the

Photo: Lexington Herald-Leader

Book buyers hunt for bargains at the Lexington Public Library's annual sale.

library was then housed in the back of his apothecary and home at Market and Short streets.

Shareholders who paid $5 were entitled to make use of the library's collection, which consisted of books that had previously belonged to Transylvania as well as 400 books that were bought with the $500 initially raised by the group that formed the Lexington Library Co. Among the earliest shareholders were Henry Clay and *Kentucky Gazette* publisher John Bradford. In January 1801 the Kentucky General Assembly incorporated the still-fledgling library, which was then open from 2 PM to 5 PM one Saturday a month.

Much of the library's early history is sketchy. We do know that, for the first century of its existence, the library, supported solely by its shareholders, frequently changed locations from one rented downtown space to another. At one point it occupied the ground floor of Mathurin Giron's ballroom. Apathy was one nemesis, and fire was another, destroying large portions of the library's collection on at least two occasions.

For several years, apparently from 1841 to 1846, Lexington's library was closed. A newspaper article on February 7, 1846, asked: "Lexington used to have a library — where is it now? Has literature bid adieu to the Athens of the West?" By June of that year the library had finally reopened.

The first "permanent" location for the library was a building at Church and Market streets, bought by the Lexington Library Co. in October 1866 with $6,000 raised from a bond sale. During the 1860s and 1870s, lotteries were held periodically to raise money for the library.

A bird's eye view of the atrium at the Central Library
in downtown Lexington

Around the turn of the century the free public library arrived in
Lexington. In 1898 the city arranged to lease the building, books and
other possessions of the Lexington Library Co. to test the feasibility of
a free library that would be available to everyone in the community.
If the experiment was a success, the public library would maintain
permanent possession. Millionaire steel tycoon and philanthropist
Andrew Carnegie came to Lexington's rescue in 1902, pledging
$60,000 to build a library, under the condition that the city provide a
site and the money needed annually to keep it operating.

In June 1905 the Lexington Public Library moved to Gratz Park,
into an elegant new classical structure designed by Herman L. Rowe
and constructed of Bedford stone at a cost of $75,000. This building
served as the main branch until March 26, 1989. Less than two weeks
later, the library moved into its current Main Street location. The
Gratz Park building, at 251 West Second Street, is now the home of the
Carnegie Center for Literacy and Learning, created to provide leadership and programs to enhance literacy throughout the state.

The new library structure, which contains more than 110,000
square feet, is five stories high with an impressive atrium extending
from the first-floor lobby to the top of the building. It was designed by
Sherman-Carter-Barnhart Architects and is built largely of granite
and glass in a post-modern style. Other highlights of the library
include a theater, a changing art gallery, a Kentucky Room with
extensive books and files of state history, numerous computers and

conference rooms.

Construction of the new library did not come without controversy. First of all, it was made possible only after Dr. Joseph M. Hayse, a local taxpayer and library patron, filed suit against the Urban County Government, charging it with inadequately funding the library in violation of state law. As a result of Hayse's suit, the local government was forced to nearly double the amount of money it allocated to the library from its property tax base.

During the actual construction, controversy again arose when it was discovered that the black granite that had been bought for use on the library's facade might have come from South Africa. After much debate, the granite remained a part of the building. Inside the lobby, a plaque in the wall reads:

"Injustice anywhere is a threat to justice everywhere."
— Dr. Martin Luther King, Jr.

The black granite on this building was purchased without the knowledge that it had been quarried in the Republic of South Africa, whose policy of apartheid is condemned by the Lexington Public Library.

Inside
Colleges and Universities

The oldest college west of the Alleghenies and Kentucky's flagship public university are the hallmarks of Lexington's higher education arena. Local universities are among the major Lexington employers. They are a major contributor to the local economy, both through the influx of students to the area each year and through the numbers of people they draw to Lexington through special events.

UNIVERSITY OF KENTUCKY

Avenue of Champions   257-9000

Started in 1865 as part of Kentucky University, a land-grant institution, the University of Kentucky today has close to 75,000 students enrolled in classes at the main Lexington campus and the 14 Community College campuses around the state. UK employs 1,600 full-time academic staff members, 98 percent of whom hold the highest degrees in their discipline.

UK's main campus comprises 17 colleges and schools: agriculture, allied health, architecture, arts & sciences, business and economics, communications, dentistry, education, engineering, fine arts, human and environmental sciences, law, library and information science, medicine, nursing, social work, and the graduate school. Academic degrees at all levels are offered in dozens of majors.

Last year, UK received $98 million in grants, contracts and gifts, about 73 percent of which were for research. *U.S. News & World Report* last year ranked the UK College of Pharmacy third best in the nation, and the College of Medicine was ranked ninth best in the nation at training primary care physicians.

The UK library system serves as a large and acclaimed research tool both for the Commonwealth and the nation. The system contains more than 2 million volumes, and it is the state's only complete depository for government publications of the United States, United Nations, European Communities, and Canada.

UK receives national attention not only in its many fields of study, but on the playing field as well. Student athletes compete in 19 sports on the national level.

The UK Wildcat basketball team under the direction of Coach Rick Pitino rarely drops out of the Associated Press's ranking of the top 10 teams across the nation. Over the years, UK has won five NCAA national championships and consistently takes championship honors

Photo: Lexington Herald-Leader

Finding a quiet place to study for finals in the dorm might be difficult, especially if your roommate has finished his exams. But the University of Kentucky's libraries, including M. I. King Library above, offer lots of space for study.

in Southeastern Conference competition (see our chapter on Big Blue Basketball).

The Wildcat football team, under the leadership of Coach Bill Curry, is working its way toward national prominence, having appeared in the 1993 Peach Bowl.

The Wildcat teams are near and dear to the hearts of Lexingtonians, and UK fans are some of the best in the country. On game days, don't be surprised if Lexington appears to be swathed in a royal blue haze. Actually, it's Kentucky Blue, and it adorns people, cars and anything else it can be attached to, draped over, or prominently displayed on. Big Blue (as the UK sports program is affectionately known) paraphernalia is hot stuff from the retail point of view. This author has yet to be successful in her quest for UK flags to clamp to her car windows.

In-state tuition runs about $1,100 per semester, and it is about $3,100 per semester for nonresidents.

TRANSYLVANIA UNIVERSITY
300 North Broadway   *233-8242*
(800) 872-6798

The oldest college west of the Alleghenies and the 16th oldest in the country, Transylvania University consistently ranks among the best institutions of higher learning in the nation. In 1989 and 1993, a survey conducted by *U.S. News & World Report* ranked Transylvania as the best regional liberal arts college in the South.

About 1,000 students attend Transylvania (called "Transy" by Lexingtonians), which is associated with the Christian Church (Disciples of Christ). Among Transy's alumni are two U.S. vice presidents, 50 U.S. senators, 100 U.S. representatives, 36

governors, and 34 ambassadors. Jefferson Davis (president of the Confederacy during the Civil War), noted abolitionist Cassius Marcellus Clay, and Stephen F. Austin, the first governor of Texas, all attended Transy.

Established in 1780 as Transylvania Seminary, the school became home to the first law and medical schools in the West in 1799. At one time, Henry Clay served as a law professor there.

Today, Transy offers bachelor of arts degrees in 23 majors: art, biology, business administration, chemistry, computer science, drama, economics, education, English, French, history, math, music, philosophy, physical education, physics, political science, psychology, pre-engineering, religion, sociology, anthropology, and Spanish. Pre-professional programs in dentistry, law, medicine, pharmacy, and veterinary medicine are also available.

Transy provides opportunities for its students to participate in a num-ber of extracurricular activities. Transy competes nationally in the National Association of Intercollegiate Athletics. Men's varsity sports include basketball, golf, soccer, swimming and tennis. Women's varsity sports include basketball, field hockey, softball, swimming and tennis. Students can also participate in one of 25 intramural sports. About 80 percent of the students participate in some form of athletics.

There are more than 40 student organizations on campus, including student government, speech and debate teams, a radio station, print publications, and eight national fraternities and sororities.

Annual tuition is approximately $10,200. A number of financial aid options are available to students, including grants, loans, work-study programs and merit scholarships.

In addition to the major institutions of higher learning, there are several business and junior colleges offering associate degree programs in everything from fashion merchandising and travel to accounting and computer programming.

SULLIVAN COLLEGE

2659 Regency Road   276-4357

Offering diploma and associate degree programs in office administration, early childhood (professional nanny), business (executive secretary, business manager, computer programmer), legal (paralegal), and travel and tourism areas, Sullivan College offers Lexingtonians a convenient, quick way to work toward a better career or to improve their position in their chosen career.

Among Sullivan's "perks" for students are the four-day week of classes (Friday is optional attendance and is used for catching up or more in-depth study), and a student apartment complex located near campus for those students living beyond commuting distance.

Tuition costs are $120 per credit hour.

The Louisville campus of Sullivan College was recently accredited to offer four-year bachelor's degree programs, making Sullivan the first private career college in the South to move from two-year to four-year accredited status. Bachelor's degree programs are in the plans for the Lexington campus later this year.

KENTUCKY COLLEGE OF BUSINESS

628 East Main Street   253-0621

An accredited junior college of business, Kentucky College of Business was founded in 1941. Today in its efforts to prepare students for positions in a variety of business and technical careers, Kentucky College of Business offers 15 diploma and associate degree programs.

The following programs are available: accounting, business management, fashion merchandising management, business administration, management information systems, data processing, word processing specialist, executive secretarial, legal secretarial, administrative office specialist, medical secretarial, receptionist, medical records technician, medical administrative assistant and travel and tourism specialist.

The six campuses of the Kentucky College of Business system are Lexington, Florence, Richmond, Danville, Louisville and Pikeville.

Classes are offered on a quarterly basis, and there are a number of scholarships and financial aid options available to students to help cover tuition and other expenses.

Tuition is $104 per credit hour.

FUGAZZI COLLEGE

406 Lafayette Avenue   266-0401

Serving Lexington since 1915, Fugazzi College names small class

Memorial Hall at the University of Kentucky

size, coupled with a good variety of associate degree and diploma programs, among its most desirable characteristics for students.

Degree and diploma programs are offered in computers, radio and television broadcasting, management, accounting, travel and tourism, medical transcription, administrative office specialist, management and business accounting.

Fugazzi also offers students employment counseling, day and evening classes and financial aid for those who qualify.

Tuition is $104 per credit hour.

LEXINGTON THEOLOGICAL SEMINARY
631 South Limestone   252-0361

Originally known as the College of the Bible, Lexington Theological seminary is the oldest ministerial school of the Christian Church (Disciples of Christ). It was founded in 1865 as one of the colleges of Kentucky University.

In 1950, the College of the Bible moved to its current South Limestone location, and in 1965 the school changed the name it had carried for a century to Lexington Theological Seminary.

Today the school offers a number of divinity and ministry degrees and programs, including a joint divinity and social work program with the University of Kentucky. The school also offers master of divinity and master of arts degrees, as well as a doctor of ministry degree. About two-thirds of the students who attend Lexington Theological Seminary are from the Christian Church (Disciples of Christ) denomination.

Lexington Theological Seminary is a member of the ecumenical Theological Education Association of Mid-America and the Appalachian Ministries Education Resources Center.

Tuition is $125 per credit hour. Financial aid is available.

Regional Colleges and Universities

Lexington has not cornered the Central Kentucky higher education market. There are a number of nationally recognized and rated private schools and state universities located in the immediate Lexington vicinity. With the exception of Centre College in Danville, all the colleges and universities listed in the following section are located in the counties highlighted in Lexington's Neighbors. Danville is highlighted in Daytrips.

In the early years of our country, Kentucky was a national leader in higher education, establishing many of the first colleges and universities on the western frontier. However, that reputation declined in the 20th century, and in recent years, the state has struggled to reestablish its reputation for academic excellence.

And these efforts have paid off. Today, small colleges like Berea, Centre and Transylvania University are continually ranked among the top small liberal arts schools in the nation. And the bigger universities have developed programs and areas of specialization that place them on the cutting edge of research and development.

Kentucky is once again coming into its own as a national higher education leader, and the schools listed below are playing a crucial role in that effort.

ASBURY COLLEGE

1 Macklem Drive, Wilmore   *858-3511*

Named for the famous circuit-riding preacher, Francis Asbury, who became the country's first Methodist bishop, Asbury College was established in 1890.

The school is governed by a 30-member board of trustees who operate Asbury according to the principles of "entire sanctification" and "scriptural holiness" taught by the Rev. John Wesley Hughes, who established the college. Although the college is predominantly Methodist in its enrollment, it is officially nondenominational, and receives neither denominational or government support for its programs.

Today, Asbury College has an undergraduate enrollment of about 1,100 students. Annual tuition for this private, four-year, coed liberal arts college is about $7,800 per year. Asbury College offers a wide range of undergraduate majors from Christian ministries and ancient languages to biology, nursing and art.

BEREA COLLEGE

CPO 2344, Berea   *1-986-9341*

"Anti-slavery, anti-caste, anti-rum and anti-sin, giving an education to all colors, classes, cheap and thorough."

This was the vision the Rev. John G. Fee had of an ideal academic institution when he founded Berea College in 1855. The famous Madison County abolitionist and politician, Cassius Marcellus Clay (cousin of Lexington lawyer Henry Clay), donated the land on which Fee built the college.

However, Fee's dream of an interracial school didn't go over too well in the tense months leading up to the start of the Civil War. He and

Some of the top football coaches in collegiate and NFL history, including Paul "Bear" Bryant, Don Shula, Howard Schnellenberger, Chuck Knox and Bill Arnsparger, were once coaches with the University of Kentucky program.

the first Berea teachers were driven from the state just before the war began. But they were not defeated. They returned after the war and opened the Berea Literary Institute which enrolled 96 blacks and 91 whites its first term.

Fee's vision was again stymied in 1904 when Kentucky passed the Day Law forbidding the education of whites and blacks together. This law was not amended to allow integration until 1950.

Even during the years of forced segregation, however, Berea College never stopped in its pursuit of Fee's vision. It founded and supported the Lincoln Institute — a separate school for blacks — near Louisville in 1904. At home, the college turned its attention to the Appalachian region, focusing its efforts on making a quality education available to needy students from the region who lacked access to such education opportunities.

Today, Berea College consistently ranks among the nation's top small liberal arts colleges. Eighty percent of Berea's 1,500 students are from the southern Appalachian region, and the remaining 20 percent come from across the country and around the world.

The mission of the college — to provide a low-cost, high-quality liberal arts education within the context of the Christian faith and ethic — remains the guiding principle for the administration of the school. To be admitted, students must demonstrate financial need, and students pay no tuition. The costs for room and board are paid in large part by the money students earn in the unique college labor program, which teaches students trades and craftsmanship as well as allowing them to earn money to pay for the non-tuition aspects of school.

CENTRE COLLEGE

600 West Walnut Street,
Danville   1-238-5350

Highly acclaimed Centre College in Danville has come a long way from its first graduating class of 1824, consisting of two students, to its current list of alumni that includes U.S. vice presidents, chief justices, congressmen, governors and business leaders.

In fact, Woodrow Wilson once said of the school in a speech at Princeton University, "There is a little college down in Kentucky which in 60 years graduated more men who have acquired prominence and fame than has Princeton in her 150 years." It was probably not a comment that made him popular at Princeton, but it does illustrate the significant role this small Central

Photo: Lexington Herald-Leader

Grounds near UK's Student Center provide pleasant areas in which to study.

Kentucky college has played in national higher education.

Centre College was founded in 1819 by the Kentucky Legislature, and it was named (as you might guess) for its central location in the state. The state turned over control of the school to the Presbyterian denomination of Kentucky in 1824.

A year later, however, a new college president began his 27-year tenure that would play a decisive role in the future of the struggling school. John C. Young became president of Centre College in 1830, and during the ensuing three decades expanded the student body from just 30 students to 225.

As with most other efforts in Kentucky, however, the Civil War drastically diverted the positive expansion of the school. Enrollments significantly dropped, and campus buildings were used by Confederate soldiers before the famous nearby Battle of Perryville in October 1862, and by Union soldiers after that battle.

But the college, like the state and the nation, recouped its losses in the years following the Civil War and slowly rebuilt its student body, gaining greater recognition for its academic excellence and its role as a training ground for many of the nation's up-and-coming political leaders.

Centre College became coed in 1926.

Today, this private, four-year, liberal arts college enrolls about 300 new freshmen each year who enter a wide range of undergraduate programs ranging from biochemistry and molecular biology to psychobiology, education, religion and foreign languages. The student body numbers about 900 full-time students. Tuition runs about $11,000 per year, and financial aid is available.

During the presidencies of Richard L. Morrill and Michael F. Adams in the past two decades, the school has achieved yet another claim to fame. During the 1980s and 1990s, the percent of alumni donating funds to the college has exceeded that of any other college or university in the United States.

EASTERN KENTUCKY UNIVERSITY
Lancaster Avenue, Richmond   1-622-1000

Eastern Kentucky University traces its beginnings back to the normal school movement in the first years of the 20th century (a "normal school" is focused on the training of teachers and educators). In 1906, the Kentucky General Assembly passed a bill establishing the Eastern State Normal School. The school's exclusive focus on the training of teachers continued into the 1920s when it began offering four-year degrees. By the mid-1920s, enrollment had reached well over 1,000 students, and the school was renamed Eastern State Teachers College in 1930.

World War II saw Eastern's enrollment drop to a fraction of its normal number, and the campus was used for a Women's Auxiliary Army Corps training school.

However the postwar boom years of the 1950s and 1960s saw enrollment triple, and new buildings sprang up across the campus. In 1966, the school was again renamed Eastern Kentucky University. Today, EKU's enrollment comprises about

11,000 undergraduate students and 2,000 graduate students in a wide variety of programs. EKU offers more than 150 majors ranging from fisheries management and computer science to forensic science, geology and broadcasting. In-state tuition runs about $1,500 per year.

EKU has distinguished itself on the playing field as well as in the classroom through its participation in NCAA competition. The football team, the Colonels, under the leadership of Coach Roy Kidd, has reached the NCAA Division I-AA national playoffs more than a dozen times in the last decade and a half, and has twice won the I-AA championship.

GEORGETOWN COLLEGE
400 East College Street,
Georgetown   *(800) 788-9985*

Georgetown College traces its history back more than 150 years to its cutting edge position in forming the backbone of the western frontier higher education community. In 1827, Georgetown College became the first Baptist college west of the Alleghenies and the sixth Baptist college organized in the United States.

The college flourished under the leadership of Howard Malcolm of Philadelphia, who became president in 1840. However, his opposition to slavery forced him to resign. His successor, Duncan Campbell, presided over the school's largest graduating class in the 19th century. However, the Civil War brought a sharp end to that period of rapid growth, when the school closed shortly after the war broke out.

The small faculty struggled to re-open the school and rebuild the academic program after the war, and the school's successes, both in the classroom and on the playing field (the school football and basketball teams are among the most successful in the National Association of Intercollegiate Athletics, or NAIA), stand as a tribute to their efforts.

Today, Georgetown's 2,000-member student body is drawn from around the world. The school offers 27 major programs ranging from information systems and medical technology to political science, music education and environmental science. Annual tuition for this private, four-year, coed Southern Baptist liberal arts college runs about $6,700 per year.

KENTUCKY STATE UNIVERSITY
East Main Street, Frankfort (502) 227-6813
Out of state   *(800) 325-1716*

Established in 1886 by a vote of the Kentucky legislature at the urging of the Colored Teachers State Association, Kentucky State University officially opened in 1887 as the State Normal School for Colored Persons.

In 1890, the federal government began providing for the development of land grant colleges for people of color, and the State Normal School for Colored Persons began instruction in agriculture and mechanics in order to qualify for federal money. The school changed its name in 1902 to Kentucky Normal and Industrial Institute to reflect this new diversity in its academic programs.

Because of its location in Frankfort, the state capital, and because of the governor's right to appoint the school's board of trustees who in turn appointed the college president, that position quickly became a highly political matter, and the leadership of the school proved mercurial at best until the early 20th century. At that time, the school's sixth president, Rufus Atwood, withdrew himself from the tempestuous arena of partisan politics and concentrated on forging the position of college president into a professionally legitimate office.

The school changed names again in 1926 to Kentucky State Industrial College for Negroes. During this time, the school's academic standards fell to an all-time low, and the college went into debt. Atwood strove to improve the school's accreditation level, and in 1939 (after again changing its name to Kentucky State College for Negroes) it was recognized as a class A college by the Southern Association Committee on Approval of Negro Schools.

By the time Atwood retired in 1960, Kentucky State had become Kentucky's preeminent black institution of higher learning. The phrase "for Negroes" was removed from the name of the school by a vote of the state legislature in 1952, and in 1972, the Kentucky General Assembly passed legislation officially establishing Kentucky State University.

Today, Kentucky State University has about 1,700 full-time undergraduate students who study a wide range of majors, from art education and criminal justice, to biology and business administration. In-state tuition is about $1,400 per year.

MIDWAY COLLEGE

512 East Stephens Street,
Midway   846-5346
                        (800) 755-0031

As Kentucky's only college for women, Midway College was founded in Woodford County in 1847 with the express purpose of preparing financially disadvantaged women for teaching careers. It was formerly known as the Kentucky Female Orphan School.

Today, equine studies and interests play a key role in the programs Midway College offers its students. The hallmark of this interest is the Keeneland Equine Education Center and the school's outdoor riding facilities, including 50 acres for cross-country riding. Midway also offers associate degrees in equine management and equine office administration.

Other associate (two-year) degrees are available in business administration, early childhood education, fashion merchandising, general studies, nursing, office administration, paralegal studies and teacher education.

In 1989, Midway began offering four-year bachelor of arts and bachelor of science degrees in several fields including nursing, accounting and equine studies.

Midway's student body comprises about 500 full-time and 300 part-time students. Tuition for this private liberal arts school affiliated with the Christian Church (Disciples of Christ) is $6,200 per year, and 87 percent of undergraduates receive financial aid.

Photo: Lexington Herald-Leader

Shopping downtown, amid quaint surroundings, tends to be less hectic than the malls.

Shop, Dine, Play, Stay

Stop in the heart of downtown Lexington and discover the Triangle Shopping District, conveniently located around Triangle Park at the intersection of Main, Broadway and Vine and within walking distance of Lexington's most picturesque historic district.

In Victorian Square and The Civic Center Shops you will find a distinctive collection of nationally-known shops blended with the delightful boutiques that give the centers a local flavor–over 40 in all. A children's museum, 3 full service restaurants and a Food Court will make your day complete.

Parking is free for 3 hours in the Victorian Square Garage or at the Civic Center Shops on High Street.

At the Radisson Plaza Hotel enjoy luxurious accommodations in 367 rooms, fine dining at Cafe on the Park, and nightly entertainment in Spirits Lounge. Make the most of your stay with a visit to our heated pool, whirlpool and exercise room. And don't forget to ask about special business class amenities. See what they mean by the Radisson Advantage.

The Triangle Shopping District is conveniently located within 10 minutes of I-64 and I-75. Shop, Dine, Play, Stay at the Triangle Shopping District connected by covered walkways at the center of downtown Lexington.

Triangle Shopping District

CIVIC CENTER SHOPS	RADISSON PLAZA HOTEL	VICTORIAN SQUARE
(606) 233-4567	606) 231-9000 (800) 333-3333	(606) 252-7575

Photo: Lexington Herald-Leader

The Woodland Arts Fair features work from artists and craftspeople from Kentucky and other states.

Inside
Shopping and Antiques

*I*f you're into shopping, you're probably pretty serious about it, and rather than skimming through a long introduction, you'd prefer we get right to the good stuff.

So here's the lowdown on the Greater Lexington shopping scene. In one day of good shopping in the area, you could purchase hand-painted dolls from Russia, pottery made from local clay, a pair of jockey's racing silks, and even a 19th-century armoire. In terms of the variety and sheer number of shopping possibilities here, Lexington and the surrounding area are a retail paradise.

In terms of superlatives, the area boasts several unusual ones, including the oldest continuously working pottery west of the Alleghenies (Bybee Pottery), the largest mall in the state (Fayette Mall), and the Wal-Mart with the state's largest retaining wall in front of it (located on Richmond Road).

This chapter loosely groups shopping options by location, with the exception of antique stores and shops, which are listed together under one heading.

If you're determined, and you have a good full day to spend, it's possible to sample the scope of what the area has to offer in the way of

stores, shops, boutiques, malls and studios. But you would probably enjoy local shopping more if you are able to spend a few days and divide your shopping excursions into categories.

For instance, you might want to take the better part of a day to go to Berea (about 40 miles south of Lexington — see Lexington's Neighbors for details) and browse through the dozens of antiques stores and malls and the many working arts and crafts studios. Then you could take another day to do the malls, and another for downtown shopping, etc.

The following listings should give you a taste of what is out there, waiting for you to find it — that one dress or pair of brass candlesticks or hand-woven shawl you just can't live without. So grab your credit cards and your walking shoes, and forge on!

Downtown

Lexington's downtown shopping district is filled with interesting and unique shopping experiences. There are also dozens of charming and delicious restaurants, coffee shops and cafes, as well as several beautiful city parks for you to enjoy on your downtown shopping excursion.

This shopping district is perhaps most obviously noted for the trio of shopping "centers" that anchor West Main Street surrounding Triangle Park and Rupp Arena. These are Victorian Square, The Market Place and the Civic Center Shops. There are a couple of parking areas where you can park free with a validation from one of the businesses located in these centers. The centers are also connected by pedways, so you don't even have to worry about traffic.

However, not all downtown shops are in this concentrated area. Dudley Square, located south of Main Street, the Clay Avenue Shops, located off East Main Street, and specialty shops carrying everything from Peruvian beads to used Levi's, are scattered throughout the area.

VICTORIAN SQUARE
401 West Main Street   *252-7575*

This block of restored Victorian buildings is a quaint and charming addition to the downtown shopping scene. Equine products, fine clothing, and beautiful gift items and collectibles are among the items you'll find here.

If you're a horse lover, or even just interested in all things equine, you'll enjoy browsing through Nags 'n Rags, a boutique for horse lovers featuring jewelry, sportswear, original equestrian art, toys, and items for the home. A Touch of Kentucky is an equestrian-themed gift shop carrying a line of fine gift items that includes brass, silver, crystal and leather, as well as accessories, jewelry, books and cards all based on the theme of horses.

Talbots Surplus Store on the first level offers a great discount of 50-70 percent on misses' dresses and sportswear sizes 4-20, and petite sizes 2-14. Talbots also features an array of belts, scarves and accessories as well as children's clothing, and some home furnishings and gift items.

Howard & Miller Clothiers to Gentlemen carries classic menswear from such designers as Corbin, Southwick, Robert Talbott and Kenneth Gordon.

Victorian Square also has Laura Ashley and Pappagallo stores, and it is the home of the Lexington Children's Museum (see Kids Stuff).

CIVIC CENTER SHOPS
410 West Vine Street   *233-4567*

At the Civic Center Shops, you can browse for hours, stop for something delicious to eat, then browse again. Among the dozens of shops and specialty boutiques, you'll find jewelry, art, clothing, stationery, and Appalachian arts and crafts.

Artique, on the Main Street level, is a colorful, artsy store filled with the creations of more than 700 American artists and craftspeople. You'll find everything from blown glass and wood accessories to whimsical and equine art, jewelry, pottery and other unique gift items.

Illusions carries a line of equine and equestrian-themed clothing and accessories, from hand-painted denim to silk jackets, sunglasses and jewelry.

Crystal, china, jewelry, sterling silver flatware, mint julep cups, and limoge and cloisonne boxes are among the treasures you'll find at Lafayette Galleries. The store also offers free gift wrapping and free

Zandale Center

Astuto • 276-0609
Residential and commercial interior design.

Baby's Room of Jack & Jill • 278-1211
Cribs, nursery furniture, bedding, strollers and infant accessories.

Bank One • 259-9480
Full-service bank.

Beneficial • 276-4835
Consumer lending with an emphasis on service.

Big Green Gene's Christmas Trees
Firs, Pines, garlands, and custom-made wreaths.

Cakes and More • 277-8360
Specializing in Parkerhouse rolls, cakes, and salt-rising bread.

Kreations by Karen • 277-6166
Floral arrangements, balloons, plants, and arrangements.

Critchfield Meats • 276-4965
Lexington's finest meats, including steaks and holiday hams.

Don's Wedding Chapel • 277-8832
Chapel performing wedding ceremonies and receptions.

Fabric Fair • 277-7914
An array of fabrics and services including custom-made draperies.

Fazoli's • 275-1955
Real Italian. Real Fast. Twelve menu items under $3.00.

Grott the Loc Doc • 233-4833
A complete locksmith service.

Harber Shoe Repair • 276-2256
Repairing shoes, purses, luggage and belts.

Howard-Knight Alterations • 278-9560
Quick, efficient alterations on men's and women's clothing.

Howard-Knight Tall and Big Men's Shop 278-7005
Brand-name big & tall men's clothing and shoes.

I Can't Believe It's Yogurt! • 278-7001
Frozen yogurt in a variety of flavors.

Jack & Jill's Children's Shop • 278-1411
Infants' and children's clothing, accessories, books and gifts.

Liberty National Bank of Lexington 253-0522
Quest 24-hour automated teller.

Mandarin Oriental Cafe & Carry Out 275-4300
Gourmet Oriental Cuisine.

Miller & Woodward • 276-6100
Jewelry Craftsmen since 1931.

Monfried Optical • 278-9497
Name-brand prescription eyewear.

Nationwise Auto Parts • 276-1481
Complete auto and truck supply store.

Natural Foods • 276-1778
Vitamins, cosmetics, healthful foods and juice bar.

Naturalizer Shoes • 276-4504
Sizes 4 to 12, widths 4A through D, for the working woman.

Rent-A-Center • 278-9557
Rent-to-own appliances, televisions, furniture and jewelry.

Sunshine Grow Shop
Indoor and outdoor flowers and plants.

The Eye of the Needle• 278-1401
Knitting and needlepoint supplies and services.

The Thimble • 277-0103
Alterations for men's, women's and children's clothing.

Visions Hair Design • 277-3957
Fashionable hairstyles at reasonable prices.

Walgreen's • 277-1947
A full-service drug store with a pharmacist on duty.

Zandale Barbershop • 277-9022
See Mack, Ben, J.B., Bill and Bob for a professional haircut.

Zandale Cleaners • 277-6971
Specializing in laundered shirts and dry cleaning.

Zandale Office Center • 277-0553
Professional business suites for lease.

delivery in Lexington.

If you're looking to satisfy your sweet tooth, Old Kentucky Candies is the place to go. Specialties of this confection connection include bourbon chocolates and bourbon cherries as well as their famous pulled cream candies. Old Kentucky Candies has several Lexington locations other than its shop on the second level of the Civic Center Shops. There are also stores in the Lansdowne Shoppes, Turfland Mall, and 450 Southland Drive. This last location is a favorite with bus tours, since the candy shop gives free plant tours and free samples.

THE MARKET PLACE
325 West Main Street   *254-9888*

The Market Place is another unique downtown collection of restaurants, specialty shops, retail stores and businesses. Formerly known as Festival Market, this center has retained its festive atmosphere since it opened in 1986. A full-size carousel inside the building adds to the atmosphere.

The Market Place has a number of one-of-a-kind shops and eateries to please every interest.

CLAY AVENUE SHOPS
Just off East Main on Clay Avenue

This unique shopping area has taken over the homes in a residential area, giving the shops, boutiques and businesses a homey charm. You can find just about everything here in the way of gifts and specialty items, from the practical to the unusual.

Animal Crackers carries a nice line of children's clothing from layette to preteen and prep. There is also a selection of baby and birthday party gifts. Among the services Animal Crackers offers its customers are baby registry, layaway and monogramming.

Peggy's Gifts & Antiques features a wide range of fine gift items, varying both in type and in price. You can find that special gift for someone at a price you can afford, whether it's luxury bath oil or hand-painted ceramic bowls from Louisiana. Unique jewelry, home accessories and furniture are also featured.

From personalized stationery to paper by the pound, The Paperweight Inc. features practically every imaginable writing-related item. Unusual colors and styles of stationery, pens, photo albums and greeting cards are also available. The Paperweight can also help you with personalized invitations and announcements, as well as business cards.

Lavender and Rose is a Victorian delight. From the moment you step through the front door, you'll know you've entered a place where romance still thrives. Natural herbal bath oils, gift baskets, and wreaths

Clay Avenue
"A Neighborly Place To Shop."

and bouquets made from dried flowers fill the walls and the shelves. Lavender and Rose also has a gift basket center where you can purchase prepared baskets or design one of your own to fit any occasion.

Thomas Harvey Salon, a full-service, skin, nail and hair care salon has been serving Lexington customers for close to four years. Thomas Harvey clients cite high-quality customer service and the personal attention of staff members as some of the top reasons they patronize this salon. Thomas Harvey also carries a full line of hair, skin and nail care products.

High Cotton is the newest member of the Clay Avenue Shops family, specializing in designer drapery and upholstery fabrics that you aren't likely to find anywhere else around town. These great fabrics are available at very reasonable prices, not because they are seconds, but because the store purchases them directly from the mill, passing the savings on to the customer. High Cotton also features custom draperies, bed dressings, pillows and trims. Reupholstery services and interior design consultation are also available.

Across the street, Serendipity is as fun a place to shop as its name implies. From American Country furniture, china, silver and glass-ware to wicker and iron porch furniture, Serendipity has an eclectic assortment of unique gift items and home furnishings. Among the shop's most popular items are the colorful and decorative banner flags representing the creations of nine different designers.

If you're looking for unusual items to complement your porch or garden, Through the Garden Gate features a great variety of unique objects, from handcrafted decorative pieces and garden supplies to statuary and garden tools.

DUDLEY SQUARE
380 South Mill (at Maxwell Street)

A dozen or so shops and boutiques, as well as one of Lexington's finest restaurants — Dudley's — are housed in this restored school building, constructed in 1881. The shops in Dudley Square feature everything from antiques and collectibles to needlepoint and cross-stitch supplies, clothing, prints and custom framing.

Other Downtown Locations

WORLDS APART
400 Old East Vine   254-6897

Worlds Apart is a clothing store for women that features its own original line of fashions. Worlds Apart

produces four collections a year, which are marketed in 500 stores nationwide. Store hours are Monday-Wednesday, Friday-Saturday, 10:30 AM-5:30 PM, and Thursday 10:30 AM-8 PM.

THE UNFINISHED UNIVERSE
525 West Short Street   *252-3289*

The restoration, repair and refinishing of fine antiques is the specialty of The Unfinished Universe. The store also carries a line of custom-made tools and refinishing supplies.

J&H LAN-MARK
515 West Main Street   *254-7613*

J&H Lan-Mark is your outdoor center, carrying many lines of well-known outdoor clothing (such as Woolrich and Ruff Hewn), hiking boots, and other recreational footware. J&H Lan-Mark also features camping and other outdoor recreational equipment. It is open Monday-Thursday and Saturday 9 AM-6 PM, and Fridays 9 AM-8 PM.

DANDELION BEAD CONNECTION
224 Walton Avenue   *231-6664*

Dozens of styles and types of beads in 300 colors from around the world is the Dandelion Bead Connection's claim to fame. Czechoslovakian glass beads and bugles, beads made from turquoise, garnet and amethyst, cloisonne beads, hand-painted beads — the selection is seemingly inexhaustible. Dandelion Bead Connection also carries jewelry parts, tools, bead hooks and more. Hours are Tuesday and Thursday-Saturday, 11 AM-6 PM, Wednesday 11 AM-8 PM. The store is closed Sunday and Monday.

AFRICAN MARKETPLACE
Robert H. Williams Cultural Center
644 Georgetown Street   *255-5066*

The African Marketplace, featuring Afro-centric and authentic African art, jewelry, fabric, books, accessories, food, and decorative items for the home, is held the first Saturday of the month from noon to 6 PM. The selections vary from month

Fayette Mall on Nicholasville Road expanded in 1993 to include another anchor store, McAlpins.

to month, often featuring the works of a particular artist, or native jewelry and art from visitors from various African nations.

BLACK MARKET

319 S. Ashland Ave.   *269-3968*

The rare and hard-to-find jewelry, home decorations, clothing and accessories you can purchase at the Black Market are not illegal, although they are unusual. This fun shop is packed full of great stuff at reasonable prices. The jewelry and accessories from around the world are diverse enough to suit even the most discriminating shopper.

Tates Creek Road Area

CHEVY CHASE

Along Euclid Avenue

Chevy Chase is one of Lexington's most unique shopping districts where you can buy every-thing from French pastries and bar-becue to silk flower arrangements, Oriental rugs, and designer cloth-ing. There are a number of good restaurants in this district, includ-ing many ethnic types of food, such as Mediterranean and Mexican. Chevy Chase covers several blocks of shops and businesses in the Ashland Avenue, High Street, Euclid Avenue and Tates Creek Road conjunction areas.

Located in Chevy Chase Plaza, Dana Kelly Oriental Rugs has been in operation longer than any Oriental rug gallery in the area. Oriental rugs add a distinctive flavor to your home decorating, and Dana Kelly has a beau-tiful assortment in all sizes, colors and prices. Cleaning and restoration, as well as trade-ins and free consulta-tion, are available.

Chatters, 312 South Ashland Av-enue, is a kids' specialty store, fea-turing a wide and colorful array of

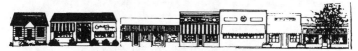

Insiders like riding the trolley through downtown
Lexington for a quarter.

clothing, accessories and gift items for the young folks in your life. The Front Porch and Oram's Florist (located in the 800 block of East High Street) feature party supplies, stationery, flower arrangements and home decorating accessories.

When you step into The Best of Flowers, located at 6 Chevy Chase Place, you may feel like you're entering an open-air, European flower market instead of a Central Kentucky florist shop. That's because the shop is filled with hundreds of unique plants, garden decorations and tools, decorative pieces, and rare fresh cut flowers. At The Best of Flowers, you'll find just about everything you need or want pertaining to flowers and plants, from gorgeous full-color books on gardening to unusual statuary, topiaries, fountains and fresh and silk flower arrangements. The Best of Flowers also carries many international fresh flowers from such exotic places as Australia and Holland.

When you step through the doors of The Galleria, at 826 E. High Street, one of the area's most beautiful gift shops, you'll immediately know you've entered a place where merchandise is of the finest quality. From the French Limoges porcelain and Italian pottery to the fine bone china from England and exquisite French crystal, The Galle-

ria is a place of beautiful pieces for the discriminating shopper. One of the newest additions to the Chevy Chase shopping area, the store offers its customers such amenities as a bridal registry, trained professional sales associates and convenient parking at the door. One of the highlights of a trip to The Galleria is a browse through the Equestrian Art Gallery, featuring original oils and watercolors, as well as fine art prints and bronze sculpture by noted equestrian artists from around the world.

Chevy Chase also has a liquor store, grocery store, drug store, paperback book exchange, laundromat, banks and gas stations. It's a convenient way to do a lot of your shopping and business in one handy spot.

TATES CREEK CENTRE
4104 Tates Creek Road   253-0000
Located at the intersection of Tates Creek Road with Man o' War Boulevard, Tates Creek Centre is one of Lexington's newer shopping centers. A grocery store, video rental store and coffee shop help generate a consistently high volume of shoppers, many of whom are drawn from the surrounding residential areas.

Tates Creek Centre has a variety of unique small shops and boutiques. Another location of The

Lexington shoppers can find a variety of discount stores, such as Wal-Mart, Kmart and Target.

Front Porch is also here and has a colorful collection of party and gift supplies, from candies to beautiful wrappings and balloons. Logan's is a clothing store for men, featuring top-of-the-line suits, sport coats, dress shirts, sportswear and accessories for the well-dressed man.

Tates Creek Centre is also home to a number of popular Lexington eateries, including Jozo's and Ramsey's.

THE LANSDOWNE SHOPPES
3369 Tates Creek Road

At The Lansdowne Shoppes, you can get everything from your groceries to a great steak dinner. This shopping center also features a deli, jewelry store, card shop and pet store. Embry's Petites is a boutique featuring designer clothing for women. Old Kentucky Candies is not a place to frequent if you want to shop at Embry's Petites, however. Offering some of

the best locally produced confections around, Old Kentucky Candies is a temptation too hard to pass up.

Picture frames, stationery, jewelry, monogrammed glassware, and seasonal items are among the huge selection of unique items available at The Hollow Stump. This gift shop has a little bit of everything, from pastas and gourmet cookies and candies to colorful, fun children's items.

Nicholasville Road Area

THE MALL AT LEXINGTON GREEN
3199 Nicholasville Road   245-1513

You can't miss The Mall at Lexington Green. It's big, and it has a big, bright green roof under which you'll find all kinds of fun shopping opportunities, as well as great things to eat.

Leather, Inc. features fine luggage and leather goods, ranging from garment bags and carry-ons to attaches, brief cases, pullmans and

wheel-a-ways. Tumi and Hartmann are among the fine lines Leather, Inc. carries.

At Winterberries Ltd., you'll discover many treasures of brass, home furnishings, fine art, lamps and unique gifts.

For the bibliophile, Joseph-Beth Booksellers is a book heaven with more than 100,000 titles in stock. You can enjoy a sandwich or a cup of coffee while you shop at Cafe Joseph-Beth, or get your children fired up about reading at Joseph-Beth Kids.

The Mole Hole is as fun to shop in as its name implies. This shop carries a charming array of beautiful and unusual items, both useful and decorative. Paper weights, fine art, brass, crystal, glassware and lamps are among the things you'll want to check out at the Mole Hole.

FAYETTE MALL

3473 Nicholasville Road   272-3493

Recent additions to and expansion of Fayette Mall have turned it into the biggest shopping mall in the state. More than 120 department stores, specialty shops, businesses and restaurants make their home in Fayette Mall. It is almost like a self-contained community — you could come to the mall when it opens at 10 AM Monday-Saturday, stay till it closes at 9 PM, and still not experience all that Fayette Mall has to offer. The mall is also open 1-6 PM on Sundays.

Fayette Mall is anchored by four large department stores — McAlpin's, JC Penney, Lazarus and Sears. Thirty-four more stores carry men's and women's apparel, including Dawahares, New Way Boot Shop, Embry's, Lane Bryant, Victoria's Secret, The Limited and The Gap.

Fayette Mall also has a cinema complex and game room, not to mention the Pavilion Food Court, which features 11 fast-food restaurants from Mexican to German to Italian to American. You can browse through dozens of book and stationery shops, check out the latest in computers and electronics, get your car fixed or book a cruise around the world.

REGENCY CENTRE
2300 block of Nicholasville Road

One of the newer additions to the Nicholasville Road shopping area, Regency Centre shops carry everything from GTE phones, golf clothes, clubs and supplies, discount clothing and books. The shopping center also includes a grocery store and restaurants.

If you're shopping for clothes, and you're looking for a bargain, you may just find it in one of the Regency Centre shops. TJ Maxx offers discounts on clothing for the entire family, while Hit or Miss features women's clothing, and S&K Famous Brands offers designer men's clothing at reduced prices.

Michaels is a potpourri of supplies for weddings, parties, silk floral arranging and crafts and art. Hobby Town has everything to fit your favorite pastimes, from kites and model cars to collectibles, such as baseball and basketball cards.

ZANDALE SHOPPING CENTER
2200 block of Nicholasville Road   278-5495

Zandale offers a wide range of retail stores and services: You can purchase toiletries at Walgreen's drug store, an oil filter at Nationwise auto parts store, knitting and needlepoint supplies at The Eye of the Needle — or get married at Don's Wedding Chapel.

Howard-Knight Tall & Big carries fine sports and dresswear for large men. And if you're interested in sewing, Fabric Fair Textile Outlet is a bonanza of fabric at discount prices. Jack & Jill carries infant and children's clothing and accessories.

NATASHA'S CAFE AND BOUTIQUE
304 Southland Drive   277-8412

With a selection of unique and unusual items from more than 50 countries, Natasha's is a treasure trove of jewelry, clothing and native crafts. While you're browsing, you can also enjoy a cup of coffee from the cafe.

THE BOOT STORE
3090 Lexington Road   885-6629

Located just across the Jessamine-Fayette county line on Lexington (Nicholasville) Road, The Boot Store is the place to go for boots, country-western furniture, and men's and women's western clothing. The Boot Store carries 123 different styles of hats as well as a full line of belt buckles, accessories, and custom-made styles of boots. Store hours are 10 AM-9 PM Monday-Saturday, and 1-5 PM Sunday.

Photo: Lexington Herald-Leader

In 1993, a pedway was built across Main and Vine streets downtown linking the Civic Center and Victorian Square.

Richmond Road Area

LEXINGTON MALL
2349 Richmond Road   269-5393

Anchored by a large department store, McAlpin's, and a large grocery store, County Market, Lexington Mall is a nice, moderate-size mall that is small enough to offer easy access, yet large enough to offer a wide range of retail stores, restaurants and businesses. Between the two anchor stores, you will find tapes and CDs, shoes, eyeglasses, sporting goods and outdoor recreational equipment, books, jewelry, popcorn balls, brownies and boots. There is also a movie theater and video arcade, as well as several restaurants. Mall hours are 10 AM-9 PM Monday-Saturday, and Sunday 1-6 PM.

PATCHEN VILLAGE
153-154 Patchen Drive   266-6664

Probably the first thing you'll notice about Patchen Village is its unique architecture. It resembles a charming old European village, an unusual site among the hustle and bustle of the city. The collection of shops, businesses and eateries you'll discover at Patchen Village run the gamut from jewelry repair and Chinese takeout to designer clothing and Pizza Hut.

Comic Connection is a fun place to visit if you are interested in the world of the fantastical and imaginative. The store features a wide selection of comic books, both rare and popular, as well as role-playing games such as Dungeons and Dragons.

Another interesting shop is Wild Birds Unlimited, a shop that caters to a popular local interest — feeding wild birds. Many people have at least one bird feeder in their yards and enjoy seeing the many varieties of birds that visit throughout the year. Wild Birds Unlimited carries all the supplies you'll need to set up your own bird feeder and bird watching hobby.

J. PETERMAN CO.

3094 Richmond Road   268-0990

The breadth and success of the J. Peterman Co. far exceeds the retail store on Richmond Road. Although many one-of-a-kind items are available only through the store, the bulk of the company's sales come from its mail-order business, which is highlighted by one of the most unique and engaging catalogs in the country. J. Peterman features an ever-changing store of goods, ranging from men's and women's fashions to unusual household items.

Harrodsburg Road Area

TURFLAND MALL

2033 Harrodsburg Road   276-4411

For the past 26 years, Turfland Mall has been one of Lexington's shopping mainstays. With 45 shops and stores, including two large anchor department stores—McAlpin's and Montgomery Ward — Turfland Mall has something for everyone, including the kids. A movie theater, arcade and kiddie rides will keep even the youngest shopper happy.

Turfland Mall hosts a number of promotional shows and exhibits throughout the year, ranging from antiques and arts and crafts to baseball cards. Mall hours are Monday-Saturday, 10 AM-9 PM, Sunday noon-6 PM. The Walgreen's here is open 24 hours a day, seven days a week.

Food and Specialty Shops

VICTORIANA GIFTS, GARDENS AND GOURMET FOODS

900 North Broadway   233-7381

Restore a 19th-century carriage house, fill it up with fruit preserves, old-fashioned relishes, soup mixes, seasonings, herbal wreaths and arrangements, Christmas items throughout the year, and herbal gardening supplies, and you have a great Victorian shopping experience. Victoriana Gifts, Gardens and Gourmet Foods also features Kentucky Gourmet Gift Baskets filled with the finest food and gift items from across the Commonwealth. It is open Tuesday-Saturday, 10 AM-4 PM.

GREAT HARVEST BREAD CO.

Stonewall Center,
3101 Clays Mills Road   223-7603
Idle Hour Center,
Richmond Road   266-2915

Made from flour stone milled each morning, Great Harvest Bread Co.'s fresh-baked loaves are to die for. From nut-raisin cinnamon rolls dripping with butter and brown sugar, to loaves of herb bread, sourdough bread and special seasonal breads such as Country Cheddar and Basil Parmesan, Great Harvest's baked goods are too delicious to pass up. Bread prices range from about $2-$4 per loaf, and other items, such as muffins, cookies, honey and gift baskets, are available.

THE NASH COLLECTION

843 Lane Allen Road   276-0161

John and Vivian Nash have always been interested in fine art. When they open the Nash Collection in the summer of 1994, they will be fulfilling one of their longtime dreams — to own a gallery for spectacular works of handmade art by artists from around the world. The Nashes are designing this gallery and

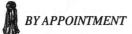

Fayette Mall on Nicholasville Road has an extensive food court.

showroom to have an uncluttered, museum ambiance. Different display areas will focus on specific types of art, from "higher end" glass, metal and wood sculpture to functional glass and signed paintings.

The Nashes want the gallery to provide people in Central Kentucky with access to international artists. Special orders and commissions from specific artists can be arranged through the gallery, which will be open Tuesday through Saturday.

FACTORY STORES OF AMERICA OUTLET CENTER
Exits 125 & 126 off I-75
in Georgetown   *(800) SHOP-USA*

This outlet mall features more than 30 factory direct outlets that offer 30 percent-70 percent off regular retail prices. Among the name-brand clothing outlets are Duck Head Outlet, Levi's Outlet by Designs, Bon Worth Factory Outlet, Bugle Boy, Van Heusen, and Aileen Factory Outlet.

Carolina Pottery offers great bargains on everything from silk flowers to wicker baskets and brassware.

The Black & Decker outlet specializes in the sale of factory reconditioned, discontinued, excess and blemished carton power tools and appliances. Socks Galore & More features more than 60,000 pairs of socks priced 25 percent-80 percent below retail. There are also outlet locations featuring thousands of varieties of ribbons, handbags, boots, paper, linens, cookware and sunglasses. Outlet Center hours are Monday-Saturday 9 AM-9 PM, Sunday 1-6 PM.

Berea

Up till this point, our shopping chapter has focused on Lexington businesses, but we felt the section would be incomplete without mentioning the one-of-a-kind shopping experience you'll enjoy in "The Folk Arts & Crafts Capital of Kentucky."

About 40 miles south of Lexington on I-75, Berea is nationally known for the more than 60 arts and crafts studios, galleries, shops and antiques shops that line the streets of this charming town set in the foothills of

Antique shops and malls can be found in most Central Kentucky towns.

the Appalachian Mountains.

While many of Berea's working craft studios and shops are clustered in two main areas — historic Old Town and College Square — there are a lot of others scattered throughout town. Part of the fun of shopping in Berea is discovering a unique shop on a quiet side street or just outside of town on a country lane.

Information about Berea artists and craftspeople, as well as antiques shops and malls, and maps of where to find them is available at the Berea Welcome Center, which is located in the old L & N railroad depot at 201 North Broadway, (800) 598-5263.

While it's not practical to detail every shop in Berea, we'll give you a taste of the scope of the treasures you'll discover in this delightful town.

Berea artists and craftspeople create dozens of traditional and contemporary pieces of art, pottery, jewelry and weaving each year. During your shopping tour of Berea, you can also find stained glass art, Shaker fur-

niture and boxes, hand-carved wooden spoons and utensils, hand-forged knives, Windsor chairs, blown glass, quilts, dulcimers made from native woods and turned wooden bowls.

As for the finest, most beautiful things from the past, you'll find many of them in Berea's more than 15 antiques shops and malls. From porcelain, china and glassware to toys, advertising pieces, lamps, trunks and furniture, Berea is an antiques lover's dream come true. Information on local antiques shops and malls is also available at the Berea Welcome Center.

Antiques

The Central Kentucky region is one rich in heritage and an appreciation for the fine craftsmanship of the past. So it's not surprising to find that there are 200 antiques shops in the area, nearly 50 of them in Lexington. Several of Lexington's antiques dealers are open by appointment only, and some shops feature antiques as part of

Photo: Lexington Herald-Leader

Home-grown products, from tomatoes to flowers, are available at
Lexington's Farmers Market.

Whether you've lived in Lexington for years or you're a newcomer, it's always nice to get something extra when you shop!

When you use our Convenience Account to subscribe to the Herald-Leader, you'll automatically receive your EXTRA! card, a valuable new way for you to save money. With your EXTRA! card, you will receive discounts and special offers at more than 500 merchants. And the EXTRA! card is free with your paid Convenience Account subscription to the Herald-Leader. The EXTRA! card is also available for an annual fee of $20. For more information, call 253-1314 or toll free 1-800-999-8881.

Photo: Lexington Herald-Leader

Find out about Berea's antiques and crafts at the Welcome Center, which is in a renovated L&N Railroad depot.

their inventory along with gift items and home furnishings.

Additionally, there are big antique shows throughout the year at several area locations, including the Lexington Loose Leaf Tobacco Warehouse on Angliana Avenue (call 255-7309 for show dates) and Heritage Hall in Rupp Arena on Main Street beside the Civic Center Shops.

Listed below you will find some of the bigger antiques shops and malls, as well as some of the shops that specialize in certain items. However, anyone who is an antiques shopper knows you often have to check out a lot of places before you find exactly what you're looking for. Of course, that's half the fun.

COUNTRY ANTIQUE MALL
1455 Leestown Road   233-0075
About 60 dealers make their home at the Country Antique Mall, located in the Meadowthorpe Shopping Cen-

ter. With four large showrooms and 14,000 feet of space, the Country Antique Mall has something to interest everyone, from babies to grandmas. Period furniture, smalls, linens, glassware and country motif items are among the thousands of antiques you can browse among here. Country Antique Mall also offers its customers two special services — clock repair by their in-house clockmaker, and antique glass and china repair. The Country Antique Mall is open seven days a week, Monday-Saturday, 10 AM-5 PM, and Sunday 1-5 PM.

GALLERY ANTIQUES
Victorian Square, second level   225-1247
An 1850s cameo carved from lava and set in gold and diamonds. A *plique-a-jour* (translucent enameling) pendant from the 1930s. A delicate limoges box with an intricate, hand-painted interior.

These are just a few of the pieces of rare and antique jewelry you will

Photo: Victorian Square Shoppes

Downtown visitors can shop and dine at Victorian Square.

discover at Gallery Antiques. In fact, Gallery Antiques features one of the largest collections of antique and vintage jewelry in the region. Their collection of old Scottish jewelry is stunning. The Gallery features pieces from periods spanning Victorian and Edwardian to Art Deco. Gallery Antiques also has an exclusive collection of the jewelry of Danish designer Georg Jensen.

Accessible elegance is a phrase that comes to mind when you step through the doors of Gallery Antiques. Unique and fascinating jewelry is available in all price ranges and styles. The Gallery also features contemporary pieces modeled after older jewelry styles, such as their

popular Russian enameled pendants reminiscent of the famed Faberge eggs, or their Celtic musical jewelry. Whether you're interested in antique jewelry, silver, or just want to take a look at the display of mementos of the Lexington Brewing Co. (the only existing display of its kind in Lexington), it is a delight to browse through Gallery Antiques.

ANTIQUE MALL AT TODD'S SQUARE
535 West Short Street   252-0296

Featuring the collections of about 20 area dealers, the Antique Mall at Todd's Square features vintage clothing, quilts, jewelry, clocks, glassware, furniture, dolls, and old advertising pieces. The mall is open

How can I get you to come to my new store every week? My fiendish plan:
a) Exotic new stuff every week (in small, quickly disappearing quantities).
b) Disconcerting price reductions every week on regular merchandise, here, there,
everywhere. Don't fight it. Don't miss it. Don't kick yourself later.

Odd, wonderful things: $11 to $16,900:

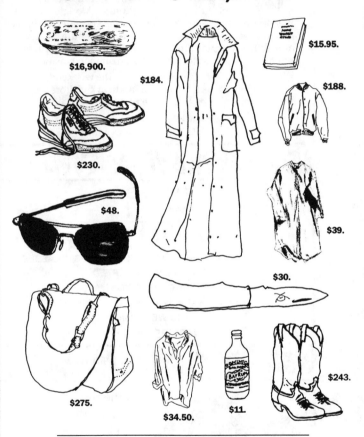

$16,900.

$184.

$15.95.

$188.

$230.

$48.

$39.

$30.

$275.

$34.50.

$11.

$243.

The J. Peterman Company Store

3094 Richmond Rd., The Village Shoppes, Lexington.

Exit 104 from I-75/I-64. Turn left at Locust Hill Drive (just past Man O' War Blvd.).

Mon.–Sat. 10am–9pm, Sun. 12pm–6pm.
(606) 268-0990. All major credit cards.

Absolute Satisfaction.
Anything less, and you get your money back. Period.

Triangle Shopping District

*V*ictorian Square is the careful restoration of a full block of 19th Century buildings. Along its meandering corridors, you'll find local specialty shops as well as famous names such as the Acorn, Laura Ashley and Talbots Surplus Store. Two full-service restaurants offer regional favorites and authentic Italian cuisine.

Whether staying for the week or just the weekend, Victorian Square is a Lexington landmark visitors won't want to miss. Three hours free parking with validation.

Hours: Mon. - Sat., 10 to 6 • Sun., 1 to 5
Open late Thurs. evenings until 8

ARTISTS' ATTIC

STUDIOS, GALLERIES, SALES, WORKSHOPS, CLASSES
COMMISSIONS ACCEPTED.
EXHIBIT CHANGES MONTHLY.
Take the elevator by Talbots to the 4th floor
PUBLIC WELCOMED!
(606)254-5501

Fine food & spirits in a comfortably elegant setting. Monday thru Sunday starting at 11... lunch, dinner and cocktails.

Free Parking
Banquet Facilities Available

259-3771

VICTORIAN SQUARE
252-7575 • 401 W. Main St. • Main & Broadway

Triangle Shopping District

Monday-Saturday, 10 AM-5 PM, and Sunday 1-5 PM.

ANTIQUE & MODERN FIREARMS
2263 Nicholasville Road   276-1419

If you are interested in antique guns, rifles and related items, Antique & Modern Firearms is the place for you. In addition to their selection of the most collected firearms in the world — Colt firearms and Winchester rifles — they also carry Civil War guns and related accouterments, including swords, holsters, bayonets and bullets. The Kentucky Rifle, a frontier firearm, is also popular among collectors, and Antique & Modern Firearms carries a selection of these rifles, along with powder horns, bullet molds, and related items. Their hours of operation are Monday-Friday, 10 AM-6 PM, and Saturday 10 AM-5 PM.

ANTIQUE MARKET INC.
760 Winchester Road   254-8350

Whether you're looking for a cherry sideboard, a miniature horse-drawn Budweiser beer wagon or a full-size English vending cart, you'll probably find it at the Antique Market. The market's 9,500-square-foot showroom houses the collected treasures of 13 dealers. There are lots of unexpected nooks and crannies filled with all kinds of hard-to-find items, kitchenware, old photographs, glassware and framed art. There is a special room showcasing unfinished furniture or furniture needing to be refinished in the back. The Antique Market does furniture refinishing and appraisals. They offer their customers free delivery in Fayette County, and delivery for a reasonable fee outside the county. Hours of operation are Monday-Saturday, 9 AM-6 PM, and Sunday noon-6 PM.

IRISH ACRES GALLERY OF ANTIQUES
4205 Fords Mill Road,
Nonesuch   873-7235

This antique gallery is as unique as the name of the little town in which it is located. Just south of Versailles off Ky. 33, Irish Acres is a sprawling, 32,000-square-foot complex with more than 50 showrooms of antiques and collectibles. Dolls, toys, lamps, glassware, furniture, marbles, vintage clothing — the list is endless. Actually, going to Irish Acres would make a nice daytrip. You can browse through some of the antique showrooms, then take a break for lunch in the on-site restaurant — The Glitz — before shopping some more. Lunch is served 11 AM-2 PM, and reservations are strongly recommended. Irish Acres is open Tuesday-Saturday, 10 AM-5 PM.

Inside
Restaurants

We hope you're hungry. If not, you're sure to work up a hearty appetite as you explore the Bluegrass. And, whether you're a world traveler with a discriminating palate or the head of a family with a limited budget, you'll find a restaurant to suit you in Lexington and its environs. You may be surprised by our diversity. Anxious to try the "regional" cuisine? We'll try to steer you in the right direction. In the mood for exotic foods from faraway lands? You can find them here, and we'll share our findings with you. Want to know the best places for a thick steak or some fresh seafood? We'll show you where *we* go.

Obviously, this is a highly subjective chapter. It's not a complete directory and was never intended to be. Personal tastes being what they are, we can't guarantee that you'll agree with everything we say. Similarly, the Bluegrass has many fine restaurants, quite deserving of your business, that aren't included here. The authors are mortal beings, on limited budgets themselves, and we must confess that we have yet to eat at *every* restaurant in the area. (We tried to arrange it when we began writing this book, but Bill, the stingy so-and-so who approves our expense invoices, nipped that plan in the taste bud.)

As a result, we had to rely on our existing knowledge, supplemented with occasional input from friends and experts. The restaurants in this chapter are the ones we personally recommend. If you have a Bluegrass dining experience that you'd like to share with us, let us know about it so we can take it into consideration when revising *The Insiders' Guide to Greater Lexington* for next year.

With a few exceptions, we have avoided the big chain restaurants, the reason being that you probably already know about them. The ones we have mentioned are the ones that we, 1) think you might not know about or, 2) are simply so wild about that we decided to mention them anyway. You might be interested to know, incidentally, that Lexington and Kentucky are the headquarters for a number of popular restaurant chains. Long John Silver's is based in Lexington, as is Fazoli's, a fast-food Italian restaurant that is growing rapidly. In 1993, PoFolks relocated its headquarters from Nashville to Mount Sterling, a town of 5,000 people about 35 miles east of Lexington. Louisville is the corporate home for Kentucky Fried Chicken, Chi-Chi's Mexican restaurants and the Rally's hamburger chain.

Restaurants in this chapter are

organized by type of food served (barbecue, Italian, seafood, steak, etc.) or, in a couple of cases, by environment (bar food, cafeterias). At times the decision was somewhat arbitrary as to which category a restaurant belonged in, but we used our best judgment. We also included a few restaurants outside Greater Lexington but within a reasonable drive.

In case you're wondering what, precisely, we mean by "regional" cuisine, we'll tell you, vaguely, that the term is a little murky. Basically, as we see it, it's food that originated in this region of the country, was perfected here or is associated with these parts. Most people would consider "lamb fries" or catfish fried in cornmeal to be regional cuisine; the hot Brown, invented in Louisville, definitely qualifies. You could also make a case for barbecue, although we have listed it as a separate category. Sushi and cannelloni, on the other hand, are definitely not regional cuisine, although you can find excellent versions of them in the Bluegrass. (For more information on regional foods and beverages, see A Taste of Kentucky Food and Drink, elsewhere in this book.)

Our pricing guide is intended as a guide, not as gospel. Menus and prices change. If you order the most expensive appetizers and entrees on the menu, your check may be higher than suggested here; by the same token, if you don't do appetizers, the total will be lower. We have tried to indicate the typical range for a basic dinner for two including appetizers, entree with two side dishes, dessert and coffee or soft drink. Alcoholic beverages and tips are not included. Lunch prices will generally be one-half to two-thirds the price of dinner.

Under $20	$
$21 to $35	$$
$36 to $50	$$$
$51 and up	$$$$

If you have any questions about prices or menu offerings, it certainly doesn't hurt to call the restaurant in advance. Most of these restaurants serve beer, wine and mixed drinks, and most accept credit cards.

Some of the more upscale restaurants suggest making reservations; we have indicated this preference in the appropriate listings. During Keeneland meets and on nights when the University of Kentucky has a basketball or football game, it's a good idea to phone ahead anyway if you want to avoid a long wait.

While dining in the Bluegrass, you'll find that, although Kentucky may technically be a border state, it's brimming with that characteristic commonly known as Southern hospitality. Don't take offense if your waitress calls you "honey" — it just means she's enjoying the opportunity to serve you. And you'll surely enjoy the fine dining experiences that await you here.

In addition, if "fine dining experience" to you connotes quantity as well as quality, you can find a variety of buffet opportunities here. This author has a particular weakness for all-you-can-eat specials.

We know you're hungry by now, so dig in. Perhaps we'll see you at one of our favorite establishments. In the meantime, *good eatin'* (that's Kentuckian for bon appétit)!

American and Regional

A.P. Suggins Bar & Grill

345 Romany Road   268-0709
$$ Visa, MasterCard, American Express

A.P. Suggins has one of the most varied menus in town: seven pages of beef, chicken, fish, Kentucky favorites, specialty burgers, salads with homemade soups and Mexican dishes. Whew! Something to please anyone in your group! And if you can't find anything that hits you in the menu, take a look at the blackboard listings of daily specials. The restaurant is open Monday through Saturday, 11 AM to 11 PM; closed on Sundays.

Applebee's Neighborhood Grill & Bar

4009 Nicholasville Road   271-9393
2573 Richmond Road   266-3327
Carriage Gate Shopping Center
Richmond   1-624-1224
$$ Most major credit cards

This increasingly popular chain has earned a reputation as a fun place to eat for kids as well as adults. It's a perfect place to go for appetizers or for a meal, with an emphasis on such satisfying "finger foods" as fajitas and quesadillas, sandwiches including blackened chicken, and the ever-popular riblet basket. There's also pasta, chicken, steak and seafood. The two Lexington Applebee's are open from 11 AM to 1 AM Monday through Saturday and 11 AM to 11 PM Sunday; the Richmond location closes at midnight Monday through Saturday.

Beaumont Inn

638 Beaumont Drive (off U.S. 127), Harrodsburg
                                  1-734-3381
$$$ Most major credit cards

The stately building, an 1845 Greek Revival brick mansion with Ionic columns, was once the Greenville Female Institute. Since 1918, however, it has been Beaumont Inn, and it is practically synonymous with Kentucky hospitality. The interior is filled with family portraits and heirlooms. The Dedman family has run the inn for four generations, serving such traditional favorites as yellow-legged fried chicken, 2-year-old cured country ham and its famous corn pudding. Meals are served in scheduled sittings. Lunch is at noon and 1:15 PM Tuesday through Saturday and at noon and 1:30 PM Sunday. Dinner is at 6 PM and 7:30 PM Monday through Saturday and at 6 PM Sunday. Reservations are recommended, especially on Saturday night.

Boone Tavern

Main Street, Berea   1-986-9358
$$$ Most major credit cards

Boone Tavern, at the center of picturesque Berea, is operated by students at nearby Berea College. The limited but excellent menu

There is a toss-up between Lynagh's on Euclid Avenue and Buffalo & Dad's on North Broadway for Best Hamburger in Town kudos.

Insiders' Tips

highlights traditional Kentucky cooking in plentiful quantities. The servers will keep you supplied with plenty of vegetables, and you'll probably want a second or even a third helping of the signature spoonbread. Open daily 7 AM to 9 PM for breakfast, 11:30 AM to 1:30 PM for lunch and 6 PM to 7:30 PM for dinner. Reservations are required.

BUFFALO & DAD'S

805 North Broadway   252-9325
$$ *Most major credit cards*

During the summer, you'll often find adult softball teams still in uniform at Buffalo & Dad's, chowing down and ordering a beer or two. The menu is surprisingly diverse for a little place with such a laid-back tavern atmosphere. You can get burgers, grilled steaks and pork chops, lamb fries, grilled or blackened swordfish, fried seafood and frog legs and more. And to ensure that you feel at home, the extensive sandwich menu even includes fried bologna sandwiches. Breakfast is served, too. Open 8 AM to 11 PM Monday through Thursday, 8 AM to midnight Friday and Saturday, and 1 PM to 9 PM Sunday.

CAMPBELL HOUSE INN

1375 Harrodsburg Road   255-4281
$$$ *Most major credit cards*

Traditional Southern fare is the specialty in the dining rooms of this longtime Lexington landmark. From the outside, the original section of the Campbell House complex, with its graceful white columns, gives the impression that it's always been there and always will be. On the inside, the food confirms that idea with such time-honored fare as lamb chops, lamb fries, Southern fried chicken, hot Browns, country ham and frog legs, as well as more mainstream items like steak, prime rib and seafood. A Sunday buffet is offered from 11 AM to 3 PM. Open 11:30 AM to 11 PM daily.

DESHA'S

101 North Broadway   259-3771
$$$ *Most major credit cards*

It's hard to miss deSha's, with its prime location at the southeast end of Victorian Square at Main and Broadway. Inside and out, this 1870s structure retains much of its Victorian charm. The dinner menu features an array of steak, chops, prime rib, chicken and seafood, plus inventive daily specials. Lunch is oriented around a tantalizing variety of soups, salads and sandwiches. You can't go wrong with the homemade soup du jour, which includes offerings like crab corn chowder. The house cornbread with honey butter, served with all dinners, is wonderful. Unusual appetizers include English "banger" sausages and mozzarella-stuffed banana peppers. Open 11 AM to 11 PM Monday through Friday, 11 AM to midnight Friday and Saturday, and 11 AM to 10 PM Sunday.

MAX & ERMA'S

153 Patchen Drive   269-5692
$$ *Most major credit cards*

Years ago, Max & Erma's had a red telephone at each table, allowing customers to call one another and making it highly popular with singles on weekend nights. The restaurant has evolved since then, getting rid of the phones and expanding the menu but retaining its popularity. Whether you go on a date or with the family, you'll enjoy the slightly quirky atmosphere and the food. The big burgers are still around; try the loaded "garbage burger" basket with fries and onion rings. You can also get several kinds of char-grilled chicken, pasta and more. Open 11:30 AM to 10:30 PM Monday through Thursday, 11:30 AM to midnight Friday and Saturday, and noon to 10 PM Sunday.

MERRICK INN
3380 Tates Creek Road 269-5417
$$$ *Most major credit cards*

The Merrick Inn serves regional cuisine, with a few Continental touches, to a loyal clientele made up largely of doctors, lawyers and other professionals. The formal dining room has a homey, colonial inn atmosphere graced by fireplaces and candlelight. Regular entrees include prime rib, Southern fried chicken, seafood and veal, and there are nightly specials. Separate menus are available for the more casual bar and, in warmer weather, the patio. Open 5:30 PM to 10 PM Monday through Thursday and 5:30 PM to 10:30 PM Friday and Saturday. Reservations are recommended.

RAMSEY'S DINER
496 East High Street 259-2708
4053 Tates Creek Road 271-2638
$$ *Visa, MasterCard, American Express*

Ramsey's serves good, old-fashioned home cooking guaranteed to "stick to your ribs." We're talking pot roast, meat loaf, country fried steak and more, served with your choice of fresh veggies. Want something different? Try the lemon-yogurt chicken breasts, available as a meal or a sandwich. Breakfast is served whenever you want it. There's a limited late-night menu on weekends. Open 11 AM to 11 PM Sunday through Thursday and 11 AM to 1 AM Friday and Saturday.

ROSEBUD BAR & GRILL
121 North Mill Street 254-1907
$ *Visa, MasterCard*

This quaint and quirky little downtown spot serves up a largely Southwestern bill of fare. Black beans and rice are everywhere on the menu: in the nachos, as a lunch item, as a side dish on the dinner menu. Enchiladas, Jamaican jerk chicken, chili and meat loaf are also regulars. There are specials daily. Open 11:30 AM to midnight Monday through Friday.

RUBY TUESDAY
The Mall at Lexington Green 273-7985
$$ *All major credit cards*

Ruby Tuesday, part of a popular chain, offers steak, chicken, fish, pasta, burgers, sandwiches, fajitas and more, as well as a fresh and immensely satisfying salad bar, in a warm and cozy atmosphere. The meatless "Gardenburger," made with whole grains, nuts and mushrooms, is one of several health-conscious selections. Open 11:30 AM to 11:30 PM Monday through Thursday, 11:30 AM to midnight Friday and Saturday, and 11:30 AM to 9 PM Sunday. Ruby is also quite a bartender, with some refreshing mixed drinks in her repertoire.

SHAKERTOWN TRUSTEES' OFFICE INN

3500 Lexington Road,
Harrodsburg   1-734-5411
$$$ Visa, MasterCard

Since the Shakers' religious sect practiced celibacy, they're no longer around. Fortunately, their dining traditions live on in the inn at Shaker Village of Pleasant Hill. The hearty regional fare — from start (relish tray) to finish (fresh-baked pies and cakes) — is served in scheduled sittings only. Buffet breakfast is served daily at 7:30 AM, 8:30 AM and 9:30 AM. Lunch is 11:30 AM, 1 PM and 2:30 PM Monday through Saturday. Dinner is 5:30 PM and 7:15 PM Monday through Saturday and 1:45 PM, 3:15 PM and 5:30 PM Sunday. Reservations are required.

SPRINGS INN

2020 Harrodsburg Road   277-5751
$$ Most major credit cards

The dining room at this locally owned motel is renowned for its Southern hospitality. The house specialties are Kentucky standards like country ham with redeye gravy, lamb fries with cream gravy and the hot Brown. There's also a generous selection of beef, poultry and seafood including whole rainbow trout. If you want a crash course in regional cuisine, try the Wednesday night Kentucky buffet, which includes burgoo, catfish, country ham, pork roast with dressing, spoonbread, bread pudding and more. Open 6:30 AM to 10 PM Monday through Saturday, 7 AM to 8:30 PM Sunday.

Bar Food

CHARLIE BROWN'S

816 Euclid Avenue   269-5701
$ Visa, MasterCard

The ultimate in coziness. Sink down in an overstuffed chair or couch near one of two fireplaces in a room lined with bookcases, and you're likely to feel as if you're sitting in the parlor of a friend who lives in an inviting old house. In addition to appetizers and a bunch of burgers and sandwiches — including a turkey burger — there are daily specials. During the warmer months, you can relax on the patio out back. Open 11 AM to 12:30 AM Monday through Saturday and 1 PM to 11 PM Sunday.

CHEAPSIDE BAR & GRILL

131 Cheapside   254-0046
$$ Visa, MasterCard, American Express

Cheapside describes its menu as "contemporary cuisine with a Southwestern flair," and this author can't think of a better description. The atmosphere in the bar area, like the building exterior, is old-fashioned.

High ceilings and lots of classic dark woods lend a certain timelessness to the place. The main dining area is more contemporary, with walls graced by minimalist art like that of local painter and bluesman Rodney Hatfield (a k a Art Snake). When weather permits, the patio is generally filled. Menu highlights include jalapeño black bean soup, smoked duck tacos, crab enchiladas and a grilled veggie sandwich. Open for lunch 11:30 AM to 2 PM Monday through Friday, dinner 5 PM to midnight Monday through Saturday, and brunch 11:30 AM to 3 PM Saturday and Sunday.

HOOTERS

3101 Richmond Road   269-8521
$ Visa, MasterCard, American Express

Forget political correctness and just have a good time. Some folks have criticized this chain restaurant for the short shorts and tight T-shirts worn by the waitresses, but it's really all in fun. This is a great place to watch a ball game on TV with friends while sharing a pitcher of beer and a plate of chicken wings. Other specialties include oysters on the half shell and steamed clams, and there's also a selection of salads and sandwiches.

LYNAGH'S IRISH PUB & GRILL

University Plaza Shopping Center   255-6614
$ Cash or local check only

Looking for the best burger in town? It may be here in the O'Round, a huge burger (the menu says it's the size of a small hubcap), chargrilled to order and topped with your choice of cheeses. You'll have to settle for potato chips on the side because Lynagh's doesn't serve fries. You really won't mind. Other stand-out sandwiches are the ribeye and the T&A, which stands for — guess again — turkey and avocado. Lynagh's also has Guinness and Watney's on tap, which gives the place extra points.

SHOOTERS BAR & GRILL

723 Lane Allen Road   278-0815
$$ Most major credit cards

As its name suggests, Shooters has a poolroom theme. A room with several tables adjoins the bar, and huge black-and-white movie stills from *The Hustler* and other flicks cover the walls. Shooters, which is owned by the same people who own Columbia's steakhouses, offers two items lifted from Columbia's menu: beef tenderloin, served here on skewers, and the simple yet wonderful Diego salad. Sandwiches include an excellent Reuben and barbecue chicken. Open 11:30 AM to 11 PM Monday through Thursday, 11:30 AM to 11 PM Friday and Saturday, and 4 PM to 10 PM Sunday.

WINNERS SPIRITS AND FOOD

348 Southland Drive   277-9872
$$ Visa, MasterCard, American Express

This low-key sports bar and restaurant is decorated with pennants and team photos and has its televisions tuned to athletic events. The food isn't flashy but it's solid, with a variety of soups, salads and sandwiches, as well as steak, chicken and chops. And the deep-fried dill pickles are an appetizer you won't find at too many places. Open 11 AM to 1 AM Monday through Saturday and 1 PM to 11 PM Sunday.

Tradition...

Have lunch or dinner at Lexington's dining tradition for 25 years.

The Coach House

*"Casually
Elegant"*

*"Ties
Optional"*

855 South Broadway, Lexington, KY • Reservations suggested 606•252•7777

Barbecue

BILLY'S BAR B-Q

101 Cochran Road   269-9593
$$$ *Visa, MasterCard, American Express*

Billy's is Lexington's original purveyor of Western Kentucky-style hickory-pit barbecue. Although the number of barbecue restaurants has increased severalfold since Billy's opened in 1978, lots of natives still swear this place is the best. You can get barbecue pork, beef, mutton, chicken or pork ribs with traditional side items like baked beans, coleslaw and potato salad. Billy's also offers several hardwood-grilled items and Kentucky burgoo. And you can bring your own turkey or pig in and have it custom smoked. Open 11 AM to 9 PM Monday through Wednesday, 11 AM to 10 PM Thursday through Saturday, and 11 AM to 8 PM Sunday.

GOOD OL' DAYS BARBECUE

620 Old Frankfort Pike, 873-9520
$ *Visa, MasterCard, American Express*

Good Ol' Days is technically in Woodford County (by a measly half-mile), but it's close enough to be considered a Lexington eatery. Barbecue beef, pork and ribs and smoked turkey and prime rib are among the specialties served in a rustic roadside setting. Near Keeneland and horse farms, Good Ol' Days has quickly become a popular stop before or after the races. Open 11 AM to 10 PM Monday through Saturday and noon to 6 PM Sunday.

RED HOT & BLUE

874 East High Street   268-7427
$$ *Most major credit cards*

Blues and barbecue complement one another perfectly at this chain restaurant, where the walls are covered with concert posters and photos of blues legends and the music doesn't stop. Memphis-style barbecue specialties include beef brisket, pork shoulder and pork ribs, which you can order "wet" (with sauce) or "dry." Open 11 AM to 10 PM Sunday through Thursday and 11 AM to 11 PM Friday and Saturday.

Insiders who love Chinese food know that most Oriental restaurants in Lexington have Sunday buffets from about 11 AM to 2 PM.

WEST KENTUCKY BARBECUE

1510 Newtown Pike   *231-0597*
$$ *Visa, MasterCard, American Express*

Western Kentucky has staked a legitimate claim to the title "Barbecue Capital of the World," and this attractive eatery hickory-smokes its beef, pork, ribs and mutton the way they do in that part of the state. Catfish and steaks are also on the menu, as well as freshly prepared side items. And those who like baloney with their barbecue can have lunch in the "Rush Room," featuring the broadcast opinions of a certain Mr. Limbaugh. Open 11 AM to 9 PM Sunday through Thursday and 11 AM to 10 PM Friday and Saturday.

Cafeterias, Family and Fast Food

BLUE BOAR CAFETERIA

Turfland Mall   *277-6180*
$ *Most major credit cards*

At peak times, like Sunday after church, you sometimes have to wait in line to eat here. But, hey, you're *supposed* to wait in line at a cafeteria. The Blue Boar doesn't disappoint. Choose from several salads, entrees, side dishes, breads and desserts daily. Standbys including turkey and dressing, roast beef and fried cod. Open 11 AM to 2:30 PM and 4:15 PM to 8 PM Monday through Saturday and 11 AM to 7 PM on Sunday and holidays.

CENTRAL CHRISTIAN CHURCH CAFETERIA

205 East Short Street   *255-3087*
$ *Cash or check only*

For more than 13 years, Mike and Debbie Silvey have been serving home-style breakfasts and lunches to downtown patrons in space leased from the Central Christian Church. These days the catering business is bigger than the restaurant business, but the cafeteria still thrives at breakfast and lunch. With entrees ranging from $1.80 to $2.50 and vegetables for 70 cents apiece, you can eat your fill for about what a fast-food meal would cost you. The chicken-and-broccoli casserole would do your mom proud. Open 7 AM to 2 PM Monday through Friday.

MORRISON'S CAFETERIA

Lexington Mall   *269-3329*
Lexington Green   *273-4470*
$ *Visa, MasterCard, American Express*

At Morrison's you can get salad, entree, two vegetables, bread, drink and dessert at a price that makes it easy to feed the whole family. Quarter broiled chicken, fried and broiled fish, country fried steak and liver and onions are among the regular features. Open 11 AM to 8:30 PM Monday through Saturday and 11 AM to 8 PM Sunday.

Columbia Steak House

SINCE 1948

Lexington Locations:

201 N Limestone   1425 Alexandria Dr.
3347 Tates Creek Rd.

I-75 Interchange - Berea   U.S. 127 South - Frankfort

KENNY ROGERS ROASTERS

4101 Tates Creek Road	245-2585
2700 Richmond Road	268-0802
Turfland Mall	277-2491
$	Cash or check only

Forget "Lucille" and "The Gambler"; this has nothing to do with Kenny's music. Even headbangers enjoy the enticing roasted chicken served by this relatively new chain. It's fast food, but it's different. The specialty is chicken marinated in citrus juices and spices, then slow-roasted over a wood fire. This process supposedly produces chicken lower in fat and healthier than the fried kind, but the bottom line is it tastes great. The side dishes are a perfect complement; this author loves the garlic-and-parsley potatoes, coleslaw and steamed veggies, as well as the sweet corn muffins studded with kernels. Open 11 AM to 9:30 PM Sunday through Thursday and 11 AM to 10 PM Friday and Saturday.

PARKETTE DRIVE IN

1216 New Circle Road NE	254-8723
$	Cash only

Drive-ins with honest-to-goodness curb service are a rare breed these days. But the Parkette continues to thrive. Just pull up to one of the big menu boards and place your order through the speaker. Your food will arrive in minutes. When Joe Smiley opened the drive-in in 1952, it was in the boonies; now it's surrounded by businesses. Today, under Richard and Marjorie Wilkins, it still serves largely the same menu: "Kentucky Poor Boy" double-decker cheeseburgers, fried chicken and seafood boxes, strawberry pies and more. The big neon sign out front welcomes you with a Bible verse. Open 11 AM to 11 PM Monday through Thursday and 11 AM to 1 AM Friday and Saturday.

Insiders love beer cheese
and fried banana peppers served at
Hall's on the River.

PERKINS FAMILY RESTAURANT

2401 Richmond Road   269-1663
$ Most major credit cards

Perkins, a great place to take the family for a variety of soups, salads, sandwiches and dinner selections, is also a favorite late-night spot because it's always open. You'll love the pasta, especially the seafood primavera and the chicken Alfredo, served in edible bread bowls. An in-house bakery makes fresh breads and desserts daily. Open 24 hours a day.

ROCK-A-BILLY CAFE

2573 Richmond Road   268-9089
$ Visa, MasterCard, Discover

Put on your letter sweater or your poodle skirt and bobbysox and bop on over to Rock-A-Billy Cafe. This bright, '50s-style soda fountain serves a variety of whimsically named burgers and sandwiches, chili fries and shakes. Your kids will love this place. Open 10:30 AM to 10:30 PM Sunday through Thursday and 10:30 AM to 12:30 AM Friday and Saturday.

Chinese

AUGUST MOON

2690 Nicholasville Road   277-8888
$$ Visa, MasterCard, American Express

Many people like August Moon for its atmosphere, which is more sophisticated than the average Chinese restaurant. The furnishings and service are elegant, and the food is consistently good. Crab Rangoon — a fried wonton filled with crab meat, cream cheese and spices — is a favorite appetizer, and there are an incredible eight soups. Spicy "five-flavored" sauce, a house specialty, is used in several dishes, including seafood, lamb, chicken, pork and steak. Open 11 AM to 10 PM Monday through Thursday, 11 AM to 11 PM Friday, 11:30 AM to 11 PM Saturday, and 11:30 AM to 10 PM Sunday. Reservations are recommended.

CHINA KITCHEN

1837 Alexandria Drive   276-2328
$ Visa, MasterCard, American Express

Tucked away in Gardenside Plaza in west Lexington is this delightful restaurant with gracious service even by Oriental standards. The menu selection is fairly standard — wor su duck, beef with broccoli and spicy curry chicken are among this author's picks — but there's nothing average about their preparation. Everything on the menu is available in large and small portions, and there's a Sunday buffet. Open 11 AM to 9:30 PM Monday through Thursday, 11 AM to 10:30 PM Friday, 11 AM to 2 PM and 5 PM to 10:30 PM Saturday, and 5 PM to 9:30 PM Sunday.

IMPERIAL HUNAN

1505 New Circle Road NE   266-4393
Hunan Chinese Restaurant
111 Southland Drive   278-3811
$$ Most major credit cards

These restaurants, in east and south Lexington, respectively, share ownership and menus. The New Circle location, in Woodhill Circle Shopping Center, is a perennial poll-winner as best Oriental restaurant. Specialties include Peking duck and seafood deluxe (shrimp, scallops, crab meat and lobster with vegetables). The extensive menu of beef, pork, chicken and vegetable dishes makes it hard to choose; fortunately, sharing is customary at Chinese restaurants, so go with several people. Both restaurants also offer a Sunday buffet. Open 11:30 AM to 10 PM Sunday through Thursday, 11:30 AM to 11PM Friday and noon to 11 PM Saturday.

SZECHUAN GARDEN

270 Southland Drive   277-4402
$$ Most major credit cards

Mandarin Szechuan cuisine is the order of the day in this colorfully decorated restaurant with a fountain and fish pond in the main room. The service is friendly and knowledgeable, so don't hesitate to ask about the ingredients or preparation of a certain dish. Mu shu pork, rolled in thin pancakes spread with plum sauce at tableside, is a treat. So are the crispy duck and the shrimp with lobster sauce. And guess what's available on Sunday? Open 11:30 AM to 10 PM Monday through Thursday, 11:30 AM to 11 PM Friday and Saturday, and 11:30 AM to 9:30 PM Sunday.

Continental

A LA LUCIE

159 North Limestone Street   252-5277
$$$ All major credit cards

This quaint and tiny downtown restaurant was deemed "a Lexington treasure" by *Herald-Leader* restaurant critic Howard Snyder, and it's earned quite a following. From the appetizers, which include three varieties of escargots, through the desserts, a la lucie makes its inventive offerings seem simple. The menu changes periodically, but you can be sure it will always be tantalizing. Recent offerings included an avocado half stuffed with lobster and grapefruit, barbecued duck burrito and Caribbean chicken with peanut sauce and pineapple. Open 6 PM to 10 PM Monday through Saturday. Reservations are recommended.

THE COACH HOUSE

855 South Broadway   252-7777
$$$$ Most major credit cards

Under original owner Stanley Demos, The Coach House long ago set the standard for Lexington culinary excellence. The current owners, Mr. and Mrs. John B. Du Puy III, continue the fine tradition. You should eat here at least once in your life, even if you have to eat Ramen noodles for the rest of the month. The Coach House is famous for its Maryland crab cakes, available as an appetizer or for lunch. Other specialties include rack of lamb and veal Oscar. The chicken topped with warm bing cherries, a truly heavenly creation, was listed only on the lunch menu at this writing; however, if you request it when you make reservations, The Coach House will gladly accommodate you. Open for lunch from 11 AM to 2:30 PM Monday through Friday and for dinner from 5 PM to 10:30 PM Monday through Saturday. Reservations are recommended.

DUDLEY'S

380 South Mill Street   252-1010
$$$ Visa, MasterCard, American Express

The centerpiece of historic Dudley Square, a former schoolhouse divided into a number of small businesses, is this comfortably elegant spot. High ceilings, simple but attractive place settings and attentive service make Dudley's a dining experience. The patio is the place to be for a business lunch or an afternoon date on a warm spring day. Lunch features a quiche of the day, and there are daily fish and pasta specials at lunch and dinner. Roasted scallops with vegetables and Niçoise sauce is a highlight, and Dudley's fresh-baked muffins start any meal on the right foot. Open for lunch daily (including Sunday brunch) from 11:30 AM to 2:30 PM. Dinner hours are 5:30 PM to 10 PM Sunday through Thursday and 5:30 PM to 11 PM Friday and Saturday. Reservations are recommended.

ED AND FRED'S DESERT MOON

249 East Main Street   231-1161
$$ All major credit cards

Ed and Fred's Desert Moon is an eclectic and intriguing blend of Southwestern and nouvelle cuisine. The place is named after its creators' fathers, who financed the place. This is the former site of Cafe Max, which had a distinct Art Deco style; the new owners have left some of the original ambience but have added an earthy Southwestern flair that complements the food. "Imagination at no extra charge," the menu says, and Ed and Fred's clearly takes the motto to heart. From appetizers like black bean enchiladas through entrees like lime chili pesto linguine and raspberry chicken, there's nothing ordinary here. There's also gourmet pizza. Open from 11 AM to 3 PM and 5 PM to 10 PM Tuesday through Thursday, 11 AM to 3 PM and 5 PM to midnight Friday, 5 PM to midnight Saturday, and 5 PM to 10 PM Sunday.

LA CUCINA

355 Romany Road   266-8704
$$ Visa, MasterCard

La Cucina offers gourmet food lovers three ways to enjoy its menu: Its gourmet and deli food can be served at little tables inside the store. The Easy Way Out! is a take-home supper service that will prepare a meal for you to eat at home (we find this is also a great way to present a freshly-cooked meal for guests — and you don't *have* to tell them you didn't make it yourself). For a special supper, call 24 hours in advance. Catering is also available. And customers can buy foods, wines, liquors, food baskets and gifts in the shop. Open Monday through Thursday from 10:30 AM to 7 PM, and Friday and Saturday from 10:30 AM to 8 PM. Closed on Sunday.

MAGNOLIAS 307 SOUTHERN BISTRO

307 South Ashland Avenue   266-6545
$$$ Most major credit cards

"Southern bistro" is an apt term for this Chevy Chase restaurant, which serves Continental cuisine with a Southern flair in a classy yet comfortable setting. A beautiful black baby grand was recently installed near the bar, and artwork and murals by local artists grace the walls. Several small dining areas, one with a fireplace, add to the coziness. At this writing, Magnolias was upscaling its menu, but a number of the signature items were remaining, including a variety of creative seafood and pasta creations and rich desserts. Adjoining the bar is a deck with a 5-foot fire pit that allows for outdoor socializing even in cooler weather. Open 11 AM to 11 PM Monday through Thursday, 11 AM to 1 AM Friday and Saturday, and 11 AM to 9 PM Sunday.

THE MANSION AT GRIFFIN GATE

1720 Newtown Road   231-5152
$$$$ Most major credit cards
The Mansion at Griffin Gate is a restored Southern antebellum mansion; you could call it Lexington's version of Tara. It offers tastefully prepared American and Continental cuisine with impeccable service. Lunch is served from 11:30 AM to 2 PM Monday through Friday. Dinner hours are 6 PM to 10 PM daily. Reservations are recommended.

THE PAMPERED CHEF

314 $^{1}/_{2}$ South Ashland Avenue   268-1005
$$$ Visa, MasterCard, American Express
With The Pampered Chef's lim-

ited hours, you may find it a challenge getting a table in the narrow, European-style dining room. It's a worthy challenge. Chef David Larsen's changing lunch menu revolves around sandwiches, salads and a freshly prepared quiche of the day. Weekend dinner offerings include the likes of tournedos of beef tenderloin in a sauce of shallots, cognac, sun-dried tomatoes, basil and creme fraiche; sauteed sea bass with red bell pepper sauce; and bouillabaisse. Open for lunch Monday through Friday from 11 AM to 2 PM; dinner is served only on Friday and Saturday from 6 PM to 9 PM. Reservations are recommended.

Delis

THE MOUSE TRAP

3323 Tates Creek Road   269-2958
$ Visa MasterCard, American Express
A friend who frequently entertains is sold on The Mouse Trap for its pâtés, including a tasty veal-chicken one. This deli in the Lansdowne Shoppes has Greek and other salads, delicious smoked salmon spread and more. Its selection of imported crackers, cookies and candies makes it something of a "gourmet supermarket," our friend says — and it also has fancy homemade cookies like almond macaroons. The Mouse Trap, which has a

small dine-in lunch area and European cafe-style tables outside, also prepares distinctive gift baskets. Open 10 AM to 7 PM Monday through Friday, 10 AM to 6PM Saturday and noon to 5 PM Sunday.

STANLEY J'S NEW YORK STYLE DELICATESSEN

Stonewall Shopping Center,
Clays Mill Road 224-3354
$ *Cash or Check Only*

In addition to your standard deli offerings like corned beef and pastrami, Stanley J's makes a variety of ethnic foods in-house, including Indonesian rice with plum sauce and ginger root, tabouli and Greek lemon soup. The ham, baked in Stanley J's own bourbon sauce, is great served on a hot or cold sandwich, and you can also get huge, one-third-pound kosher hot dogs and bagels and lox. And, of course, New York cheesecake for dessert. Open 10:30 AM to 8 PM Monday through Friday and 10:30 AM to 5 PM Saturday.

Three popular downtown-area delis are the **Park Plaza Deli**, 120 East Main Street, 252-0153; **Pottinger's Deli**, 113 Cheapside, 254-6865; and **Stella's Deli**, 598 Ballard Street, 252-3263.

In addition, all of the larger groceries in town have delis with varying selections of meats and cheeses, salads and plate lunches. The Kroger, Randall's and Winn Dixie delis, for example, have good varieties of hot and cold foods. Most of them can prepare party trays to order and also have ready-to-cook en-

trees that make it easy for you to throw a dinner party without actually doing that much work. Visit the one nearest you.

Italian and Pizza

BRAVO'S OF LEXINGTON

Victorian Square,
401 West Main Street 255-2222
$$$$ *Most major credit cards*

Originally called Bravo Pitino, this authentic Italian restaurant was sure to become a hit when it opened, simply because the beloved UK basketball coach was a partner and the place was modeled after his favorite Big Apple eatery. Rick Pitino has reduced his involvement, and the restaurant has modified its name, but it still serves elegant cuisine in an atmosphere to match. Tender fried calamari and a filling antipasto are just the beginnings. Entrees include six varieties of both chicken and veal (including osso buco), grilled salmon and "Pitino's pasta," a savory blend of tomato fettucine, crab meat, shrimp and vegetables in a sauce of white wine and herbs. Lunch is served in the bar and grille from 11:30 AM to 1 PM Monday through Friday; dinner is 5:30 PM to 10:30 PM Monday through Saturday. Reservations are recommended.

JOE BOLOGNA'S

120 West Maxwell 252-4933
$$ *Most major credit cards*

Since moving into a beautifully restored old church building several years ago, Joe B's, as it is affectionately known, is no longer the dive (in the best sense of the word) it used to be when it was just up the street at the

corner of Maxwell and Limestone. The scratchy old jukebox has been replaced with a CD jukebox, and stained-glass windows let the sun in. One thing that hasn't changed, however, is the fantastic pizza, which is available in traditional round, Sicilian pan and specialty versions. You can also get meat or vegetable lasagna, manicotti and other pasta dishes, salads and sandwiches. Whatever you order, start off with one of Joe B's famous bread sticks (if you're on a diet, you can get the garlic butter on the side). Open 11 AM to 11 PM Monday through Thursday, 11 AM to midnight Friday and Saturday, and noon to 11 PM Sunday.

LEXITALIA RISTORANTE
1765 Alexandria Drive   277-1116
$$$ *Most major credit cards*

Joe DiMaggio, Billy Joel and James Caan have savored Lexitalia's Italian specialties. A special order was once rushed to Elton John's private jet as it waited to take off from Blue Grass Airport. The casually elegant atmosphere — stucco interior walls, a handful of Italian paintings — is reminiscent of an Italian courtyard. And the food? Glad you asked. There are good reasons for all the celebrity patronage. Lexitalia's assortment of pastas, veal, beef, chicken and seafood is *magnifico!* The homemade sausage, grilled with onion and peppers in olive oil, is excellent. Or try the rich pizza bianco, topped with a cream sauce and a blend of cheeses. Lunch hours are 11 AM to 2 PM Monday through Friday. Dinner is served from 5 PM to 10 PM Sunday through Thursday and 5 PM to 11 PM Friday and Saturday.

PAISANO'S
2417 Nicholasville Road   277-5321
$$ *Most major credit cards*

This hideaway in the inconspicuous Stone Square shopping center features numerous traditional Italian favorites, from pasta and pizza to veal, chicken, seafood and steak. Baked ziti, eggplant parmesan and Florentine rolls (available with or without meat) are among the specialties. The warm bread is a perfect complement to any meal. Lunch 11 AM to 2 PM Monday through Friday, dinner 5 PM to 10 PM Monday through Thursday, and 5 PM to 11 PM Friday and Saturday.

PIZZERIA UNO

2547 Richmond Road   266-8667
$$ Visa, MasterCard, American Express

This chain, which originated in Chicago, specializes in Chicago-style deep-dish pizza. Freshly made dough and choice ingredients make such creations as the spinoccoli (spinach and broccoli) and the four cheese exceptional. Uno's also serves pasta, steaks, ribs, chicken and burgers. Open 11 AM to midnight Monday through Thursday, 11 AM to 1 AM Friday and Saturday, and 11:30 AM to 11 PM Sunday.

Japanese

NAGASAKI INN

2013 Regency Road   278-8782
$$$ All major credit cards

If you've never been to a Japanese steakhouse, you should know that it's more than a dining experience — it's a show. At least that's the case with Nagasaki Inn, which prepares steak, seafood, chicken and vegetables right in front of you on a specially designed table. The action takes place at large tables, where your party is likely to be seated with another party or two; for extra enjoyment, go with a large group. Open 4:30 PM to 10 PM Monday through Thursday, 4:30 PM to 11 PM Friday and Saturday, and 4:30 PM to 9:30 PM Sunday.

TACHIBANA

785 Newtown Court   254-1911
$$$$ Visa, MasterCard, American Express

This is Toyota's place—what more recommendation do you need? The location just off I-75 makes it a quick commute for executives from the Georgetown plant. And, especially if you're in the mood for sushi, it's worth a drive from anywhere else in Central Kentucky. Especially recommended are the tuna rolls and the yellowtail, a form of mackerel. And if, like Travis Tritt, you like your sushi Southern fried, you can go the tempura route with deep-fried seafood and veggies. Tachibana also has a room where you can get Japanese steakhouse-style cuisine, show and all. Lunch 11:30 AM to 1:30 PM Monday through Friday, dinner 5:30 PM to 10:30 PM Monday through Saturday.

Mexican

GALVAN'S

825 Euclid Avenue   266-1683
$$ Visa, MasterCard, American Express

Galvan's, like many of Lexington's authentic Mexican restaurants, is a family operation. The food at this Chevy Chase cantina is freshly prepared and delicious. The pollo Picada, which is grilled chicken topped with fresh vegetables and served with flour tortillas, is one of this author's favorites (it's also available with steak instead of chicken), as is the Mexican shrimp. Combination dinners and a la carte items are also offered. Try the tamale or the relleno dinner with your choice of one or two rellenos. Open 11 AM to 10 PM seven days a week.

JALAPEÑO'S

285 New Circle Road NW   299-8299
$$ Visa, MasterCard, American Express

Jalapeño's offers traditional favorites as well as some truly inventive creations, all served amid festive surroundings. The camarones Pacificos — shrimp stuffed with jalapeño pepper and cheese, rolled in bacon and grilled — are mind-blowingly delicious. There are also several other fish items on the menu. Open 11 AM to 10 PM Sunday through Thursday and 11 AM to 11 PM Friday and Saturday.

MESA VERDE

The Mall at Lexington Green   272-3311
$$$ Visa, MasterCard, American Express

Mesa Verde is best known for its sizzling fajitas, available with steak, pork, chicken, shrimp or garden vegetables. Mexican-style grilled swordfish and Tex-Mex items like mesquite-grilled baby back ribs and barbecue chicken are also popular. Open 11 AM to 10 PM Sunday through Thursday and 11 AM to 11 PM Friday and Saturday.

RINCON MEXICANO

818 Euclid Avenue   268-8160
$$ Most major credit cards

In a city blessed with an abundance of good, authentic Mexican cooking, Rincon Mexicano faces perhaps its toughest competitor right across the street at Galvan's. But this second-floor restaurant, above Charlie Brown's, holds its ground. If you like your Mexican food really hot, you must try the chile Colorado, tender chunks of beef in a fiery red sauce, served with flour tortillas. Rincon Mexicano, which translates

as "Mexican corner," also offers several vegetarian combination dinners. Open 11 AM to 10 PM Monday through Thursday, 11 AM to 10:45 PM Friday, noon to 10:30 PM Saturday, and noon to 9 PM Sunday.

Seafood

CHARLIE'S FRESH SEAFOOD & CARRY-OUT MARKET

928 Winchester Road   255-6005
$ All major credit cards

You can't eat *at* Charlie's, and even the carry-out menu is very limited, but you can't beat the price or the generous portions. Whitefish sandwiches and shrimp and clam dinners are the extent of the menu. The market, however, has a bounty of fresh and frozen seafood — including oysters, shrimp, tuna, halibut, salmon, swordfish, Alaskan king crab legs, crawfish tails and more — for wholesale and retail. Serving hours are 9:30 AM to 6 PM Tuesday through Friday and 9:30 AM to 5 PM Saturday.

ET-R HOUSE OF SEAFOOD

2628 Richmond Road   269-4316
$$$ All major credit cards

ET-R's seafood (Get it? "Eat our seafood") is fresh and delicious. It may seem a little pricey for a restaurant that doubles as a fish market, or vice versa, but atmosphere isn't really the point here. The grilled yellowfin tuna dinner, also available as a sandwich at lunch, is excellent. Other specialties include mesquite-grilled soft-shell crabs, barbecued shrimp and scallops Provençale. Soups include bouillabaisse, gumbo and conch chowder and more, although availability varies. Lunch is served

11:30 AM to 3:30 PM Monday through Saturday and dinner 5:30 PM to 10 PM Wednesday through Saturday. The retail business is open every day.

HALL'S ON THE RIVER

1225 Athens-Boonesboro Road
near Boonesboro   255-8105
$$$ *Visa, MasterCard, American Express*

Hall's may be most famous for its beer cheese and its fried banana peppers but that doesn't mean its seafood isn't something special as well. Catfish is a specialty, as are frog legs. And Hall's location on a bank of the Kentucky River provides a great view. Open 11:30 AM to 9 PM Monday through Thursday, 11:30 AM to 11 PM Friday and Saturday, and noon to 8 PM Sunday.

THE KETCH

2012 Regency Road   277-5919
$$$ *Most major credit cards*

The Ketch has several fresh catches daily, with choices like tuna, swordfish and mahi mahi grilled or blackened Cajun-style. You can also get shrimp, scallops, frog legs and several varieties of oysters. Most of the items are available fried or broiled. The whitefish is extremely popular as a meal or a sandwich, and the seafood chowder is also a winner. New York strip, filet mignon, chicken and ribs are available for landlubbers. Open 11 AM to 10:30 PM Monday through Thursday, 11 AM to 11:30 PM Friday and Saturday, and 11 AM to 10 PM Sunday.

L&N SEAFOOD

Lexington Green   273-7875
$$$ *Most major credit cards*

L&N, part of a growing chain, recently reworked its menu. There are still fresh catches and grilled specialties, but there also are plenty of new items. The pasta selections now include linguine and shrimp marinara, fettuccine Alfredo with shrimp and more. The smoked tomato-jalapeño catfish is a bold and spicy menu addition. One warning: If you're not careful, you'll get filled up on the "bottomless bowl" of house salad and the unlimited supply of hot and fluffy homemade biscuits. A Sunday buffet brunch, served from 11 AM to 2 PM, features Belgian waffles, omelets, sausage, shrimp and more. Open 11:30 AM to 10 PM Monday through Thursday, 11:30 AM to 11 PM Friday and Saturday, and 11 AM to 9 PM Sunday.

LEO'S SEAFOOD SHACK

825 Lane Allen Road   278-2402
$$ *Most major credit cards*

For years, Leo's has served some of Lexington's best cooked-to-order seafood from an unpretentious, no-frills little building — it really is a shack — in the Garden Springs neighborhood. At this writing, however, the building was for sale. But don't worry: The owners assure us that, if they lose their lease, Leo's will reappear in a new location. Oysters are the specialty, and you can get them rolled, pan-fried, Rockefeller or on the half-shell. You also can't go wrong with the whitefish, whether you like it fried, broiled or on a sandwich. Open 11 AM to 9 PM Monday through Thursday, 11 AM to 10 PM Friday, and 11 AM to 2 PM and 5 PM to 9 PM Saturday.

LINC'S, SPRINGFIELD

1007 Lincoln Park Road,
Springfield   1-336-7493
$$ Visa, MasterCard

Linc's lovers don't mind driving nearly an hour to reach this seafood haven off Ky. 555. Shrimp, oysters, scallops, catfish and frog legs are highlights, and there is a selection of broiled seafood items. A big draw is the Friday and Saturday night buffet offering crab legs, steamed and fried shrimp, oysters on the half shell, fried and broiled whitefish, barbecue ribs and more. Non-seafood menu items include ribeye and filet mignon.

NEW ORLEANS HOUSE

1510 Newtown Pike   254-3474
$$$$ Most major credit cards

Be sure to wear loose-fitting clothing when you visit the New Orleans House in Griffin Gate Plaza. And be sure to take your appetite with you. This isn't your typical seafood buffet, with the emphasis on fried fish. At New Orleans House, most of the seafood is broiled, Louisiana style. The buffet's "cold" station features Norwegian smoked salmon, peel-and-eat shrimp and oysters on the half shell. The seafood chowder, stocked with oodles of fish and shellfish, is marvelous. Then there's Alaskan crab legs, tasty broiled scallops, steamed shrimp and clams, mussels cooked in wine, frog legs and much more. Open 6

PM to 9 PM Monday through Thursday and 5 PM to 10 PM Friday and Saturday. Reservations are required.

TIPPEDORE'S CAFE

French Quarter Suites,
2601 Richmond Road   269-4316
$$$ Most major credit cards

Tippedore's, located inside the courtyard/atrium at French Quarter Suites, looks onto a New Orleans-like scene of antique lamps, wrought-iron gates and balconies and a gazebo bar. The menu, with a few exceptions, concentrates on soft-shell crab, scampi, and Creole-style seafood such as shrimp etouffee. Prime rib is available alone or in combination with shrimp or lobster. Lunch is served 11 AM to 2 PM seven days a week, dinner 5 PM to 10 PM Sunday through Thursday, and 5 PM to 11 PM Friday and Saturday.

Steakhouses

CLIFF HAGAN'S RIBEYE

941 Winchester Road   253-0750
I-75 interchange, Berea   1-986-3639
Franklin Square, Frankfort   (502) 227-2380
$$$ Visa, MasterCard, American Express

Cliff Hagan, who led the Kentucky Wildcats to an NCAA basketball championship in 1951 and an undefeated '54 season, founded his restaurant after retiring from the

Insiders like eating carrot soup at the Atomic Cafe on Limestone Street.

NBA in 1970. As you might expect, UK athletics photographs cover the walls. Grilled, well-seasoned ribeye is the specialty and can be ordered in cuts up to 32 ounces. The slow-roasted prime rib is bursting with flavor. Other choices include barbecue ribs, chicken and halibut. A varied all-you-can-eat soup and salad bar is included with each meal. Open 5 PM to 10 PM Sunday through Thursday and 5 PM to 10:30 PM Friday and Saturday.

COLUMBIA STEAK HOUSE

201 North Limestone Street	253-3135
1425 Alexandria Drive	233-4185
3347 Tates Creek Road	268-1666
$$$	Visa, MasterCard, American Express

The Columbia Steak House special — a thick, round tenderloin of beef broiled to order in garlic butter — has been one of Lexington's finest steaks for decades. In fact, it's the only entree this author has ever ordered here, even though T-bones, prime rib, lamb fries, chicken and seafood also are available. The Diego salad, a simple mixture of lettuce and tomatoes mixed in big bags with a secret seasoning, is a must. The original Limestone location has the funkiest and best atmosphere; when Smitty, the maitre d', calls for your party, you'll know you're someplace special. Hours vary by location.

DEL FRISCO'S

164 South Eastern Avenue	252-2992
$$$$	All major credit cards

The owners like to boast that you don't need a steak knife to cut their beefsteaks. They're not lying. In addition to melt-in-your-mouth ribeye, filet mignon, sirloin and prime rib, Del Frisco's has a selection of seafood and poultry. Celebrate a special occasion or create one with the chateaubriand for two. Vegetables are à la carte. The house vegetable, Green Phunque Casserole, is a mixture of chopped spinach, eggs, mushrooms, onion, bacon and cheddar cheese. Try it. Open 5 PM to 10 PM Monday through Thursday and 5 PM to 11 PM Friday and Saturday. Reservations are recommended.

LOGAN'S ROADHOUSE

1224 Harrodsburg Road	252-4307
$$$	Most major credit cards

This Western-style saloon/steakhouse charcoal-grills steaks, ribs, chicken and seafood in plain view in the center of the restaurant. If you're in the mood for something deliciously different with your meal, order the baked sweet potato. The hot, freshly baked bread is also a must. On weekend nights, the place is packed, but waiting isn't so bad if you can find a seat in the bar, where they'll give you a bucket of peanuts in the shell to tide you over. You're encouraged to throw the shells on the floor. Open 11 AM to 1 AM Monday through Saturday and 11 AM to 11 PM Sunday.

Other Ethnic

THE ATOMIC CAFE

265 North Limestone Street	254-1969
$$$	Visa, MasterCard

This author has never been to the Caribbean, but when he does, he hopes he can find conch fritters, coconut shrimp and jerk chicken as good as those served here. Owner Linda Hoff wanted to remind people of their island vacations, so she created a casual restaurant and bar featuring a huge tropical mural, reggae music and menu items adapted from Jamaica, the Bahamas, the West Indies and other exotic locales. The Atomic Cafe also has plenty of options for vegetarians, like Latin carrot soup from Cuba, an eggplant "caviar" appetizer from Trinidad and a vegetarian sampler dinner. Key lime cheesecake is one of several tempting desserts. Open 4 PM to 10 PM Tuesday through Thursday and 4 PM to 11 PM Friday and Saturday.

INDIAN CUISINE AND NATURAL FOODS

Nicholasville Road at
Arcadia Park   278-6327
$ Visa, MasterCard

This tiny shopping-center storefront across from Central Baptist Hospital offers zero frills: plastic chairs, tables with laminated woodgrain tops and undecorated pink walls. But don't worry about the decor; you're in for a real treat. A vegetarian buffet is offered daily for lunch and dinner, with items that this author can't spell, pronounce or, in some cases, even identify. No matter, they're all good. Some of the curried dishes are fiery, so make sure you have some sweet chutney or yogurt on your plate to balance the taste. If you want meat, you can order curried chicken or goat. And you want to talk about personal service? On the author's first visit, planned as a business lunch, he and his companion were joined by the proprietors for an illuminating discussion of Hinduism. Lunch 11 AM to 2 PM Monday through Friday, dinner 5 PM to 9 PM Monday through Saturday.

JOZO'S BAYOU GUMBO

4053 Tates Creek Road	273-9229
384 Woodland Avenue	254-7047
115 Locust Hill Drive	268-4700
$	Cash or check only

One of the great things about Cajun and Creole food is that even the names of the dishes are a treat for the tongue. Jambalaya. Gumbo. Chicken fricassee. Shrimp etouffee. They all just seem to roll musically off the tongue. And wait until you taste them. With its generous servings and bayou bargain prices that even a college student can afford, Jozo's (pronounced YO-zo's) will give you more than you can eat for about $4. Thank goodness for those take-home boxes! All dishes are served over rice and include crusty French garlic bread. Crawfish and alligator are available in season. For dessert, treat yourself to a slice of peanut butter pie or a rich praline. Open 11 AM to 9:30 PM Sunday through Thursday and 11 AM to 10 PM Friday and Saturday.

MARIKKA'S

411 Southland Drive	277-9801
$$	Visa, MasterCard

German restaurants have always been risky ventures in Lexington, but Marikka's has been going strong for more than two years now. One reason for the success is the authentic German cuisine — including Weiner schnitzel, jaegerschnitzel, sauerbraten, knackwurst and bratwurst — cooked up by Marikka Tackett from family recipes. The adjoining bar is a beer lover's dream, with more than 300 brews from around the world. The restaurant is open from 11 AM to 10 PM Monday through Thursday, 11 AM to 11 PM Friday, and 4 PM to 11 PM Saturday. Die Bier Stube, which draws a fun-loving crowd, is open until 1 AM Monday through Saturday.

NATASHA'S CAFE

304 Southland Drive   277-8412
$ Most major credit cards

Natasha Williams, a Russian native, and her American husband, Gene, opened Natasha's Cafe and Boutique in December 1991. The cafe features Russian and Greek dishes and exotic coffees. Vegetarian specials include an Armenian cheese roll filled with feta and cream cheeses, black olives, green peppers and cilantro. The adjoining boutique has an array of clothing, gifts and jewelry from around the world. Open 11 AM to 10 PM Monday through Thursday, 11 AM to 11 PM Friday and Saturday, and 5 PM to 6 PM Sunday.

THE OASIS

868-B East High Street in
Chevy Chase Place   268-0414
$ Cash or check only

Lexington's only Mediterranean restaurant, at this writing, offers plenty of options for meat-lover and vegetarian alike. Greek specialties include gyros, spinach pie, tabouli, falafel and stuffed grape leaves. Open 11 AM to 8 PM

Monday through Wednesday, 11 AM to 4 PM Thursday, 3 PM to 10 PM Friday, and 11 AM to 10 PM Saturday.

OLD SAN JUAN

247 Surfside Drive   278-2682
$ Visa, MasterCard

Had a good Cuban sandwich lately? You know, with roast pork, ham, cheese, butter and pickles all between two slices of crusty Cuban bread? No, it's not exactly low cholesterol, but you should have one anyway. Or at least a bowl of black beans and rice with a side order of fried plantains. Come as you are. Old San Juan is nothing fancy, just a few tables at the front of a Cuban/Puerto Rican grocery. The owners are friendly, the food is cheap, daily specials are offered and you can't get a good Cuban sandwich just anywhere, you know. Open 9 AM to 9 PM Monday through Wednesday and 9 AM to 10 PM Thursday through Saturday.

SIAM THAI RESTAURANT

126 New Circle Road NE   231-7975
$$ Visa, MasterCard, American Express

Siam Thai specializes in spicy dishes such as Thai chili and pad Thai, both of which are available with chicken, pork, beef or shrimp. The spring roll appetizer is a good way to start things off. Vegetarian dishes are available. Lunch 11 AM to 2 PM Monday through Friday. Dinner 5 PM to 9:30 PM Monday through Thursday, 5 PM to 10:30 PM Friday, 4 PM to 10:30 PM Saturday, and 4:30 PM to 9:30 PM Sunday.

Vegetarian

ALFALFA

557 South Limestone Street   253-0014
$$ Cash or check only

This restaurant across from the main entrance to the University of Kentucky gained its reputation in the '60s as a primarily vegetarian hangout for the coffeehouse crowd. Times have changed since then, and so have the patrons, but they keep coming back. And Alfalfa continues to serve old favorites as well as inventive new creations. Lunch 11 AM to 2 PM Monday through Friday. Dinner 5:30 PM to 9:30 PM Tuesday through Thursday and 5:30 PM to 10 PM Friday and Saturday. Saturday and Sunday brunch is served from 10 AM to 2 PM.

EVERYBODY'S NATURAL FOODS & DELI

503 Euclid Avenue   255-4162
$ Visa, MasterCard

During lunchtime at Everybody's, a storefront cafe with health-food products lining the wall shelves, you'll find everybody from suit-and-tie professionals to hippie types in tie-dyes and sandals. The food is healthy and cheap, and there are daily specials. Regular offerings include a meatless whole-grain "veggie burger"; tofu, falafel and tuna salad (dolphin-safe, of course) sandwiches; pasta salad; and tabouli. Friday night is Gourmet Night, with a changing menu. Open 11 AM to 8 PM Monday through Thursday, 11 AM to 9:30 PM Friday, and 11 AM to 8 PM Saturday.

Delivery

Want a restaurant meal but don't feel like going out? Your options aren't limited to that old stand-by, pizza. Here are a couple of alternatives.

CAFE EXPRESS

873-2233
Visa, MasterCard

Menu items from nearly three dozen restaurants are available from Cafe Express. Order steak, prime rib, Chinese, Mexican, Italian, barbecue, sandwiches and more, and it will generally be delivered in less than an hour. Drivers use insulated Mylar bags to keep the food warm. You pay a delivery charge of $3 if you live within the designated delivery area and an additional 75 cents for each mile outside it. Gratuity isn't included, but you know you should tip generously, just as you do at a restaurant. Pick up a menu book at any participating restaurant, or call Cafe Express and one will be mailed to you. Delivery hours are 11 AM to 11 PM, Monday through Saturday, and 5 PM to 10 PM on Sunday.

STEAK-OUT

125 Southland Drive   277-2669
V, MC $$

Steak-Out offers a variety of charbroiled items including steaks, chicken and burgers, along with side dishes, generally delivered in a half-hour to 45 minutes. The current delivery area is between Versailles and Richmond roads out to Man o' War Boulevard. Plan are to open another Steak-Out on Richmond Road sometime in 1994.

Caterers

It isn't difficult to find a caterer around here. What's hard is *choosing* one. Whether your event is a wedding reception, a corporate luncheon or a Super Bowl party, there is a wide range of businesses that specialize in catering. In addition, nearly three dozen restaurants of all types — from fried chicken to pizza to haute cuisine — also provide catering services. Check the Yellow Pages under "caterers," and you'll probably find someone who can provide the appropriate food for your party. We've listed a handful who have gained popularity in the Bluegrass.

CATERING BY GEORGE
178 North Upper Street   252-3688

DUPREE CATERING
McCORMICK CATERING
223 North Limestone Street   231-0464

PHIL DUNN'S COOKSHOP
431 Old East Vine Street   231-0099

PURPLE COW CATERERS
447 Lexington Road, Versailles   873-8379

THE TICKLED PALATE
147 North Limestone Street   255-4911

A Taste of Kentucky Food and Drink

When you're dining in the Bluegrass, it is quite possible that you will encounter certain menu items that, while not unpronounceable like some snooty French dish, are simply unfamiliar to you. Things like "lamb fries," for example, or "hot Browns." Should you order them, or should you steer clear? And just what do we mean when we talk about "country ham"—are we trying to distinguish it from pork raised in the city? This chapter is designed to help you answer such questions.

From the perspective of worldwide culinary recognition, Colonel Harland Sanders' "finger-lickin'-good" creation might be the food that most people associate with Kentucky. If you go to Corbin, about 80 miles south of Lexington, you can visit the very first KFC establishment, which opened in 1930. But if your knowledge of Kentucky cuisine is limited to fried chicken, then you're in for a surprise. (Sanders, incidentally, was born in Indiana. As any market researcher worth his salt will tell you, however, "Indiana Fried Chicken" would never have flown.)

A number of influences, including Native American, Irish, Scottish, French and German, have come together to create the smorgasbord of tastes known as Kentucky cuisine, regional cuisine or "country cookin'." All in all, it's hearty fare, heavy on the meat and potatoes. And second helpings are encouraged!

Restaurants offering "regional" cooking are likely to serve such delicacies as fried catfish, country ham with beaten biscuits and redeye gravy, grits, fried chicken, barbecue and burgoo. It's true that many of these dishes can be found throughout the South, but Kentucky cooks take special pride in the way they prepare these delicacies. More recent additions to the state's diverse menu include beer cheese, fried banana peppers and the aforementioned hot Brown.

With good bourbon in such plentiful supply, the native liquor is used not only as a beverage but also as a flavoring agent for a number of recipes. Commercially bottled preparations such as bourbon steak sauce can be found in groceries throughout the state, and Kentucky-made chocolate candies sweetened with bourbon are popular around the country, especially during the holidays.

Lexington Herald-Leader food writer Sharon Thompson has graciously shared a handful of the Kentucky-style recipes she has accumulated over the years, and we have included them in this chapter just in

Photo: Lexington Herald-Leader

A mint julep is a traditional Southern drink made with bourbon.

case you're inclined to whip up a few of these dishes yourself. As with just about any regional dish, numerous variations are possible, so you may see different versions of these recipes elsewhere. Experiment with your own versions; we don't care.

Of course, if Bluegrass cuisine is a new experience for you, you may feel more comfortable letting the so-called experts do the cooking. Either way, do sample some Kentucky-style home cookin'. While everything on our varied menu may not be to your liking, you'd have to be a mighty picky eater not to find something that suits your fancy, especially when it's served with such fine hospitality. If you leave a Bluegrass dinner table hungry, it's nobody's fault but your own.

COUNTRY HAM

A Kentucky country ham is distinguished from your run-of-the-meal variety by its preparation, which involves curing with salt or sugar for a period of anywhere from six months to three years. Before you cook your country ham, you'll first want to remove some of the salt it acquired in curing (not necessary when the ham is sugar-cured) and restore moisture lost in the aging process. To accomplish this, the ham is usually boiled instead of baked. Some cooks set a glaze on the outside by baking it briefly after boiling. Here's one way to fix a country ham.

10- to 16-pound aged country ham
1/2 cup cider vinegar
1 bottle beer or 1 1/2 cups ginger ale (optional)
Whole cloves (optional)
1 cup brown sugar
1/4 cup cornmeal
1 tablespoon dry mustard
1 tablespoon freshly ground black pepper
2 or 3 tablespoons bourbon, pineapple juice or apple juice

Put the ham under cold running water and scrub with a stiff brush to remove any loose mold. Place the ham in a large container and add cold water to cover. Allow to soak for 24 hours.

Drain off the water and scrub the ham again, then wipe with a cloth soaked in vinegar to remove any remaining mold.

Place the ham in a large kettle or deep roasting pan with enough water to cover it completely. Add the vinegar and beer, if desired, to help neutralize the salt flavor.

Bring to a boil, cover and simmer gently for 3 to 3 1/2 hours. Keep the ham covered with liquid by adding boiling water as needed. The ham is done when the small crossbone in the shank is pulled out easily.

Let the ham cool to room temperature in its cooking liquid. This will take several hours.

Preheat the oven to 400 degrees.

Remove the cooled ham from the liquid. Cut off all of the rind except for a small band around the shank end that will serve as a handle when carving.

Trim off the fat, leaving only a 1/4- to 1/2-inch-thick layer. You may score the fat in a diamond pattern.

To glaze the ham: In a bowl, mix together the brown sugar, corn-meal, mustard and pepper. Moisten the mixture with the bourbon.

Spread the mixture over the ham and bake for 20 minutes or until the glaze is bubbly and nicely browned. Watch the ham carefully during glazing to make sure the glaze doesn't burn; pour a cup or two of water into the pan if necessary.

Country ham is best served at room temperature, sliced very thin with the grain. Eat it with biscuits.

If you want redeye gravy with your country ham: Fry it instead of baking it. After boiling, slice the ham into thicker slices and fry it in a skillet. Take the juice left from frying, stir in a little water (use your own judgment) and, if desired, a spoonful of coffee (no grounds, please). Spoon the mixture over your ham and biscuits.

BURGOO

The meat in burgoo, according to a popular joke, consists of "whatever didn't make it across the road the night before." That's a bit of an exaggeration, but the fact is that you can add virtually any type of domestic or wild beast that you might imagine. The policy on vegetables is also quite liberal. This concoction — something like a thick and spicy vegetable soup or beef stew — is tasty and filling. It's popular at Kentucky race tracks and is especially good on warm evenings.

There are a number of theories about the origin of burgoo. Although the name is the same, this slow-cooked, labor-intensive and ultimately satisfying delicacy is not to be confused with the thick but bland oatmeal group once served to sailors, who quite likely went wild with gastronomic abandon whenever they reached shore. No, tasty Kentucky-style burgoo apparently was the creation of rugged, hearty 19th-century folks who filled their continuously simmering stockpots with the bounty from the men's hunting trips: squirrel, rabbit, venison, fowl and sometimes even bear.

Gus Jaubert, a member of Gen. John Hunt Morgan's cavalry, is sometimes credited with first using the word "burgoo" for meat-and-vegetable stew, which he prepared for the troops in massive quantities from field rations. Variations of Jaubert's dish later became a hit at political rallies, and that tradition has continued. J.T. Looney, a Lexington grocer and Jaubert protege, later became known as "the burgoo king." In 1932, a horse named Burgoo King won the Kentucky Derby and the Preakness.

It is common knowledge that you should always make enough burgoo to serve an army. The following recipe, which contains nothing you have to go out and shoot, was created to serve "at least 25" — or six to eight members of this author's family.

2 pounds lamb shank, bone in
2 fresh pork knuckles, about 1 1/2 pounds
1 veal shank, about 2 1/4 pounds
5 pounds of beef shank, bone in
4 to 4 1/4 quarts of water
2 teaspoons salt
2 bay leaves
Handful of celery tops
1 tablespoon black peppercorns
3 dried red pepper pods (optional)
1 large onion, quartered
3 to 4 cloves garlic, peeled

Put all the meat and bones in a 12- to 15-quart kettle with a lid. The bone-in beef shank is a huge piece; unless your pot is huge, you'll probably need to cut the meat off the bone in two or three pieces so both the bone and the meat will fit comfortably into the pot.

Cover all the meat and bones with water. Add all the other ingredients. Bring to a slow boil, skim, lower the heat, cover and simmer for 2 1/2 to 3 hours, until the meat is falling off the bones.

Take the pot off the heat and let it cool. Take out the meat and strain the broth. Discard any gristle on the meat.

With a small spoon or knife, dig any lingering marrow out of the bones and put it, along with any loose marrow, back into the stock. Discard the bones. Refrigerate the stock and the meat separately in covered bowls. The next day the stock will have jelled, and the top layer of fat can be removed. Return the stock to the pot and bring slowly to a high simmer. Then add:

1 3 1/2- to 4-pound chicken, cut in quarters
2 cups diced carrots
2 cups diced onion
2 cups diced celery
2 cups diced green peppers

Photo: Lexington Herald-Leader

Burgoo, a tasty stew, is popular Kentucky dish.

Let simmer, partially covered, for an hour. Take out the chicken and set it aside to cool slightly. To the still-simmering stock, add:

4 cups diced potatoes

In about 15 minutes, when the chicken is cool enough to handle, pull off and discard the skin and bones, cut the chicken into small pieces and put it back into the pot along with:

All of the reserved meat, shredded or finely chopped

4 cloves garlic, minced

6 cups fresh corn kernels, or three 10-ounce frozen packages

4 cups baby lima beans, or two 10-ounce frozen packages

4 cups okra, or two 10-ounce frozen packages, cut into 1-inch pieces

1-pound can tomato puree

4 cups tomatoes, skinned and chopped, or 2 pounds canned plum tomatoes, drained

Stir all these ingredients together while they simmer about 15 minutes, until the lima beans are cooked and the okra has thickened the stew. Now it's seasoning time, that crucial point at which you mold the character of your burgoo — and it should go without saying that you want your burgoo to have character. You will need the following:

3 tablespoons Worcestershire sauce

2 teaspoons salt to taste (optional)

Cayenne pepper to taste

Black pepper to taste

Tabasco sauce to taste

1 bunch curly parsley, stems removed and leaves minced

Add everything except the parsley. Burgoo is supposed to be on the fiery side, so be liberal with the Tabasco sauce, while taking into consideration the tolerance levels of your guests and yourself. Cook gently for about 10 more minutes, stirring to blend the flavors. Stir in the parsley and serve with biscuits.

THE HOT BROWN

The hot Brown, an open-faced sandwich made with turkey and cheese, is so named because, 1) it was created at the Brown Hotel in Louisville in the 1920s and, 2) it is served hot.

In later years, various chefs at the Brown Hotel introduced their own hot Brown variations. The recipe that follows is for the original hot Brown.

4 ounces butter

Flour to make a roux (about 6 tablespoons)

3 to 3 1/2 cups milk

1 beaten egg

Rebecca Ruth Candies in Frankfort is one of Central Kentucky's makers of bourbon balls.

6 tablespoons grated Parmesan cheese
1 ounce whipped cream (optional)
Salt and pepper to taste
Slices of roast turkey
8 to 12 slices of toast (may be trimmed)
Extra Parmesan for topping
2 strips cooked bacon

Melt butter and enough flour to make a reasonable roux (enough to absorb all of the butter). Add milk and Parmesan cheese. Add egg to thicken sauce, but do not allow to boil.

Remove from heat. Fold in whipped cream. Add salt and pepper to taste.

For each hot Brown, place two slices of toast on a metal or flameproof dish. Cover the toast with a liberal amount of turkey. Pour a generous amount of sauce over the turkey and toast. Sprinkle with additional Parmesan cheese.

Place entire dish under broiler until the sauce is speckled brown and bubbly.

Remove from broiler, cross two pieces of bacon on top and serve immediately. Makes 4 servings.

Subsequent versions of the hot Brown have included such variations as sliced chicken or country ham instead of turkey, Romano and American cheeses, sherry and tomato, to name a few. Today you can order some version of the hot Brown just about anywhere you go in Kentucky.

Beer Cheese

Beer cheese, which varies in spiciness according to the maker, is popular when served with crackers or veggies as a snack or an appetizer. Here's one of many versions.

1 pound aged Cheddar cheese
1 pound natural Swiss cheese
1 cup beer
1 teaspoon dry mustard
2 teaspoons Worcestershire sauce
Red pepper to taste, or a little chopped jalapeño pepper
Garlic to taste

Grate cheese; mix in a little garlic, pepper, dry mustard and Worcestershire sauce. Gradually beat in enough beer until mixture is well blended. Serve at room temperature. Makes about 1 quart.

Corn Pudding

Kentucky pioneers, influenced by the Indians, displayed endless creativity in finding new uses for corn, a staple in their gardens and on their tables. Today corn is consumed on the cob, off the cob, in cornbread and "Johnny cakes," as hominy and grits and in many other forms, including as grain for livestock and as a key ingredient in the mash that is fermented to make bourbon.

Corn pudding is a rich casserole that Harrodsburg's long-lived Beaumont Inn has down to an art form. Here's how Beaumont Inn makes its legendary corn pudding.

2 cups white whole kernel corn, or fresh corn cut off the cob
4 eggs
8 level tablespoons flour
1 quart milk
4 rounded teaspoons sugar
4 tablespoons butter, melted
1 teaspoon salt

Stir into the corn the flour, salt, sugar and butter. Beat the eggs well; put them into the milk, then stir into the corn and put into a pan or Pyrex dish. Bake at 450 degrees for 40-45 minutes.

Stir vigorously with long-pronged fork three times, about 10 minutes apart, while baking, disturbing the top as little as possible.

Lamb Fries

WARNING: If you're easily offended or grossed out, please skip this section.

Lamb fries are a Kentucky delicacy, but they're not for the squeamish. They're tasty enough — until you learn that they are actually, ahem, lamb testicles, sliced thin, breaded, fried and served with cream gravy. Despite the origin of the dish, sometimes called "Kentucky mountain oysters," it remains popular enough that a number of restaurants throughout the Bluegrass offer lamb fries on their menus. Everyone can't be ordering them for the first time. Some people are simply nuts about them.

We don't have a recipe for lamb fries to share with you, but you can get them at the Campbell House, Columbia's, the Springs Inn, The Coach House and many other fine dining establishments in the Bluegrass.

THE MINT JULEP

As a whole, Kentuckians and visitors alike are ambivalent about the mint julep, a Kentucky beverage tradition and the "official" drink of the Kentucky Derby. "It's a terrible thing to do to good bourbon" is a typical complaint. A joke recipe for the drink instructs the unsuspecting novice to — after preparing the needed mint syrup from mint leaves, sugar and water — throw the sticky-sweet mixture away and drink the bourbon straight, on the rocks.

Nevertheless, thousands of mint juleps are served each year on the first Saturday in May at Churchill Downs and at weekend Derby parties around the Bluegrass (my editor corrected me here and said that this concoction is served all over the country during Derby parties, as she had had "only a couple" at such a party in Richmond, Virginia). Again, there are many variations, the merits of which can be hotly debated. Anita Madden, the queen of Derby parties, uses this recipe:

1/3 cup sugar
2 tablespoons mint syrup (instructions follow)
1 1/2 to 2 ounces bourbon
Crushed ice
Fresh mint
Powdered sugar

To make mint syrup, bruise a "whole handful" of mint leaves and combine with 1/3 cup sugar dissolved in 1 cup water. Boil for 5 minutes and strain.

Pour mint syrup in sterling silver cup. Add bourbon. Mix.

Fill cup with crushed ice. Rub fresh mint around rim of cup.

For garnish, dip fresh mint sprig in powdered sugar and insert in ice.

CHOCOLATE-CHIP-AND-NUT PIE

Another popular Bluegrass dessert is the Derby Pie, a rich, chocolate-chip-and-nut-filled trademark of Louisville-based Kern's Kitchen. Rivaling this treat in popularity are its many generic versions, known by a variety of names including Kentucky pie, Pegasus pie, Keeneland pie and Run for the Roses pie. Kern's Kitchen does not take trademark infringement lightly.

This variation is known as Oldham pie.

1/4 cup margarine (not butter)
1 cup sugar
3 eggs
1/4 teaspoon salt
3/4 cup light corn syrup
1 teaspoon vanilla
1/2 cup chocolate chips
1/2 cup chopped black walnuts
2 tablespoons bourbon
1 unbaked pie shell

Cream margarine. Add sugar and beat with a mixer. Add eggs and syrup. Then add salt and vanilla. Mix well. Add chocolate chips, nuts and bourbon. Pour into pie crust. Bake at 350 degrees for 45 minutes. Serve warm with whipped cream.

BOURBON BALLS

Even teetotalers enjoy a bourbon ball or six during the holidays. Rebecca Gooch and Ruth Hanly, the founders of Rebecca-Ruth Candies in Frankfort, are credited with inventing bourbon balls. Variations are many, and the choice of bourbon is up to the cook. Here's one recipe.

1 cup pecans
4 tablespoons bourbon
1 stick butter or margarine
1 pound powdered sugar
1/2 box semisweet chocolate
1/2 rectangle paraffin

Combine pecans and bourbon and allow to sit for 3 hours. Cream butter and powdered sugar with mixer, adding pecan mixture. Roll in small balls and chill. Melt chocolate in double boiler, adding shaved paraffin. Dip balls into chocolate mixture, using fork. Put on waxed paper to dry.

Weisenberger Mills, in a scenic location at 2545 Weisenberger Road near Midway (254-5282), makes and sells 70 products including many types of flour and biscuit, pancake and hushpuppy mixes. The historic water-powered flour mill, the oldest commercial mill in Kentucky, is in its fifth generation of operation by the Weisenberger family. Please take note that, although you are welcome to visit the adjoining store, no tours are available.

Insiders' Tips

Inside
Distilleries and Breweries

*K*entucky is the top producer of bourbon whiskey, which was recognized by Congress in 1964 as a distinctly American product. That means no "bourbon whiskey" can be imported into this country. The potent brew is distinguished from other whiskeys in that the mash used to make it contains at least 51 percent corn.

Bourbon is distilled in a number of Kentucky towns, including Frankfort, Lawrenceburg, Louisville, Loretto and Bardstown, which is often referred to as "Bourbon Capital of the World." But it is no longer legally distilled or sold in the county that probably gave the beverage its name because Bourbon County is "dry." Conversely, you can buy bourbon in Christian County.

A number of Kentucky counties, including Scott, Bourbon and Jefferson, claim to be the site of the first bourbon whiskey production. Many people claim it was Georgetown minister Elijah Craig who first stumbled upon the secret, but there are several other people who might also have done it first. At this point in time, it seems unlikely that we will ever know the truth. So, to paraphrase a popular beer commercial, "Why ask who?"

Because whiskey served as currency in the time of the early set-tlers, converting the state's plentiful supply of corn into spirits made sound economic sense. As a result, distilleries have long played a major role in the Kentucky economy. As early as 1775 or 1776, whiskey was being distilled in the territory that is now Kentucky, and the Old Pepper Whiskey distillery was operating in Lexington in 1780.

The number of distilleries has declined significantly since the early 19th century, when as many as 2,200 were producing whiskey in the state. Even today, however, Kentucky continues to be the nation's largest producer of distilled spirits, including not only whiskey but also vodka, gin, brandy and assorted liqueurs. According to some estimates, the state produces 70 percent of the world's distilled spirits.

In addition to being the "bourbon capital of the world," Bardstown also is home to:

THE OSCAR GETZ MUSEUM OF WHISKEY HISTORY
114 North Fifth Street, Bardstown   *(502) 348-2999*

This museum contains a collection of whiskey artifacts and documents, including Abraham Lincoln's liquor license for a tavern he operated in Illinois in 1833. You can also

Photo: Lexington Herald-Leader

Shirley Ruley dips bottles of Maker's Mark bourbon into a vat of "Wildcat Blue" wax. The bottles are usually dipped into trademark red wax, but the blue wax was used during the '93 SEC tournament for bottles that later became collector's items.

You can't buy bourbon in Bourbon County, but you can buy liquor in Christian County.

see an authentic moonshine still, numerous antique bottles and jugs and memorabilia relating to Carrie Nation, the Kentucky-born woman who traveled throughout the country with a hatchet in her bid to eliminate the evils of alcohol. The whiskey museum is housed, along with the Bardstown Historical Museum, in historic Spalding Hall. Hours are 9 AM to 5 PM Monday through Saturday and 1 PM to 5 PM Sunday from May 1 through October 31. From November 1 to April 30, the museum is open from 10 AM to 4 PM Tuesday through Saturday and 1 PM to 4 PM Sunday. Admission is free.

Distilleries

Here are just a few area distilleries where you can get a glimpse into the making of one of the state's most famous products. Even for people who don't enjoy whiskey, these tours provide a fascinating look into an integral facet of Kentucky's history and its economy.

ANCIENT AGE DISTILLERY
Wilkinson Boulevard,
Frankfort   (502) 223-7641
Bourbon production at this facility began as early as 1869. Free tours are offered on the hour from 9 AM to 3 PM Monday through Friday year round. You'll see a video and walk through parts of five buildings,

including bottling, warehouse and the Blanton building where the company's award-winning premium Blanton brand is produced.

JIM BEAM DISTILLERY
Clermont, near Bardstown   (502) 543-9877
Free tours are offered seven days a week at Jim Beam's American Outpost adjacent to the distillery. Although the distillery itself is not open for tours, you can see a 10-minute film on how bourbon is made and take a short walking tour that includes what is said to be the oldest moonshine still in the country. Hours are 9 AM to 4:30 PM Monday through Saturday and 1 PM to 4 PM Sunday. To get to Clermont, take the Bluegrass Parkway to the first Bardstown exit, get on Ky. 245 and follow it about 18 miles to the distillery.

HEAVEN HILL DISTILLERIES
Bardstown
Tours: Call Bardstown/Nelson County Chamber of Commerce   (502) 348-4877
Heaven Hill, which bills itself as "America's largest family-owned distillery," produces Evan Williams bourbon whiskey as well as other distilled spirits. The free tours cover the entire bottling process, and visitors can take home a souvenir barrel bung (the cork or stopper in the barrel) soaked in bourbon. Take the Bluegrass Parkway to the first Bardstown exit and then take Ky. 49 to Heaven Hill.

MAKER'S MARK DISTILLERY

Loretto   (502) 865-2099

Free tours are offered hourly from 10:30 AM to 3:30 PM Monday through Saturday in March through December and Monday through Friday during January and February. The tour includes the still house, where the smooth bourbon is made; the bottling house, which includes the wax-dipping operation; and the warehouse. To get to the distillery from Lexington, take the Bluegrass Parkway to the first Springfield exit and go left toward Springfield. At Springfield, take a right onto U.S. 150, go for about 1 mile, then turn left onto Ky. 152. Go about 11 miles until the road becomes Ky. 49, and continue or about a mile into Loretto. There 49 runs into 52, which you take east for about 2 1/2 miles. Turn left on Burks Spring road, which will take you to Maker's Mark.

WILD TURKEY DISTILLERY

Lawrenceburg   (502) 839-4544

Free tours of the plant, which produces 8-year-old, 101-proof Wild Turkey bourbon, are conducted Monday through Friday at 9 AM, 10:30 AM, 12:30 PM and 2:30 PM. Groups of 20 or more should make reservations. To get there from Lexington, take U.S. 60 west to Versailles, then get on U.S. 62 west and follow the signs.

Breweries

Kentucky's claim to drinking fame is bourbon, not beer. But that could be changing, as there appears to be a trend toward microbreweries that brew small quantities of pre-mium beer on the premises and serve them along with food and sometimes entertainment.

OLDENBERG BREWERY

Interstate 75 at Buttermilk Pike,
Fort Mitchell   1-341-2804

Oldenberg's distinctive beers are bottled and sold in a growing number of locations around the country. Daily tours include the microbrewery; the American Museum of Brewing History & Arts, with more than 500,000 bits of brewing beer memorabilia; and a tasting of Oldenberg products. The complex also includes a seasonal outdoor beer garden and a country-western dance hall. To get there, take I-75 north to Exit 186, 5 miles south of Cincinnati.

SILO BREW PUB

630 Barret Avenue
Louisville   (502) 589-2739

Silo serves a variety of freshly brewed beers, some of which are available with unique added flavorings such as raspberry, in a large complex that also includes a restaurant and offers live entertainment.

BLUEGRASS BREWING COMPANY

3929 Shelbyville Road,
Louisville   (502) 899-7070

Bluegrass Brewing, Kentucky's newest microbrewery at this writing, makes five varieties of German-style draft beer, which are served fresh on the premises. The restaurant also serves a range of appetizers and entrees.

Photo: Lexington Herald-Leader

Some of Lexington's nightspots offer two-step and other dance classes.

Inside
Nightlife

*T*hey roll up the sidewalks at 1 AM, which means you'll probably beat the cows home. But, until you find out where those blasted cows are partying, you'll have to deal with the early closing times. In the meantime, there's plenty of variety on Lexington's nightlife scene to keep you groovin' past midnight.

As far as bars are concerned, there are plenty of good ones in Lexington, many of which are located in restaurants. What we have done in this chapter is list some of the highlights, those establishments that offer something noteworthy in the way of entertainment and/or ambiance. There are also establishments that provide entertainment and activities for people who aren't into the "bar scene." We think there's something for everybody here, regardless of musical preference, age or social status.

You can dance or simply listen to music served up by live bands or by disc jockeys. Play pool in a bar or in an alcohol-free pool-only atmosphere. Play bingo while benefiting a local charity. See a first-run blockbuster movie or an avant-garde foreign film.

Keep in mind that, in most cases, you must be 21 years of age to gain admittance to Lexington's night-

clubs. There are some exceptions. The Wrocklage, for example, occasionally has all-ages shows on Sunday night when no alcohol is served. But if you're planning to use a fake ID, take our advice and don't do it. Local bartenders and bouncers have become increasingly sophisticated in their ability to detect frauds, and you could find yourself with a major hassle to contend with. Similarly, you should know that drunken driving is taken very seriously by the Lexington police department and its special Traffic Alcohol Patrol, which monitors the streets in a fleet of unmarked Ford Crown Victorias.

Concerts and Shows

For lovers of music and culture, living in Lexington means there's always some momentous event going on within easy driving distance. When Lexington doesn't have much live entertainment, there's usually something on in Louisville or Cincinnati. Most of the major rock and country tours hit one of these three cities, as do Broadway touring productions and other shows.

Tickets to many area concerts can be ordered by calling TicketMaster at 281-6644, a local number.

Keep in mind that a fair number of national acts also play smaller places like The Wrocklage in Lexington, which you'll find below under bars/nightclubs/restaurants.

RUPP ARENA

430 West Vine	233-4567
Ticket information	233-3566
Charg-A-Tick	233-3535

If there's a more popular year-round public place in the Bluegrass, somebody's gonna have to tell us about it. First, of course, you have Kentucky Wildcat basketball, which packs the 23,000-seat arena roughly 15 times a year. Then you have an impressive schedule of concerts and shows featuring some of the biggest names in the biz. Highlights of the last couple of years, for example, have included two rapidly sold-out Garth Brooks concerts on successive nights, Rod Stewart, Clint Black with Wynonna, Metallica, Bruce Springsteen and a double bill featuring Vince Gill and Mary-Chapin Carpenter.

BOGART'S

2621 Vine Street,	(513) 872-8801
Cincinnati after 11 AM	
Concert line recording	(513) 281-8400
TicketMaster	281-6644

This comfortable 1,300-seat venue near the University of Cincinnati features a wide range of artists who, for assorted reasons, don't play arenas. Some of them are up-and-coming stars, some are veterans whose arena days are behind them, still others are bands with cult followings or "alternative" heavy-weights. Recently, for example, you could have caught such shows as B.B. King, Warren Zevon, Los Lobos, Smashing Pumpkins, The Lemonheads and De La Soul. If someone you like is playing Bogart's, it's well worth the drive from Lexington.

RIVERBEND MUSIC CENTER

6295 Kellogg Avenue,	
Cincinnati	(513) 232-6220

Riverbend is nestled, appropriately enough, in a bend in the Ohio River. Concertgoers can choose covered pavilion seats or save a few bucks and sit farther away from the stage on the sloping lawn. This highly popular place for summer concerts covers all the bases, from pop, rock and country to blues, jazz, Big Band and even comedy. Jimmy Buffett played five sold-out shows in 1993. Other hot tickets were the Steely Dan reunion tour, Sting, Van Halen, Bette Midler and Billy Ray Cyrus.

TIMBERWOLF AMPHITHEATRE

Paramount's Kings Island	
Kings Mills, Ohio	
Interstate 71	(513) 573-5700

During the summer, TimberWolf at Kings Island, located 24 miles north of Cincinnati, offers concerts under the stars by nationally known pop, rock and country acts. The Moody Blues, the Beach Boys, James Taylor and Sharon Lois & Bram all usually make TimberWolf a stop on their summer tours. If you really want to get your money's worth, buy a combination ticket that lets you spend the day at the amusement park and then catch the show at night.

KENTUCKY CENTER FOR THE ARTS
5 Riverfront Plaza, Louisville (502) 562-0100
For tickets   (502) 584-7777

The beautiful Kentucky Center for the Arts building, on Main Street between Fifth and Sixth streets, offers a variety of cultural opportunities. With 2,479-seat Whitney Hall; Bomhard Theater, which seats 622; and the flexible MeX black-box theater, which can seat up to 139, the center has something for everyone. Five resident groups — Stage One, the Broadway Series, the Louisville Ballet, the Louisville Orchestra and the Kentucky Opera — present several programs apiece each year. The center's award-winning "Lonesome Pine Specials" series, which airs on Kentucky Educational Television and on other public TV stations around the country, has featured critically acclaimed folk, blues, jazz and "world music" artists from around the globe.

RIVERFRONT COLISEUM
Cincinnati   (513) 241-1818

FREEDOM HALL
Louisville   (502) 367-5001

LOUISVILLE GARDENS
Louisville   (502) 587-3800
Charge tickets by phone   (502) 584-7777

Those arena acts that don't hit Rupp Arena on a given tour will very likely be playing one of these venues.

NORTON CENTER FOR THE ARTS
Centre College, Danville   1-236-4692

This often-overlooked treasure, in a town with a population of 12,500 about a half-hour from Lexington, offers a wealth of big-city culture. Ballet. Opera. Tony Award-winning Broadway musicals and plays. Orchestra concerts. Classical soloists. Jazz. A classic-film series. The Norton Center's consistently top-notch offerings are not surprising when you consider Centre College's nationally acknowledged academic reputation and the fact that the school has produced vice presidents, U.S. Supreme Court justices and many other leaders in all walks of life.

To keep updated on what's happening on the rock 'n' roll concert scene in the area, call WKQQ's concert line, a recording, at 259-3398. For country info, call WVLK's recorded line at 253-5993.

Bars/Nightclubs/ Restaurants/Etc.

A1A SANDBAR & GRILLE
2660 Wilhite Drive   276-4513

By the time you read this, A1A might be in a new location. The Wilhite site was bought by Bob Evans, which planned to use it as a Mexican restaurant. A1A, which is popular with young professional singles of

Country music fans will enjoy Austin City Saloon, where John Michael Montgomery got his start.

Insiders' Tips

both sexes, offers two separate clubs under one roof. One side is a Florida-theme sports bar. An outdoor deck bar, open from April to October, has two volleyball courts that are host to league play. Inside you can watch sports on big-screen TV or play interactive trivia, pool or darts. On Thursday through Saturday night, Robbie and Joel Parker play acoustic guitar music by the likes of Jimmy Buffett, who is phenomenally popular in these parts. The other side of A1A is a nightclub with a disc jockey playing popular music; on Sunday night country line dance lessons are offered. The nightclub has a cover charge; the sports bar doesn't.

ALFALFA RESTAURANT
557 South Limestone Street   253-0014

Low-key acoustic music ranging from folk, pop and jazz to Appalachian bluegrass and New Age is performed in an intimate, bohemian coffeehouse atmosphere. Performances are offered from 8 PM to 10 PM Friday and Saturday night.

AUSTIN CITY SALOON
2350 Woodhill Shopping Center   266-6891

Country music fans who appreciate history-in-the-making will appreciate the fact that this is where rising star John Michael Montgomery got his start. To show his appreciation, he filmed his video, "Beer and Bones," here. Montgomery has moved on to the big time, but Austin City Saloon continues its long tradition as one of the top places in Lexington to catch local country bands.

THE BAR
224 East Main Street   255-1551

The Bar, once known as Johnny Angel's, is a long-lived downtown nightclub that serves a primarily gay clientele. Patrons dance to industrial and dance music played by a disc jockey in a discotheque atmosphere, and weekly shows by female impersonators are featured.

BLUE MOON OLDIES SALOON
815 Euclid Avenue   268-0001

Dance cheek to cheek with your baby while a DJ spins hits from the '50s, '60s and '70s at this popular Chevy Chase nightclub that has had several previous incarnations. If you dig dancing to the original versions of the oldies, this is the place to be in Lexington.

THE CAMPBELL HOUSE
1375 Harrodsburg Road   255-4281

The Campbell House nightlife is primarily aimed at an older crowd, but anyone is welcome. Pianist Claire Vance entertains from 7 PM to 9 PM Monday through Saturday in the dining room. In the Gallery Lounge, karaoke lets you be the singer from 7 PM to 9 PM Tuesday through Friday, followed by a variety band such as National Velvet until closing.

CHEAPSIDE BAR & GRILL
131 Cheapside   254-0046

Blues, jazz and zydeco, as well as rock, are the musical cornerstones of this immensely popular bar and restaurant in the heart of downtown. It can sometimes be a yuppie haven, but when the music is hot — as it generally is — the clientele is diverse and sometimes sweaty, espe-

For a nice, romantic, cheap (OK, *free*) date, it's hard to beat a nighttime stroll around Triangle Park. Sit for a spell and gaze at the well-lighted fountains of water cascading down a series of steps.

cially those who crowd into the tiny dancing area in front of the band. The bar section is a dark, loud, smoky joint and packed on weekends, literally standing room only — you'll have to be lucky or quick to snag a table. During the summer, the action spills out onto a brick patio where you can have a conversation without screaming. Cheapside also is known for its inventive Southwestern-tinged menu. Simultaneously hip and down-to-earth.

CHUCK'S JAZZ CAFE
153 Patchen Drive   268-2250

Chuck's Jazz Cafe, formerly Laffitte's Rendezvous, features live jazz along with French and Cajun food nightly in a New Orleans-style setting. The dining room, which is separate from the narrow bar, is on a lower level and provides an intimate atmosphere for enjoying some cool jazz.

CIRCLE H
9079 Old Richmond Road,
Clays Ferry   263-9944

Country stars such as Keith Whitley and Alan Jackson, in town for concerts, have sat in with the band at the Circle H. But even without celebrity cameos, this bar on the Kentucky River at Clays Ferry would be a hot place for country music. Owner Earl Watkins and his County

Line band play Thursday through Saturday. The joint is closed the rest of the week because, as Watkins says, "I like my four-day weekends."

COMEDY ON BROADWAY
144 North Broadway   254-5653

Its ads proclaim that it was "voted one of the top five comedy nightclubs in North America" by New York's Professional Comedians Association. Up-and-coming funnymen and -women are featured, as well as local talent such as Alex Bard. The atmosphere is as intimate and laugh-friendly as anything you'll see on cable television, with a brick wall behind the stage and tables arranged in a circular pattern around the stage. A warning: If you're easily embarrassed, don't sit near the stage, as some comedians tend to single out individuals for ridicule. And would-be hecklers take heed: No matter how witty you might think you are, it's hard to win a verbal battle when the other guy has a microphone and you don't. During the week, Comedy on Broadway offers one show nightly. There are two shows Friday night and three Saturday night.

COMMON GROUNDS COFFEE HOUSE
343 East High Street   233-9761

Acoustic music, which starts about 9 every Monday night, is in the coffeehouse tradition with a variety that runs from folk to Celtic to New Age. Every other Monday night is open microphone from 7 PM to 9 PM, followed by the regular entertainment.

CONTINENTAL INN
801 New Circle Road NE   299-5281

The Revere Lounge features Top 40 and variety dance bands for a mixed crowd. Downstairs at the Someplace Else lounge, a DJ spins the hits for a slightly younger crowd. Blackjack tables, with play money, are open for action beginning at 8 PM nightly.

GAZEBO LOUNGE
In French Quarter Suites Hotel
2601 Richmond Road   268-0060

Top off your French or Creole dinner at Tippedore's with a visit to the Gazebo Lounge, which features jazz by area musicians. The courtyard-like atmosphere is casual, with a fountain, trees, a gazebo bar and wrought-iron tables and chairs sprinkled around the band area. Pianist Keith McCutchen and local sax legend Duke Madison are among the musicians who frequently play here.

HEMMINGWAYS
3101 Clays Mill Road   223-5751

Hemmingways, in Stonewall Shopping Center in south Lexington, features live bands on Friday and Saturday night. The musical style varies, as does the clientele.

JDI (JEFFERSON DAVIS INN)
102 West High Street   233-9107

JDI is housed in a historic South Hill building where the future president of the Confederacy lived while attending Transylvania University in 1823-24. The close-quartered dining and entertainment area, in a level several steps below the bar, features a variety of Lexington's best-known blues, hard rock and "alternative" bands.

THE CAFE JOSEPH-BETH
The Mall at Lexington Green   273-2911,
In cafe   271-0062

Not that you needed any additional reasons to visit Joseph-Beth Booksellers, but here is yet another: live music. Acoustic performances on such instruments as piano, harp, dulcimer and fiddle draw a diverse crowd on Friday and Saturday nights from 7 PM to 9:30 PM. Music is played in a cozy, fireplace setting near the popular cafe, which serves espresso, cappuccino, soups, salads, sandwiches and desserts. Looking for a place to take the whole family at night? The kids can browse or read in the expanded children's section while everyone enjoys the music. On the other hand, The Cafe Joseph-Beth is also a popular spot for literate singles who spurn the bar scene and want to chat over a cup of espresso and a pastry.

LYNAGH'S BLUES EMPORIUM & MUSIC CLUB

University Plaza Shopping Center   255-6614

Just two doors down from the great hamburgers at Lynagh's Irish Pub & Grill, you can find some of the top bands in town performing. Originally opened as a blues venue, Lynagh's gradually began expanding its repertoire to include a wider range of music, from funk-metal to rock 'n' roll to country. The Metropolitan Blues All-Stars are regulars here, as are the hot sounds of 10-Foot Pole. Lynagh's has also featured occasional national acts such as Texas singer-songwriter Jimmie Dale Gilmore.

NEW MORNING COFFEE HOUSE

504 Euclid Avenue   233-1190

Yes, it's a coffee house, but it's probably a lot more diversified than you might think. In addition to folk music, which you'd expect, you can also hear other types of music like reggae and rap being performed for a somewhat bohemian clientele.

THE SPRINGS INN

2020 Harrodsburg Road   277-5751

The Springtide Lounge here is a happening place for anyone who appreciates a variety of danceable music spanning from the Big Band era to rock 'n' roll oldies to modern country. Live music Wednesday through Saturday features the house band, the Phil Gunning Group, and occasionally other local musicians. The clientele ranges from about 35 on up. If you're younger, this is the type of place you might take your parents dancing for a special occasion.

STAR OF LEXINGTON CRUISE BOAT

9070 Old Richmond Road,
Clays Ferry   263-7827

The *Star of Lexington*, a 500-passenger riverboat, offers two-hour dinner and dance cruises on the Kentucky River. Cruises may not be available every night if a sufficient number of reservations have not been made. The dinner cruise, from 7 PM to 9 PM, features live entertainment and cash bar; musical styles vary from night to night. Cost is about $30 a person. Also available on Friday and Saturday night is a dance-only cruise with DJ and cash bar for $7.95 a person. The *Star of Lexington* contains two fully enclosed decks and one open deck on the top level.

SUNDANCE, THE BREWERY

(Formerly Breeding's)
509 West Main Street   255-2822

The line-dance phenomenon sparked the 1993 transformation of Breeding's, a Lexington live-music tradition, into this "country disco." You'll find two lighted dance floors, video screens and lots of people in cowboy hats and boots. Free line-dance lessons are offered from 8 PM to 9:30 PM Tuesday through Friday and 8 PM to 9 PM Saturday. Upstairs at the Brewery, things remain pretty much the same on the weekends, with Larry Redmon playing Jimmy Buffett covers and country crowd-pleasers to an appreciative audience.

TODD'S DINING AND DIVERSIONS

1938 Stanton Way   259-1311

Todd's, in the Ramada Hotel off

Newtown Pike, has developed a following of people who like to come for dinner and stay for mingling and dancing. A free happy hour buffet is served from 5 PM to 8:30 PM, with offerings varying nightly: One night it might be Mexican and another night ribs or steamship round of beef. After 9, when a DJ starts spinning Top 40 dance hits for the largely single adult crowd, there is a $3 cover charge.

TWO KEYS TAVERN

333 South Limestone Street   254-5000

"The Keys," a popular college hangout since it opened in the 1920s, is at the corner of the University of Kentucky campus. Original and cover bands play primarily college-oriented rock Wednesday through Saturday night. On Tuesday night, you can catch national comedians during WKQQ's Laugh Track Live. Two Keys' bar menu includes club sandwiches, Reubens, burgers, soups and salads.

UNDER MAIN RESTAURANT & BAR

269 West Main Street   255-3119

Under Main is Lexington's newest blues joint, albeit an upscale one. The basement location of this tavern formerly known as Mainstreets — combined with touches like carpet, mirrored columns, murals and a lot of glass — adds to its big-city charm. There's live entertainment Wednesday through Saturday nights, featuring such reliable blues practitioners as Lexington's own Metro Blues All-Stars and Louisville's Curtis and the Kicks. The dinner menu, which includes a variety of appetizers, sandwiches and entrees, is served until late.

THE VIRTUAL

117 South Upper Street   281-4142
                              231-1529

Lexington's only all-ages club is open Friday and Saturday nights from 10:30 PM to 4 AM. Disc jockeys play primarily industrial and other types of modern music in an atmosphere best described as "underground." Although Virtual's clientele is underage college students and other people too young to get into nightclubs, anyone can come and dance into the wee hours. No alcohol is served.

THE WROCKLAGE

361 West Short Street   231-7655

The Wrocklage, formerly The Bottom Line, is an old downtown dive that serves as Lexington's primary "alternative" music haven. Don't let the alternative label scare you, though, because such labels are usually meaningless. This is just an alternative to the same old music you hear on your tightly programmed radio stations of whatever format. The clientele can range from preppies in button-down shirts to grungy skateboarder types and black-lipsticked "gloom" rockers. There are a few tables, but unless you get there early, you'll probably end up standing when the band hits the stage. It's hard to dance when sitting at a table, anyway. In addition to some of the Lexington area's hottest young bands — a diverse bunch that ranges from the furious metal-tinged funk of 10-Foot Pole to the melodic pop of Candy Says to the countryfied sounds of The Yonders — The Wrocklage in recent years has also featured such national acts

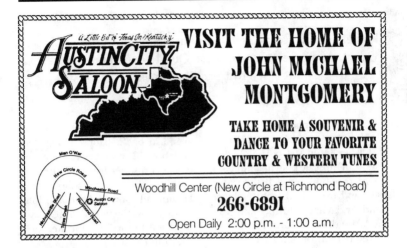
as The Replacements, Jason and the Scorchers, Uncle Tupelo and The Cactus Brothers. All-ages shows are often held on Sunday night. By the way, check out the big mural on the wall.

Karaoke

If you're repulsed by the idea of sitting in a bar and listening to people who, after a drink or two, think they're the next Sinatra, Garth Brooks or Whitney Houston, then you're probably not a good karaoke candidate. On the other hand, if you're convinced that you could hit the big time with a decent break or two, or if you just want to let your hair down and have a little fun, then give it a shot. Hey, don't knock it until you've tried it! Just pick a song, grab the microphone and sing along to the lyrics displayed on the video screen. You probably won't be seen by a talent scout, but this isn't "The Gong Show," either, so you'll at least get to finish your song.

For better or worse, karaoke seems to be a growing craze. In Lexington you can do the karaoke thing at several places, depending on the night. They include:

THE CAMPBELL HOUSE
1375 Harrodsburg Road   255-4281

CHINOE PUB
Chinoe Village Shopping Center   269-9557

SPIRITS LOUNGE IN THE RADISSON
369 West Vine Street   231-9000

Pool and Billiards

BLUEGRASS BILLIARDS
South Limestone and Pine streets

Toby Kavanaugh's poolroom features pool only, no bar. If you're lucky, maybe you can get a few pointers from the man who taught Walter Tevis, the late author of *The Hustler* and *The Color of Money*, how to play the game. (See the oral history on Kavanaugh at the end of this chapter.)

Insiders' Tips

Insiders let off steam by engaging in high-tech warfare at Laser Quest. And on weekends, Laser Quest is open until midnight. (See Kid Stuff for details.)

YESTERDAYS

410 West Vine Street   231-8889

Owner Karen McCool bills Yesterdays as an "upscale pool hall" for baby boomers of both sexes. It also serves food and drink and features blues bands Friday and Saturday night. Rising Atlanta blues guitarist Tinsley Ellis played here in December 1993.

THE RACK CLUB

235 Woodhill Drive   266-9942

The Rack Club, also a restaurant and bar, features blues, rock and country bands Wednesday through Sunday night.

SHOOTERS BAR & GRILL

723 Lane Allen Road   278-0815

Shooters has just a few tables but an inviting pool atmosphere. It also has great food.

ALL STAR BILLIARDS

987 Winchester Road   252-9591

STEEPLETON BILLIARD CENTER

1431 Leestown Road   252-9135

BUSTER'S

164 West Main   231-5076

Cinemas

KENTUCKY THEATRE

214 East Main Street   231-6997

This beloved downtown landmark is *the* place to go for foreign, offbeat and classic films. All movies are $3.75, or $2.50 for senior citizens and those 12 and younger. An acoustic concert series featuring the likes of Arlo Guthrie, Leon Redbone, John Hammond, Don McLean and John Sebastian, was instituted in 1993. (See the "oral history" on the Kentucky after this chapter.)

TURFLAND CINEMAS

2025 Turfland Mall   277-2825

These cinemas show second-run movies for $1.

CROSSROADS CINEMAS

119 East Reynolds Road   277-2825

These cinemas also show second-run movies for $1.

CINEMARK THEATRES

Lexington Green 8, Nicholasville and New Circle roads   271-2070
Man o' War 8, Man o' War Boulevard and Richmond Road   266-4645
Richmond Mall 8, Eastern By-Pass, Richmond   1-623-8215

LOEWS THEATRES

South Park, 3220 Nicholasville Road   272-6611
North Park, 500 New Circle Road   233-4420
Fayette Mall, Nicholasville and New Circle roads   272-6662
Lexington Mall, 2361 Richmond Road   269-4626

FRANKLIN SQUARE CINEMAS 6

Frankfort   (502) 875-9000

Bingo

BLUEGRASS BINGO CENTER
3340 Holwyn Road   *223-9467*

To quote Clint Eastwood, sometimes you've got to ask yourself: Do I feel lucky? If so, you might want to head over to the Bluegrass Bingo Center, off Clays Mill Road in south Lexington. And even if you don't feel lucky, you'll be helping a good cause. Games are sponsored by a variety of nonprofit organizations, which reap the benefits. There is play every night, with doors opening at 6 PM, "early bird" games at 7 and main events starting at 7:30. On Sunday afternoon, door open at 1 and main events begin at 2:30. And on Wednesday mornings, doors open at 10, early birds are at 11 and main events at 11:30 AM. The minimum cost for the night sessions is $20 for 12 "faces" for 17 games. Winning amounts vary from night to night.

Shocking Revelations

Psst! It's only fair to mention that Lexington does have several establishments at which young — and, in some cases, not so young — women shed a good portion of their clothing. If you're inclined to visit this sort of place, you'll find your way there one way or another. This author, unfortunately, can provide no additional information lest he arouse the suspicions and/or wrath of his generally understanding wife. In the service of equal rights, we must also reveal that some Lexington nightclubs are also host occasionally to traveling bands of Tarzan-like young men who apparently exhibit brazen disregard for local dress codes. Watch your newspaper for details.

Toby Kavanaugh:
"A profitably misspent youth"

About any day of the week after 4 PM or so, if you go to Bluegrass Billiards at the edge of the University of Kentucky campus, you can find Toby Kavanaugh, the one to whom Walter Tevis dedicated his 1984 novel, *The Color of Money*, which like its predecessor, *The Hustler*, was made into a hit movie. "To Toby Kavanaugh," the dedication reads, "who taught me how to shoot pool."

Bluegrass Billiards, which Kavanaugh owns and operates, is about what you'd expect . And, then again, it isn't. It's well lighted, smoky when it's crowded and sometimes a bit loud with laughter and the thwack of balls hitting. There's a Coke machine, but no alcohol or food is sold. With the exception of a homeless woman who sits in a metal chair near the front of

Toby Kavanaugh

the room — she's a regular when it's cold outside — people come here for one reason.

The players are a fairly diverse mix: college kids and middle-aged men, blacks and whites and Hispanics, a couple of grandmotherly types who admit they haven't played in years. There's a former cop who comes in about every night. There's Joe, a heavyset and jovially outspoken computer expert who was working at NASA when the Challenger blew up and who now makes his own pool cues. Many of them call Toby, who's about 65, by his first name.

The poolroom owner is genial but doesn't tolerate misbehavior. He also doesn't hesitate to dispense unsolicited advice to players he thinks are in need of it. The smiling, freckle-faced kid at the front table is in need of it. Several times in about a one-hour span Kavanaugh calmly calls out pointers:

• "Pool has nothing to do with hitting the ball hard. It has to do with making it go where you want it to go."

• "Forbidden shot. You've got a little ways to go before you get into that — especially on my new cloth on my front table. To learn how to play well, you've got to learn how to make the easy shots."

At one point, a little old lady asks about the price. When Kavanaugh tells it's $1.50 an hour for men and half price for women, the visiting writer makes a joking comment about equal rights. Kavanaugh has heard it before.

"I had one girl in here who was a feminist or something. When I charged her half price, she was insulted. She said, 'Listen, our day is coming . . .' and she started all this soapbox stuff. And I said, 'You can pay full price if you want to.' My reason for doing it is that there are a lot of potential customers who don't feel like they should be playing pool. When I started this, a lot of girls were hesitant to come in here and play, and I figured this would encourage them. It's not philanthropy; it's good business. Where the girls are, that's where the guys are going to be. So it's worked out. I've got a bunch of girls who play, and some of them have gotten pretty good."

Toby Kavanaugh loves the game and the business. He also loves to talk.

"I was born about a hundred yards from here, right across the street at Good Samaritan Hospital. So I've come a long ways. I've always lived right here in Lexington. I lived on Ashland Avenue for about 50 years. My dad was a doctor, and he was one of the founders of the old Lexington Clinic. It was the first clinic in Kentucky, I think, where all the doctors got together and divided up the fees and had one building where you could get lab work and everything done. It was sort of a new idea way back about 1920. That's when he met my mother, and they were married.

"My grandmother built that home out on Ashland Avenue. People thought she was crazy — why'd she want to move way out there in the country? It was the only paved street from Limestone on up at that time. It was the only street in Ashland Park that was paved back in 1915. I lived there in my grandmother's home most of my life until after she passed away and we sold it. I moved out on Versailles Road by Calumet Farm, a quiet subdivision. I miss that old home on Ashland, though. It was sort of palatial. Stucco with big white columns out front. It was designed by a French architect from Cincinnati named DeJardin or something; it was a right fancy home for that time. They had a fire once, and when they remodeled it, the guy said it would take about $750,000 to build a home like it using the same materials. I think it cost about $15,000 to build in 1915, back when you could buy a beer for a nickel.

"I went to the public schools here, Ashland and Morton. Went to Henry Clay for a while, then went away to school for a couple of years up in Pennsylvania, then came back to UK. I met Walter Tevis in the sixth grade at Ashland Elementary School; he'd just moved here from California. We were sort of brother intellectuals. There were a lot of rednecks in school, and we sort of took a liking to one another because we thought the same way. Tevis was a pretty smart boy. Everybody sort of praised him for his writing, but he was a pretty good photographer. And he was also a pretty good woodworker. He did a little amateur painting, and he was a pretty good mechanic, fixing kitchen gadgets and things like that. He was what you might call a junior Renaissance man.

"We met in sixth grade and went through school there. I went to Morton Junior High School for three years, and then I went to Henry Clay with him for one year. Then he went in the Navy for a couple of years, and I went away to school. When he got out of the service, I'd been at UK for a year, and he had about three-and-a-half years on that old G.I. Bill. So he went to school, and when he first started he stayed over at our house, then he got a place down in his aunt's basement. That's when he started writing *The Hustler,* on a little typewriter down under the furnace. Typical starving artist.

"We were pretty close buddies. I was best man at his wedding. He was teaching school over in Carlisle, Kentucky, and he met his wife, who was teaching home ec over there. He taught at two or three little schools around here. I went to visit them in Irvine and stayed over with them. He had his son by then. He taught high school for three or four years, off and on, before he got to the point where he could make some money writing.

He got a little confidence when he sold a couple of short stories to *The Saturday Evening Post* and *Collier's*.

"The movie *The Hustler* was first a short story in *Esquire,* and he expanded it into a novel, and then they made it into a movie. He got $25,000 for the movie rights, which was big money to him. He didn't know they were going to cast Paul Newman and Jackie Gleason. It turned out to be a big hit movie. He felt like he'd done pretty well. I don't think he got but about $10,000 for the hardback. He made some more out of the paperback after the movie came out.

"Walter didn't have much money for a long time. His dad worked at Bluegrass Ordnance in Richmond. He went to Model High School over there for a little while. They never did have anything fancy. He liked to dress well, and he never could do it. I know later on, when he finally made some money, he got his cashmere sweaters and nice suits and everything. It's kind of ironic: When he started making his big money, it wasn't long after that that he passed away.

"He was in his mid-50s. He was a heavy smoker, sort of a nervous, high-strung person. I assume it was lung cancer, although when he was young, he had problems. He had rheumatic fever or something. When he was young in San Francisco, he was in the hospital about a year, and he did a lot of reading there, played a lot of chess, and that kind of developed his intellect.

"He wrote one book that was something like *The Hustler* except it was about chess. It was a young girl prodigy, and he had her starting out in sort of an orphanage type of hospital, which he'd been in and didn't like. He had feelings that his family had rejected him because they'd put him in a hospital and he was confined there for that time. So he wrote a story. A lot of his stuff was slightly autobiographical. He picked people he knew and invented roles.

"He wrote some science fiction. We were big on science fiction. Me and my younger brother got him started on science fiction. We read all those old pulp magazines when we were kids, and when he started hanging around the house, he started reading them. And he ended up writing some pretty good science fiction. He wrote one called *Mockingbird.* They never have made a movie out of it. His second wife has all the rights and everything.

"Walter was inducted into the Billiard Hall of Fame, which is really exclusive. Up to his time, it had only been pool players — Willie Mosconi and Willie Hoppe and a few people like that. But they inducted him for his influence; you know, he changed the face of pool. In the flyleaf of my copy of *The Hustler,* he wrote, 'Many thanks for a profitably misspent youth.' And I wrote him back later, 'Many thanks for adding to my profitable pool business.' It helped. Of course, it helped everybody, because it made pool more nationally acceptable. After the movie of *The Color of Money* came out, I noticed all these kids in here playing, spinning cue sticks with their fingers, emulating Tom Cruise. Monkey see, monkey do. So it did help me.

"I'd help Walter a lot. Our family was pretty well off, and Walter didn't have anything, and I sploshed him meals and things once in a while. When he was living with his aunt down in that basement, he was eating vegetables at the cafeteria over here. The G.I. Bill was something like $120 a month. He graduated in three-and-a-half years because that's when it ran out. But then he came back and got his master's. Luckily, he took a class from A.B. Guthrie on creative writing. Guthrie was impressed with his work and got him this agent up in New York. Walter sent him stuff, and he sent him some advice back, and he sold his things to *Esquire* and these places and got him going. He and Guthrie were instrumental in getting Tevis' writing career started.

"Tevis' teachers all knew he had talent, but he was kind of lazy. He and I liked to slip off and go down to the Phoenix Hotel poolroom and play pool instead of being in class. We started playing pool when he first came here. Dad had bought a pool table from the old Lafayette Hotel and had it down in the basement over on Ashland Avenue. I'd played a little, but I wasn't too good. My dad wasn't much of a pool player, and I didn't play anybody else much. We didn't really get started until we got old enough to get into the Phoenix — you know, 16 or 17, and we might not've supposed to been in there then. But the Phoenix was like he said in the front of *The Hustler*: It was a poolroom. It wasn't a restaurant, like 99 out of 100 poolrooms are. It wasn't a video-game place. It wasn't a bar. The Phoenix didn't sell anything but pool. Those services were available in the hotel, but in the poolroom there was nothing but 17 pool tables.

"And they did big business with those 17 tables. A lot of times they were full, and a lot of the people who played in there were well-known local people. People like Ollie Hurst of the printing company, he liked to play. There was another old fellow named Uncle Ollie; I think he was president of Second National Bank at that time. A lot of businessmen played in there. Of course, the hustlers came through and played, too. During the Keeneland meets, especially in the spring, they all came here from Hot Springs. The Derby weekend was the hustlers' big weekend; there was a lot of loose money. They gambled among themselves and whoever else wanted to play around here for about three weeks while the races were here. All the best players in the country just converged here.

"Back then, there weren't many tournaments. All these real good players just had to go out on the road and gamble to make any money. They had to find games and challenge people. Now there are enough tournaments where a lot of them don't have to do that. They had one here in Lexington at the Continental Inn a few weeks ago, and the total prize money was about $40,000, about $10,000 for the winner. So there was enough money there that you didn't have to sneak around and try to inveigle somebody into a game for money.

"I got to know a lot of those real good old-time players. Of course, they all had their yarns about how they'd get people to play. One old fellow, Texas Puckett they called him, heard about a real good player up here in Irvine or somewhere around Lexington. He was a farmer, but he had money and would gamble. So this Puckett went and bought a couple of coonhounds and an old station wagon and some hip boots and old clothes. He let the two dogs out on the edge of town, and he came up to the poolroom. He got a big roll of money out and said he'd lost his dogs and he'd give these kids $10 or $20 apiece if they'd find them. After everybody'd seen all that money, he sat down and said, 'Well, I guess I'll just have to wait around here and see what happens.'

"Sure enough, he started playing somebody for a few dollars and lost it to him or didn't do too well. And they sent for this farmer because he had all that money. So the end of the story is: He gave somebody the coonhounds that the kids found and took I-don't-know-how-many thousand dollars with him. He traded that old station wagon back in and left.

"It was like *The Sting*. That's the way they all operated. A lot of times one of them would come into town a week ahead of the other and win some money. Then this other guy would come in and play him, and they'd bet on this guy who'd won the money, and he wouldn't be as good, and they two would divide it up after they left. They had all kinds of crooked ways. They played good, but there just wasn't that much 'action,' as they called it, to make it on the up-and-up, so they devised all these schemes to get people gambling. You know, the classic shooting poorly until somebody bets more and then, all of a sudden, taking a chance on getting your thumbs broken. Like Tevis' hustler, you know; that's what happened to him.

"I've been lucky. I've never had much fighting or anything in my place. I'm pretty strict about it. They had two or three at the Phoenix. I don't know how much they amounted to. I was young then, and, of course, when you're young, you like something like that. When you're older and you get a little smarter, you don't like it, especially if you're connected with the business. Woody always hated that down there.

"Woody worked for the Phoenix Hotel, which owned the poolroom. Back during the Depression, the poolroom was the only thing that turned a profit in the whole Phoenix. The rooms and the bar and the dining room and everything were losing money, but the poolroom was making money. Of course, it was partly because there were a lot of people in there out of work with time on their hands. But it was a pretty good business for the space it took up, just to be pool only. That's the way this is, just pool.

"The last year the Phoenix poolroom was open, I worked for Woody. I got a summer job there. That was the summer of 1950. I worked down there that last summer they were open, helped take the tables out when they closed up and everything. Woody went back to work there after they remodeled. Kentucky Utilities took over the space where the poolroom had been. The poolroom ceiling went as high as the second floor of the rest of the hotel. The side of the poolroom went down Limestone Street from Main back to Water Street. When they remodeled, that was all gone. Woody went to work on the desk, greeting people and checking them in and out. He stayed with the business. The people who ran the hotel liked him because he ran the poolroom right.

"When the Phoenix poolroom closed, a little poolroom called Sports Center opened on Upper Street close to the railroad tracks. Woody worked there for two or three months, and when he went back up to the hotel, I took that job. I quit school. At that time I was a second-semester senior, and I dropped out of school, so I'm still a second-semester senior. I'd made up my mind I was going to do my thing. So I worked down there for two or three months, and that guy closed up and sold out.

"There was a bowling alley, Bluegrass Lanes, where Kennedy Book Store is now. In the bottom of it was a bowling alley, and up above it there was nothing; it was unfinished. A fellow named Jones came in there about 1948 and opened up a poolroom named Bluegrass Billiards, and that's still my trade name. I bought it from him in 1951. Jones was getting older and wanted to sell out and move to Florida. I used to play there a little, and I ended up buying it from him. I got my parents to borrow some money, and I opened up in late March of '51. He was a pretty good businessman; he taught me a lot about business.

"One of his favorite expressions that I remember him saying — when people were getting ready to practice, and he had clocked them in, he'd say, 'Remember one thing: Every time one of those balls rolls on one of those tables, it's costing you money.' That tells you how tight he was. When those balls roll on there, they wear out the table sooner or later. That's why he didn't let anybody practice; he clocked them in as soon as they got to the table. He was all business. But he didn't make the kind of money I did because he didn't get along with younger people. I was 23 then, and I got along with all the students.

"Anyhow, that's when I got the poolroom. I stayed there from '51 to '64. And Mr. Kennedy wasn't a bad businessman, either. He'd bought the building, unbeknownst to me, and when my lease ran out it wasn't renewed. He needed my space. So I was out of business for about a year in 1964. I looked around, bought this property here, tore down an old house and built this. Since '65 I've been here. Everybody calls this place Toby's. But it's actually Bluegrass Billiards.

"I had the sabbatical for about one year, but I was busy. I'd move all my equipment — tables and everything — out of that second floor above Kennedy's, store it in this big basement over on Ashland Avenue while they were building this, dismantle it and then bring it all back up here.

"My parents saw that I was hell-bent on doing it. I think my dad figured that it was a fad or something. Dad passed away about 1955, only about four years after I'd had it, but I'm sure he realized by then that I was serious about it and I was making money. I was living at home, but I was supporting myself. If he were around now, he'd see that it wasn't just a passing fancy. And my mother was a pretty understanding person; she figured let people do what they want to do.

"My mother always liked Walter. When Tevis was young, he came over to our house to eat a lot because he didn't have anything to eat at home. We had a maid, Liza, and she'd say, 'Here comes that worthless Tevis boy again. I guess he's going to stay over here and eat now, Toby.' And my dad would say, 'Yeah, I don't think he'll ever amount to anything.' I wish he were alive to see what happened. My mother was always Walter's champion. She always took up for him and encouraged him to write. Walter thought a lot of her, and he came down from New York for her funeral.

"There are a lot of underprivileged kids who are pretty brilliant. If you dig them out, find out who they are and get somebody who can see it. . . . You know, a lot of times it goes unnoticed. A lot of people who could be pretty smart just keep that candle under a bushel.

"Walter came to work for me about a year after I got up to the poolroom there. I'd had a couple of old guys working for me who were skimming a little or wouldn't get there on time. He'd come back to get his master's then — it was '52 or '53 or something like that — and he worked for me in the poolroom. It was about that time he got this idea about writing. He was making notes. I'd go over to his house real late at night, and we'd sit down there in the basement. We'd have a drink, and he'd get out all these typewritten pages and get me to read them and see what I thought.

"He kind of had the plan then, these three or four short stories about pool. He had one in *Collier's,* one in *The Saturday Evening Post,* one in *Esquire* and one in *Playboy.* He knew he was going to write a little more about pool. He always said that'd be a good subject because nothing had been done on it. . . . He did write science fiction and some other things in different fields, so he wasn't one of these people who just have one subject in them. He was accomplished enough, and he got enough out of some of those good teachers over at UK. He was real fond of English literature: Chaucer, Byron and all those poets, Shakespeare. He was real high on Milton. He memorized 'The Raven' by Edgar Allan Poe. He was just fascinated with words and the English language and storytelling. You wonder what else he might have done if he had survived.

"I was a little critical, but that was just sort of needling him. I wasn't serious about it. I was impressed when he got that first $350 check from *Esquire* because I had it in my mind to do something on my own rather than work for somebody else. That's part of the way he felt, he always told me when we worked for Professor Webb at UK, cataloging skeletons and so forth. He was restless when he was on a time clock. He and I worked for a while at the stockyard on Versailles Road. We were what they called 'lamb boys'; we chased them around with a can full of rocks and put them in pens. Buyers would come in for the auction, then we'd help load them on the freight cars. Tevis wasn't into physical labor; he was into getting ahold of some money some way or another. We went to work in tobacco one day, and he quit after the day was half over. I was ashamed to quit, but I didn't want to be left out there by myself, so I left, too. We had to hitchhike back home. I didn't like it much.

"I think that's why some people, when he was young, thought he was going to be a ne'er-do-well. They couldn't see what was buzzing around in his head. He was the butt of some jokes. He had a bit of an Ichabod Crane look, and he wasn't real popular among the football player types. He had a little San Francisco accent when he got here, and like any intellectual in gym class, he kind of got picked on when he was young. They didn't bother him later on.

"Most of his characters, like Fast Eddie Felson, the hero of *The Hustler* and of course the other movie, too, were sort of a composite. There was a guy named Eddie Taylor who was a great hustler and a terrific player; he was inducted into the Hall of Fame not too long ago. When he was young, he used to travel all over the country winning money off people. Later on he won some tournaments and got too well known to do that. Of course, he's an older man now. When he was inducted, I saw that he was 75, and I didn't realize he was that old. He doesn't play pool much anymore.

"There was an old Slavic guy who had a lot of homespun philosophy. Tom Smith, from Cincinnati. He lived till he was 99, and he gambled on pool till he was about 85. He played a boy one night, I remember, and they had a big long session in one pocket. Tom beat this boy, who was about 25 and thought he was a hotshot player. After Tom left, the boy's friends were ribbing him: 'You let that old man beat you?' And he said, 'Hell, I could've beat that old man, but I got tired.' He really didn't know what he was saying. We thought that was hilarious. He was playing an 85-year-old man, and his alibi for losing was he got tired!

"That's where Tevis' stuff came from, these characters we ran into around the poolroom. But you can't take one person; they don't fit your story. You take parts of Eddie Taylor, maybe his name or how he shot certain shots, but then you take another guy who did this or that. You mold a character, which is your own improvisation. You take three or four people, put them together and get what you want. It's a new person, but he's got these attributes.

"That character Fats, you know, always had a running threat to sue Tevis. He said he was who the movie was made after. And he wasn't. He was a fat guy who played pool, so he was called Fats. He was called New

York Fats back then; his name was Rudolph Wanderone. He lived in New York all his life. New York Fats was quite a character. He didn't play as good as the top players. He *claimed* he did. And just as soon as Tevis' book came out, suddenly he said, 'That's me! *I'm* Minnesota Fats.' He quit being New York Fats and Rudy Wanderone. He said Tevis was really writing about him, which he wasn't.

"He didn't sue, but he kept talking about it. He had a lot of hot air. He was a good talker and a pretty smart gambler, but he wasn't quite as good a player. In the movie, Minnesota Fats was supposed to be the champion. But, like one of his pool-hustling friends told me, 'Fats has probably never been in Minnesota.' But he adopted it and cashed in on it. He put out Minnesota Fats cue balls and chalk, pool tables, and he got a show on TV where he played pool with celebrities.

"I think Eddie Taylor double-crossed him. He was supposed to go up there and have an interview and play a game. Fats was king of the hill and was supposed to win, but Eddie beat him. Needless to say, he never got back on the show!

"*Sports Illustrated* sent Tevis to Dayton to do a little article on a tournament up there, because of his notoriety from *The Hustler*. He invited me to go with him. When Tevis and I walked in, Fats started some big argument. He said, 'There's the guy who says I'm not this, that and the other.' And Walter just said, 'Fats, let's not bring all that up now. Just forget about it,' and walked on by him. That's the way Fats was. He could have been in a story, but it probably wouldn't have been a very flattering story. . . .

"I don't play as much as I used to — because I'm back here behind the counter, for one thing. I still like to play. I used to gamble a lot on pool, but I'm getting a little older, getting a little mellow. I teach a little, play with some young people who are starting to play pretty good. I pick on them, criticize them a little. Yeah, I still like to play. Not like I did when Tevis and I were playing. We'd cut classes to go to the poolroom or go over to my house to play, and my dad would come down in the basement and say, 'Don't y'all know what time it is?'

"Tevis' coordination wasn't real good. I think it had something to do with his early physical troubles. He had the savvy, knew what he was supposed to be doing, but his body just wouldn't always do what he told it. He got to be a fair player, competent, but he never got outstanding. I got what you'd call good, but then there are hundreds of people better, tournament players and people who do all that. I've got a big table at home, but I don't play on it much. It's sort of like taking a busman's holiday: You don't go on a bus ride.

"The game itself is a little like chess. You never know it all, and new things keep coming up. However good you get or how much you learn about it, there's always more to it. . . . You meet some real fine people when you're in a business like this, but you also meet some of what the poets call the 'dregs of humanity.' But I've got a lot of students and young people; that kind of keeps me young. I've always admired good pool players and still like the game. No, I haven't burnt out on it. Of course, at this stage, what would I do — go sell used cars?

"People always ask me when I'm going to retire. I feel well. If I retired, I'd kind of vegetate. I'm used to being around something going on. If you feel well, I don't think it's a good idea to retire, unless you're crazy about golf or tennis or unless you're real lazy or you've got something else that you're going to do a whole lot of. In other words, I don't dread coming down here to work. I mean, every business has its problems. I've got problems with taxes and bureaucracies and the government, and every now and then the customers and equipment. But as a rule, I can come up here and sort of relax and listen to the radio and do a little of my homework, bookkeeping and things.

"A lot of the people who come in here know me and have played pool around here for years. I've got some buddies about my age who are old-time customers. I get some doctors, lawyers and Indian chiefs. Every now and then you get a few of what you expect to see when you come into a smoky room — you know, the opinion of pool like it used to be. But now girls and everybody plays. It's easier on me. It was more like people thought it was back at the Phoenix in the '50s, with fights and gambling and everything.

"Of course, pool is an ideal medium for local color. You get characters around the poolroom. Sometimes respected citizens are good players, too, gamblers and things like that. There was a real top-notch pool player who lived in Lexington for years. Everybody used to hang around Main and Limestone, where the poolroom was. He was out on the street a lot. He was kind of a ladies' man, and he'd been a good boxer when he was young. He was a terrific pool player, but the old demon rum got the best of him. Everybody knew him, and talked to people he didn't know; he was just a gregarious person.

"There was an old tobacco auctioneer who was down there all the time. He was a big drinker. He wasn't a good pool player, but he always came down there to watch and kibitz on the games. He'd get drunk, and he'd reach in his pocket, pull out a big ball of money and say, 'Hey, I've got plenty of money, haven't I?'

"Tom Smith, that older fellow, would come to Lexington every now and then to play pool. He made his living doing stuff like that. He hung around the Phoenix. He'd lived in Yugoslavia, and he left right before the first World War broke out. His family sent him to this country, and he came to some small town around Cincinnati and went to work as a blacksmith. This was in the early 1900s. Of course, I'm talking about him playing in the '50s; he was an older man then. When he was about 35, he was kind of worn out doing this heavy work. He'd go to a place and drink beer, and they had a pool table. And he always told us a story.

"He says, 'I walk into poolroom. I see these two men pushing these balls around. One of them hands the other one $5. They play a little longer, and he hands him another $5. I don't make but *$5 a day!* I go back and quit. I'm going to learn how to do *this*.' So he started playing pool when he was about 35, and by the time he was about 45, he was an accomplished player. He went all over the country gambling with people. He made his living that way.

"That was Tom Smith. His real name was Siccic, I think. He told me he had a grandmother who was 102 over there, and several aunts up in their 90s. He looked like he'd never die. When he was 80 or 85, he was just as erect and well dressed. He was a homespun philosopher. He'd tell you, 'You know what keeps those pool balls on that table?' Kids would scratch their heads, and he'd say, 'It's atmospheric pressure.' And he'd say: 'You take a dollar, and you plant it in the ground. What do you get back? Not a damn thing. You plant a potato in the ground, and you get back a bushel.' That was his kind of talk. He had worked hard and always depended on himself. He never drew Social Security or anything. He said, 'I am man enough to support myself.' You don't hear much of that anymore. . . .

"All of these big cities now have these elaborate, extremely expensive, disco-type of poolrooms with every kind of upscale equipment. Of course, they're charging $5 or $10 an hour to play. I had an article here that had pool prices from five or six of these places in New York. Every time somebody'd say something about the prices, I'd say, 'You'd better go up to New York where it's cheap.'

"I've outlasted four or five competitors. Now Lexington just has about three poolrooms that are pool only. Bar pool tables take up a lot of the business. A lot of good players like to play in the bars because that's where you can gamble and win money, because people are drinking. I don't care about selling alcohol. I've been here long enough that I value my sanity more than a few extra dollars. When I was young, I'd want the dollars. Now I just want a peaceful existence.

"I'm a Lexingtonian. Like I said, I was born right across the street. I've never lived anywhere but Lexington. I went away to school for a couple of years and have been to Europe a couple of times, been to Florida and California. Been around, but I've lived right here. I'm one of these people who kind of like for things to stay the same. I'm a little conservative. I've found my niche, and I'm satisfied with it."

The Story of the Kentucky Theatre — "The Show Must Go On"

*F*rom midnight sell-out screenings of *The Rocky Horror Picture Show* and a patron who insisted on bringing his pet goat to the movies with him, to the devastating downtown fire that heavily damaged the theater, forcing it to close down for several years, Fred Mills has seen it all.

During his past 30 years as manager of the Kentucky Theatre on Main Street, Mills has handled crowd control for the theatre's many sell-out shows, popped and sold popcorn, planned programming, and has even taken special care of "special" patrons.

Like the one young man who didn't get up to leave when the last show was over. Mills said he and the staff did everything they could think of to wake the man up, but he had been drinking and could not be roused. Mills said he couldn't just leave him there, but to top it all off, it was a terrible winter night with bad snow and wind, and the police were too busy coping with the effects of the storm to come and get the man.

So Mills did what any good theatre manager would do. He checked the man's wallet to make sure he had some cash, dragged him out to his car and drove him to a local motel where he got the man a room and deposited him. Mills said he bets that man wonders to this day how he ended up in The Downtowner that night.

The 1,100-seat Kentucky Theatre opened on October 4, 1922, with a great deal of fanfare and festivity. A musical overture performed on the Wurlitzer Organ (at the time, the second largest organ south of Chicago), a rousing rendition of "My Old Kentucky Home," and a dedication speech by Kentucky Gov. Edwin P. Morrow preceded the showing of the theater's first feature film, the historical romance *The Eternal Flame* starring Norma Talmadge.

That was a little before Fred Mills' time, but the grandiose promotion and presence of the theater has become the stuff of local legend.

To compete with the other major theaters in town, which included the Ben Ali, the Strand, and the Ada Meade, the Kentucky boasted the most modern conveniences housed in the most luxurious surroundings. Oil paintings, plush carpeting, tapestries, mirrored doors, a foyer graced by matched marble that cost $18,000, and hand-carved wood-

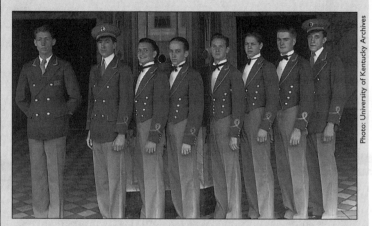

Photo: University of Kentucky Archives

A group of Kentucky Theatre ushers spiffed up and ready to help folks to their seats in 1931.

work created an aura of elegance inside, while 4,000 light bulbs in the marquee outside proclaimed the Kentucky's presence to all of Lexington.

At 10 cents for kids and 25-30 cents admission for adults, the Kentucky charged more than other local theaters, but the Lafayette Amusement Company, which owned the theatre, claimed it was worth the price — "Every Patron an Honored Guest" was the theatre's motto. Not only did the theater management vow to show "only the best and cleanest productions," it also kept its patrons cool and comfy with its state-of-the-art ventilation system. In the attic, tons of ice were shipped in and huge fans blew air over the ice, through the vents, cooling the entire theater.

Another innovative feature of the theater, according to the Kentucky's "exploitation manager" (what is today a publicity manager), R.R. Russell, was that it was the only theatre in the country that owned its own railroad siding. A train track large enough to hold five railroad cars on the theatre property gave it the ability to accommodate large road shows.

In April of 1927, the Kentucky was the first local theater to introduce Warner Brothers' Vitaphone sound films, and by the following winter, the theater was featuring all the new "talkie" movies.

Mills traces his experience with the Kentucky back to the 1950s, when, as a 10-year-old kid, he was impressed by the theater's huge stained glass dome that to this day dominates its rear ceiling. He also

Photo: University of Kentucky Archives

The Grand Opening of the Kentucky Theatre on October 4, 1922, was one of the gala events of the season in Lexington. Here, the fanfare is about to begin.

recalls the burgundy urinals in the men's room, a distinctive feature of the theatre that was phased out during the post-fire renovations in the late 1980s.

Those urinals were, for a long time, a great source of conversation and humor. Mills recalled a male patron who came up to him one evening to ask how to get the drinking fountains in the bathroom to work.

Mills began work as an usher at the theater in the summer of 1964. That was the summer that "The Sound of Music" sold out every day for three months.

Over the last three decades, the Kentucky Theatre has metamorphosed right along with the rest of Lexington. Major renovations in the 1950s and the 1980s (both before and after the fire), changes in management, and changes in the types of movies it features are among the major modifications the Kentucky has undergone.

In 1987, a devastating fire in a next-door restaurant did heavy smoke damage, although not much structural damage, to the Kentucky. The theater was closed for more than four years. After a great deal of vocal interest from the Lexington community, the Kentucky finally reopened in April of 1992 under the management of the Kentucky Theatre Group Inc., of which Mills is one of three owners.

It was in the late 1970s that the Kentucky changed to what is now more or less its current format as a repertory theater or "revival house."

Today, the Kentucky offers Lexington theater-goers an interesting range of movies, from the classics such as *Casablanca* and *Oklahoma!* to second-run, foreign and art films or first-run films other Lexington

Photo: University of Kentucky Archives

"Every patron an honored guest" was the motto of the Kentucky Theatre when it opened in 1922. The plush, elegant interior reinforced that claim, as is evident in this 1933 photograph.

theatres don't show. Admission prices are lower than most Lexington theatres, with special rates for kids and senior citizens.

When the theater reopened after the fire, the stage had been restored and enlarged, cutting down the number of seats to 810, but giving the facility the capacity to feature live productions and concerts. Last spring, the theater introduced the Troubadour Classic Unplugged Concert Series, whose sell-out shows have featured everyone from Lucinda Williams, Richie Havens and Arlo Guthrie to Taj Mahal and Leon Redbone.

It's not the same flamboyant motion picture house that took Lexington by storm in the 1920s, but the Kentucky Theatre continues to be a beloved and unique feature of Lexington's entertainment scene.

Inside
Hotels and Motels

*F*rom a New Orleans-style inn to resort hotels with golf courses and fine dining to your more traditional kids, pets and pool motels on the interstate, Lexington is likely to have an accommodation option that will suit your needs.

Lexington's more than 50 hotels and motels have more than 6,000 rooms and suites available for visitors to the area. While Lexington is not typically known as a resort area, we do have a nationally known resort hotel and golf club. Marriott's Griffin Gate features a championship 18-hole golf course designed by Rees Jones and listed by *Golf Digest* as one of the 75 top resort golf courses in the country. For more information about this course, see our chapter on golf.

The Bluegrass AAA has awarded its prestigious Four Diamond rating to three Lexington hotels and motels, and these are listed first in our description of places to stay in the area. The AAA discount is offered at these hotels to members. The other hotels and motels we highlight in this section are roughly grouped by location for your convenience. For more information about accommodations not detailed here, contact the Greater Lexington Convention & Visitors Bureau at 233-7299 or

(800) 84LEXKY.

One note of warning: There are times during the year, especially in spring and fall, when Lexington's hotels and motels are pretty well all booked. This usually happens on weekends when there is a University of Kentucky home football or basketball game and horse racing or horse sales going on at the same time. Lexington is also host to a number of large conventions throughout the year, so it is advisable to call ahead early for reservations.

The average nightly rates for two adults at the hotels and motels listed in this section are indicated by a dollar sign ($) ranking as follows:

$25 - $50	$
$51 - $75	$$
$76 - $100	$$$
$101 - $125	$$$$
$126 - $150	$$$$$

MARRIOTT'S GRIFFIN GATE
RESORT AND GOLF CLUB
1800 Newtown Pike   231-5100
$$$$$ *(800) 228-9290*

Marriott's Griffin Gate is the ultimate place to stay in Lexington if you're an avid golfer. In addition to sporting one of the finest 18-hole championship golf courses in the nation, this resort hotel and award-winning restaurant (The Mansion) offer guests to Lexington all the creature comforts, with a lot of luxuries thrown in for good measure.

Conveniently located near the intersection of highways I-64 and I-75 and just 15 minutes from the Blue Grass Airport, Marriott's Griffin Gate has 388 guest rooms and 21 luxurious suites. In addition to the golf course, there are three lighted tennis courts, indoor and outdoor swimming pools, a hydrotherapy pool and health club. You can even get a massage when you're through recreating.

When you get hungry, the resort has several dining options. The Mansion, Kentucky's only AAA Four Diamond restaurant, features elegant dining in a restored 19th-century home. Pegasus specializes in steaks and seafood, Griffin Gate Gardens features family-style dining, and Pegasus Lounge offers dancing and entertainment in the evenings.

If you're in town on business, Marriott's Griffin Gate has 14 meeting rooms that can accommodate 12 to 1,400 people. The resort also offers complimentary van service to and from the airport.

As you might expect, you do have to pay for all these conveniences. Rates depend on the number of people and how far in advance you make your reservation. The resort offers special weekend and event packages throughout the year. Some of the services, such as massages, cost extra. Pets also cost $20 extra per stay. All major credit cards are accepted.

RADISSON PLAZA HOTEL LEXINGTON

369 West Vine Street   *231-9000*
$$$$ *(800) 333-3333*

As the only AAA Four Diamond hotel in downtown Lexington, the Radisson Plaza is an ideal combination of top-notch service and comfort and convenience and accessibility to the greater Lexington business and financial district. Situated about equidistant from I-75 and Blue Grass Airport, the Radisson Plaza has all the perks that make it even better — in some cases — than a home away from home.

Located just across the street from Rupp Arena and the Civic Center, the Radisson Plaza is surrounded by unique shopping and dining opportunities. You don't even have to go outside to visit the interesting shops and eateries in the Civic Center and Festival Market which are connected to the Radisson by skywalk. Picturesque Triangle Park, with its 100 lighted fountains, fronts one side of the hotel, and horse-drawn carriage

Insiders' Tips

When you're in the right part of Lexington and the wind is blowing your way, you can step outside and breathe in the rich, warm, tantalizing aroma of roasted peanuts. This is the smell of Jif peanut butter being made at the Procter & Gamble plant on Winchester Road.

rides through Lexington's historic district leave from the hotel's Vine Street entrance.

In addition, during your stay at the Radisson Plaza, you can enjoy free and pay movies in your room, a small heated indoor pool, sauna, whirlpool and exercise room. Health club privileges are available for an additional fee. Transportation to and from Blue Grass Airport is provided to guests of the Radisson as well.

The Radisson's fine dining restaurant — Cafe on the Park, overlooking Triangle Park — is located off the lobby, and in the evenings you can enjoy live entertainment in Spirits Lounge.

The Radisson Plaza has 367 guest units. There is a discount for senior citizens, and in conjunction with some discount and special packages, rooms are available for as little as $79 per night. The hotel accepts most major credit cards. Pets are not allowed.

FRENCH QUARTER SUITES

2601 Richmond Road   268-0060
$$$$ (800) 262-3774

Lexington's third AAA Four Diamond-rated hotel takes you back to the quaint Southern charm of New Orleans. From the indoor courtyard filled with exotic trees, fountains and wrought iron furnishings to the live jazz performances each weekend, the French Quarter Suites offers its guests a unique and charming accommodation option.

Ideally located just 10 minutes from I-75 and from downtown, the French Quarter Suites are near many unusual and interesting restaurants and shopping areas, including Lexington Mall.

The hotel's 155 guest rooms feature hot tubs and refrigerators as well as free and pay movies. Many rooms open onto the picturesque courtyard. A swimming pool and exercise room give you a great opportunity to work out or just ease away tension. When you get hungry, Tippedore's Restaurant in the lobby features the finest French and Cajun cuisine. Live jazz is performed on Friday and Saturday nights in the Gazebo Lounge.

Airport transportation is available to guests, and pets are not allowed. All major credit cards are accepted.

North (Off I-75 exit 115)

COURTYARD BY MARRIOTT

775 Newtown Court   253-4646
$$$

Located conveniently near both I-75 and downtown Lexington, the Courtyard by Marriott gives you easy access to the greater Lexington area. Courtyard is in an ideal setting on a quiet side street off one of the main feeder roads from I-75 into Lexington. You can feel free from the hustle and bustle of traffic while still being accessible to most area attractions.

A heated indoor pool, whirlpool and exercise room are available for your recreational enjoyment. There are also free and pay movies in the room, and a coin laundry available for guest use.

Courtyard has 146 units, and special weekend rates are offered November through February. Most major credit cards are accepted. Pets are not allowed. A

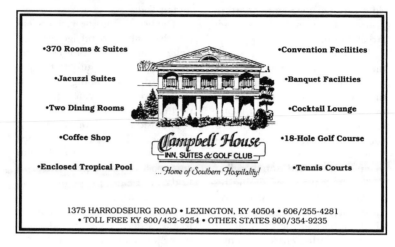
restaurant, with entrees priced $8-$13, and a lounge with TVs are located in the hotel lobby.

RESIDENCE INN BY MARRIOTT
1080 Newtown Pike   231-6191
$$$$$

The Residence Inn by Marriott truly offers all the comforts of your home away from home. Its 80 apartment units are spacious and beautifully decorated. Many units have fireplaces, and some even have two bathrooms. All apartments have refrigerators, cable TV and movies. VCRs are available for rental.

For recreation, a heated pool, whirlpool and sports court will keep you entertained. Several nearby restaurants, including one next door, make eating out convenient.

Pets are allowed, but a substantial deposit is required. Rates are slightly higher during the Keeneland race meets in April and October. All major credit cards are accepted.

HOLIDAY INN - NORTH
1950 Newtown Pike   233-0512
$$$ (800) HOLIDAY

With its convenient location just off I-75, Holiday Inn - North is easily accessible to most of the big area attractions, including the Kentucky Horse Park just to the north. For golfers, it is an ideal location adjacent to the nationally ranked Griffin Gate Golf Club. There is also a putting green at the hotel.

The Holidome recreation center includes an indoor heated pool, sauna, whirlpool and exercise room. And a restaurant, with entrees priced from $8-$13, and lounge in the hotel mean you really don't have to go far to get anything you'll need during your stay.

All major credit cards are accepted, and pets are allowed.

LA QUINTA MOTOR INN
1919 Stanton Way   231-7551
$

Situated just off I-75 near the Griffin Gate Golf Club, La Quinta

Motor Inn offers travelers convenience, comfort and cable TV.

The motel has a heated pool and your can bring your pet (though not to the pool). A restaurant is located opposite the motel, and several are nearby, offering a nice choice in places to eat. This is a nice, comfortable place to stay.

The rates are pretty reasonable, too, and are even slightly lower from mid-November to February. All major credit cards are accepted.

North Central
(Off I-75 exit 113)

HARLEY HOTEL
2143 North Broadway   299-1261
$$

If you're looking for lots of ways to recreate without leaving your hotel, the Harley Hotel is the place to be. A heated outdoor pool and an indoor pool, a wading pool for the kids, saunas, whirlpool, putting green, exercise room and two lighted tennis courts will keep even the most active traveler busy for awhile.

A dining room, with entrees priced $7-$14, is located in the hotel lobby, and there you can also get a cocktail and enjoy live entertainment.

Harley Hotel has 146 units, and there is a discount for senior citizens. No pets are allowed. The hotel accepts most major credit cards.

East Central
(Off I-75 exit 110)

HAMPTON INN
2251 Elkhorn Road   299-2613
$$

It's new and attractive, and it's conveniently located near I-75. Hampton Inn is a nice place to stay if you're in the market for a clean, comfortable, moderately priced motel.

You can enjoy movies and cable TV in your room, or take a dip in the motel swimming pool. Then when you get hungry, there are several restaurants within close walking distance, ranging from fast food to country cuisine.

Hampton Inn has 125 units. All major credit cards are accepted, but pets are not.

SIGNATURE INN EAST
2381 Buena Vista Drive   299-0302
$ (800) 822-5252

Just a quarter of a mile from I-75, and kids 17 and younger stay free with their parents — what more could you ask for from a motel?

But there's more. When you stay at Signature Inn East, you also get a free Breakfast Express and a free newspaper each morning, plus you get cable TV, movies and a swimming pool. You can even rent a VCR for use in your room. No pets are allowed.

Signature Inn East has 124 units. All major credit cards are accepted.

WILSON INN

| 2400 Buena Vista Drive | 293-6113 |
| $ | (800) WILSONS |

It's a traveler's dream come true: a refrigerator in every room, you can bring your pet, and your teens stay free in your room. Plus, when you stay at Wilson Inn, you get a free breakfast and free fax service.

There is a restaurant adjacent, but if you feel like just staying in the room, about half of them come equipped with microwave ovens.

Wilson Inn has 110 rooms and suites. All major credit cards are accepted.

BEST WESTERN REGENCY/ LEXINGTON INN

| 2241 Elkhorn Road | 293-2202 |
| $ | (800) 528-1234 |

Convenience, attractive rooms, and a lot of fast food and regional cuisine restaurants within close walking distance are some of the perks of staying at the Best Western Regency/ Lexington Inn.

In addition, you get cable TV and movies in your room, access to a coin laundry and a recreation area that features a pool, sauna and whirlpool.

Best Western Regency/Lexington Inn has 112 guest rooms. A special rate is offered mid-December through the first of March, and a senior citizens discount is also available. All major credit cards are accepted.

South Central
(Off I-75 exit 104)

HOLIDAY INN SOUTH
5532 Athens-Boonesboro Road   263-5241
$$

Conveniently located just off Lexington's southernmost I-75 exit (hence the name) Holiday Inn South offers all the perks at a pretty reasonable rate.

Cable TV, free and pay movies, plus a pool, sauna, whirlpool and exercise room are all provided for your recreational pleasure. You can even bring your pet!

A dining room — entrees priced $8-$13 — is located off the lobby, and there you can also enjoy a cocktail and live entertainment. All major credit cards are accepted.

Central
(Within New Circle Road)

HYATT REGENCY LEXINGTON
400 West Vine Street   253-1234
$$$$

If you want to stay right downtown where all the action is, from college basketball to harness racing to banking, Hyatt Regency Lexington is the place to be. It is located in the heart of downtown and is attached to the Civic Center, a shopping and restaurant complex, and Rupp Arena, home to major rock 'n' roll and country music acts as well as the nationally ranked University of Kentucky Wildcats basketball games.

The Glass Garden restaurant, located in the hotel lobby, is well known for its great Sunday brunch. Plus you get free and pay movies and cable TV in your room, and access to a heated indoor pool and health club. Pets are not allowed.

Hyatt Regency Lexington has 365 guest rooms (one for each day of the year if you wanted to stay that long). Senior citizens discounts are available, and all major credit cards are accepted.

CAMPBELL HOUSE INN,
SUITES AND GOLF CLUB
1375 Harrodsburg Road   255-4281
$$$$ *(800) 354-9235*

A longtime Lexington tradition, Campbell House Inn, Suites and Golf Club has a lot to offer its guests. If you golf, there's an 18-hole course adjacent to the hotel (greens fees apply). But you may also want to play tennis on one of the hotel's two courts or take a swim in either the indoor pool or the heated outdoor pool. An exercise room is also available for guest use.

Campbell House Inn has two restaurants, with entrees priced $9 to $20, and a coffeeshop, plus a lounge area and live entertainment.

The hotel has 367 guest units, with some whirlpool suites. All major credit cards are accepted, but pets are not.

GRATZ PARK INN
120 West Second Street   231-1777
$$$$ *(800) 227-4362*

If you're looking for a unique and interesting place to stay, Gratz Park Inn might be a good choice. Located in the heart of one of Lexington's most historic districts (just a few blocks from Transylvania University, the first college west of the Alleghenies), Gratz Park Inn is surrounded by some of

Insiders enjoy the old fieldstone sheep fences that line much of Paris Pike.

the finest and most historic architecture in town.

Another plus about staying at this inn is that it's just a couple of blocks from Main Street, so you have the convenience of being downtown plus the quiet and peacefulness of staying in a more residential area.

Gratz Park Inn has 43 rooms furnished in 19th-century antique reproductions. Transportation to and from Blue Grass Airport is available to guests. Most major credit cards are accepted. Pets are not allowed.

South (Outside New Circle Road)

HILTON SUITES OF LEXINGTON GREEN

3195 Nicholasville Road   *271-4000*
$$$$ *(800) HILTONS*

Part of the uniqueness of the Hilton Suites of Lexington Green is that you are located right in the heart of some of the best mall shopping in town. Lexington Green shopping center features a number of unique stores (including Joseph-Beth Booksellers, one of the largest book stores in the region) and great restaurants, plus Fayette Mall, the largest mall in the state, is just down the road. Add to that three major movie theaters and at least a dozen restaurants ranging from fast food to Mexican to Chinese, and you're

talking major convenience.

But even if you don't want to set foot out of your hotel, you can enjoy food and drinks at Polos Cafe and Chukker's Lounge right inside the hotel. Hilton Suites has 174 guest rooms and suites, many of which have refrigerators in them. You also get free and pay movies, a swimming pool, sauna, whirlpool and exercise room available for your use. Pets are not allowed, but kids stay free with their parents. All major credit cards are accepted.

SHONEY'S INN - LEXINGTON

2753 Richmond Road   *269-4999*
$

Located right in the heart of one of Lexington's prime shopping, business and restaurant districts, Shoney's Inn is convenient, comfortable and affordable. Shoney's Restaurant is adjacent to the motel, but if you're in the mood for something more exotic, there are Italian, Oriental and steakhouse restaurants located nearby.

Shoney's Inn also has a pool, cable TV and movies in your room, plus kids younger than 18 stay free with their parents. You can't bring your pet, however.

Shoney's Inn's 102 rooms are moderately priced, and all major credit cards are accepted. A senior citizens discount is also available.

Inside
Bed and Breakfast Inns

Most of them don't sport the kidney-shaped swimming pool with a slide for the kids. And you'd be hard-pressed to find soda or ice machines out in the hall.

But there's a certain charm about staying in a bed & breakfast that just can't be matched by your super-highway-kids-eat-free motel chains. The absence of humming, neon-lit food and drink machines is a big part of that charm. The "&" in the name also plays a big role: You get a meal with your room.

Bed & breakfasts are places you can feel free from the drudgery of daily, hand-to-mouth existence, yet still feel at home when you're on the road.

The more than two dozen bed & breakfasts in Lexington and the surrounding Bluegrass area capture that sense of being a "home away from home" while they regale visitors with the awesome charm of true Southern hospitality.

The ones mentioned here are located in Lexington or in towns in the surrounding counties (which are featured in our chapter on Lexington's Neighbors). Rooms fill up fast, so it would behoove you to make reservations as far in advance as possible, especially during the summer vacation season.

For more detailed information about personalizing your bed & breakfast stay in Central Kentucky, contact one of the following organizations.

BLUEGRASS BED & BREAKFAST
Rt. 1 Box 263,
Versailles, KY 40383   873-3208

Bluegrass Bed & Breakfast represents about 20 lodgings in Lexington and the surrounding region.

KENTUCKY HOMES
BED & BREAKFAST
1507 S. Third,
Louisville, KY 40208   *(502) 635-7341*

This organization represents about 80 bed & breakfasts across the state.

THE BED AND BREAKFAST
COLLECTION OF LEXINGTON
1099 South Broadway   252-3601
                          800-526-9801

The Bed and Breakfast Collection of Lexington is a group of individually owned and operated bed and breakfasts in the Lexington area, ranging from locations in historic downtown houses to suburban cottages and scenic horse farms. Rates range from $59 to $129 per night.

There is also a toll-free number you can call to get information from the Bed & Breakfast Association of Kentucky — (800) 292-2632.

Photo: Lexington Herald-Leader

Visitors to downtown Lexington can see unique architectural details such as the window on this Romanesque Revival house.

Area bed & breakfasts are listed below by town. All phone numbers are in the "606" area code unless otherwise noted. A "1" in front of the number indicates the call is long distance from Lexington.

Lexington

547-A B & B

547 North Broadway   *255-4152*

547-A B & B puts you right downtown Lexington in the heart of one of the city's most historic districts near Transylvania University and Victorian Square. It has one small, private apartment in a Victorian home, and features a sunny bay window in the eating area and a large, modern bathroom. Kids are welcome, and there is a small extra room off the main room that can be opened up for them. Rates are $60-$65/night. Checks are accepted, credit cards are not — and neither are pets.

B & B AT SILLS INN - THE COTTAGE

1099 South Broadway   *252-3601*
(800) 526-9801

B & B at Sills Inn offers a variety of modern amenities in a charming setting in a historic area of downtown Lexington. Among these are double Jacuzzi suites and a full gourmet breakfast. Rates for the two private rooms are $59-99/night. Checks and all major credit cards are accepted. Pets are not allowed, and children are permitted with caution.

CHERRY KNOLL FARM

3975 Lemons Mill Road   *253-9800*

Built in 1855 and situated on 28 acres of beautiful Bluegrass farmland, this Greek Revival home is listed on the National Registry of Historic Places. The country location makes it a great place for walking and enjoying the great outdoors in a peaceful setting. Special events are planned at Thanksgiving and Christmas. The guest rooms at Cherry Knoll Farm are somewhat flexible in nature, ranging from a room with a fireplace to a suite with a couch and sitting area that can be opened up to include another room, with the combined space sleeping six guests. Room rates are $79-$130 (for the large suite)/night. Pets are not allowed but kids are. Checks and major credit cards are acceptable payment methods.

Richmond

BARNES MILL

1268 Barnes Mill Road   *1-623-5509*

This Victorian home built in the early 1900s has been beautifully restored to its original elegance and Southern charm. Barnes Mill B & B offers a peaceful country setting less than a mile from I-75. Its private room and shared room are priced $50-$60/night. MasterCard, Visa and American Express are welcome, as are personal checks. Children 12 and older are welcome, pets are not.

Berea

THE MANSION HOUSE

U.S. 25 South   *1-986-9851*

The Mansion House B & B, which can accommodate 10 guests, was remodeled and decorated in a way that offers a pleasant mix of Southern living and English tradition. The

Bed & Breakfasts

547—A Bed & Breakfast

547 N. Broadway
Lexington KY 40508

Apartment with well—stocked kitchen in Victorian home near downtown.

Hosts: *Ruth & Joseph Fitzpatrick*
606/255—4152

Breckinridge House (1820)

201 S. Broadway
Georgetown KY 40324

Georgian home, 2 suites w/BR, sitting room, kitchen & bath.

Hosts: *Annette & Felice Porter*
502/863—3163

Albion Farm

1490 Woods Road
Nicholasville, KY 40356

Rest and Relax on a working thoroughbred horse farm.

Host: *Cassandra Baker*
606/273—0037

Cedar Haven Farm

2380 Bethel Road
Nicholasville KY 40356

Working farm in relaxed setting. Full country breakfast served.

Hosts: *Irene & Jim Smith*
606/858—3849

Barnes Mill Guest House

1268 Barnes Mill Road
Richmond KY 40475

Restored Victorian home with old South charm. Off I—75 Exit 87

Hosts: *Christine & Euzenith Sowers*
606/623—5509 or 623—0543

Jordan Farm

4091 Newtown Pike
Georgetown KY 40324

Carriage house jacuzzi suites on working thoroughbred horse farm.

Hosts: *Becky & Harold Jordan*
502/868—9002 or 863—1944

Blackridge Hall

4055 Paris Pike
Georgetown KY 40324

Charm & elegance of a southern colonial mansion with suites.

Host: *Jim D. Black*
800/768—9308 or 502/863—2069

The Mansion House

123 Mt. Vernon Road
Berea KY 40403

Typical English style B&B in southern colonial home.

Christine & Malcolm Egglesden
606/986—9851

Call or write individual

of the Bluegrass

Pineapple Inn (1876)

645 S. Broadway
Georgetown KY 40324

*Beautiful antiques, full
breakfast, comfortable rooms.*

Les Olsen & Muriel Konietzko
502/868–5453

Rosedale

1917 Cypress St. Paris KY 40361

*A charming Civil War–era home
filled with antiques, situated on
three peaceful acres.*

Hosts: Katie & Jim Haag
606/987–1845

Rose Hill Inn

233 Rose Hill
Versailles, KY 40383

*Downtown 1800's home with
gourmet breakfast in room.*

Hosts: Kathy & Mark Miller
606/873–5957

Sandusky House

1626 Delaney Ferry Road
Nicholasville KY 40356

*An 1850 Greek Revival home amid
horse farms, minutes from Lexington.*

Hosts: Linda & Jim Humphrey
606/223–4730

Scott Station Inn

305 East Main
Wilmore KY 40390

*Real southern hospitality
near Asbury College.*

Hosts: Sandy & Mike Jansen
606/858–0121

B & B at Sills Inn

270 Montgomery Ave.
Versailles KY 40383

*Victorian home, jacuzzi
suites, historic shops &
horse farms.*

Sills Inn — "The Cottage"

1099 S. Broadway
Lexington KY 40504

*Jacuzzi suites,
gourmet breakfast,
Lexington attractions.*

B&B
Collection of Lexington

"A reservation service for
a collection of horse farms
to downtown homes."

Host: Tony Sills

Lexington: 606/252–3601
Versailles: 606/873–4478
FAX: 606/873–4726
1–800–526–9801

B&B *for brochure or rates.*

five guest rooms, priced at $50/night, have queen-size beds and cherry furniture. The Mansion House offers a full English breakfast, and there is no book-in or book-out time. Kids are welcome, pets are not. The Mansion House accepts cash, checks, MasterCard and Visa.

HOLLY TREE

210 Chestnut Street   1-986-2804

Holly Tree B & B is in a three-story house built in 1929. Located in the heart of historic Berea, it features a large porch and comfortable living room. It was recently renovated to add two bathrooms, central air, and a deck across the back. Up to 12 guests can be accommodated in four rooms priced $50-$60/night. MasterCard, Visa, cash and check are acceptable payment methods. Kids are not encouraged, and pets are not allowed.

MORNING GLORY

140 North Broadway   1-986-8661

Located in the heart of historic Old Town Berea, Morning Glory B & B is housed in a turn-of-the-century building that has, over the years, served as a grocery store, pharmacy, church, and auto parts store. The two guest units are furnished with the works of 35 area artists and craftspeople. Rates are $25-$50/night. American Express, cash and checks are acceptable payment methods. Kids are welcome. Pets are not.

Nicholasville

CEDAR HAVEN FARM

2380 Bethel Road   858-3849

Cedar Haven Farm B & B is on a

working Bluegrass farm. It has two shared rooms priced at $35/night, and offers all the charms of a country setting, including fresh-baked breads and homegrown fruits and vegetables. Personal checks, kids and pets are accepted. Credit cards are not.

SANDUSKY HOUSE

1626 Delaney Ferry Road   233-4730
231-1522

Sandusky House B & B features two private guest rooms priced at $65/night. The house, Greek Revival style, was built in 1850. The farm on which it stands was from a 1780 land grant from Patrick Henry to Revolutionary War hero Jacob Sandusky. Sandusky House accepts major credit cards and personal checks. Kids and pets are not allowed.

ALBION FARM

1490 Woods Road   273-0037

This bed and breakfast inn is on a working horse farm in the lush bluegrass of Central Kentucky. Call for specific rate information.

Versailles

B & B AT SILLS INN

270 Montgomery Avenue   873-4478
(800) 526-9801

This B & B features six private rooms priced at $59-$99/night. Double Jacuzzi suites and a full gourmet breakfast are some of the perks of staying at B & B at Sills Inn, which is housed in a restored Victorian home. Personal checks and all major credit cards are accepted. Kids are not encouraged and pets and smoking are not allowed.

Photo: Lexington Herald-Leader

Shopping in turn-of-the-century Lexington might have included a stop at Court Day on Cheapside.

ROSEHILL INN

233 Rose Hill   *873-5957*

This spacious country estate was built in the early 1800s in what is now downtown historic Versailles. The four guest rooms with exquisite private baths are priced $69-$89/night. A nutritious gourmet breakfast is served to you in your room. Personal checks, all major credit cards and kids are welcome. Pets are not.

SHEPHERD PLACE

31 Heritage Road   *873-7843*

Centrally located just 4 miles west of Keeneland race track and the Lexington airport, and 10 miles from downtown Lexington, Shepherd Place B & B combines the charm of country living with the convenience of the city in a picturesque pre-Civil War home. Its two private rooms are $69/night. Personal checks and major credit cards are accepted. Pets and kids are not.

Georgetown

BLACKRIDGE HALL

4055 Paris Pike   *863-2069*
                                (800) 768-9308

With its three private rooms and two private suites with Jacuzzis, Blackridge Hall B & B offers the charm of an old Southern Colonial mansion mixed with the luxuries of modern amenities. Room rates are $89-$159/night, and cash, checks and most major credit cards are accepted. Kids and pets are not allowed.

HISTORIC BRECKINRIDGE HOUSE

201 South Broadway   *863-3163*

If you're looking for historic significance, Breckinridge House B & B may just be the place. This 1820 Federal style house was home to John C. Breckinridge who was Buchanan's vice president, and who ran against Lincoln for president. Guest accommodations feature two suites, priced at $65/

night, which are filled with wonderful antiques. Cash, checks, MasterCard and Visa are accepted for payment. Kids, smoking, and pets are all allowed.

LOG CABIN

350 North Broadway   *863-3514*

Log Cabin B & B offers a unique frontier perspective. Built around 1809, this Kentucky log cabin has chinked walls and period furnishings, along with a fireplace and fully equipped kitchen. Its central location — just 5 miles from the Kentucky Horse Park and 12 miles from Lexington — makes it an ideal vacation spot. Log Cabin has two bedrooms, and the rate is $64/night. You may pay by cash or check, and kids and pets are welcome.

JORDAN FARM

4091 Newtown Pike   *863-1944*

This unique B & B is in a restored carriage house on a Central Kentucky horse farm. A nearby fishing lake and acres of beautiful Bluegrass countryside enhance your stay in this idyllic spot. Jordan Farm has three guest rooms, all with Jacuzzis and wet bars as well as private baths. Cash and check are acceptable payment methods. Kids are not encouraged, and pets are not allowed.

PINEAPPLE INN

645 South Broadway   *868-5453*

Built in 1876, Pineapple Inn is listed on the national Registry of Historic Places. It is filled with many antiques and features a Country French dining room, large living room, and two private and two shared guest rooms, priced at $55/night. You may pay by cash or check. Pets are not allowed, but kids older than 12 are welcome.

Wilmore

SCOTT STATION INN

305 East Main Street   *858-0121*

This century-old farmhouse features six guest rooms, each done in a different style, from a sewing loft to an Oriental theme. Scott Station is a family oriented B&B, featuring a playroom for the kids with videos and games. Pets are not allowed. Rates are $39.95 per night for a room with a shared bathroom, and $49.95 per night for a room with a private bathroom. The inn accepts cash, checks and major credit cards.

Winchester

WINDSWEPT FARM

5952 Old Boonesboro Road   *1-745-1245*

This 150-year-old Greek Revival home offers guests a true taste of the Bluegrass region with its picturesque setting among the rolling hills of the surrounding farmland. Windswept Farm has three shared rooms priced at $45/night. Personal checks and kids are welcome. Pets are not. Swimming and tennis facilities are available for guest use.

Inside
Campgrounds

*O*ne of Kentucky's biggest claims to fame is the magnificence and purity of its natural resources. One of the finest state parks systems in the nation, along with a widely varied geography featuring mountains, rivers, lake systems, and forests, makes outdoors in Kentucky a true delight for the whole family. A fairly temperate climate makes camping enjoyable throughout much of the year.

In addition to many privately owned campgrounds in the region, the state parks system has 26 parks with campsites equipped with utility hookups and dump stations. Primitive sites are also available at many of the parks.

Following is a listing of camping facilities available at state parks in the I-75 region (the main north-south highway corridor in Kentucky). Most campgrounds along this corridor are within two to three hours of Lexington and are readily accessible to the interstate.

Rates for camping in state parks are $10.50/night for two people at sites with utility hookups, and $8.50 for primitive sites. Each additional person older than age 16 is $1 more. There is a 15 percent discount for senior citizens.

Privately owned and operated campgrounds in Central Kentucky follow the state parks listings. For more information on sports and recreational activities at area state parks, see The Great Outdoors.

State Parks

KINCAID LAKE STATE PARK
Rt. 4 Box 33, Falmouth
41040-9203 1-654-3531

Located northeast of Lexington on Ky. 159, Kincaid Lake State Park features 84 camping sites with utilities on its 850 acres. The campground is located on the 183-acre Kincaid Lake, and has a pool, multipurpose building and boat dock. Drinking water, flush toilets and showers are also available. It is open April 1-October 31.

Kincaid Lake State Park also has 125 primitive camping sites. To get there, take I-75 north from Lexington and take exit 14 Ky. 330 to Morgan and on to Falmouth.

BIG BONE LICK STATE PARK
3380 Beaver Road, Union
41091-9627 1-384-3522

The prehistoric world meets the present at Big Bone Lick State Park, where thousands of years ago great herds of giant mastodons, mammoths and bison came to enjoy the

• **267**

warm salt springs in the area.

This 525-acre park has year round camping at 62 sites with utilities. Fishing, hiking and swimming in the park pool are some of the recreational activities the whole family will enjoy. To get there, take the Ky. 338 exit off I-75.

GENERAL BUTLER STATE RESORT PARK

Box 325 Carrollton,
41008-0325   (502) 732-4384
                          (800) 325-0078

Featuring the state parks system's only snow ski area, General Butler State Resort Park is an ideal site for year round outdoor recreation. The park offers 20 acres of ski trails, a large lake for summer activities, a nine-hole golf course, tennis courts and a pool. General Butler also has 111 campsites with utilities that are available throughout the year.

To get to General Butler State Resort Park, located 44 miles northeast of Louisville, take the Carrollton exit off I-71. To get to I-71, take I-64 west from Lexington to Louisville.

LEVI JACKSON WILDERNESS ROAD STATE PARK

998 Levi Jackson Mill Road, London,
40741-8944   1-878-8000

Step back in time 200 years as you visit historic Levi Jackson Wilderness Road State Park, which is located on two pioneer trails: Boone's Trace, blazed by Daniel Boone from the Cumberland Gap to the Kentucky River, and the Wilderness Road, which led the way for more than 200,000 settlers into Kentucky.

Levi Jackson Wilderness Road State Park has 146 campsites with utilities and 15 group camping cabins, all of which are available year round on the park's 896 acres. To get there, take I-75 south from Lexington to exit 38, just south of London.

GENERAL BURNSIDE STATE PARK

PO Box 488, Burnside,
42519-0488   1-561-4104
                          1-561-4192

Kentucky's only island park, General Burnside's 430 acres are located amid the beautiful waters of Lake Cumberland southwest of Lexington. The area was patrolled by Union General Ambrose Burnside and his troops during the Civil War. Today, the park is ideal for many outdoor activities, including boating, golfing, fishing and swimming.

General Burnside State Park has 94 camp sites with utilities and 16 primitive sites, all of which are available April 1-October 31. Each campsite has a fire pit and metal grill, picnic table and paved tent pad. To get there, take U.S. 27 south from Lexington, through Somerset to the park.

Insiders' Tips

A good way to spend a Sunday afternoon is to take a hike through Raven Run Nature Sanctuary, stopping to enjoy the breathtaking view of the Kentucky River palisades.

CUMBERLAND FALLS
STATE RESORT PARK

7351 Highway 90, Corbin,
KY 40701-8814   (800) 325-0063
                      (606) 528-4121

A magnificent 60-foot waterfall that boasts the only moonbow in this hemisphere is the crowning glory of Cumberland Falls State Resort Park. Whitewater rafting, fishing, horseback riding and hiking are just a few of the outdoor activities you can enjoy during your stay at this unusual state park.

Cumberland Falls State Resort Park has 50 campsites with utilities that are available April-October.

FORT BOONESBO STATE PARK

4375 Boonesb Road, Richmond,
40475-9316   1-527-3131

Camping at the site of Daniel Boone's second pioneer settlement is a unique way to experience and enjoy this part of American history. A reconstruction of Boone's fort here along the Kentucky River, as well as fishing, boating, miniature golf and swimming, make Fort Boonesborough State Park a great place for the whole family.

There are 167 campsites with utilities on this 153-acre park. To get there, take exit 95 off I-75 and go east on Ky. 627.

PINE MOUNTAIN
STATE RESORT PARK

1050 State Park Road, Pineville,
40977-0610   (800) 325-1712
                    1-337-3066

Located atop a mountain overlooking Kentucky Ridge State Forest, Pine Mountain State Resort Park became Kentucky's first state park in 1924. The Mountain Laurel Festi-

val is held here the last weekend of every May when the beautiful laurel blossoms are in full bloom.

There are 24 tent camping sites at this 1,519-acre park, located 15 miles north of Middlesboro off U.S. 25E in Pineville.

BLUE LICKS
BATTLEFIELD STATE PARK

PO Box 66, Mount Olivet,
40164-0066   1-289-5507

The site of the last battle of the Revolutionary War in Kentucky, Blue Licks Battlefield State Park offers miniature golf, hiking and swimming to its visitors. There are 51 sites with utilities at this 150-acre park, located northeast of Lexington on U.S. 68.

NATURAL BRIDGE
STATE RESORT PARK

General Delivery, Slade,
40376-9999   (800) 325-1710
                    1-663-2214

A spectacular sandstone arch 78 feet long and 65 feet high gives Natural Bridge State Resort Park its name. The park's 18 miles of hiking trails are some of the most spectacular in the state. You can hike up to the bridge or take the sky lift.

This 1,900-acre park, located in the heart of the Daniel Boone National Forest, has 95 campsites with utilities and 10 primitive sites. To get there, take I-64 east from Lexington to the Mountain Parkway and then to Ky. 11.

GREENBO LAKE STATE PARK

H.C. 60, Box 562, Greenup,
1144-9517   1- 473-7324

Another hiker's paradise, Greenbo Lake State Park covers 3,300 acres of secluded forests in

Cave Run, a man-made lake near Morehead, about 55 miles east of Lexington, is considered by many fishing experts to be the nation's best spot to catch muskie.

Greenup County, home of the poet Jesse Stuart. Fishing, especially for rainbow trout and largemouth bass, is a favorite activity at this beautiful state park.

Greenbo State Park has 64 campsites with utilities, and they are available April 1-October 31. There are also 35 primitive sites. To get there, take I-64 east from Lexington to the Grayson exit and then to Ky. 1.

Privately Owned Campgrounds

Privately owned and operated campgrounds also abound in the Central Kentucky area. Those in the immediate Lexington area are listed below by the town nearest to where they are located. Most of these campgrounds are not as scenic as those at the state parks, but they are usually more accessible to main roads and cities.

Lexington

KENTUCKY HORSE PARK
I-75, exit 120   233-4303
There are 260 campsites with utilities at the Kentucky Horse Park. Rates March 15-November 1 are $14.50/night (which includes water and electricity) for up to four people. November 21-March 14, rates drop

to $11/night for up to four people. There is a $1 charge for each additional person. Senior citizens get a discount — rates are $11 in peak season, $9 off-season.

Located at the exciting Kentucky Horse Park (folks camping here get a discount off admission to the horse park), this campground features a number of amenities, including a pool, dump stations, tennis and basketball courts, volleyball, horseshoes, and a recreation area.

Berea

OH! KENTUCKY CAMPGROUND
I-75, exit 76 to Ky. 21   1-986-1150
Oh! Kentucky Campground has 90 sites with utilities, and a number of primitive sites. Rates are $7/night for tent sites, $10/night for sites with electric and water, and $12/night for electric, water and sewer hookups. Each additional person costs $1.

Oh! Kentucky is located in the beautiful foothills of the Appalachian Mountains in the Folk Arts and Crafts Capital of Kentucky. Amenities at the park include two pools, basketball courts, activities room and plenty of nearby churches.

WALNUT MEADOW
I-75, exit 76   1-986-6180
If you're planning on camping with a large group of people (for a

family reunion, for instance), Walnut Meadow is the place to stay. The campground provides entertainment and a potluck dinner for groups of 25 or more.

But even if you're just out with the family or friends, this Berea campground offers amenities such as a pool, volleyball court, playground for young children, laundry and bath house to all campers. Additionally, the Barn is available for use by campers for grilling out or holding gatherings. The Barn is also equipped with a small kitchen so you can prepare food for your group as well.

Walnut Meadow has about 100 sites with utilities. Rates for sites with full hookups (water, electric and sewer) are $11/night. For electric and water only, the rate is $10/night. These rates are based on two adults, and each additional adult is charged $2.

Frankfort

ELKHORN CAMPGROUND

U.S. 460   *(502) 695-9154*

Adjacent to picturesque Elkhorn Creek, Elkhorn Campground offers campers all the comforts of home away from home. There's a swimming pool, miniature golf, shuffle board, a playground, basketball court, volleyball, horseshoes and video games. An on-site camp store with food and supplies, and a laundry facility are among the other creature comforts available.

The 125 campsites with utilities at Elkhorn Campground are priced as follows: $13/night with water and electric; $15/night with water, elec-

tric and sewer; and $17.50/night with water, electric, sewer and cable TV hookups.

KENTUCKY RIVER CAMPGROUND

U.S. 127 N.
(Steele Branch Road)   *(502) 227-2465*

With its prime location on the banks of the beautiful Kentucky River, Kentucky River Campground is ideal for those who enjoy water sports. An on-site boat ramp allows campers to play on the river during the day, then return immediately to their traveling "homes." Campground features include basketball courts, picnic shelters, volleyball and horseshoes. There are also a laundromat and supply store open throughout the year.

Kentucky River Campground has 104 sites with utilities. Rates are $13/night with water, sewer and electric, $77/week, and $180/month.

STILL WATERS CAMPGROUND

U.S. 127   *(502) 223-8896*

Still Waters Campground is located on Elkhorn Creek and the Kentucky River. Water sports play a big part in activities at this campground. Boats and canoes are available for rent, and on weekends when there is a new moon or full moon, the campground has a guided starlight or moonlight "float" with a cookout after. The cost is $13. Other campground amenities include volleyball, horseshoes, croquet, Frisbee golf, a bath house and dump station.

Open April-October 30, Still Waters Campground has 29 sites with utilities and 32 primitive sites. Rates are $6/night for primitive sites, $8/night with water and electric, $11-

12/night with water, electric and air conditioning.

Richmond

BLUE GRASS CAMPGROUND
I-75, exit 95 (Ky. 627)   *1-623-4843*

Located in the rolling farmland of scenic northern Madison County near the stately mansion of famed abolitionist and U.S. statesman Cassius Marcellus Clay, Blue Grass Campground is primarily an RV park. A store, laundromat and bath house are available for campers' use.

There are 35 sites with utilities available for $15/night with electric, water and sewer.

CLAY'S FERRY LANDING
I-75, exit 97   *1-623-1569*

The Kentucky River is the site of yet another Central Kentucky campground — Clay's Ferry Landing. For entertainment purposes, there is a nightclub nearby, and the campground is located next to the Star of Lexington riverboat cruise. For recreation, campers can enjoy horseshoes, volleyball, croquet, video games, a playground and a recreation hall. There are two bath houses and a supply store. The laundromat is open in season.

Clay's Ferry Landing has 100 sites with utilities and 15 primitive sites. Rates are $8/night for primitive sites, and $10.50/night for sites with electric and water, not on the river. Riverside sites are $13/night with water and electric, and $15/night with water, electric and sewer. Weekly and monthly rates are $65 and $256 respectively.

SOUTH LEXINGTON CAMPGROUND
I-75, exit 97   *1-624-9342*

Convenience is a key word to use when describing South Lexington Campground. It is not far off the interstate, located almost equidistant between Richmond and Lexington. That means you can enjoy the serenity of the rolling hills around the Kentucky River, while still being close enough to "civilization" that you won't feel cut off.

South Lexington Campground has 48 campsites with utilities, 10 with full hookup (sewer, water and electric). The rates for these sites, as well as for sites with electric and water only, are $13.50/night or $200/month. Sites with electric only are $12/night, and primitive sites are $10/night.

Tours are available at Waveland, an historic site between Lexington and Nicholasville.

Photo: Lexington Herald-Leader

The Shillito Creative Playground, dedicated in 1992, is one of three creative parks in Lexington. The parks have physical challenges that keep kids occupied for hours.

Inside
Parks and Recreation

Go fly a kite.

If that doesn't interest you, sign up for a basketball or soccer league. Fish. Swim. Hang upside down on a jungle gym. Walk, jog or run. Play tennis. Sail or pedal across a peaceful lake. Play a friendly, or not so friendly, game of softball. Enjoy a quiet picnic or an enthusiastic family reunion. Learn how to tap dance.

In Lexington, your recreation possibilities are virtually unlimited. Whether you prefer active or passive recreation, you can most likely find what you're looking for in the Bluegrass. In many cases, you'll find city-run programs offering what you want; in other cases, you'll have to look elsewhere. But you'll probably find it somewhere.

The authors had some difficulty in deciding which activities to include in this chapter and which to put in the chapter on The Great Outdoors. Some of our decisions were fairly arbitrary. This chapter includes the municipal parks and the assorted programs associated with them, along with some participatory sports, some of which are played indoors and others outdoors. The YMCA and YWCA are also here. The Great Outdoors chapter, meanwhile, is geared more toward traditional, more "woodsy" outdoor ac-

tivities such as fishing, hunting and hiking.

Public Parks, Playgrounds and Programs

Lexington has a generous supply of green parks and playgrounds filled with activities for all ages. Parks and Recreation, a division of the Lexington-Fayette Urban County Government, is responsible for operating and maintaining nearly 100 parks on more than 3,000 acres in Fayette County.

The division also offers, sponsors or co-sponsors a wide range of athletic leagues; instructional and recreational programs, including after-school classes, at Lexington elementary schools and community centers; and annual events for children and adults.

Special recreation programs are available for individuals with disabilities and special needs.

After-school youth classes, which vary seasonally and from site to site, include arts and crafts, ballet, baton, creative dance, drama, modern dance, sports activities, tap dance and tumbling. Costs for the youth classes are nominal, about $6 for a 10-week class. Adult classes, which cost a little more than the youth programs but are still reasonable, include art, ballroom dance, ceramics, clogging, crafts, fencing, pottery and step aerobics.

Athletically speaking, Parks and Recreation offers adult and youth softball, youth T-ball and baseball, youth football and cheerleading, youth and adult basketball, tennis; volleyball, and other activities. For sign-up times, watch for announcements or call the department at 255-0835.

(Parks and Recreation also maintains and operates four public golf courses. For details, see the chapter on Golf.)

Below, we have described some of Lexington's larger and more popular parks. There are many more, but we couldn't list them all. If you live in Lexington, there's bound to be at least one in your vicinity, and others may be on their way. Don't feel bad if your neighborhood park isn't mentioned here. In fact, you may want to let it remain your little secret; we love parks, and some of them get a little crowded at peak times.

For information about any of the municipal parks or programs, visit the Division of Parks and Recreation, 545 North Upper Street, or call the information office at 255-0835. The office is open Monday through Friday from 8 AM until 5 PM. There's also a 24-hour recorded hot line, 253-2384, offering news about events, activities and meetings.

CASTLEWOOD PARK
201 Castlewood Drive

In addition to a community center offering a range of activities (see below), Castlewood Park has a swimming pool, basketball courts and baseball and softball fields.

DOUGLASS PARK
726-798 Georgetown Street

Mention Douglass Park to many Lexingtonians, and two words come to mind: Dirt Bowl. Now, to be fair, this 27-acre park about a mile north of downtown has plenty more to offer, including a swimming pool and facilities for baseball, football, tennis and volleyball. But its claim to fame, especially among much of the black community, is the Dirt Bowl Summer Basketball League. Since its founding in 1967, the Dirt Bowl has featured a number of UK basketball stars and other high-grade players, some of whom have played in the NBA. Former Wildcats Jack Givens, James Lee, Dirk Minniefield and Melvin Turpin and Duke's Vince Taylor are among the stars who have left their marks on the court here. The Dirt Bowl's climax comes in July, when Super Sunday draws thousands of people to watch the games amid a festive atmosphere. (See the oral his-

Insiders' Tips

Insiders enjoy renting a pontoon or other boat for a day at Herrington Lake.

tory with Melvin Boyd Cunningham at the end of this chapter.)

GARDEN SPRINGS PARK
2005 Dogwood Drive

This 4 1/2-acre park in southwest Lexington is easily accessible from Garden Springs Drive; just turn into the Garden Springs Elementary School parking lot and drive to the back of the school. You'll find two baseball diamonds, a pool, a batting cage and more.

IDLE HOUR PARK
212 St. Ann Drive, behind Lexington Mall

With several basketball courts, this park is a popular spot for competitive hoops action. It also has baseball, softball and football fields, tennis courts, a picnic area, and a playground.

JACOBSON PARK
4001 Athens-Boonesboro Road

Drive into this 216-acre park on practically any Sunday afternoon and you'll quickly realize how popular it is. An attractive, 47-acre lake provides opportunities for fishing (license required), sailing or being captain of a two-passenger pedal boat, which can be rented at the marina. The park also contains Lexington's newest and largest creative playground (see the chapter on Kid Stuff). Seven picnic shelters, some of which have electricity, can be reserved by calling the Division of Parks and Recreation at 288-2900. The cost is $15 a day.

Jacobson Park also contains Camp Kearney, a two-week summer day camp for children. Four sessions are offered, with the first beginning in mid-June and the last beginning at the end of July. Times vary, but are generally from about 8:30 AM to 4:30 PM. The cost is $50, which includes transportation, lunch, snacks, insurance and supplies. Scholarships are available.

MASTERSON STATION PARK
3051 Leestown Road

Equestrian programs, including horseback riding lessons, clinics and

Photo: Lexington Herald-Leader

Thousands of runners and walkers turn out every July 4th for the Bluegrass 10,000 race in Lexington.

lectures, are among the offerings of this 660-acre park. (See the chapter on Horses for more information.) You'll also find an entertainment area where concerts are sometimes performed, fields for soccer and football and a jogging and walking trail. Masterson Station, which contains picnic areas and dog runs, is also the site of the Bluegrass Lions Club Fair each June.

SHILLITO PARK
3399 Brunswick Drive, off Reynolds Road

You can almost work up a sweat just thinking about this 120-acre park behind Fayette Mall. It contains numerous softball, baseball soccer and football fields, 13 tennis courts, a 50-meter swimming pool and a fitness trail. Picnic shelters with tables and grills can be reserved. Shillito Park is also home to one of three creative playgrounds in the city (see the chapter on Kid Stuff).

VETERANS PARK AT HICKMAN CREEK
Off Tates Creek Road just south of Man o' War Boulevard

This still-developing park, one of Lexington's newest, contains 200 acres with spectacular vistas of hillsides, woods, meandering streams and spacious meadows. The park features a "passive" recreation area with bicycle and jogging trails, picnic shelters, play equipment and benches. The "active" recreational facilities include ball diamonds and tennis and basketball courts.

WOODLAND PARK
601 East High Street

This park near downtown is an athletic and cultural magnet. In addition to a swimming pool, basketball and tennis courts, football and soccer fields, volleyball, playground equipment and picnic areas, Woodland Park also features an amphitheater that is used for the annual

Shakespeare in the Park festival and other events (see the chapter on Arts).

golf, tennis and martial arts; summer camps for youth; and much more. Call for a program guide.

Community Centers

Lexington's community centers, with an array of programs that varies from site to site, are:

BELL HOUSE SENIOR CITIZENS CENTER
Sayre Avenue   233-0986

CASTLEWOOD COMMUNITY CENTER
Castlewood Drive   254-2470

CHARLES YOUNG COMMUNITY CENTER
540 East Third Street   252-1955

DUNBAR COMMUNITY CENTER
545 North Upper Street   288-2941

KENWICK COMMUNITY CENTER
313 Owsley Avenue   266-6405

THE "Y"
YMCA OF CENTRAL KENTUCKY
239 East High Street   254-9622
YWCA of Lexington
1060 Cross Keys Road   276-4457

The YMCAs and YWCAs in Lexington and in surrounding counties offer an array of programs for children and adults. Programs include recreational sports leagues; swimming lessons and lifeguard certification; scuba instruction; classes in

Annual Athletic Events

In the Bluegrass, it seems there's always some major athletic event going on. The ones listed below, while hardly the only events, are representative because they offer something for people of all ages. If you live in Lexington, whatever your age, you have no excuse for not having a good time.

BLUEGRASS 10,000

The Bluegrass 10,000 foot race, sponsored by Parks and Recreation in conjunction with the *Lexington Herald-Leader*, is held every July 4 and is open to all ages. Many families participate together, some of them with strollers. Although many participants will be going all out to finish in the fastest time possible, others take a more casual approach and do it for the enjoyment. In addition to the 10,000-meter (about 6 1/4 miles) race around the streets of downtown Lexington, there also is a "fun run," as well as other related events. This popular race annually attracts thousands of runners from Kentucky and other states. We guarantee that between now and next July 4 you will have

Insiders like the great photo opportunities among the bronze horse statues at Thoroughbred Park on the corner of Main Street and Midland Avenue.

Insiders' Tips

Photo: Lexington Herald-Leader

Pedal boats can be rented at the Jacobson Park marina.

ample opportunities to register and get your very own commemorative Bluegrass 10,000 T-shirt.

A MIDSUMMER NIGHT'S RUN

1994 is the 10th year for A Midsummer Night's Run, sponsored by Central Baptist Hospital. The main event is a 5-kilometer race, but there are several other activities, including a 1-mile fun walk/run, a Baby Derby, fastest-kid-in-town contest and entertainment. A Midsummer Night's Run is held downtown each year in late August.

BLUEGRASS STATE GAMES

This annual summer event is our own version of the Olympics. The Bluegrass State Games, started in August 1985, constitute the state's largest amateur sporting event. They are open to all ages and skill levels. Games are held over one weekend at various locations around the state, depending on the sport. Participants, who must be Kentucky residents, are limited to one sport, but they can participate in as many events as they desire in that one sport.

Events in 1993 were: archery, basketball (three on three), bowling, canoeing and kayaking, chess, croquet, cycling, darts, diving, equestrian, fencing, golf, gymnastics, horseshoes, karate, racquetball, shooting, soccer, softball, swimming, table tennis, tennis, track and field, volleyball and wrestling. The 1994 offerings should be similar. Special categories are available for athletes with disabilities. Watch the newspaper and local TV stations for announcements.

LEXINGTON SENIOR GAMES

These games for Lexington residents age 55 and older are a more low-key version of the Olympics. The Lexington Senior Games feature not only competition in such events as basketball shooting, billiards, bowling, cards, croquet, fishing, horseshoes, shuffleboard and table tennis

Insiders' Tips

Insiders enjoy renting pedal boats and cruising the lake at Jacobson Park. They also enjoy playing hide-and-seek in the creative playground.

but also social events such as a nature walk, a party and a dance. For more information call 288-2900.

KENTUCKY SPECIAL OLYMPICS

Kentucky began holding this statewide competition for mentally retarded people in 1970. Leading up to the state championships in June, as many as 12,000 participants ages 8 through adult compete in 22 sports, including swimming, diving, track and field, weight lifting, gymnastics and bowling. Every four years, qualifiers are eligible to participate in the International Special Olympics. This competition helps develop self-esteem among the competitors; and, as anyone who's ever been involved as a volunteer or spectator will tell you, it's a very rewarding cause — rewarding enough, in fact, to warm the heart of the most jaded sports fan.

Participatory Sports

LEAGUES

Leagues in baseball, softball, volleyball, tennis and other sports are offered through the Division of Parks and Recreation of the Lexington-Fayette Urban County Government (288-2900), the Y's (see above section on YMCA and YWCA) and other sources. There is a variety of options

for adults and youth. In many cases, adults can join as individuals or as teams; you may want to get together with a bunch of friends or a group from your workplace. Many churches also have their own leagues.

A number of instructional and competitive baseball and softball leagues are offered through The Ball Diamond (150 Dennis Drive, 277-6305).

Bars are getting into the volleyball scene, which for some people means not having to wait until the game's over to hoist a cold one. A1A Sandbar & Grille (2660 Wilhite Drive, 276-4513) and Marikka's Restaurant und Bier Stube (411 Southland Drive, 275-1925), for example, have outdoor volleyball courts that see a lot of action, and A1A is known for its competitive leagues.

Soccer has really taken off in the Bluegrass in recent years, especially among youth. The Lexington Youth Soccer Association, popularly known as LYSA, runs an excellent program; for information, call 223-5632.

RUNNING GROUPS
TODDS ROAD STUMBLERS

This nonprofit group, founded in 1975 by Alex Campbell, is the largest running organization in Central Kentucky. It's a very informal group, with no dues or anything: Simply meet, run and then socialize for a while if you like. During nice weather, up to 100 people meet between 7 AM and 8 AM Saturday at the clubhouse on Todds Road. Six-, 9-, 12- and 15-mile courses are marked off on rolling hills in the country. First-time completers of the 6-mile course receive a free Todds Road T-shirt. Afterward, coffee and donuts are served in the clubhouse.

Those who are interested in joining should call Becky Reinhold at 268-2701 or show up on Saturday morning.

BICYCLING

Lexington cyclists have been pushing for more trails for years. So far, only a handful of roads are marked with bicycle lanes or designated for bicycle use. They are Rose Street, Alumni Drive and Bellefonte Drive, all of which run partly on the University of Kentucky campus, and Old Squires Road, which is closed to automobiles.

A number of city parks have bike trails, where traffic isn't a problem at all. These include Kirklevington, Lansdowne, Merrick, Veterans and Waverly. Most Lexington neighborhoods also feature wide streets suitable for safe cycling, if proper caution is exercised. And people who like to get away from the suburban traffic and into a more scenic environment enjoy such roads as Walnut Hill, Delong and Old Richmond, as well as Parker's Mill and any other rural road with "Mill" in its name.

Those who really like roughing it prefer mountain biking on their rugged, thick-tired vehicles. Mountain biking trails can be found at Cave Run Lake near Morehead (1-784-6428), in the Daniel Boone National Forest near London (1-864-4163) and at Red River Gorge in Stanton (1-663-2852).

Here are some good places to get a bike in Lexington:

CYCLE SPORTS & FITNESS
1965 Harrodsburg Road   277-6013
3101 Richmond Road   266-8937

PEDAL POWER BIKE SHOP
401 South Upper Street   255-6408

SCHELLER'S SCHWINN CYCLING
(formerly Everybody's Bike Shop)
212 Woodland Avenue   233-1764

TENTH GEAR BICYCLE SHOP
828 Lane Allen Road   278-1053

TENNIS COURTS
Tennis courts are all over Lexington, most notably in city parks and at apartment complexes.

There's bound to be one near you. The Lexington Tennis Club (at 410 Redding Road, 272-4546) is a private facility with indoor and outdoor courts, an Olympic pool, weight room, whirlpools and saunas.

BOWLING

COLLINS BOWLING CENTER — EASTLAND
786 New Circle Road   252-3429

COLLINS BOWLING CENTER — SOUTHLAND
205 Southland Drive   277-5746

JOYLAND BOWL & PARK
2361 Paris Pike   293-0529

GEORGETOWN BOWLING LANES
Lexington Road, Georgetown   863-9756

FITNESS AND HEALTH CLUBS

BODY INVESTMENT
3340 Holwyn Road   223-3773

FORD'S FITNESS CENTERS
151 West Zandale Drive   276-1151
2100 Oxford Circle   252-5121

GOLD'S GYM, AEROBICS & FITNESS
Fayette Place
4001 Nicholasville Road   271-1900

JAZZERCISE CENTER OF LEXINGTON
4750 Hartland Parkway   272-4455

JEANNIE THÉ FITNESS STUDIOS
2573 Richmond Road   269-8437

LEXINGTON ATHLETIC CLUB
3992 West Tiverton Court   273-3163

LEXINGTON SPORTS CLUB
230 West Main Street   281-5110

SHAPES NEW DIMENSIONS HEALTH & FITNESS CENTER
South Park Shopping Center   273-6881
Village East Center   299-8441

SIN THÉ GYM
284 Gold Rush Road   275-2148

MARTIAL ARTS INSTRUCTION

ATA TAEKWONDO KARATE SCHOOL
1833 Alexandria Drive   276-2425

DAVE VOSSMEYER'S TAEKWONDO CENTER
820 Lane Allen Road   277-5425

INTERNATIONAL KUNG-FU ACADEMY
3341 Holwyn Road   224-0623

LEXINGTON TAEKWONDO CENTER
537 Waller Avenue   255-4137

SIN THÉ KARATE SCHOOL
284 Gold Rush Road   275-2148

TAEKWONDO PLUS KARATE CENTER
3120 Pimlico Parkway   245-1733

TRACY'S KARATE STUDIOS
373 Codell Drive   266-3734

SPORTING GOODS

JOHN'S BLUEGRASS RUNNING SHOP
321 South Ashland Avenue   269-8313

John's offers professional, experienced help in selecting the right walking and running shoes and accessories for your needs.

NEW HORIZONS DIVING CENTER
2566 Regency Road   277-1234, 277-6349

In addition to scuba equipment sales, service and rental, New Horizons offers professional scuba instruction and booking of underwater expeditions.

PHILLIP GALL'S

Woodhill Plaza   266-0469
1555 New Circle Road NE

Phillip Gall's, which recently moved from Lexington Mall to right behind it, has a wide selection of sleeping bags, tents, stoves, knives and other camping and outdoors equipment.

PLAY IT AGAIN SPORTS

120 Richmond Road   269-4556
820 Lane Allen Road   276-3299

Play It Again buys and sells used sporting goods, which makes it a good option for the novice golfer who doesn't want to drop a fortune on a set of clubs.

ALLIED SPORTING GOODS

Idle Hour Shopping Center,
2010 Richmond Road   268-4600
North Park, 500 New Circle
Road NW   253-3222

Richmond Mall, 830 Eastern By-Pass, Richmond
1-624-8100

ALLSPORTS

Fayette Mall   282-8656
Lexington Mall   269-4361

BOB DANIELS SPORTING GOODS

1400 Alexandria Drive   255-0104

BOBICK'S NEVADA
BOB'S DISCOUNT GOLF

101 Mount Tabor Road   269-4443

KENTUCKY SPORTING GOODS

501 West Main   252-5825

THE LOCKER ROOM SPORTING
GOODS

739 Lane Allen Road   276-1101
304 South Limestone Street   252-8312

SOCCER CENTER

451 South Ashland Avenue   269-1100

SPORTS UNLIMITED

3650 Boston Road   223-4211

Melvin Boyd Cunningham: "We were doing something we believed in"

"My position here is director of the Carver Neighborhood Center. We are a social-service building run by the Urban County Government. Within the building we have various agencies that provide nonprofit services to the city of Lexington. We have a clothing bank that is run by Community Action. We take in clothes and redistribute them free of charge. We have been doing this for a number of years now, and it is a worthwhile and much-needed service. Even though we are located on the south side of town, we are open to the whole city.

"We have a Parks and Recreation Department here. We provide basketball, volleyball, ping-pong, aerobics, dancing, arts and crafts, drill teams, cooking and sewing. So we have a variety of activities. We keep the kids busy for nine months, from August till school is out at the last of May, and then we take our recreation programs outside to the playground for the summer.

"The Micro-City Government is housed here. We provide summer youth jobs, GED programs. We have a recreation and fun room with a TV and pool tables, and we have club meetings and so forth in that room.

"I've been here for a total of 14 years — the first two as assistant director and the past 12 as director. So I've spent the last 14 years being involved in various programs all over the city.

"I was born and raised in

Melvin Boyd Cunningham

Lexington and went to Booker T. Washington Elementary School over on Georgetown Street. Then I graduated from the old Dunbar High School on North Upper Street. I left there and went to college at Kentucky State University in Frankfort. I graduated from there in 1962.

"I played intramural basketball in high school and college. That's where my involvement in basketball comes from. But I also had a love for track and field, so I was on the track team at Dunbar High School for three years, and then I ran varsity track at Kentucky State for four years. After college I became heavily involved in working with youths in basketball and developed a college placement program and the Dirt Bowl. That was the end of my track and field involvement.

"From 1963 until 1967, I was teaching high school in Charleston, South Carolina. My mother got sick, and I came back to Lexington to help here. I had intentions of maybe staying a year and going back to Charleston. But in the meantime, I secured a job at Kentucky State University as director of the student center. It was there that I kind of developed this idea of the Dirt Bowl, and I took it to a friend of mine, Herbert Washington, who was working for Parks and Recreation at that time. He was also a full-time employee at IBM.

"I went to him with this idea of forming a real rigid type of organized outside basketball league. He was very receptive to the idea, and we formed a partnership with his cousin, Marvin Washington. The three of us got together and had a series of meetings and kicked around all kinds of ideas.

All sorts of rules: where it would be played, who we could get to volunteer to be coaches, how many kids would be on a team, what age groups they would be, who we could get that would be effective referees. . . .

"We wanted it to be under game conditions in terms of scorekeepers, time-clock operators and that type of thing. So we went to work. We talked on the telephone every day, and we would meet at one another's houses and kick around this idea. It was then that we picked Douglass Park as a site.

"Every day when we got off work, we would have meetings and formulate names of referees and coaches and players. We would get in the car and go around knocking on the doors of these guys we had selected, to see if they would volunteer their time to help us get started. We were very lucky that a lot of people wanted to be a part of it.

"One of the keys to the Dirt Bowl, one of the things that made it so popular and successful, was that from day one, the three of us had this vision that it would be a training ground for the young kids to develop from junior high to high school all through college. We had basically three purposes in mind: It would serve as a training ground for the players, the referees and the coaches.

"We were very fortunate with that, even today. Guys like Donnie Byars — you've probably seen him on TV. He has moved all the way up from the Dirt Bowl to being a licensed referee for the Ohio Valley Conference. This guy Bernie Jenkins — he calls the state tournament just about every other year, and he also is a licensed referee in the Ohio Valley Conference.

"Steve Chandler, who won three state tournaments in baseball at Lafayette, played in our Dirt Bowl every summer while he was in college at Vanderbilt playing baseball. Steve played for The Bronx, probably the most popular team ever to play in the Dirt Bowl. That's the team that James Lee played on, one of the most popular players to ever play in the Dirt Bowl. Steve was a player-coach, so he got some experience way back then in terms of handling and disciplining players. It carried over for him. He was very successful. Of course, he resigned his teaching position at Lafayette, and now he is a minor-league scout full time for the New York Yankees.

"We've had just a slew of outstanding players who have participated in the Dirt Bowl year in and year out. We still place kids in college, and the Dirt Bowl has expanded now into a women's Dirt Bowl division, a junior Dirt Bowl, a senior Dirt Bowl and a Sun Bowl for little kids. It has survived all these years, and it will go on and on forever. After I'm dead and gone, it will still be here.

"We still get scouts to come in as much as possible, but not as much as we did in the old days because the rules have changed, and the NCAA is real strict now on these camps and summer leagues that go on all over the country. So the college coaches can no longer flock in and out of these summer leagues any time that they want to; they have certain periods that they can scout these camps and leagues. So I personally take it upon myself to give them a call or write them a letter to give them tips on who is doing well and who they should get involved with. It's still what they call an official NCAA-sanctioned outdoor summer league.

"One of the keys to making the Dirt Bowl stable was that, when Herb Washington, Marvin Washington and I got together, we made it a serious business. It was no joke. All three of us told our wives what we were going to be doing at night when we got off work. We told them that it was in some way going to infringe upon our time with them and the children in terms of not being able to come home every night at 5 o'clock for dinner. We were trying to do something that we believed in, and we were dead serious about it.

"*USA Today* picked up on it and ran some stories. Two books were written: *The In-Your-Face Basketball Book* and *The Back-in-Your-Face Guide to Pick-up Basketball.* Believe it or not, the guys who wrote those books and stories and helped us get off the ground . . . they got jobs out of it, and one of them is kind of famous now, Alexander Wolff. He calls me every time he comes to Lexington, and, of course, he's making big money; he's a top writer for *Sports Illustrated.*

"Back in the summer, ESPN covered, live, one of those Dirt Bowl leagues in Southern California. I watched that back around the last part of June. Dick Vitale did the commentary on it. That's how enormous this thing was.

"Even to this day, the players and the coaches and the administration take this thing very seriously. I gave up my active position on the Dirt Bowl . . . but the people who are now involved take it very seriously. I'm sort of an adviser to them, and I'm an everyday spectator. I lend my support any way I can.

"The team that I had was called the Cunningham Stars; I named it after myself (laugh). They have tryouts now. At the time I was actively involved, each coach was instructed to go out and recruit his own players. Recruit the best team that you possibly could to make the league highly competitive every summer. If you did not do that, if you did not get involved to the point where you wanted to have a competitive team, you were not invited to coach the following year. If the team was not competitive, it made for a bad league.

"I went around and recruited all young players. My thing was developmental, getting the kids ready to play for their high school teams. So I had people on my team like Melvin Turpin (who later starred for the University of Kentucky) and Fred Emerson, who played for Henry Clay and went on

Teams from all over the city play in the annual Dirt Bowl tournament.

to play for Boyd Grant at Fresno State. I had Leroy Byrd on my team at that time, before he went to Las Vegas (and later returned to play for UK). So we had what we called the 'new kids on the block' type of team.

"The Dirt Bowl at that time did not have divisions. The younger kids had to play against the older, college kids. And the fans liked the underdogs. So my team was popular. We used to pack that arena week after week. We fed off the crowd. It was a David and Goliath type of thing.

"James Lee used to pack the house. They used to come to see James Lee and his thunder dunks, you know. He was highly competitive. He put his whole heart and soul into Dirt Bowl and summer league ball. A lot of kids who had a future in playing college ball — the summer was something they took lightly. But James Lee took that Bronx team that he played on to heart.

"Back during the early days, the famous kids from Kentucky State were a big contributor to the Dirt Bowl, and they made it highly competitive. I'm talking specifically about Billy Ray Bates, who went on to play for the Portland Trailblazers in the NBA. He played guard for them for about three years. Billy Ray Bates may be the most popular player and the most forceful player to ever play in the Dirt Bowl.

"Travis Grant played in the Dirt Bowl back in the first few years. Elmore Smith played; we're talking about a 7-footer way back in those days. Elmore Smith went on to play for the Cleveland Cavaliers, and Travis Grant played for the Los Angeles Lakers.

"The coaches became fascinated by recruiting, getting the players to compete. We would have our organizational meetings in the winter, around February, to start planning for the Dirt Bowl. From February till the league started on June 15 — once we got sanctioned, June 15 was the starting date every year — the coaches would recruit the high school players they wanted, players from Eastern, Morehead, Transylvania, UK. They would start mentioning to them: 'If you're going to be around this summer, I'd like for you to be on my team. I've already talked to this player, and he has agreed to play, and we think we can win the whole championship this year.'

"The coaches got a taste of what it was like to talk to people, to go into people's homes and meet the mothers and fathers and explain to them that 'Your son is going to be playing for me, and this is what I expect of him,' and what it was like to be rejected. Like, 'Hey, I've got other plans for my son, and I don't want him to be playing outside.' See, there's always that fear that with outside basketball you'll get hurt, but playing in the gym you won't.

"The coaches learned to accept rejection, and they learned not to put all of their pennies in one bag. If you recruit *him,* you better recruit somebody else because, when the time comes, something else could come up. That fear of getting hurt, or the kid's parents have something else planned for him. A kid will tell you he's going to play for you, and then when he finds out his buddy is on another team, then he prefers to play on the team with his buddy. So I would always get a real good feel for the kids who want to play for me, and then at the end of the summer I would have a team meeting and explain to my kids that, if you didn't get a chance to play and you were not satisfied, if you want to jump teams, that's fine. I have no problems with it. There was no league rule that if you played on one team one year, you had to play on the same team next year. You were free to jump teams. But once the league started, you had to play for your team for the rest of that summer. If you chose to quit, that was fine, but you could not join another team once the league had started.

"It's a shorter schedule now than it was. We ran it from June 15 up until a week before school started. So we probably had a 10-week schedule. We scheduled it so that each team would play two games a week. You get stale and rusty playing one game a week. If you have too many teams, you can't get two games in. We wanted the people to have fun and develop, and one game a week is just not enough to keep it exciting.

"We fixed it so everybody would play everybody, so you couldn't dodge the good teams. We set our rosters at 10 per team so you wouldn't have a lot of kids sitting on the bench who didn't get to play. We instructed the kids not to join a team if they didn't think they were going to play. If you were 15 years old, in high school, and you joined the Bronx team just out of excitement and you're going to be on the team with James Lee and Jack

Givens, you're not going to get a chance to play. So you need to be on a team that has your interests at heart and wants to work with you and develop you and get you to a different level.

"That was part of my job, to remind the kids. And then remind the coaches: If you don't think a kid can play, don't put him on your team. You're not obligated to put a kid on your team. And you've got to be strong and stand up to the kid and the parents. I've had parents come to me and say, 'You've got a very good team, and I've watched your kids, and they all speak highly of you, and they all seem to be happy, and they win, and they're having fun and I'd like for my son to play for you.'

"And I would have to tell them, you know, that 'I've seen your son play. And for what we're doing, he's not quite ready. I've got a friend who's got a team, and I'll speak with him. What you do is you start your son off with my friend's team, and then next year, he should be ready for my team. This is not a slap in the face, and don't take it the wrong way, but this is just the way sports is. Sports is development and moving from the bottom to the top.'

"Super Sunday comes in the middle of the league. That's the biggest event that you have, basically, in the city of Lexington because of the enormous amount of people who have come out and supported that down through the years. When you say 'Super Sunday,' it takes on a citywide meaning. It is not for the Dirt Bowl; it is not for the people on the west side of Lexington because the park is located there. It is a citywide project, and it's for the people of Lexington. And it has been able to maintain its enthusiasm and popularity.

"Herb Washington is the one who came up with the name. We were talking one day at a little staff meeting between the three of us, and we were just fantasizing about the NCAA tournament and the Super Bowl and the World Series and things of that nature, and he said, 'Hey, let's have a big day where we invited people in not only to watch basketball but to pitch horseshoes, play volleyball, go swimming, have baseball games. And let's just bring people out: people in wheelchairs, people with disabilities. Let's try to have people out there who have not been in the parks for years. Let's think of something that will bring the people back to where they used to be years ago, when they were kids.'

"So he came up with this idea of Super Sunday. We would take one Sunday in the middle of the season, and we would sit down and look at every team's record, and we'd match games. The concept of Super Sunday was entertainment, show biz. You had to be good in basketball, and you had to have proved that you had something the people wanted to see.

"A lot of people felt it was unfair because some of your weaker teams wanted to share in the glory and the spotlight, too. And as the years went on, we were very sensitive to that. Now the weaker teams are woven into

Super Sunday, and the girls are woven in. We have at least one girls' game to give them the opportunity to play before the big crowds and share in the thrills. We got complaints and were criticized for having the stars or the same teams every year. But we still had the featured games. You've got to have superstars.

"We have a beautiful court out there. They redid it last year. They have new baskets and new posts and all the equipment, the time clocks. The surface is brand new. We used to paint it every year to represent one of the high schools in Lexington. We'd rotate it. One year it would be red and white for Lafayette, the next year it would be yellow and blue for Henry Clay, then green and gold for Bryan Station. . . . We would include the two old black high schools that used to be here: One year it would be green and white to represent Dunbar, and the next year it would be blue and gold to represent Douglass, which had colors similar to Henry Clay's.

"As a staff we had a lot of respect for Mr. S.T. Roach. He was our biology teacher at Dunbar. And Herbert Washington played varsity basketball for Mr. Roach at Dunbar. So we always invited him to the big affairs, and we kept him up to date on what we were doing. And we would be open to any suggestions that he would have. Because of his popularity and other activities, he didn't always have time to be involved with the Dirt Bowl, but we relied on him for advice, and we respect him for the contributions he's made.

"One of the persons who made a giant contribution was Ted Hundley, who played at Bryan Station with Jack Givens (and went on to play for Morehead). And Bob Daniels, who has Bob Daniels Sporting Goods, when he retired from coaching at Kentucky Wesleyan and moved to Lexington to open up his store, he put his sons in the Dirt Bowl and he coached for years. He had a team called the All-White Team that we admitted to the Dirt Bowl right after we got it started.

"From day one, most of the teams that were in the Dirt Bowl had white kids on them, even though they might have been predominantly black. The people who played on the teams had white friends who played basketball, and they were invited to be on the teams also. I recruited white kids who went to college like Kenny Southworth. He played for me and at Bryan Station, and he went on to play at Central Missouri for Lynn Nance, who used to be an assistant coach under Joe Hall at UK. And we had kids like Paul Collier, who went to Central State of Oklahoma. Little Junior Johnson, who played on a state championship team at Lafayette with Dirk Minniefield, played in the Dirt Bowl. And he went on to play at the University of Cincinnati. He's a very successful businessman now, in the burglar alarm business.

"The Dirt Bowl would not have reached its popularity as an all-black league. Because of its physical location on the west side of Lexington and in Douglass Park, then naturally the black connotation would be placed upon it, but its intent was never to be all black. From day one, we had white coaches and white teams. And the black teams had white players. And that holds true today.

"It didn't cause any problems. When the all-white teams played the all-black teams, the park was so packed you couldn't get in. The white teams had a great fan following, and they had good players. And the black teams had a great fan following. So that was a monumental thing when the teams like Bob Daniels' team played and when Ervin Stepp's team played. And there never were any racial problems with the Dirt Bowl. Never. Never. Never. That is a complete blessing, with the racial tensions that you had in Lexington, in Kentucky and in America, that we have been able to bring the blacks and whites together in Douglass Park for over 20 years, and there has not been one single racial incident concerning basketball. That is a blessing.

"Summer-league basketball all over the United States — especially in places like New York, Chicago and Detroit — was a recruiting heaven for Division I schools like Marquette and Las Vegas. On the playgrounds, you had the 'pimps,' guys who hung around and actually were peddling off kids for money to junior colleges and places all over the United States. The NCAA did not have restrictions on that, and those things were getting out of hand. So the NCAA came up with this idea that there should be some control over these Dirt Bowls and summer leagues and that they must be sanctioned. Now, when they went to that, it meant that only certain leagues all over the country were granted sanctions.

"In order to be sanctioned, there was a license. The NCAA had to come to your place, and we had to write proposals and prove that we were running a legitimate summer-league program. We had applications that were kept on file in Shawnee Mission, Kansas. I was the director, so they had to know about me: Who is this guy? Is he a pimp, a con man? Who will be supervising these kids? Do these referees have enough experience and training that it won't get out of control? Are the physical facilities big enough and safe enough to conduct a program of this magnitude? Do you have bathrooms and water fountains? Because we're talking about playing in 90-degree heat. Do you have first-aid kits? Are your basketball goals legitimate, 10 feet high? That kind of thing.

"Those first few years, they only granted a few all over the United States. So when the rules changed and college kids had to go out and recruit at these summer leagues, a lot of them had been disbanded. The NCAA provided an official sanctioned list. The college coaches would look at the list and decide where to go. That's when coaches started calling me.

"So the Dirt Bowl gave summer-league basketball the credibility on a nationwide level. See, everybody in the state knew that, even in the days of segregation and your all-black high schools, Kentucky was loaded with good gobs of white players and black players. And these summer leagues were always carried on, but they never rose to the level of New York and Chicago and Detroit. Now here was little Lexington, Kentucky, that was doing something out of the ordinary for a town this size. So the Dirt Bowl gave Lexington the credibility and respect that these other places had. It put us on a new level.

"And when other cities wanted to develop Dirt Bowls to the magnitude that we did, they called Parks and Recreation. They even flew people in. And it gave the high school coaches so much confidence that they could put their kids in a program where the kids could develop.

"And it really helped to ease a lot of the racial tension with the high school coaches and programs. Up until then, they were leery of putting their kids in this type of program because they knew of the leagues in Chicago and Detroit, and that's all-out war. Well, when this thing leveled off, then a guy at Lafayette would say, "Hey, I've got this little kid in 10th grade. What they're doing out there is great. I have no problems with sending this kid over there for the summer." It was a big race-relations factor — and, even today, it brings the blacks and whites together to do something in the summer, when it's 95 degrees."

Today, even though Melvin Boyd Cunningham is no longer "actively" involved with the Dirt Bowl, he remains involved with the kids as a counselor and motivator. He stresses the importance of academics, especially for those who hope to play college ball and must meet Proposition 48 requirements. He provides them with inspirational stories of others who have succeeded. And, through his connections, he is often able to help place kids in colleges and junior colleges around the country.

"Your average high school kid doesn't read the paper. A lot of them don't watch college games; they watch cartoons on Saturday morning. So when a kid comes in and I talk to him about his grades, I show him. I say, 'You know that even though you were qualified last year, this Prop 48 is going to change. You need to know this, and I'm going to make you a copy of this newspaper article to take home to your mother and father.'

"So I'm still involved in the recruiting and counseling aspect. . . . I keep saying I'm going to quit. And then every time I get my mind set to quit, there's somebody who just needs some help, and because I'm able to do it, I do it."

Inside
Kid Stuff

*O*h, to be a kid again!

Lexington is a great place to be a kid. And, whatever your age, you can be a kid in Lexington. Most of the attractions mentioned in this section are open to all ages. To fit in, all you need is a willingness to have fun and approach life as an adventure.

If you're a parent, you'll be happy to know that your children can learn while they're having fun at many of these places, such as the Lexington Children's Museum, the Lexington Public Library, Safety City and the YMCA and YWCA. Heck, you might even learn a few things yourself.

We have gone the extra mile to lend some perspective to this section of the book. We consulted a recognized expert on children's activities: a genuine 7-year-old boy with a slightly dirty (but smiling) face. The resulting selection of things to do is versatile enough to satisfy almost any interest — even interests that are accompanied by short attention spans. Most of the attractions mentioned in this section are within the confines of Lexington proper, and there's nothing more than two hours away.

We've got animals and arts and astronauts . . . balls and books and bugs . . . a castle and climbing and clowns . . . dinosaurs and drama and driving . . . magic and music and Mickey Mouse . . . playgrounds and parades and pumpkins. We could go on, but by now you're probably about ready to pile into the station wagon with your family and start exploring the area on your own, so we'll cut to the chase.

First, a note of explanation: Some of the children's attractions listed could easily have been included in other parts of the book, such as the Shopping section. Some *are* mentioned elsewhere. Because of their appeal to the younger set, however, we thought it appropriate to include them here. For additional activities that the entire family can enjoy, refer to the sections on campgrounds, parks and recreation, sports, fishing, horses, museums, the arts and, frankly, just about anything else.

As we said, Lexington is a great place to be a kid. So here are the details on a bunch of neat stuff for Bluegrass kids to do, from amusement parks to zoos.

Amusement Parks

Although there are no amusement parks in the immediate Lexington area, two very good ones are located less than two hours away.

Photo: Lexington Herald-Leader

The castle above is located on U.S. 60 between Lexington and Versailles.

KENTUCKY KINGDOM

Kentucky Fair and Exposition Center,
Louisville (502) 366-7508

This park at the Kentucky Fair and Exposition Center in Louisville opened briefly in 1986 and closed the same year. When new owners reopened it in 1990, it was vastly improved. Kentucky Kingdom's 40-plus acres now are home to a number of thrilling rides, including a wooden roller coaster that *Amusement Business* magazine called the most terrifying in North America. There's also a 15-story Ferris wheel, a kiddie section, a water park with slides and wave pool, and a variety of stage shows.

Tickets in 1993 were $16.95, with seniors and children shorter than 4 feet tall getting in for just $9.95. The regular season is June 5 to August 18; the park is also open on weekends in May and from August 19 through Labor Day. Regular hours, from June through mid-August, are 11 AM to 9 PM Sunday through Thursday, 11 AM to midnight Fri-day, and 11 AM to 11 PM Saturday. Hours are extended during the Kentucky State Fair in late August. The park is also open on weekends in May and through Labor Day in September. To get to Kentucky Kingdom from Lexington, take I-64 west, exit on I-264 west and follow the signs to the Fair and Exposition Center.

PARAMOUNT'S KINGS ISLAND

Kings Mills, Ohio
Interstate 71 (513) 398-5600

A little farther away — 24 miles north of Cincinnati — lies a longtime regional favorite. This 185-acre park, known for its Hanna-Barbera cartoon characters and its Beast roller coaster, was bought in 1992 by the Paramount movie studio. In addition to The Beast, one of the longest and best wooden roller coasters in the United States, there are several other coasters and thrill rides. The new Hollywood connection resulted in a Top Gun ride for 1993, and a Days of Thunder racing ride is coming in 1994. Milder rides include the enchanting, air-conditioned Smurf's Voyage for all ages. Kings Island also offers a "safari" monorail ride, a petting zoo and an adjoining water park. And let's not forget International Street with its one-third-scale model of the Eiffel Tower.

In addition to live shows throughout the park, Kings Island also has an amphitheater that regularly features concerts by popular national acts. General admission is $23.95; seniors and children ages 3 to 6 get in for $11.95 and those 2 and younger get in free. Discount coupons are available through area Kroger stores. The park is open Saturdays and Sundays in April and May, then opens daily from Memorial Day to Labor Day. In September and October, it is open on selected Saturdays and Sundays when corporations do not have the park rented for private use. Hours vary some but are generally from 10 AM to 10 PM.

General Fun Spots

THE BALL DIAMOND
150 Dennis Drive   *277-6305*

The Ball Diamond, which bills itself as "Kentucky's largest indoor batting range," appeals to virtually all ages with its variety of instructional and recreational activities and leagues. For sports-minded boys and girls, it is a popular site for birthday parties. Children can play whiffleball on an indoor diamond that quickly converts to a basketball court, take batting practice in a cage with a pitching machine, practice their putts on a small artificial green or play one of a handful of pinball and video games. Prices vary.

"THE CASTLE"
U.S. 60 between Lexington and Versailles

Technically, this isn't a kids' attraction, or even an attraction at all. You can't go in it, or even get any closer than 300 yards from it without trespassing, so we can't tell you what it's like on the inside.

But the anachronistic Gothic structure has been the subject of more speculation than any other building in the Bluegrass, and it's great fuel for a child's imagination. Visitors stop along the highway daily to have their pictures taken in front of the castle, which businessman Rex Martin began building in 1969 for his wife. They have long since divorced, and the castle, which has been mentioned as a possible museum site, is for sale.

CHAMP'S ROLLERDROME
2555 Palumbo Drive   *268-3888*

Champ's, Lexington's only roller-skating rink, is another frequent site

of birthday parties. A disc jockey keeps things interesting, periodically interrupting the regular action for special activities such as adult skating, backwards skating, the limbo and the hokey-pokey. Rental skates and individual lessons are available, and novice skaters with sore posteriors can take a break with a large selection of video games. General prices for skating vary from $3 to $5, and kids 5 and younger can skate for $1.

CHUCK E. CHEESE'S
1555 New Circle Road NE   268-1800

Yet another popular party site is this franchise pizza restaurant formerly known as Showbiz Pizza Place. The motto is "where a kid can be a kid"; fittingly, food is secondary to entertainment. The play area offers a range of games and activities, including a pit filled with plastic balls where young ones can burrow to their hearts' content. In front of a dining area filled with long tables, a stage features a mechanical animal

rock band led by Chuck E. himself. Chuck, a mouse, also wanders about, greeting children and singing "Happy Birthday."

CREATIVE PLAYGROUNDS

Lexington has three creative playgrounds: huge, wooden structures packed with nooks, crannies and physical challenges that can keep easily bored kids occupied for hours while causing their parents to say, "Why didn't they have neat stuff like this when *I* was a kid?" These playgrounds, built by community volunteers, can be found at Shillito and Jacobson parks and at Picadome Elementary School.

THE DISNEY STORE
Fayette Mall (McAlpin's wing)   271-6077

This is the place to find the latest in official Disney merchandise ranging from Mickey Mouse watches and clothing to dolls and figurines. Youngsters and their parents are captivated from the moment they

Photo: Kentucky Kingdom

Hurricane Bay and the 15-story giant wheel are part of the fun going to Kentucky Kingdom amusement park in Louisville.

enter this colorful world where big video screens feature clips and music from Disney films. You can also stock up on videocassettes of those movies, from classics like *Old Yeller* through recent gems like *Beauty and the Beast.* When the store opened in 1993, people were waiting in line to get in; it's a small world, after all.

GARRETT'S ORCHARD & COUNTRY MARKET

3360 Shannon Run Road
(Ky. 1967 South)   873-3819

The ideal time to visit Garrett's is on a fall Saturday afternoon a week or two before Halloween. The air is crisp but not too cool, the sun is shining, leaves are turning, kids are planning jack-o-lanterns and you're mulling the idea of taking a thermos of hot spiced cider to tonight's UK football game.

So you go to Garrett's, where the kids pick out their own pumpkins.

After sampling some fresh, free cider, you buy a couple of gallons along with some spices and seven-bean-soup mix and Indian corn and a caramel apple and a few other things. If you're lucky, you might even get to see the cider being made. Added bonus: the scenic drive. Just go out Versailles Road, turn left across from the castle (see above) and follow the signs for 3 1/2 miles.

A GOOD PLACE FOR FUN

(also known as Lexington Ice Center)
560 Eureka Springs Drive   269-5681

A wide range of sporting activities is available at A Good Place for Fun, Lexington's only spot for ice skating (except for those rare occasions when your backyard pond freezes solid). Lessons are available for would-be ice skaters. If ice skating isn't your idea of fun, you can play in one of three gymnasiums, pray for a hole-in-one on one of three 18-hole miniature courses with biblical themes, step up to the plate in a batting cage or head for the game room. Prices vary.

A Good Place for Fun is also the site of the University of Kentucky hockey team's home games, which are played on Fridays at midnight in season.

JOSEPH-BETH KIDS

The Mall at Lexington Green   271-4031

The expansion at Joseph-Beth Booksellers has resulted in more things for everybody, and kids are no exception. The children's section now has its own entrance, its own phone number and a wide selection of books and other fun/educational items for all ages. There's even a comfortable "amphitheater" area where the little ones can sit and read, and special readings and other programs are also offered.

KIDS PLACE

3992 West Tiverton Court   272-5433

Kids Place, in the Lexington Athletic Center, bills itself as "the world's largest indoor playground." We can't vouch for that, since there are a couple of indoor playgrounds in Singapore that we have yet to visit. We can tell you, however, that kids love it. The two-story-high playground, which fills an entire gymnasium, includes three slides, three "ball baths," a rope bridge, a "Tarzan climb" and plenty of other climbing

and jumping activities. After-school, day-care and summer programs are available, and it's also a great place for a birthday party. Admission, $5.95, includes unlimited play.

LASER QUEST

224 Bolivar Street   225-1742

Looking for a way to vent some of your pent-up anger? Put down that handgun and head for Laser Quest, which provides a thrilling but safe outlet for all your shoot-'em-up tendencies. Laser Quest, located in a renovated warehouse at the edge of the University of Kentucky campus, is space-age warfare a la *Star Wars*, and it's good fun for kids and adults. Participants, equipped with laser guns and sensors, set out on a mission amid a dark labyrinth filled with enemies intent on deactivating them. Points are gained and lost depending on number of foes hit and number of times hit by foes. The cost is $6 for a 20-minute game; with $25 annual membership, you play for $5 a game. One caution: On weekends, you may face as much as a two-hour wait. May the force be with you.

LEXINGTON CHILDREN'S MUSEUM

Victorian Square   258-3256

"Hands-on" is the rule at this two-story, 14,000-square-foot museum. Kids can explore a cave, walk on the moon, participate in an archaeological dig, sit in an actual military flight simulator, wander through a huge model of the human heart and lungs, fight a fire on Main Street, visit foreign countries and travel back in time — and still be home for supper.

Other enjoyable activities include blowing giant soap bubbles, walking across the keys of a large floor piano like Tom Hanks did in the movie *Big,* rolling around the floor inside a giant turtle shell on wheels and trying to solve a series of brain-twisting puzzles. Enthralled children might not even realize they're *learning* about subjects like anatomy, archaeology, biology, geography, history, physics and social studies. And most adults we know could stand to brush up on a few of those subjects as well. Whatever your age, visit the Children's Museum, even if you have to rent a kid for a few hours. Admission $2.50 for adults, $1.50 for children, free for those 2 and younger.

LEXINGTON CHILDREN'S THEATRE
161 North Mill Street   254-4546

Lexington Children's Theatre, a professional company that has been around since 1938, presents five fully staged plays each season for children and their parents. A special touring company performs for school groups around the state. Productions in recent years have included *Romeo and Juliet, Peter Pan, Androcles and the Lion, The Jungle Book* and *Most Valuable Player,* the Jackie Robinson story. Dickens' holiday classic, *A Christmas Carol,* is performed annually. The nonprofit theater group also has an Acting Company for Teens and a number of educational programs. Call for a schedule.

LEXINGTON PUBLIC LIBRARY
Main branch, 140 East Main Street	231-5500
Branches at:	
101 North Eagle Creek Drive	231-5560
Lansdowne-Emrath,	
3317 Tates Creek Road	231-5580
Northside, 1737 Russell Cave Road	231-5590
Southside, 3340 Holwyn Road	231-5570

Each branch of the Lexington Public Library offers a variety of programs targeted at children. Although schedules change, here are some examples of the type of programs available: storytelling sessions for toddlers, "small folk" and "big girls and boys"; videos; traditional dance; puppet making; dinosaurs; postcard design; sidewalk art; and make-your-own comic strips. Call for a schedule. Of course, each branch also has a stimulating selection of books, audiotapes and videos to check out.

LIGHTER THAN AIR
136 Southland Drive   272-7777

Clown shows. Magic. Fire eating. Balloon animals and decorations. Owner Johnathan Pinczewski can bring it all to your place, with shows tailored to any age group, including adults. Prices range from $65 to $150. Lighter Than Air's offerings also include singing telegrams and other deliveries. Pinczewski, who teaches clowning, balloon decorating and fire eating, also sells animal balloons and other party accessories at his store.

LIVING ARTS & SCIENCE CENTER
362 N. Martin Luther King Boulevard 252-5222

The Living Arts & Science Center, which celebrated its 25th birthday in 1993, was created to promote education in the arts and sciences for young people. Ask your kids if they care. Didn't think so. Now, ask them if they'd like to go to a big, old house where it's cool to touch things and they can draw or paint or make their own masks or cartoons or wander around outside in a natural urban habitat with birds and bats and other wild things. OK, now, that's better!

Since 1970, the center has been located in the Kinkead House, an antebellum mansion that is on the National Register of Historic Landmarks. In its 7,000 square feet of indoor space, you'll find two art galleries featuring local artists, a science gallery with hands-on exhibits, a library, classrooms, a darkroom and a media center. Through an ever-changing variety of art and science classes — sculpture, bugs, cooking, pottery, ecology, outer space, dinosaurs and calligraphy, to name just a few — children are encouraged to express themselves, ask questions and solve problems creatively.

Class fees range from $35 for child members to $65 for teen and adult nonmembers. Exhibits are free to all. The Living Arts & Science Center is closed on summer weekends.

MARKET PLACE MERRY-GO-ROUND
325 West Main Street   254-9888

Need to take a short break from downtown shopping or relax after a hard day at the office? A charming carrousel awaits you on the third floor of the Market Place. For 75 cents, you can pick yourself a worthy steed, forget about life's troubles for a few minutes — and promise that next time you'll take the kids.

NATURAL WONDERS
Fayette Mall   245-2313

This eclectic shop is filled with unusual books, puzzles, games and toys, many of them relating to nature and science. Sure-to-please gifts recommended by our discerning kid stuff consultant include rear-vision sunglasses, real wooden boomerangs, "squiggly writer" pens, holograms, kaleidoscopes and plenty of dinosaur merchandise.

PARADES

Lexington has a number of annual parades, including Christmas and St. Patrick's Day, and Lexington's neighbors also like a good parade now and then. See Festivals and Annual Events for more details.

SAFETY CITY
Red Mile Place   258-3636

A miniature version of Lexington is the scene for a 4 1/2-hour course that teaches children some of the most important lessons they'll ever learn. Safety City, which cost $400,000 to build, is the first such facility in Kentucky and probably the finest one in the country.

The highlight comes when the little ones get to drive miniature, battery-powered cars through a residential section and a downtown area, complete with sidewalks and working traffic signals. There's even a small-scale, two-story "Big Blue" office tower. Children watch a short film on safety, which teaches them about fire prevention, looking "left-right-left" before crossing the street, calling 911 and not talking to strangers, among other things.

A warning: Safety City is open to groups only, by appointment only. Most pupils in Fayette County Public Schools participate in the program when they are in first or second grade.

TOYS R US
South Park Shopping Center   271-6374

Sure, it's a big chain. But our 7-year-old consultant calls it "the most amazing toy store in Lexington."

After he recited a potential wish list that included ball gloves, G.I. Joes, Ninja Turtles, Batman and bikes, we suggested he include some girls' toys. Before reluctantly adding Barbies and some other dolls to the list, he muttered, "It's not like girls can't play baseball or ride bikes." Frankly, we're not sure this entry is politically correct, but our consultant knows what he likes.

Toys R Us also includes an extensive selection of board games, as well as Nintendo and Sega Genesis cartridges.

VALLEY VIEW FERRY
Tates Creek Road at Kentucky River

The river isn't wide at this point, where it separates Jessamine County from Madison County, but the $2.50 ride on a paddle-wheel-powered ferry is worth the price for historical value alone. The Valley View Ferry is officially the state's oldest continuously operated business, having been granted its title by the Virginia General Assembly in 1785, seven years before Kentucky became a state.

The short trip across the river is sure to be a treat for the kids, especially ones who have never experienced a ferry. Catch it before 7 PM Monday through Saturday and before 6 PM Sunday.

YMCA OF CENTRAL KENTUCKY
239 East High Street   254-9622
YWCA OF LEXINGTON
1060 Cross Keys Road   276-4457

The "Y" is a great place for the whole family to get in shape or just have fun. The YMCA and YWCA also give you the chance to acquire a whole range of new skills. Possibilities include swimming, lifeguard training, country-western dancing, CPR, first aid, basketball, soccer, karate, cheerleading, aerobics, ballet, babysitting, cooking and yoga. Call for a schedule.

Zoos

As with amusement parks, Lexington doesn't have its own zoo, unless you count the end zone at a UK football game. But you have only to go as far as Louisville or Cincinnati to find a good one.

LOUISVILLE ZOO
1100 Trevilian Way   (502) 459-2181

The Louisville Zoo draws more visitors every year than Churchill Downs, making it the city's most-visited attraction. It has nearly 400 breeds of animals, a third of which are endangered species. Highlights include a realistic indoor re-creation of a tropical rain forest — complete with real snakes and other jungle flora and fauna. Live shows daily feature zoo inhabitants in sessions that are informative, entertaining and often eye-opening. All your favorites, such as lions and tigers and bears (oh my!) are there; and, if you like, you can even ride an elephant or camel.

The Louisville Zoo is open year-round. Hours from April through Labor Day are 10 AM to 6 PM, with extended hours on Wednesdays and Thursdays through August. The rest of the year it is open from 10 AM to 5 PM. Admission is $5.50 for ages 12-59, $3.50 for seniors, $2.75 for ages 3 to 11, and free for those 2 and younger.

CINCINNATI ZOO AND BOTANICAL PARK

3400 Vine Street   *(513) 281-4700*

This zoo has long been known for its white tiger collection as well as its outdoor gorillas. Its insectarium is the only one of its kind in the country, and in 1993 it added an Asian and African rain forest exhibit.

Cincinnati Zoo is open year round from 9 AM to 6 PM. Admission is $6.75 for adults, $4.50 for seniors, $3.75 for children ages 2 through 12, and free for those younger than 2.

Inside
The Great Outdoors

"There are no finer forests in the world than the natural parks of the 'Blue-grass region' of Kentucky," wrote Cassius Marcellus Clay in his 1886 autobiography. We know what he means. The good Lord has blessed Kentucky with a generous supply of natural beauty in the form of lush woodlands, rolling hills and valleys, scenic waterways, spectacular rock formations and vast caves — all of which cry out to anyone who enjoys communing with the outdoors.

Whatever type of outdoor activity you prefer, you can find it here in Central Kentucky or within about two hours' drive. Hunting. Fishing. Hiking. Camping (see the chapter on Campgrounds for details). Swimming. Boating. Snow skiing. Spelunking.

Kentucky's state parks system is widely recognized as one of the finest, if not the finest, in the nation. There are 44 state parks, the majority of which have facilities for outdoors activities. Some of them are listed in this chapter, and you'll find others under Daytrips. The state also has one excellent national park, Mammoth Cave.

Remember that this is *not* an exhaustive list of outside activities. If it were, this book would be too heavy for you to lift. The author has selected several of the most popular sites and some personal favorites, with special emphasis on the ones closer to Lexington, and organized them semi-arbitrarily according to activity.

In The Water

Kentucky has more miles of running streams than any other state except Alaska. We have more than 50 man-made reservoirs, which provide such benefits as recreational opportunities, fish, flood control, water supplies and electricity.

Kentucky anglers love to pursue bass, which are abundant here. The spotted bass, the state's official game fish, is known nationwide as the Kentucky bass. Largemouth and smallmouth bass are also popular targets. But there's much more — more than 200 native species, at least 40 of which are considered game fish — in Kentucky waters.

It's a good state for catfish (and you haven't eaten fish until you've had Kentucky-style catfish pan-fried in cornmeal; see A Taste of Kentucky Food and Drink). Other favorites are crappie, bluegill, muskie and walleye. The Kentucky Department of Fish and Wildlife Resources, through its fisheries division, has

Photo: Lexington Herald-Leader

Herrington Lake is one of the many nearby lakes and rivers worth fishing.

also introduced brown trout and rainbow trout in state streams.

Kentucky's fishing season is year-round. Size and creel limits, which vary from site to site, are generally posted. For more information, write the Kentucky Department of Fish & Wildlife Resources, #1 Game Farm Road, Frankfort, KY 40601, or call (502) 564-4336 between 8 AM and 4:30 PM Monday through Friday.

Kentucky's waters are suited for a wide range of boats and activities. More than 100 marinas statewide provide docking space for motor-boats, houseboats and pontoons, and rentals of all kinds are available. In addition, you'll find ample opportunities for canoeing, kayaking, rafting, sailing and water skiing.

Paddlers can test their skills over 114 miles of designated Kentucky Wild Rivers — scenic, undeveloped and free-flowing sections of nine rivers, ranging from smooth to Class V whitewater. Parts of the 75-mile-long Rockcastle River, the Red River Gorge area of the Red River, the Cumberland Falls area of the Cumberland River and the Green River are among the best. Information on Kentucky's Wild Rivers is available through the Kentucky Division of Water, 14 Reilly Road, Frankfort, KY 40601, (502) 564-3410.

KENTUCKY RIVER

Many sections of the Kentucky River in the Bluegrass area, particularly between Boonesboro and Frankfort, are used extensively for fishing and boating. This area is notable for its palisades, scenic limestone cliffs that rise high above the river.

From Lexington, the nearest operational Kentucky River boat ramp is at Clays Ferry. Take I-75 north about 15 miles and get off at Exist 99, the Clays Ferry exit. You'll find the ramp below the bridge.

STONER CREEK

Stoner Creek, in Bourbon County, winds through picturesque horse farm country, including Claiborne and Stone farms. In this peaceful setting, ideal for fishing, you're also likely to see ducks, muskrats, raccoons and other animals.

At Stoner Creek Dock, 387 Chambers Street, 1-987-3625, you can rent canoes, fishing boats with trolling motors and pedal boats. Or you can bring your own boat and use one of two ramps for $3. To get to the dock, take Paris Pike out of Lexington into downtown Paris. When you get to where the road becomes one-way,

near a Hardee's, turn right at the first stop light. Go one block, turn left onto Pleasant and then right onto Duncan. At the next four-way stop, veer onto Scott Avenue. Chambers Street is the third street on the left, and you'll see Stoner Creek Dock's sign.

HERRINGTON LAKE

Herrington Lake, a 1,860-acre reservoir created in 1925 when Kentucky Utilities dammed the Dix River, was Kentucky's first major lake. This popular site for fishing and boating touches Boyle, Garrard and Mercer counties in Central Kentucky and is about 30 miles south of Lexington.

To get to Herrington Lake, take U.S. 27 (Nicholasville Road) south. Once you cross the Kentucky River at Camp Nelson, your route will depend on which of the nearly dozen marinas you're going to. The two closest marinas, reached via Ky. 152, are Kamp Kennedy (1-548-2101, open year-round) and Chimney Rock (1-748-9065, March through October). The newest, Herrington Marina (1-548-2282, year-round), opened in April 1993; to get there, turn right from U.S. 27 onto Ky. 1355 4 1/2 miles past the bridge, drive through Homestead Herrington subdivision and follow the signs. Other major marinas are Sims Mid-Lake (1-748-5520, April through October) and Gwinn Island Fishing Resort (1-236-4286, April through October).

Other popular lakes within a couple of hours' drive from Lexington include:

• Taylorsville Lake State Park. This relatively young lake, on Ky. 44

near Taylorsville in Spencer County, was created in 1982. To get the marina, take I-64 west to the second Shelbyville exit and go south on Ky. 55; when you hit Ky. 44, you're practically there. Call (502) 477-8766 for more information.

• Cave Run Lake in Bath County. Two marinas operate year-round: Longbow, on Ky. 1274 near Frenchburg, at 1-768-2929; and Scott Creek, on Ky. 801 near Morehead, at 1-784-9666. Take I-64 east to either the Frenchburg or Morehead exit, which will be approximately a one-hour drive, and then follow the signs.

• Grayson Lake State Park, which surrounds a 1,512-acre lake in Carter and Elliott counties. Take I-64 east from Lexington to the Grayson exit, about 100 miles, and follow the signs. Grayson Lake Marina, 1-474-4513, is on Ky. 7

• Lake Cumberland State Resort Park. This park, near Jamestown in Russell County about 100 miles south of Lexington, offers some of the best fishing in the state. To get there, take U.S. 27 south to Somerset, then go west on the Cumberland Parkway. Take the Jamestown-Russell Springs exit and get on U.S. 127 south, which will take you straight into the park. The State Dock, (800) 234-3625, is open year-round.

BILL'S LIVE FISH FARM
1588 Carrick Pike, Georgetown   863-4269

This pay lake provides a good opportunity for exposing the family to the joys of fishing with minimal hassle and drive time. No license is required. Five ponds are stocked with farm-raised channel catfish ranging from a pound and a half up to 3 or 4 pounds. You pay only for what you catch: $1.45 a pound, and you can have your fish cleaned and fileted for an additional 30 cents a pound. Bill's Live Fish Farm is open March through October from 8 AM until dark. To get there from Lexington, take Russell Cave Road out of town for about 11 miles — a scenic drive, by the way — until you come to Carrick Pike. Turn left onto Carrick and go about 2 more miles, and you'll find Bill's on your right.

FISH & WILDLIFE GAME FARM
U.S. 60, Frankfort   (502) 564-5448

Two fishing lakes are available at this site operated by the state Department Fish and Wildlife Resources. There is no charge, but you do need a license. When you get tired of fishing, you can check out bears, buffalo, cougars, coyotes, deer and other wildlife native to the state. The game farm is open daily from dawn to dusk.

Insiders like biking on country roads around Lexington.

Insiders' Tips

Hunting

Kentucky hunters have a wide range of options in season, including deer, squirrel, rabbit, quail, wild turkey, grouse and waterfowl. Deer season is divided into bow, crossbow, muzzle-loading firearms and modern gun seasons, with some of the dates overlapping. Seasons and limits vary from year to year.

Kentucky has a number of wildlife management areas, which are open for hunting during regular statewide seasons. Many of the areas, however, have their own restrictions, so you should check with the area manager of the state Division of Wildlife, at (502) 564-4406. Before hunting on private land, always get permission from the landowner.

For more information, write the Kentucky Department of Fish & Wildlife Resources, #1 Game Farm Road, Frankfort, KY 40601, or call (502) 564-4336 between 8 AM and 4:30 PM Monday through Friday.

LICENSES

Hunting and fishing licenses are available in Room 107 of the county clerk's office, 162 East Main Street, 253-3344, as well as at various sporting-goods stores around town. Licenses are good through December 31. If you're a resident who hunts and fishes, your best bet is to get a combination license for $20. Other costs are:

Statewide hunting license, $12.50 resident, $95 non-resident; five-day non-resident hunting license, small game only, $27.50; junior hunting license (age 16 and younger), $6.25;

statewide fishing license, $12.50 resident, $30 non-resident; statewide joint fishing license for resident husband and wife, $22.50; 15-day non-resident fishing license, $20; junior deer hunting permit, $12.50; wild turkey hunting permit, $17.50; trout stamp, $5; waterfowl stamp, $5.25. License fees are subject to change.

Boat licenses, required for all motorboats, are also available through the county clerk's office and at many sporting goods stores. Fees vary according to size of boat and motor.

Hiking

With all the woodlands throughout Kentucky, hiking and backpacking come naturally. For maximum viewing satisfaction, may we suggest an autumn expedition. In the fall, especially during October, our trees explode into a kaleidoscope of vibrant reds, oranges and yellows. Of course, you can find scenes of great beauty any time and anywhere in the state, including three extremely popular areas not far from Lexington. In fact, the first of these areas is in Fayette County.

RAVEN RUN NATURE SANCTUARY
Jacks Creek Pike   272-6105

Raven Run, which recently acquired additional land giving it a total of nearly 500 acres, has 7 miles of hiking trails. History and nature peacefully coexist in this sanctuary highlighting the beauty of the Kentucky River palisades region. You can find nearly 400 species of wild-

Photo: Lexington Herald-Leader

All types of boats float by the Kentucky River palisades during the annual Admiral's Day parade.

flowers — sorry, no picking of plants, so future hikers can enjoy them — growing amid Raven Run's meadows and woodlands and along its creek beds.

The aesthetic highlight is probably the Kentucky River overlook, which provides a stunning view of the palisades from more than 100 feet above the river. Rock fences, a lime kiln, part of a mill and other artifacts from the state's pioneer days are also found within the boundaries of Raven Run. The sanctuary's nature center features displays and exhibits of the area's flora and fauna and maps of the trails. A number of special programs, including night hikes and group activities, are available.

Raven Run is open Wednesday through Sunday year-round. Hours vary by season and sometimes are subject to weather and trail conditions. Before visiting, particularly on weekends, call to be sure Raven Run is open.

To get to Raven Run Nature Sanctuary from Lexington, take Tates Creek Road south until you reach the tiny community of Spears, distinguished by a gas station and a grocery. You'll see a sign pointing the way: Make a sharp left turn onto Spears Road, go about a mile and a half until the road runs into Jacks Creek Pike, turn right, and Raven Run is ahead on your left.

NATURAL BRIDGE
STATE RESORT PARK

Slade   663-2214
For reservations   (800) 325-1710

You can easily combine these next two sites into one trip. Natural Bridge is a 65-foot-high, 78-foot-long arch constructed of sandstone, with no artificial ingredients added, through thousands of years of erosion. If you think the bridge is awesome from the ground, wait until you look down from atop it. You have a choice of how to get there: Hike a mile and a half or take a sky lift. We suggest the hike.

Natural Bridge, part of the Daniel Boone National Forest, is in Powell County. To get there from Lexington, 57 miles away, take I-64 west to the Mountain Parkway, get off at Exit 33 and follow the signs.

The lodge and dining room, incidentally, are among the most popular in Kentucky's park system.

RED RIVER GORGE
Slade

On the other side of the Mountain Parkway, just a few minutes away, is the Red River Gorge Geological Area. This entire area is filled with scenery that you can't miss and wouldn't want to, whether you're walking or driving. A 30-mile scenic drive circles through the area, providing breathtaking views of the Red River as it winds through the gorge. If you really want to exercise your hiking skills, take on nearby Clifty Wilderness, which is as rugged as its name implies.

Spelunking

MAMMOTH CAVE NATIONAL PARK
Cave City   (502) 758-2328

The surface area of this highly popular tourist site about 130 miles south of Lexington covers 80 square miles, but that is literally just scratching the surface. Mammoth Cave, the centerpiece of Kentucky's only national park, is part of the world's

longest cave system with more than 330 miles of underground passages. During the summer, as many as nine guided tours are offered, including one that's accessible to disabled visitors. Structure your visit to fit your own interests, physical abilities and sense of adventure. For the more adventurous, a guided "wild cave" tour through unlighted portions of Mammoth Cave provides more of a true caving experience.

Also available is a demanding, self-guided tour through Ganter Cave. This tour is restricted to groups of four to nine who meet age, fitness, experience and equipment guidelines; reservations for the Ganter Cave tour must be made through the chief ranger's office.

Often called one of the wonders of the Western Hemisphere, Mammoth Cave was named a World Heritage Site by the United Nations in 1981. In recent years, it has drawn nearly 2 million annual visitors, who come to see such awe-inspiring sights as Floyd Collins Crystal Cave, Crystal Lake, Frozen Niagara and, of course, the multi-level main cave. You'll find stalactites, stalagmites and numerous other types of rock formations. Echo River, which runs through Mammoth Cave and is still making changes to it, is home to rare, eyeless fish.

Mammoth Cave's history is nearly as intriguing as its features. Evidence shows that prehistoric Indians visited the cave. According to some accounts, a hunter in pursuit of a wounded bear in the late 1700s was the first white person to discover the cave. During the war of 1812, a commercial saltpeter-mining operation provided gunpowder for the American troops. A few years later, the public was flocking to take in the cave's natural splendor. It became a national park, the nation's 26th, in July 1941.

Crystal Cave was discovered in 1917 by Floyd Collins, a good spelunker with a fatally bad run of luck. Collins received worldwide attention in February 1925 when he became trapped in Sand Cave while trying to find a passage linking it with Crystal Cave. Pinned in a narrow passageway by a rock that would-be rescuers could not reach, he eventually died.

If that kind of story keeps you out of caves, we're sorry for telling you; stay on the guided tours and you'll be fine, and you'll be glad you took the tour. But even if you steadfastly *refuse* to set foot in a cave, you'll still enjoy the park. You can hike more than 70 miles of forest trails, camp and take a canoe or cruise boat down the Green River. And there are plenty of picnic shelters.

To get to Mammoth Cave from Lexington, take U.S. 60 (Versailles Road) west to the Bluegrass Parkway, get on I-65 south at Elizabethtown, then take the Cave City exit.

CARTER CAVES STATE RESORT PARK
Near Olive Hill   1-286-4411
For reservations   (800) 325-0059

More than 20 caves, some of them still unchartered, are scattered about this park's 1,350 acres. The squeamish might want to avoid Bat Cave, which is home to thousands of protected Indiana bats. Other caves include Laurel Cave; Cascade Caverns, which features a 30-foot underground waterfall; and Saltpeter Cave.

Both Bat Cave and Cascade Caverns are designated state nature preserves.

Like Mammoth Cave National Park, Carter Caves includes attractions for a variety of skill and tolerance levels. If you don't mind crawling on your hands and knees with only a flashlight to lead the way, you can truly find great adventure and rekindle that forgotten pioneer spirit. Just pretend you're a modern-day Tom Sawyer or Becky Thatcher (they didn't have flashlights).

Still other caves can be found on private land in the vicinity. If you're up to a real challenge, track down a local who can tell you about Jarvie Roark's Cave, a multilevel labyrinth that will seriously test your stamina and your orientation skills. Just be sure to get permission from the landowner to explore the cave.

Other activities include camping, fishing, canoeing and hiking. Carter Caves also has a lodge, cottages, swimming pool, golf course and tennis courts.

To get to Carter Caves from Lexington, take I-64 east for about 80 miles to the first Olive Hill exit and follow the signs.

Snow Skiing

GENERAL BUTLER
STATE RESORT PARK
Near Carrollton   (502) 732-4384

This park contains the only public area for snow skiing in the state. Ski Butler, which is generally open from mid-December through March, provides 23 acres of downhill skiing.

Photo: Lexington Herald-Leader

Golf pro Gay Brewer, who grew up in Lexington, returns to the area for the annual Bank One Senior Golf Classic at Kearney Hill.

Inside
Golf

After winning Lexington's Bank One Senior Golf Classic in 1993, South African-born PGA veteran Gary Player told a reporter for local television station WKYT: "This is my favorite spot on the tour. I don't care where we go; this is my favorite spot because I am a great lover of horses. Actually, I am a horse nut. Sometimes when you're not from an area, you notice things that others don't. I've traveled more than any athlete that's ever lived, and I've never seen a more beautiful part of the world (than) right here in Lexington."

Our gently rolling hills, so ideal for horses, also make the Bluegrass a naturally appealing place for golf, and the number of courses continues to grow. This area has given rise to a number of outstanding professional golfers.

Gay Brewer grew up in Lexington, working as a caddie, winning a record three straight state high school championships at Lafayette High School in 1949-51, attending the University of Kentucky and distinguishing himself as an amateur before going on to become a persistent PGA champion.

Myra Van Hoose Blackwelder is a Lexington native who learned golf at Big Elm Country Club (now the Campbell House course) and won four consecutive state high school championships while at Lafayette. Fort Knox native Larry Gilbert, former club pro at The Champions, has lived in Lexington since the mid-'80s. Russ Cochran grew up in Paducah but attended the University of Kentucky before beginning his PGA career. From elsewhere in the state have come such notables as Frank Beard and Jodie Mudd.

Lexington is the site of the annual Senior Classic, which has drawn such heavyweights as Player, Jack Nicklaus, Arnold Palmer, Lee Trevino and Chi Chi Rodriguez. In 1993, the University of Kentucky was host of the 1993 NCAA Men's Golf Championships, played at The Champions course in Jessamine County. The Children's Charity Classic, an annual event since 1982, regularly attracts a lineup of television, movie and sports stars who have teed off to raise nearly $1 million for charity.

Area courses fall into three general categories: public, semiprivate and private. We have devoted most of this chapter to the public and semiprivate courses. Four public courses — the regulation Kearney Hill Links, Lakeside and Tates Creek, plus par-3 Meadowbrook — are owned and operated by the Lexington-Fayette Urban County Government's Division of Parks and Recreation. The Lexington City Championships are played each year at the three regulation municipal courses.

Some of the remaining public courses offer memberships, which basically amount to prepaid greens fees. The semiprivate courses are open to the public, but members are given first priority for tee times. The private courses, which include country clubs, are open only to members and their guests.

All yardage figures are measured from the back tees. Unless otherwise indicated, all courses are 18 holes and all rental carts are electric.

Public and Semiprivate Courses

CABIN BROOK GOLF COURSE
2260 Lexington Road (U.S. 60)
Versailles   873-8404
This 25-year-old public course is mostly flat, but its fairways are lined with pine trees. The 7,000-yard course is par 72. Memberships are available. Weekday greens fees are $10 for 18 holes, $7 for nine; on weekends it's $12 for 18 holes and $8 for nine. Cart rental is $8 for nine holes.

CAMPBELL HOUSE INN, SUITES & GOLF CLUB
Parkway Drive, off
Harrodsburg Road   254-3631
The Campbell House golf course formerly was part of Big Elm Country Club. The inn bought the property in 1990 and changed the course

from private to semiprivate. There are now about 300 members, who get dibs on tee times, but anyone can play here. The 6,300-yard, par-70 course is marked by speedy little greens and plenty of water hazards. Fees, including cart, are $25 weekdays and $30 weekends.

CONNEMARA GOLF COURSE
2327 Lexington Road
Nicholasville   885-4331
Connemara, a converted horse farm on a rolling hillside between Lexington and Nicholasville on U.S. 27, is one of the area's newer golf courses. This 6,559-yard, par-71 public course is designed for enjoyment rather than difficulty, with open fairways and few traps. Still, a pair of 450-plus-yard par 4s and a 572-yard par 5 can present a challenge. Members can reserve tee times whenever they want; nonmembers can make reservations no more than one week in advance. Fees, which include carts, are $16.95 for 18 holes weekdays before 11 AM, $19.95 after 11 and $24.95 weekends.

HIGH POINT GOLF COURSE
1215 High Point Drive, off Union Mill Road (Ky. 169)
Nicholasville   887-4614
For the time being, this new course, another former horse farm, consists of just nine holes, but it will have 18 before too long. Seven of the current holes are on the eventual front nine, while the other two will end up on the back nine. These holes amount to a par 35 over 3,200 yards; the complete course will be par 72. High Point maintains a horse-farm atmosphere with three lakes,

Photo: Lexington Herald-Leader

LPGA pro Myra Van Hoose Blackwelder, who learned to golf at what is now the Campbell House course, helps run Plantation Links Golf Center near Nicholasville.

two creeks and three natural springs. Highlights of the course, which has no blind shots or sand traps, are the 556-yard 14th hole, a par 5, and the 7th hole, a par 3 with an elevated tee and a 70-foot drop to the green. High Point is a public course that offers memberships. Greens fees are $9 for 18 holes and $5 for nine holes on weekdays and, on weekends and holidays, $12 for 18 holes and $7 for nine holes. Cart rental is $4 a rider for each nine holes.

JUNIPER HILLS GOLF COURSE
800 Louisville Road,
Frankfort   (502) 875-8559

Built-up greens present a challenge on this 6,147-yard, par-70 public course. The terrain is slightly hilly, with one water hole. Memberships are available. Fees are $10 for 18 holes, $6 for nine.

KEARNEY HILL LINKS
3403 Kearney Road
(off Georgetown Road)   253-1981

Since its opening in October 1989, this 6,987-yard, par-72 municipal course has quickly acquired a reputation for excellence. Designed by noted course architects Pete and P.B. Dye, Kearney Hill Links has been rated by *Golf Digest* as the fourth-best golf course in Kentucky and as one of the top 100 places to play in the country. Since 1990, it has been the site of the high-profile

Bank One Senior Golf Classic. Greens fees are $20 for 18 holes; cart rentals are $8.

LAKESIDE GOLF COURSE
Richmond Road   263-5315

This 6,844-yard, par-72 municipal course alongside Jacobson Park's lake is one of the area's most popular. The 18th hole is one of the three longest in the state at 653 yards. For 18 holes, the greens fee is $10; a cart will cost you an extra $14.

MARRIOTT'S GRIFFIN GATE GOLF CLUB
1800 Newtown Pike   254-4101

This 6,300-yard, par-72 course is semiprivate. It is characterized by gently rolling hills, with water on eight holes. Four sets of tees make the course adaptable to a variety of skill levels. Greens fees are $44 Monday through Thursday and $49 on weekends. Daily after 3 PM, $32 lets you play to your heart's content on a course that was the site of the Senior Classic for seven years before the tournament was moved to Kearney Hill Links.

MEADOWBROOK GOLF COURSE
400 Wilson Downing Road   272-3115

This 2,235-yard municipal course has 17 par-3 holes and one par-4. The slightly rolling terrain makes Meadowbrook a nice, relaxing course to learn the game or to hone

Insiders' Tips

Insiders like watching the stars at the PGA Senior Classic.

your iron and putter skills. Greens fee is $7 for nine or 18 holes. Pull cart rental is $3. You can also rent a bag with 3-, 5-, 7- and 9-irons, a putter and a 3-wood for $3; ID is required.

PLANTATION LINKS GOLF CENTER
2080 Lexington Road
Nicholasville   *885-1254*

Plantation Links, a 3,100-yard, par-58 public course across the road from Toyota on Nicholasville, is a short course designed to provide plenty of challenges in a shorter amount of playing time. The owners call it "executive par 3," with four par-4 holes thrown in. It also includes a heated driving range and will soon have a bent-grass putting course. Memberships are available for the course as well as for the practice facility. Owners say Plantation Links will soon have the area's first nine-hole, bent-grass putting course. An added attraction is the opportunity to take private lessons from Myra Blackwelder. Greens fees, including cart rental, are $10 before noon on weekdays and, at other times and on holidays, $10 to walk and $16 to ride.

PLAYERS CLUB
4850 Leestown Road   *255-1011*

The semiprivate Players Club, a relatively new addition to Lexington's golf scene, is currently a 6,800-yard, par-72 course. But plans are to make it a 27-hole course by summer 1994. The course contains the only island hole in the area and perhaps in the state, the par-3 8th. Ten ponds and lakes and more than 90 sand traps add a tough dimension to the course, especially from the most distant tees

(there are five sets per hole). Players Club was designed by owner Danny McQueen, who also has been involved in the design of the Andover Golf & Country Club and Cabin Brook courses. Greens fees for 18 holes, including cart, are $25 weekdays and $30 weekends.

SHADY BROOK GOLF
444 Hutchinson Road
Paris   *1-987-1544*

This 2,632-yard course is par 35 for its nine holes. It's a fairly flat course, but trees and three water holes keep things interesting. Greens fees, without cart, are $6 for nine holes and $8.50 for 18 on weekdays; add a dollar on weekends. Cart rental is $8 a twosome for nine holes.

SPORTLAND GOLF COURSE
U.S. 60, Winchester   *(800) 273-5001*

This rolling, par-72 course about 10 miles east of Lexington has a total yardage of 6,828 yards from the back tees. There's a lake on the 18th hole, and a small creek running through the center of the course comes into play on five holes. Greens fees vary: Weekends, with a cart, the cost is $25.50 for one duffer and $35 for two. Weekdays, with an even number in the group, it's $12.50 a person; otherwise it's $20.25 each. Without a cart, the fees are $10 on weekdays, $13 on weekends and holidays.

TATES CREEK GOLF COURSE
Gainesway Drive   *272-3428*

This hilly municipal course — 6,283 yards, par 72 — features several holes with water. Greens fees are $10 for 18 holes; the 60-and-older crowd can play for $3 Monday through Friday before 3 PM. Cart rental is $7 a person. Reservations can be made one week in advance for threesomes and foursomes; singles and twosomes are scheduled from a daily standby list.

Private Courses

THE CHAMPIONS GOLF CLUB
20 Avenue of Champions,
Nicholasville   *223-7275*

Since opening in June 1988, The Champions, a 7,081-yard, par-72 course, has twice been the site of the Kentucky Open and has also been host to the U.S. Senior Individual Challenge and the Women's Western Amateur. The 1994 U.S. Senior Amateur Championship will be played at the course Sept. 12-17. This course has tight fairways, plenty of hazards and a high slope rating.

Country club courses include **Andover Golf & Country Club**, 3450 Todds Road, 263-4335; **Greenbrier Golf & Country Club**, 2179 Bahama Road, 299-2811; **Idle Hour Country Club**, 1815 Richmond Road, 266-7901; **Lexington Country Club**, 5211 Paris Pike, 299-4388; and **Spring Lake Country Club**, Sandersville Road, 254-9646.

Instruction

MAN O' WAR GOLF
Man o' War Boulevard at
Parkers Mill Road   *259-4653*

This recent addition to Lexington's golf scene provides a number of tools to help you improve your game. A 9,000-square-foot putting green, more than 300 yards of grass teeing area, a "short game" area and a video instruction room are among the facilities at Man O' War Golf, which is open year-round. Three instructors are available during the summer, one during the winter. Range fees are $5.50 for a large bucket of balls, $3.50 for small. A short game is $8. There is no charge for using the putting area. Memberships are available.

BETTER GOLF FOR EVERYONE
332 Colony Boulevard   *269-7628*
Outside Lexington   *(800) 264-7628*

John Rood offers year-round indoor/outdoor instruction. Group discounts are available.

Miniature Golf

A GOOD PLACE FOR FUN
(Lexington Ice Center & Miniature Golf)
560 Eureka Springs Drive   *269-5681*

A biblical theme highlights 54 holes of miniature golf. The cost for 18 holes is $3.75 a person Monday through Thursday, $4 Friday through Sunday. Or you can have unlimited play for $5.50 Monday through Thursday and $7 Friday through Sunday.

PUTTER'S PLAYGROUND
2009 Family Circle Drive   *255-7888*

Lexington's only indoor miniature golf course is open year-round. The cost for all ages — except those 5 and younger, who play free — is $2.50 for one game and $3.50 for all you can play. If you're in a group of four or more, you get an even bigger break: $2.50 a person for as many games as you like.

Photo: Lexington Herald-Leader

The final round of the annual City Golf Tournament is played at Kearney Hill Links; Buddy Bryant, left, clinched the victory there in 1992.

Photo: Lexington Herald-Leader

UK has returned to Final Four contender status under Coach Rick Pitino,
who began his tenure in 1989.

Inside
'Big Blue' Basketball and Other Spectator Sports

*T*hroughout Kentucky, people take their sports seriously. Whether the sport in question is one of the big three — basketball, football and baseball — or among the many other athletic possibilities, people in this part of the country root hard for their favorite teams and play hard when they're actually competing.

This chapter covers spectator sports. Horse racing, however, is in the chapter on Horses. Participant sports are covered in the chapters on Parks and Recreation, Golf and Fishing and Hunting.

Incidentally, greater Lexington does have other spectator sports besides University of Kentucky basketball. So why all the emphasis on UK hoops? If you have to ask, you haven't been here long enough. You'll get used to it.

Basketball

So what if organized baseball came to Kentucky in 1865 at the end of the Civil War, football followed about 15 years later, and basketball wasn't even *invented* until 1891? That doesn't matter. Only a few years after James Naismith first hung a peach basket from a Massachusetts gymna-

sium balcony, basketball had become king in Lexington and in the rest of the state.

The names associated with Bluegrass basketball could fill a Who's Who; we'll name some of the most notable. There's Adolph Rupp, the legendary "baron" of the Kentucky Wildcats whose record as the winningest coach in college basketball still stands. Carey Spicer, an All-America member of Rupp's first UK team in 1930-31. Ellis Johnson, an exceptional athlete who led Ashland High School to the 1928 national championship (yes, they really had such a thing in high school back then) and then, at UK, was a basketball All-American in addition to starring in football, baseball and track.

There was Rupp's "Fabulous Five" — Cliff Barker, Ralph Beard, Alex Groza, Wah Wah Jones and Kenny Rollins — the team that won the 1947-48 NCAA championship and then the Olympic gold medal. In 1965-66 came "Rupp's Runts," who came within one game of an NCAA title; that team featured such notables as Pat Riley and Louie Dampier. Other stars have included Cliff Hagan, Cotton Nash, Dan Issel, Jack Givens, Sam Bowie, Kenny Walker, Rex Chapman

Photo: Lexington Herald-Leader

Coach Adolph Rupp and radio announcer Cawood Ledford, who retired in 1992 after 39 years as the voice of the Wildcats, are two of the most respected figures in UK Wildcat basketball history.

and Jamal Mashburn. And that's a mere sampling.

Perhaps no UK team played with more heart against greater odds than did the 1991-92 Wildcat team, led by a core of Kentucky natives who stayed with the team while it served a two-year NCAA probation for illegal payments to players. Homegrown boys Richie Farmer, John Pelphrey, Deron Feldhaus and fellow senior Sean Woods of Indianapolis anchored a team that came within a miraculous last-second shot of beating Duke in the NCAA semifinals. In an exceptional break with school policy, UK retired the jerseys of the four seniors at the end of the season.

(If we were so inclined, we could also list some of the basketball movers and shakers associated with Louisville, a river town about 75 miles west of Lexington. We could mention names like Junior Bridgeman, Denny Crum, Wes Unseld — but we won't. Why? Because this is a guide to the Lexington area. You're not supposed to like both the Cats and the Cardinals; in fact, many UK fans swear that their two favorite basketball teams are Kentucky and whoever happens to be playing Louisville. And, as if that weren't enough, our painstaking research has turned up convincing evidence that Louisville is actually in Indiana.)

Basketball fever in this state is undoubtedly at its most delirious when it involves the UK Wildcats. But unless you are a student, have season tickets or are willing to pay scalpers' prices, gaining access to the hallowed, 23,000-seat shrine called Rupp Arena will most likely be difficult. Although scalping is illegal in Kentucky, violations are frequent and fairly blatant. Fortunately, the majority of UK basketball games are televised.

If you don't have the money, connections or luck to procure UK basketball tickets, you still have a chance to see the Cats live. Your opportunity comes in the form of "Midnight Madness," an annual October event that lives up to its name. Midnight Madness is the first practice session of the year, and it's scheduled to begin at the earliest possible moment allowed under NCAA regulations.

Should you be hardy enough to accept the Midnight Madness challenge, you should head for Memorial Coliseum, the Cats' practice facility and formerly their home court, as soon as possible. Once there, you'll find a crowd of eager fans already waiting, some of them covered with cobwebs, in hopes of snaring a prime location among the coliseum's 11,000 seats.

It would be stereotypical and incorrect to say all natives are UK Wildcat fans. Without evidence to the contrary, however, when planning any social events involving new friends in Kentucky, you're probably better off assuming that they *are* fans. In other words, don't feel offended if a friend skips your wedding because it conflicts with a UK game. Even many out-of-staters who move to Lexington have fallen under the spell of "Big Blue" basketball, which has returned to Final Four contender status under Coach Rick Pitino.

Another noteworthy aspect about the Pitino era, which began in 1989, was the naming of Bernadette Locke (now Locke-Mattox) to the coaching staff in June 1990, making her the first female assistant basketball coach for an NCAA Division I men's team.

UK's women's basketball team is coached by Sharon Fanning. The Lady Kats play their home games in Memorial Coliseum.

And remember, UK isn't the only university in town. Transylvania University fields a very respectable NAIA basketball team under Coach Don Lane.

"March Madness," the name often used to describe the postseason NCAA basketball tournament, also applies to the boys' state high school tournament, which rotates between Lexington's Rupp Arena and Louisville's Freedom Hall. Also known as the "Sweet Sixteen," the tournament field is made up of the winner of each of the 16 regions in the state. The girls' state high school tournament is also held each March, with the site changing from year to year.

RUPP ARENA

430 West Vine Street
UK ticket office, Memorial Coliseum, Avenue of Champions 257-1818

Although the Kentucky Wildcats play their home games at Rupp Arena, the facility is owned by Lexington Center Corp. and is not on the campus. Calling the Rupp Arena phone number won't help you get UK basketball tickets. Call the ticket

Fans mobbed Rodrick Rhodes and the rest of the UK basketball team after they returned home with the Mideast Regional tournament title in 1993.

office at Memorial Coliseum.

McALISTER AUDITORIUM
Transylvania University
300 North Broadway   233-8202

McBRAYER ARENA
Eastern Kentucky University
Richmond   1-622-2122

ALUMNI GYMNASIUM
Georgetown College,
Georgetown   863-8115

SEABURY GYM
Berea College
Berea   1-986-9341 ext. 5424

BELLE GYMNASIUM
Kentucky State University
Frankfort   (502) 227-6509

Football

University of Kentucky football

fans know that the pigskin will forever play second fiddle to the roundball in this state. Paul "Bear" Bryant, the legendary Alabama coach, realized basketball's pre-eminence when he was at the helm of the Wildcats from 1946 to 1953. Bryant resigned because, despite building the team into a national power, he was continually overshadowed by basketball coach Adolph Rupp.

The football Wildcats, who draw respectable crowds at 58,000-seat Commonwealth Stadium, earned a berth in the 1993 Peach Bowl, which they lost 14-13 to Clemson. The program is slowly but surely returning to respectability under Bill Curry, a former Alabama coach who has run a football program marked by integrity if not by inspiring performances, as did his predecessor, Jerry Claiborne. As each season opens, it is always accompanied by optimism. Curry is a motivator who expects the best from his players both on and off the field.

Other Bluegrass colleges have also earned fine gridiron reputations. Roy Kidd, the longtime coach at Eastern Kentucky University, has made the Colonels consistently one of the top NCAA Division II programs in the country. Meanwhile, in nearby Georgetown, the Tigers have also been an NAIA powerhouse in recent years.

National Football League fans can catch the Cincinnati Bengals about 80 miles away in Riverfront Stadium, (513) 621-3550. During the 1993-94 season, however, watching the Bengals was a painful experience and not recommended; the best part was watching rookie place-kicker Doug Pelphrey, a former UK star.

COMMONWEALTH STADIUM
Cooper Drive, University of Kentucky campus
Ticket office, Memorial Coliseum, Avenue of
Champions   *257-1818*

HANGER FIELD
Eastern Kentucky University   1-622-2122

McFERRAN STADIUM-HINTON FIELD
Georgetown College   863-8115

RIVERFRONT STADIUM
Pete Rose Way, Cincinnati
Bengals ticket office   (513) 621-3550

Baseball

The UK baseball team, coached by Keith Madison, plays its home games in the Shively Field complex off Cooper Drive.

The highly paid Cincinnati Reds, who went rapidly downhill after breez-

ing through the playoffs and the World Series in 1990, are a little over an hour away. Or you can drive to Louisville to catch the minor-league Redbirds in Cardinal Stadium.

RIVERFRONT STADIUM
Pete Rose Way, Cincinnati
Reds ticket office (513) 421-4510, Ext. 300

CARDINAL STADIUM
Kentucky Fair and Exposition Center, Louisville
Ticket office   (502) 361-3100

Hockey

The University of Kentucky Cool Cats, the hockey team that was formed in 1983, draw a loyal and often rowdy crowd of more than 1,000 to their home games. Not bad, especially considering that the games are played at midnight.

LEXINGTON ICE CENTER
(a k a A Good Place for Fun)
560 Eureka Springs Drive   269-5681

Other Sports

The University of Kentucky also fields a women's volleyball team, which plays at Memorial Coliseum. There's soccer, rugby, tennis, golf, swimming, wrestling and more. For more information on these sports, call UK Sports Information at 257-3838.

For information on other Transylvania sports, call 233-8270. For Eastern Kentucky University, call 1-622-2122; Georgetown, 863-8115; Berea, 1-986-9341 Ext. 5424; Kentucky State University, (502) 227-6509.

Photo: Lexington Herald-Leader

Polish-born aviation executive Henryk de Kwiatkowski made the high bid for Calumet Farm in 1992 and saved the horse farm from being auctioned off in parcels.

Inside
Horse Country

"You were a lord if you had a horse," wrote D.H. Lawrence in 1931. "Far back, far back in our dark soul the horse prances.... The horse, the horse! The symbol of surging potency and power of movement, of action, in man."

Lawrence's words seem appropriate to introduce this section on Kentucky's most prized animals. Lexington and its surrounding areas comprise the most renowned and most concentrated horse-breeding grounds in the world. Kentucky each year is responsible for the production of more thoroughbreds than any other state, and Lexington itself is Thoroughbred Central. Visitors from all over flock to the Bluegrass to drive past rolling, picturesque horse farms, visit the Kentucky Horse Park, bet on races and enjoy other equine attractions.

The horse has a long and glorious history within the state's borders, having been brought by settlers in the late 18th century. A Fayette County census in 1789 recorded an equine population of 9,607, compared with a human population of only 9,000. Even back then, horses were used for racing as well as for more mundane tasks, such as farm work and war. There is historical record of three-day race meet-

ings being held in 1791. Seven years later, the first Jockey Club in the state was formed at a local tavern.

The glamorous thoroughbred, star of the most spectacular and most hyped two minutes in sports, gets most of the attention. But, however much we associate this sleek horse with the Bluegrass, it was developed more than 300 years ago by Europeans who bred their own horses with a trio of Arabian stallions. The only breed of horse that is actually native to Kentucky is the American saddle horse, a sturdy and spirited breed that originated in the 19th century as a direct descendant of Denmark, a thoroughbred who was in John Hunt Morgan's cavalry.

You might be surprised to find that the thoroughbred is not the most abundant horse in Kentucky. An equine census conducted by the American Horse Council in 1987 found 36,000 quarter horses to 32,000 thoroughbreds. Next, in descending order, came Arabians, saddlebreds and standardbreds.

Even without the presence of the thoroughbred, horses would play a highly visible role in Lexington's economy, its culture and its day-to-day life.

For example, in Lexington you can:

- Bet on standardbreds at The Red Mile, the fastest harness racing track in the world.
- Take a romantic horse-drawn carriage tour through the center of town.
- Go horseback riding.
- Watch or participate in steeplechases, polo matches, Three Day Events and horse shows.
- See mounted police patrolling downtown streets.

Other locally prominent breeds of horses are the Morgan, the Tennessee walking horse, the Appaloosa and a variety of show horses, work horses and ponies. At the Kentucky Horse Park, you're likely to see, depending on the occasion, such diverse breeds as Lipizanners and miniature horses.

But, without a doubt, it is the thoroughbreds — and the farms where they are bred and raised — that most visitors have come here to see. They are the horses that bring the big money into town. Should you and your bank account be so inclined, you might plunk down several million dollars for a horse as some of the richest and most glamorous people in the Bluegrass, the world (Sheik Mohammed bin Rashid al Maktoum and his brothers from oil-rich Dubai) and even the galaxy

("Star Trek" star William Shatner, who owns a farm in Woodford County) look on.

The Bluegrass thoroughbred is recognized and cherished worldwide for its beauty, speed and stamina. The plentiful calcium and phosphorous in the limestone deposits that feed the soil apparently help the horses develop strong skeletons perfectly suited for the strenuous sport of racing. The land itself — rolling, firm, well-drained — is ideal for training. As producing fine wines seems to come naturally to the people of France, so is it with fine thoroughbreds in and around Lexington. There must be something in the water indeed.

No wonder those with the wherewithal to do so are willing to pay dearly for these animals. Shakespeare, taken out of context, might have been referring to the Keeneland or Fasig-Tipton thoroughbred auctions when he wrote in *King Richard III:* "A horse! a horse! my kingdom for a horse!" When you look at the top thoroughbred prices, including a world record $13.1 million paid for a son of Nijinsky II and My Charmer in 1985, you begin to think that many kingdoms probably *have* been exchanged for the opportunity to achieve track immortality

Insiders' Tips

A thoroughbred stallion named Lexington won six of seven races during a brief but impressive 19th-century career, then became ever more productive as a stud. Lexington was the nation's top sire for a record-setting 16 years, producing 84 stakes winners and 11 champions.

Keeneland's six weeks of racing a year — three in April and three in October — draw thousands of spectators and bettors.

with one of these regal beasts.

When your horses are worth that much, you do whatever you can to keep them healthy. To that end, the Maxwell H. Gluck Equine Research Center was opened on the University of Kentucky campus in 1987. This center, acknowledged as the finest equine research facility in the country, has resulted in a number of discoveries related to vaccination and disease control, blood testing and breeding efficiency.

Look up "Horse Farms" in the Lexington Yellow Pages, and you will find nearly 200 entries, thoroughbred as well as standardbred and saddlebred. The names of the famous ones, of which there are many, trip off the tongue. Calumet (ever notice how much that sounds like Camelot?), the first horse farm that people generally see when they fly into Lexington. Castleton. Claiborne. Darby Dan. Domino

Stud. Donamire. Elmendorf. Gainsborough. Gainesway. Hamburg Place, long known for its horses as well as its extravagant pre-Derby parties. Lane's End, where Queen Elizabeth II stays when she visits Central Kentucky. Stoner Creek Stud. Three Chimneys. Walmac International. Walnut Hall. The list goes on and on.

Calumet, which in 1991 was bankrupt and at risk of being auctioned off in parcels, was rescued from such an inglorious fate by Henryk de Kwiatkowski, a Polish-born aviation executive. De Kwiatkowski — who paid $17 million for the farm plus $250,000 for the right to use the name and logo — vowed not only to refrain from changing the character of the storied farm but also to return Calumet to its glory days.

Of the first 119 Kentucky Derby winners, 89 — or 75 percent — were foaled in Kentucky. So were eight of

VINERY
1994
STALLION ROSTER

BEAU GENIUS

BLACK TIE AFFAIR

CRYPTOCLEARANCE

DIXIE BRASS

DIXIELAND BRASS

FARMA WAY

FLY TILL DAWN

FRED ASTAIRE

GILDED TIME

HERMITAGE

LOST CODE

LOST OPPORTUNITY

MARQUETRY

METFIELD

RED RANSOM

RUNAWAY GROOM

SILVER GHOST

STRIKE THE GOLD

TWILIGHT AGENDA

VINERY

Mr. and Mrs. Ben P. Walden, Jr. (606) 846-5214
Fax (606) 846-4671 • Weisenberger Mill Pike, Midway, KY 40347
All Vinery stallions are nominated to the Breeders' Cup

See races during spring and fall meets at Keeneland Race Course.

the 11 horses that have captured the elusive Triple Crown by winning the Derby, the Preakness and the Belmont Stakes. In light of such impressive pedigrees, it's only natural that Lexington be entrusted with maintaining the sacred American Stud Book, a register of all thoroughbreds foaled in the United States, Canada and Puerto Rico. The computerized data base contains the names of more than 1.6 million horses.

For years, during the 1930s, the *Lexington Herald* had a standing offer to give subscribers free papers on any day that no horse bred within a 50-mile radius of Lexington won a race at any major track. At that time, there would be periods during the year when only one track in the country would be running, which greatly increased the odds that no Kentucky horse would win on a particular day. But no one can remember it ever happening.

That a newspaper would even make such an offer is indicative of the pride many Central Kentuckians feel in being able to live in such a special place. You don't have to be involved in the horse industry to feel it.

Of course, lots of people are attracted to the racing scene simply because it provides a fabulous excuse for a party. In the Bluegrass you will find, especially around Derby time, some of the most extravagant parties anywhere, where beautiful people in tuxedos and glittering evening gowns mingle and champagne flows freely. Anita Madden's

Insiders' Tips

A great way to start a day is by watching the early morning workouts at Keeneland and eating breakfast in the track kitchen. To catch all the action, it's best to get there by 8.

Kentucky Thoroughbred Association, Inc.

Before There Was A Field of Dreams, There Was a Sport of Kings

Horse racing was America's favorite pastime before most professional sports were invented. If you'd like to experience firsthand the thrill of victory or learn more about this exciting industry, the KTA is available to assist you. Call (606) 278–6004 for more information.

K
T
A

P.O. Box 4040 Lexington, KY 40544

Photos by Midge and Stidham & Assoc.

annual Derby Eve blowout at Hamburg Place in Lexington is perhaps the grandest of them all. Should you rate as a "somebody" important enough to merit an invitation to one of these gala events (so far, we haven't), you may find yourself rubbing elbows with famous actors and actresses, rock stars, sports legends or perhaps even a president or two.

Elsewhere, we "regular" people hold our own Derby celebrations, which while substantially less stylish are characterized by no less enthusiasm. Most of us tend to steer clear of Churchill Downs itself on the first Saturday in May, but we can make a daylong party out of the two-minute race on our televisions.

Then there are the brave souls who do travel to Louisville to experience the Derby amid that strange world known as the infield. On the big day, the area inside the track is packed with humans, a sizable percentage of whom are of the "party animal" species. They will tell you

that it is entirely possible to attend the Run for the Roses without seeing an actual horse. Some have their vision obscured simply because they are surrounded by taller people and are a prohibitive distance from the action on the track. Others have theirs obscured by perhaps a few too many mint juleps. This is not advisable.

If you would like to see, feel, ride or learn about the many varieties of horses in the Bluegrass, there are numerous places and events in Greater Lexington that will allow you to do so.

Racecourses

KEENELAND
4201 Versailles Road   254-3412

With its manicured, meticulously landscaped grounds, its paddock shaded by dogwood and many other colorful trees, and its historic setting, Keeneland has been called the most beautiful racecourse in the world. With its lack of PA system, it's

The Red Mile is named for the harness track's red soil.

Photo: Lexington Herald-Leader

also one of the quietest; yet, in the six short weeks of races it has each year — three weeks in April and three in October — it makes a big noise in the racing world. The Blue Grass Stakes, for example, is one of the major pre-Derby races for three-year-olds. The 1 1/16-mile course, which opened in 1936, also features a 7 1/2-furlong turf course. On Saturday afternoons during the racing season, Keeneland is the place to be seen, a social occasion even for those who think the Daily Double is a drink served during happy hour in the clubhouse. Keeneland is also the only American track whose races

have been attended by Queen Elizabeth II.

Keeneland's influence continues to be felt when horses aren't racing there. No fewer than 12 future Derby winners have been acquired through Keeneland's July and September yearling sales, which also were the occasion for the record $13.1 million sale in 1985. The training facilities are open year round. If you haven't been to Keeneland, a National Historic Landmark, then you haven't really been to Lexington.

The spring racing season typically opens the second Saturday in April and runs six days a week for

Don't feel bad if you didn't receive an invitation to Anita Madden's Derby Eve blowout at Hamburg Place. Neither did we.

three weeks, with no racing on Mondays. The fall season opens the second Saturday in October and runs five days a week for three weeks, with no racing on Mondays and Tuesdays. The 1994 season runs April 8-29 and October 8-29. General admission is $2; preferred parking is $1, and free parking is available for those who don't mind walking. For $3 more, you can get a reserved seat in the grandstand — but, frankly, the rails and the paddock area are better if you're into the sport of people-watching. Availability of reserved tickets varies: During the week, you can generally get them at the gate, but on weekends and for major stakes races, you'll probably have to order them in advance. Incidentally, if you want to eat at the Keeneland restaurant, you should make your reservations as far in advance as possible.

THE RED MILE
1200 Red Mile Road   255-0752

The Red Mile is the fastest harness track in the world, and the oldest existing racecourse in Lexington. Compared with Keeneland, this track named for its red soil is a horse of a different color. Harness racing is naturally slower than thoroughbred racing, but it's just as exciting in its own way to watch the trotters head into the stretch, drivers perched precariously (so it seems) behind them in

their two-wheel sulkies, the race being announced from within a car that races along beside the pack of horses. The track, the oldest stop on the Grand Circuit race series, is also host of the Kentucky Futurity, which with the Hambletonian and the Yonkers Trots makes up the Triple Crown of trotting.

The original version of The Red Mile opened in Lexington in 1875. It has since changed locations and gone through two grandstands, but it retains much of its old-fashioned flavor. In the grandstand and along the rail, the atmosphere is casual. A clubhouse allows more formal dining while watching the races. The Paddock Park area is used for concerts, and the infield is the site of the annual Memorial Stakes Day and other events.

The Red Mile's operations also include the Tattersalls standardbred auctions three times a year. The 1994 spring racing schedule was set to run Wednesdays through Saturdays during April 29-July 2, post time 7 PM. The fall schedule will be September 26-October 7, post time 1 PM. Schedules are subject to change, so it's wise to call first, or check out the billboard at South Broadway and Red Mile Road. Admission is $1 during the spring meet and $2 during the fall meet.

CHURCHILL DOWNS
700 Central Avenue,
Louisville   (502) 636-4400

Lexington has the horses, but Louisville has the home of the greatest — or at least the most famous — two minutes in horse racing. The Kentucky Derby, which first ran in 1875 and offered a purse of $2,850, now attracts more than 100,000 fans every year to Churchill Downs, and millions more watch the race on television. The track's twin spires adorn the Kentucky license plate and are recognized all over the world.

The 1994 spring meet will run from April 30 through July 4; the fall meet is October 31 through November 27. Admission is $3.50 for clubhouse, $2 for grandstand. Reserved seats are $2 extra. Parking is $2. There is a long waiting list for Derby tickets, but you can be part of the mass of humanity that packs into the infield. If you really want to enjoy Churchill Downs, however, you're much better off going at a more sane time than the first Saturday in May.

Other Equine Attractions

KENTUCKY HORSE PARK
4089 Iron Works Pike   233-4303

The Kentucky Horse Park, which opened in 1987 at a cost of $35 million, is the only equestrian theme park in the world. Its lush, rolling 1,032 acres provide a comprehensive look at the importance of the horse in Kentucky and the rest of the world. The legendary Man o' War, who failed to win only one race in his career, is buried beneath a statue of himself at the park entrance. After viewing the wide-screen films *All the King's Horses* and *Thou Shalt Fly Without Wings* in the information center, visitors can tour the park on foot, aboard shuttle or horse-drawn carriage or on horseback. They also can witness day-to-day operations of a working horse farm, see representatives of more than 30 breeds of horses in the Breeds Barn and the Parade of Breeds, and pay tribute to racing and show greats in the Hall of Champions.

The Horse Park, which includes a 3,500-seat arena, is the site of many world championship equestrian events each year, including the annual Rolex Three Day Event, the High Hope Steeplechase and the U.S. Open Polo Championships. Other horse shows and polo matches are held regularly on the grounds. The International Museum of the Horse, contained within the Horse Park, traces the history of the horse and also features the huge Calumet Farm Trophy Collection. A camping resort area includes swimming pool and tennis facilities.

The Kentucky Horse Park is open from 9 AM to 5 PM daily except from November 1 through mid-March, when it is closed Monday and Tuesday. One-day general admission is $8.95 for adults and $4.95 for children ages 7 through 12. A combination ticket, $10.20 for adults and $5.25 for children, also includes admission to The American Saddle Horse Museum (see below). A one-hour guided trail ride on the outskirts of the park is $10 a person.

THE AMERICAN SADDLE HORSE MUSEUM

4093 Iron Works Pike   *259-2746*

Kentucky's only native breed is also the oldest registered American breed of horse. Saddlebreds, the result of breeding thoroughbred stallions with a number of other breeds, are used for a variety of purposes in addition to their main one as show horses. Museum officials like to point out, for example, that Gen. Robert E. Lee rode a saddlebred and that Mr. Ed was one. The museum offers a variety of multi-media presentations and exhibits, including one that allows visitors to picture themselves riding famous saddlebreds. They also can take a scenic trail ride aboard a saddlebred and watch a horse show. The American Saddle Horse Museum is open 9 AM to 6 PM Memorial Day through Labor Day and 9 AM to 5 PM September through May. Admission is $2 for adults, $1.50 for seniors and $1 for children ages 7 through 12. (See above for info on combination tickets with Horse Park admission.)

KENTUCKY HORSE CENTER

3380 Paris Pike   *293-1853*

A one-mile training track and a 900-seat sales pavilion are the highlights of this working thoroughbred training complex. A 1 1/2 hour tour gives visitors a behind-the-scenes look at the industry. Tours are offered at 9 and 10:30 AM and at 1 PM Monday through Friday from April 1 through October 31. Cost is $10, $5 for children younger than 10.

MASTERSON STATION PARK INDOOR ARENA COMPLEX

3051 Leestown Road   *253-0328*

This indoor arena, operated and maintained by the Division of Parks and Recreation, provides opportunities for riding lessons, shows, seminars and clinics. It features a 20-by-60-meter arena that seats 200 people, a judges stand, four large workout mirrors and a 32-stall attached barn. Groups can also rent the facility for their own equestrian events. Hourly rentals, available from November 1 through March 31, must be made at least 48 hours and no more than seven days in advance. Exclusive use of the arena complex is $25 an hour; time share, with three horses maximum, is $10 an hour.

LEXINGTON LIVERY CO.

171 Saunier Avenue   *259-2500*

The Lexington Livery Co. offers horse-drawn carriage tours. For $25, up to four people can enjoy a 25- to 30-minute ride through the streets of historic downtown Lexington. This makes a romantic addition to any evening, or it can be part of an enjoyable and relaxing night out with the family. You can make reservations in advance, or simply catch one of the carriages in front of the Radisson after 7:30 PM.

THOROUGHBRED PARK

Main Street and Midland Avenue

The newest of Lexington's downtown parks is a tribute to the spirit of the thoroughbreds and their jockeys. The focal point is a life-size freeze-frame of a race in action, seven bronze horses streaking toward the finish line. Their jockeys are seven

Photo: Lexington Herald-Leader

Patrick Valenzuela is one of many high-profile jockeys astride winners at Keeneland.

of the greats: Randy Romero, Pat Day, Bill Shoemaker, Jerry Bailey, Don Brumfield, Chris McCarron and Craig Perret. Lexington sculptor Gwen Reardon took three years to sculpt the richly detailed figures. In a grassy meadow above the "track," six more horses graze: brood mares, foals and, in the center, the stallion Lexington. Fountains and a still pool complete the $8 million park, which was dedicated in April 1992. Four of the jockeys who later visited the park were impressed with its realism. More telling, however, is the report that real horses have seen the statues and been spooked.

Horse Farm Tours

Horse farm visitation policies differ from farm to farm. Many are not open to tours, while others permit visitors at selected times. Because of the uncertain and often hectic nature of the business, policies are subject to change from day to day. We have listed a few of the farms that are open to the public, as well as some companies and individuals that provide tours. If you are interested in other farms, call them and ask whether visitors are allowed. In fact, to avoid disappointment, you should call any horse farm before visiting.

CLAIBORNE FARM
Winchester Road, Paris   233-4252

The great Secretariat, who won the Triple Crown in 1973 and whose world record of 2:24 for a mile and a half has yet to be matched, is buried at this farm where he was retired to stud and sired more than 300 sons and daughters. Claiborne Farm offers tours from 9 AM to 2 PM Monday through Saturday, but you must call in advance.

THREE CHIMNEYS FARM
Old Frankfort Pike   *873-7053*

The eight stallions who stand at stud at picturesque Three Chimneys include 1977 Triple Crown winner Seattle Slew and three of his sons: Slew o' Gold, Capote and Fast Play. Thousands of people annually visit Three Chimneys, which is generally open year-round. But, again, you should call first.

VINERY
Weisenberger Mill Road,
Midway   *846-5214*

Although it's not one of the better known Bluegrass farms, Vinery is home to 1991 Derby victor Strike the Gold, 1992 "Horse of the Year" Black Tie Affair, as well as 1987 Florida Derby winner Cryptoclearance. If you call in advance, the farm owners will make an effort to let you see these horses up close.

HISTORIC & HORSE FARM TOURS
3429 Montavesta Drive   *268-2906*

This tour company has a monopoly on Calumet, the farm distinguished by its track record of eight Derby winners and for its white barns trimmed in red. Several other well-known Bluegrass horse farms also can be visited through this company. Tours of two-and-a-half to three hours are offered seven days a week, with the agenda changing daily. The normal tour visits Calumet, then Keeneland and finally a brood mare farm. Reservations are suggested. The tour van picks up visitors at most hotels and motels in the Lexington area. Locals can catch the van at a designated hotel or motel. Two tours a day, at 8:30 AM and 1:30 PM, are offered. Cost is $18. A couple of cautions: There is sometimes a two- to three-week wait for Calumet tours, and tourgoers are generally restricted to the van.

BLUE GRASS TOURS
1116 Manchester Street   *233-2152*

Blue Grass Tours, Lexington's oldest tour and charter company, offers two daily tours at 9 AM and 1:30 PM. Each tour includes a stop at Keeneland, The Red Mile or both; a drive through horse farm country; and a tour through the historic downtown area, including the bronze statues at Thoroughbred Park. Tours are $18 a person, and reservations are required. Seniors get a $2 discount. The Marriott's Griffin Gate Resort is the main point of departure, but the bus will pick up passengers at any Lexington hotel for an additional $2. UK basketball fans might be interested in knowing that Blue Grass Tours is owned by former Wildcat star Wallace "Wah Wah" Jones.

KAREN EDELSTEIN
                                266-5465

Karen Edelstein has been in-

Runners can enjoy the scenic beauty of Calumet Farm, on U.S. 60 between Lexington and Versailles, while they get their exercise.

Photo: Lexington Herald-Leader

volved in the horse industry for a number of years and was a hostess at Calumet for several years. Now she offers customized private "step-on" tours. You drive the car and she talks. You'll pick up a wealth of fascinating information about breeding, training, racing and more. You'll probably get a chance to meet a legendary stakes-winner-turned-stud like Seattle Slew or Nureyev and talk with a trainer or groom. Edelstein's basic rates, which include a glossary of horse terms and additional printed material, are $50 for a minimum of two hours for up to four people and $10 an hour after that. Take a few extra dollars and enjoy breakfast in the Keeneland kitchen.

JOAN COMBS
269-1721

Joan Combs also offers customized private tours filled with insight about the horse industry. Like Edelstein, she'll show you Keeneland

from trackside to trainers' barns and, if you have a specific farm in mind, will do what she can to let you see it. Prices vary, starting with a basic two-hour car tour for about $40.

Riding and Instruction

DEER RUN STABLES
2001 River Circle Drive,
Richmond   1-527-6339

Surprisingly, this is about the only place we know of in the area where you can just go rent a horse and ride for a while on your own. The reason, instructors say, is rising overhead and insurance costs. Deer Run offers unguided or guided 3-mile tours along a gorgeous, varied trail that takes you up and down hills, through woods and along a creek. The ride generally takes about 45 minutes. Horses, which are available to accommodate all levels of experience, range from docile to more spirited. Riders must be at least 6 years old. Cost is $10 a person.

To get to Deer Run Stables, take I-75 south from Lexington to exit 97, then follow the winding, scenic two-lane east about 4 1/2 miles, keeping your eyes peeled for signs in residents' yards. As one rider says, "It's a little hard to find, but it's well worth the trouble."

Z ACADEMY
1522 Shannon Run Road (Ky. 1967 South), Versailles   873-9376, 281-5765

Instructor Lynn Zaske specializes in lessons for beginners; even if you've never been astride a horse, she will quickly put you at ease. She can also provide advanced lessons for those who want to learn show horse skills. No formal attire is required. Instruction is offered year-round in an indoor area at Jack Noble Stables. Cost is $20 a half-hour for private lessons, $15 a half-hour for semiprivate. Beginners must take at least ten private lessons before qualifying for semiprivate.

CHAMPAGNE RUN
5991 Old Richmond Road   263-4638

A variety of training — including dressage, eventing and hunter-jumper — is available. Champagne Run has indoor and outdoor arenas, as well as a cross-country course with fields and jumps. Private lessons are $20 for a half-hour, semiprivate (two people) lessons are $18 for 40 minutes, and instruction for groups of three to six is $15 for an hour.

FILLONGLEY EQUESTRIAN CENTER
1415 Pinckard Pike (Ky. 169)
Versailles   873-3337

Fillongley, which has trained Olympic athletes and provides horses for them, offers basic riding instruction, as well as dressage, combined, hunter-jumper and Western, in a relaxed atmosphere with all certified instructors. The center has an indoor arena, outdoor dressage arena, two outdoor jumping rings and a cross-country area. Riding lessons range from $7.50 an hour to $25 an hour. The center also specializes in lessons for children and families, with emphasis on grooming and getting to know a horse.

KENTUCKY BELLE STABLES
Ash Grove Pike   272-2611

Kentucky Belle, located just inside Jessamine County past the Hartland subdivision, offers private lessons for beginning, intermediate and advanced riders, with horse care emphasized. Advanced lessons are given on American saddlebred show horses. Western-style training is available, but most lessons are English-style riding. The facility has an indoor arena and an outdoor arena; trails are available for students only. Individual one-hour lessons are $22, or you can get ten one-hour lessons for $200.

CENTRAL KENTUCKY RIDING
FOR THE HANDICAPPED
4089 Iron Works Pike   231-7066

This nonprofit organization, with the motto "Ability . . . not disability," provides lessons at the Kentucky Horse Park. Commander, a gentle, 27-year-old Morgan horse, is a star of the program, which is open to any interested rider. Scholarships are available.

Instruction is also available at **Castle Hills Farms**, 235 Pisgah Pike in Versailles, 873-7534; **Gold Spring Farm**, 3065 Spurr Road, 252-5650; **Robert Murphy Stables**, 5531 Parkers Mill Road, 255-3422; and **Windy Knoll Farm Riding School**, 3263 Cleveland Road North, 299-7410.

Equine Annual Events

EQUIFESTIVAL
This October event, started in 1991, revolves around the opening weekend of Keeneland's fall racing season. Highlights over a period of several days include a Parade of Breeds in downtown Lexington, a foot race through horse farm country and a family breakfast at Keeneland.

LEXINGTON JUNIOR
LEAGUE HORSE SHOW
200 Market Street   252-1893

The American saddle horse is the star of this weeklong show, the largest outdoor horse show in the country. Each July the Junior League Horse Show, first held in 1937, features the world's finest specimens of Kentucky's only native breed. The event is held at The Red Mile.

FESTIVAL OF THE HORSE
Georgetown   863-2547

The annual Festival of the Horse is held the third full weekend each September in downtown Georgetown. Its three days of events honoring the horse industry include food and craft booths, free entertainment and carriage rides, a tennis tournament, children's games, a parade with more than 200 horses and two horse shows.

Jesse N. "Sonny" Wigginton:
"I want to play this game"

Horse trainer Jesse N. "Sonny" Wigginton has seen numerous changes at Keeneland over the years, and he's liked them all. He is a lifelong resident of Lexington who stables his charges at the Keeneland Training Center. Although he races around the country, "there's no place in the country like here."

The reasons are simple: "Class. Relaxation. Home."

A conversation with Sonny Wigginton on a November morning unfolds at a leisurely pace with a stop at the track kitchen for breakfast, a visit to the fabled track itself and then a return to the barn where his horses are stabled. Personal reminiscences are intertwined with bits and pieces of track history and observations about the state of the business. The visiting writer occasionally prompts comment with a question, but he prefers just listening.

"I can remember being here in the early '40s. Around '43 I can remember being out here, and probably was here earlier than that. Before the war even started, I would have had to have been here. Dad stabled down close to where the new kitchen is now. I guess they vanned out and raced a little bit then. When the war was over in '45, all of a sudden we were coming back out here and racing horses. There was great excitement that the war was over and all the trainers were coming back. They just stepped right back in and took over their horses.

"The changes I've seen at Keeneland have always been for the good. They made more room. The clubhouse used to be separated from the grandstand. There was a big yard there with benches — a great big, grassy place, very relaxing, but wasted space for the crowds they were starting to get. So they connected those two things. I know they've moved the finish line once in the years I've been out here. It may have been moved twice, because they changed the length of the grandstand.

"Most of the masonry and stone work that they've done up there now — beautification of the place — is just unreal, when you compare what it used to look like with what it looks like now. Not that it wasn't beautiful before then, but what they've done now up here, you'd have to go a long way to match it. . . . You just think, well, they couldn't do anything more up there to make it any prettier. And then they'll come up with something else. The turf course was a major, major accomplishment. For the public and for the true grass horses that can run only on grass, it's added another total dimension to racing here. . . .

"The old Keeneland kitchen was a very good place for the towns-people to eat at that time. You'd see people coming out from being out very late at night when they'd catch the horsemen just coming in. They'd be very well dressed up, eating in that place to get an early breakfast. It was as well known a kitchen as there was in the country. Racetracks are noted for having either bad kitchens or good kitchens. And the original Keeneland kitchen was a place that people sought to eat."

Despite his early introduction to the horse world, Wigginton's career in the business was far from guaranteed. In fact, it took a reintroduction when he was in college to make him realize what he wanted to do with his life.

"When I was a freshman at UK, Dad had died, and we'd sold all the horses and everything and were living in town. I got a job here in the old clubhouse. They had two guys over here — me and another guy my age — and we were messengers. We'd go to people's tables who didn't want to get up and walk to the window and make a bet. We wore our black uniforms with orange trim and everything, and we had this book, were authorized to write these tickets.

"The tips were — oh! I mean, for the next four or five years, all I lived for was these Keeneland meets because I'd make enough money to almost carry me. And if this isn't an introduction to the racetrack — it's where you *will* make money, you know. And I had this grand job. When I started, I was the second guy; the other guy was the head guy. He only lasted one more year, and I got the job as head man. Then they put a guy in that I kind of broke in. And you got to meet all these fantastic people that you'd only read about in *The Racing Form* and in books. They'd all be up here in the clubhouse having lunch, and they'd get to know you. And the next thing you know, hell, you know every damn race person in the country on a first-name basis because you're running their bets for them! It was a fantastic introduction into that end of the business.

"When I went in the Army, I had to let the job go. But before I did, I'd already bought a horse when I was 19. And I was successful with him. And that first horse being so successful, that capped it! Since then, from the time I was 19 years old, the only time I didn't own a horse was when I was in the Army. I've had something, and mostly multiple ownerships — you know, like, have at least three going. We'd put together little partnerships; four of us would buy a horse. Get the volume up and everything.

"I train for everybody, anybody. Those private jobs, they're very, very good. But they can be very, very dangerous. Because if you've got all your eggs in one basket and you have a falling-out with that man,

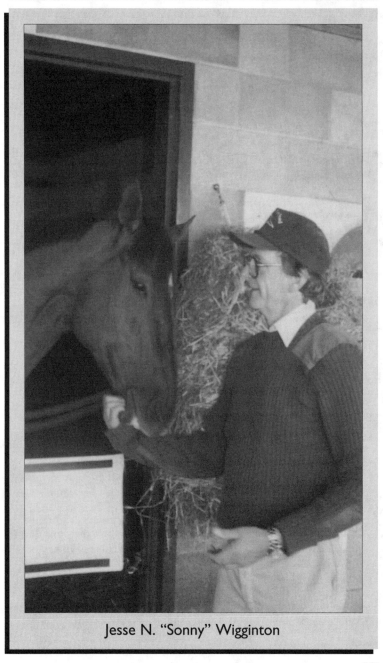

Jesse N. "Sonny" Wigginton

the next thing you know, you don't even have a horse. The good end of it is, chances are if you're a private trainer, the guy's got a better-than-average bunch of horses, and you don't have to look for but one guy to collect your money. And the job security, as far as that goes, is pretty good until it ends. If I'm training 10 horses, I'd just as soon have five owners with them. They all can't get mad at you on one day.

"From the time I was 10 out here, for the next 10 or 15 years, those riders were like *gods* to you. You know, here's Steve Brooks, who was one of the world's best riders. He was, in his day, what Donnie Brumfield was in later years to this racetrack. There were many other good riders; I just don't recall them. But Steve Brooks I can recall as being one of the grandest riders ever to ride this racetrack. In later years, Donnie Brumfield took over as Keeneland's all-time leader, and then Pat Day has surpassed him. You just watch these guys come out of the paddock when you're that young, and you say, 'I want to play this game with them. I want to be right in the middle of it.' And, luckily, I got to do it. Even before I bought that first horse, I'd just get that feeling: 'I *will* be playing this game.'

"A rider is a guy you hire to do a job for two minutes. You might have him come to the barn and get on a horse one time. But we, as a routine, do not do that. Now and then we'll get lucky with one rider; we'll use him for a while, but we'll go to another racetrack and he'll go to another racetrack. So you don't get too personally involved with them. They're all good at a certain level; they're all on a parity. A good rider is not hard to come by. If you didn't get your first choice, your second choice is probably equally as good.

"We go through their agent. We might not talk to that rider because he wouldn't be so accessible. We'd have the agent's phone number, and we'd call a few days ahead and say, 'Look, we're going to go in this race next Saturday. Are you open?' They'd look and say, 'Let me call you right back. I have a tentative thing there.' They'll call you back and say, 'Put me on' or 'If my horse doesn't get in, we'll ride yours.' They work with you very much, and they'll help you find somebody else.

"As trainers, we handle everything. In only a few instances would an owner come in and say, 'I will get the rider.' If you had the situation, you'd already be in trouble because they really need to be calling those shots. The trainer really needs to. We're hired to get the rider that will fit that horse best.

"Each track has a set fee for what they call a jock mount. It's scaled. From the latest purse, which averages around $5,000, up to maybe a $10,000 purse, it's a flat fee of approximately $50. That's a horse if he gets beat. If he runs second, he gets a little more, and if he wins, the rider is credited from the winning purse, 10 percent of what the horse won, automatically. The track has a horseman's bookkeeper who takes that money out, and that's how jockeys are paid.

"I've had a lot of favorite horses. Every time I say one ought to be my favorite, another one comes along and does something to make me think, 'Well, *he's* my favorite.' But in the last six or seven years, I've had a stake horse in the barn at all times. It makes life a lot easier because those horses are pumping more money in — my percentage of those wins. And when you can relax about money in this game and aren't worried about income, you can do a better job. So all of those stake horses have been my favorites lately. The last two years have been fantastic. At one time this year alone, in 1993, I only had 10 horses in the barn, but three of them were Grade I stakes winners. They hadn't necessarily won Grade I stakes when I had them, but they had been Grade I stakes winners, so they were running for pretty good money.

"I've had eight or 10 *really* nice horses. There's a difference. Around the racetrack, when they say, 'That's a racehorse,' they mean it's something exceptional. That's a real racehorse. You're going to see 500 before you seen one real racehorse. The rest of them — they have their use, and they are fun, but a real racehorse is hard to come by. If you've got one in the barn, you're really lucky.

"Any victory is very jubilating, even at the lowest level. It's a thrill that you just can't imagine unless you're right in the middle of it. . . . But Gold Spring, the horse that we had that was going to go to the Breeders' Cup this year and got injured, probably his win in the Aristides at Churchill Downs was a turning point for me because I thought, from here on, with the people I had behind me and the money they had, that we would probably be able to play consistently at this level. I thought we — and when I say 'we,' I mean the team I work with — had proven we could buy horses and race against the best with them. That victory was a turning point. And that was a good feeling.

"Gold Spring is a horse that one of my owners allowed us to buy for him in Argentina last winner. We brought him up here and won three straight stakes races with him. He was the 1991 sprint champion in Argentina. And he was injured severely here just before going to the Breeders' Cup. He could possibly have been very effective. Now his career is in doubt.

"It's horrible to lose a horse. You've been around them. You can't help but be involved in their personalities, good or bad. So if they get hurt, it's like your child getting hurt. You're responsible. You may not own the horse, but you're directly responsible for his well-being, so it actually hurts you as bad as it hurts the owner. Or worse, because you're sitting there looking at it. We've had a few die in action. And it's a tragedy, but so minute compared with the numbers that we race. You could probably count on one hand the deaths, and only maybe three of those were on the track. We've had some horses contract some mysterious things; their intestinal system is so delicate that we couldn't save them. Before we could get them to a vet, they'd contract something they couldn't overcome. A horse'll die in a hurry; you'd be surprised at how quick they'll go down. But I am emotionally involved with them. A lot of people say they aren't, but I am. From the cheapest horse on up, you feel responsible."

What does Wigginton like most about the horse business?

"I guess the bottom line would be the word 'action.' Even if it looks like you're just training and treading water, you're watching these horses getting *ready* to be in action. It's just the action of racing — the preparation and going and doing it. It lifts your body. You just can't imagine being involved in this damn thing. You want to get everybody and say, 'Come on in here, because it's *fun.*' Even when it's horrible, you're always optimistic that the next one is going to be a winner. And if you try hard enough, you will be."

When he has a horse racing at Keeneland, "if it's really crowded, I won't go much past the paddock area because the crowd's so bad that if you did win it, you can't hardly get back down there. So if it's really crowded, I'll watch it right down there (near the Winner's Circle). Otherwise, my cousin's got a box right on the finish line, and on a quiet day, I just like to go up there. I much prefer to watch them alone, win or lose. I like to be alone. I just like to wander off. When we ran in the stakes race here on opening day, my wife was out here, and it was very crowded. And I didn't know she knew me this well, but she turned to me and said, 'Where are you going to hide?'" Wigginton laughs at that.

"She's got a career as a schoolteacher, and she stays totally occupied. We don't get in each other's way; we're not jealous of what the other person does. It's a very good relationship.

"I race at Keeneland, Churchill Downs, River Downs, Turfway Park, Beulah Park. We go to Arlington. We've been to Saratoga this year. We've been to Omaha this year. If the horse dictates to go that far, we can do it. And if you've got good horses, you won't be able to sit still. You'll have to go to all these points where the big races are. They'll run one of the big races at one track, and then 30 days later they'll run equal for that type of horse at another racetrack, so you'll have to go the other way."

How easy is it go make a living in this business?

"It's not easy at all. . . . I owned horses so far before I trained them, so I had all that before me. That experience was paid for. All experiences cost you money. When I went into it right on the track, I had a fairly solid base to work off of. That's helped me stay, because there have been a lot of lean periods. A barn basically loses money unless you're winning a number of races to pump that extra commission in there. You're just treading water."

In Lexington, the writer suggests, when somebody acquires some money, it would seem to be a natural inclination to get involved in the horse business, much as that same person might jump into the stock market.

"You'd be surprised. The new coach comes to town, and the next thing, he's got horses. He's in playing because coaches have that sport in their blood. So very few of them are not involved some way. And it reverberates through the stockbrokers or sports, because they're gambling. Of the whole broad spectrum of people in Lexington, there's probably very few people of some means who aren't exposed to the opportunity to join in a partnership on a horse. It doesn't take a lot of talking to talk somebody into a share in a horse with a friend. That makes our work easier; for the pool of available clients, there's no better place in the world than here. Because it's ingrained in the society; racing is saturated into the fiber of the city. You shouldn't run out of work if you can keep a few clients happy."

Asked whether he'd ever yearned for the experience of being a jockey, Wigginton says: "Absolutely. I showed horses, and we had all the thoroughbred rejects on the farm. I rode them all the time, but I was growing like crazy, and I was just getting into the serious jumping when Dad died. So that just all fell apart. We moved back into town, and horses just weren't a part of my life from 13 to 19. And from then on. . . .

"In those years between 13 and 19, horses weren't that much on my mind. But, you know, as you get older and are able to drive a car, you get out and meet a few more people. And at 19, as you know, you're dumber than a rock. But I got this itch to be around these people. And this job at Keeneland had a lot to do with that. Although I didn't have my hands on the horse, I was connected with the horse people, and I liked what I saw. I liked the lifestyle."

If he wasn't doing this, the writer asks, what would Wigginton be doing?

"God forbid. I couldn't think of anything. What you do, I guess."

But, again, Sonny Wigginton has been lucky, he says. He has

survived and become successful in a business that has undergone numerous changes, especially in the amount of money involved.

"The gimmick betting has changed. I can remember when this track didn't even have a Daily Double. It was all over the country, but they didn't have a Daily Double here until like the middle '50s. Now there's not only a Daily Double, there's a Late Double, there's an Exacta on half the races and a Trifecta on the rest of them. And the astronomical payoffs and the different combinations of betting have increased the income for the track because they take a higher percentage of those bets out. The crowds get bigger, the per capita betting goes up, and where this might have been deemed casual racing 15 years ago, this is a major leader in some of the innovations that are coming. They will soon probably have a sports spectrum here for off-track betting year round, and it will probably be one of the nicer ones around. The one in Louisville is already operating.

"If somebody had said five years ago that I was going to see a crowd of people standing at Keeneland racetrack in the middle of the winter betting on horse races that were coming in on a TV and that it was going to be a constant thing, it would have been pretty hard to digest. Now it's matter-of-fact way of life. It's ingrained into racing and into this operation. And every track in the country is following suit on it or already in it. Major, major changes."

Is Wigginton a good bettor?

"Not very good. Never. I don't try. The focus. I can't focus on gambling on my horses or anybody's horses, and focus on what I'm doing. It's not a good habit to me. If you're more worried about the bet, then you're going to take your mind off the horse. It's the last thing on my mind. And if I do turn around and go to bet, the line's usually so long by the time I make my mind up that I couldn't bet anyway. When I was younger I thought the sun rose and set on gambling at the racetrack, but the more you're in it physically, the less important betting becomes. I'd say most trainers don't bet a lot, if any. It's just so insignificant to what they do. I really think that would be the rule and not the exception. I'll win a race, and the horse will pay a giant price. People will say, 'Boy, we know you've got the money now.' And I'll say, 'I didn't even have a dime on it,' and mean it. I do well enough with the fees and everything, and you can't go plowing that money into bets and lose it. You cannot beat this game as far as consistently betting, so I don't even try."

Near a row of betting windows on the first floor of the grandstand, Wigginton points out another change that modern times have brought to Keeneland.

"In the '40s and early '50s, before they had all the TV cameras and monitors here, say you came out here the third race and you wanted to know who won the first race. They had a guy on a catwalk running right across here, with a giant chalkboard. He was a very good letter man, and he'd put the number of the horse and what he paid. They'd do it all day long until they had all the races up here. That was a unique thing."

Wigginton walks around the corner to a wall covered with televisions.

"Now, as modern as it is, you can come out here the sixth race and still see the first race run. So they've come a long way.

"One other thing: Before they had a photo-finish camera, right down front they had a stone area where three placing judges would walk up about four steps above the track. They'd have a searchlight shooting down on the finish line for the last race because they didn't have daylight saving time then, and by the last race it'd be almost pitch dark. And these three placing judges had to call the finish; that's who determined who won the race. And there was a lot of bitching. You know, it's hard to do. There's got to have been a lot of wrong calls. Everybody would crowd in on the finish line because you weren't going to stand way over here and ever get an idea of what really happened if it was tight. Boy, they'd all be around those guys, and those guys would be there watching, and just as the horses turned into the stretch, this searchlight would be clicked on to light the finish line up.

"The reason they had three judges is there can't be a tie. And they don't call it, either; they write it. I did it for a year at a small track. And the reason I know that they make a lot of bad calls is because we had a camera backing us up, and I worked with two pros. And we'd have tight races, and every damn time I'd have the wrong horse. They'd say, 'You've got to judge that wire; you're judging the wire wrong.' I was useless to them. But we had the camera backing us up."

Back at the training center, Wigginton is asked about competitiveness among trainers.

"I'd say everybody's trying to help each other. If you need some help, there just isn't enough that they couldn't do to help you. No dead-on 'I want to beat this guy' or stuff like that. It might be in the lightest form, but if you took this spread out here at the training center, everybody is pulling for everybody else. . . . It is a big family."

To illustrate his point, he talks about claiming races, in which each horse is subject to being bought at a previously fixed price by anyone else who has entered a horse in that race and who has made a bid before the start of the race.

"You're looking at these people's horses all the time, and you know everything about them because they're training right in front of you. But you wouldn't dare claim one of them; you wouldn't even think about doing it. It'd be the biggest slap in the face. And since I've been out here, to my knowledge, there has never been a horse claimed from anybody that was stabled here. Nobody in Barn A has ever claimed a horse off of somebody in Barn B. And when we were all over on the other side and there were 34 barns over there, I never saw it happen. A guy in Louisville might claim your horses, and chances are it's going to happen. And you could go up there and claim one of theirs, or go to Ohio and grab one. But nobody in here ever did that to somebody else here. You'd go to a guy and say, 'Do you want to sell this horse?'"

At the time of this conversation, Wigginton has nine horses in his stables and is half-owner of one of them. It's an unusual situation, he says; usually he is training more horses that he owns in part or in full. But it's a good situation because he gets a fee for training other people's horses. His own horses bring in money only when they win races.

"Our routine doesn't change much. I get here at 6. But the people on my team get here a little after 5. The first thing they'll do is go in here and pull all the tubs out and check the feed. See who ate and who didn't. They'll have a little report for me when I get in here. If a tub isn't cleaned up, they don't dump it. We see what the horse left. If a horse doesn't eat everything, you might need to just check his temperature or something. And the night before, I will have left them a starting schedule because I'm 30, 40 minutes behind them. They can already know the first horses out, who each one will have out first to go to the racetrack. The rider comes at 6, and at that point the horse is already walking in this shed row with his saddle on him, ready to go to the racetrack. The rider just walks in, and in two minutes he's on the track, and the day begins.

"If you get up over eight or nine horses, you've got to have two riders. We've just got one man now, Dean Moore. He's an ex-jockey, a good rider. We've been lucky to have him here for a good while. He can handle anything we've got.

"As each horse comes in, we've got two hot walkers waiting. They take turns. After they're done walking all the horses, they gather up all the leather, all the dirty laundry, clean the tack (racing equipment). The two people taking care of the horses have their designated horses here in a row. They'll clean them up about in the order they took them out.

"From 9 o'clock on till 11, the veterinarian's doing pre-races or any long-range treatments on horses. They'll make a call here every day. We have two vets we work with consistently.

"Three of the horses here now didn't go to the track because two of them are injured and the other one ran two days ago. You give them an average of about two days' rest. He'll go back to the track tomorrow. Each one of them that went out went to the racetrack and did some form of training. When they come back, Pat takes four and Eric takes four. They bandage the legs, clean the feet. As you can see, she's all brushed off and everything. A blanket will go back on them tonight. They changed all the bedding while we were out, changed the water and all that. Then they'll eat in about 30 minutes, and they'll eat again tonight about 5 o'clock. Much more tonight, three or four times what they do in the morning."

Wigginton lives in Lexington but has a small farm in Scott County that he uses for breeding on a small scale.

"It's an old family place, tobacco and cattle. We've got a little part of it fenced in where we can raise a couple of horses. I just do it because it's not that expensive for me to maintain a mare down there and raise a foal. I've got one foal on the ground and a mare in foal right now. My old brood mare died last year. She must have had 12 or 14 foals over her lifetime. And I just kept breeding her. They were successful. . . . It's not a market operation. The mare is usually some mare that I knew could run better than she actually ever did run. Injured or something. But I knew what the potential was."

One of the great memorials in the Lexington Cemetery is the Dr. Sophonisba Preston Breckinridge grave, in memory of the first woman admitted to the Kentucky Bar and a former dean of the School of Social Administration of the University of Chicago.

Inside
Historic Sites and Monuments

Lexington is fortunate both in that it is rich in history dating back to pioneer days, and that most of its important historic sites were left relatively unscathed by fighting during the Civil War.

The historic architectural resources of the area are abundant as well as well preserved and, in many cases, open to the public either daily or by appointment.

One of the most pleasant ways to experience much of Lexington's historic architecture is to embark on the Lexington Walk, a picturesque walking tour that hits many of the high points of Lexington's historic places. Maps of the tour, which include one for the Bluegrass Driving Tour as well, are available at the Greater Lexington Convention and Visitors Bureau in the Lexington Civic Center at 430 West Vine, Suite 363, Lexington, KY 40507. If you can't get downtown to the visitors bureau, call 233-1221 in Lexington or (800) 84-LEX-KY.

The Lexington Walk is about 2 miles long, but there are plenty of pleasant places to stop and rest or maybe even chat awhile. It incorporates some of downtown Lexington's nicest parks and most unique shopping areas. Triangle Park on Main Street is highlighted by 100 fountains and flowering pear trees. Gratz Park, a few blocks up North Mill Street from Main Street, was originally the campus lawn of adjacent Transylvania University. It was at one time the focal point of one of Lexington's most prominent and wealthiest neighborhoods. Both the Bodley-Bullock House (used as a Union headquarters during the Civil War) and the Hunt-Morgan House (home of a famous Confederate Civil War general) face Gratz Park.

The walking tour also takes you past Henry Clay's law office on North Mill Street, the Lexington Children's Museum, Victorian Square shopping area, Transylvania University and the Lexington Opera House, which was dubbed "the best one-night stand in America" after its opening in 1887. Famous people who have performed there over the years include Al Jolson, Will Rogers, Fanny Brice, Lillian Russell and the Barrymores.

Several of the following historic sites are included in the walking tour, but you'll probably have to drive to the others. Oh, and don't forget to take special note of the statue of Confederate General John Hunt Morgan (that's right, the one whose family home is in Gratz Park) astride a stallion, instead of his most well-known mount Black Bess, on

Henry Clay

the lawn of the Fayette County Court-house.

POPE HOUSE

326 Grosvenor Street   *253-0362*

The John Pope House is one of Lexington's most recently opened historic homes. It is one of three surviving houses by early 19th-century architect Benjamin Henry Latrobe. Latrobe immigrated to the United States from England in the late 18th century. After befriending

many of America's founding fathers, he was appointed architect of the U.S. Capitol by Thomas Jefferson, in which position he created such impressive neoclassical spaces as the old Senate Chamber and the House Chamber, which is now Statuary Hall in Washington, D.C.

One of the most interesting architectural features of the Pope House is the rotunda set in the middle of the square house plan. While the house is still in the process

Photo: Lexington Herald-Leader

Ashland, estate of Kentucky statesman Henry Clay from 1811 until 1852, was extensively renovated in 1992. Visitors can stroll the house's 20 acres, which include a beautiful garden.

of restoration, exhibits are focusing on ongoing conservation work, as well as on Latrobe and Senator John Pope, the house's first owner.

The Pope House is open to the public for tours Saturdays, 10 AM-4 PM; admission is $4.

HOPEMONT
(HUNT-MORGAN HOUSE)

201 North Mill Street   253-0362

Built in 1814 by the first millionaire west of the Alleghenies, John Wesley Hunt, this Federal-style house is in Lexington's historic Gratz Park. Prominent Hunt family members include John Hunt Morgan, the "Thunderbolt of the Confederacy," and 1933 Nobel Prize-winner Thomas Hunt Morgan.

The house is open to the public, and guided tours are offered March 1-December 22, Tuesday-Saturday, 10 AM-4 PM, Sunday, 2-5 PM. Admission is $4 for adults, $2 for ages 6-12.

MARY TODD LINCOLN HOUSE

578 West Main Street   233-9999

As the first site restored in America to honor a First Lady, Lexington's Mary Todd Lincoln House offers a unique glimpse into the early years of the life of this wife of America's 16th president, Abraham Lincoln. The house was originally a brick tavern constructed in 1803. Mary's father, Robert Todd, renovated the tavern into a family dwelling in the 1830s, and the family moved there in 1832.

The house contains many fine period furnishings, as well as a collection of Mary's personal belongings. Public tours of the home are offered April 1-December 15, Tuesday-Saturday, 10 AM-4 PM. Admission is $4 for adults, $1 for ages 6-12.

ASHLAND (HENRY CLAY MANSION)

Richmond and Sycamore roads   266-8581

Ashland was the estate of the "Great Compromiser," Henry Clay, from 1811 until his death in 1852.

Clay, a Lexington lawyer, played a prominent role in U.S. politics throughout his lengthy career, serving as U.S. senator, speaker of the House, secretary of state, and three-time presidential candidate.

One of the nicest features about a visit to Ashland is exploring the beautiful, extensive grounds around the house. The 20 acres of the Henry Clay estate are filled with ancient and unusual trees, including a ginkgo tree (a species that Clay imported to Kentucky) near the house's entrance. There are also several original outbuildings, including a pair of 19th-century round ice houses and a smokehouse.

Ashland is open Tuesday-Saturday, 10 AM-4 PM, Sunday, 1-4 PM, with tours of the home starting on the hour. Admission is $5.

WAVELAND STATE HISTORIC SITE
225 Higbee Mill Road   272-3611

This Greek Revival mansion built in 1847 by Joseph Bryan, a relative of Daniel Boone, is a good example of the lifestyle of the landed gentry in antebellum Kentucky.

Waveland is open to the public March-December, Tuesday-Saturday, 10 AM-4 PM, Sunday, 2-5 PM. Guided tours of the home and grounds are offered throughout the day. To get to Waveland, drive south on Nicholasville Road past Man o' War Boulevard, and take the next right onto Old Higbee Mill Road.

BODLEY-BULLOCK HOUSE
200 Market Street   259-1266

One of the most stunning features of the Bodley-Bullock House is its grand staircase, one of the few cantilevered staircases left in the state. This Kentucky Federal-style house was built around 1814 for Lexington Mayor Thomas Pindell. Pindell in turn sold the house to General Thomas Bodley, a hero of the War of 1812. The house was used as Union headquarters during the Civil War, and one popular story has it that Union troops painted one of the beautiful hardwood floors red, white and blue in celebration of a victory.

While the Bodley-Bullock House is open by appointment for tours Monday-Friday, 9 AM-1 PM (admission $4 for adults, $1.50 for kids older than 5), one of its most popular uses is as a rental space for parties, weddings, receptions and board meetings. Lovely and ornate gardens, as well as a beautifully restored interior, make the house a favorite in Lexington. The Bodley-Bullock House is also the current headquarters of the Lexington Junior League. Be sure to see the Bullocks' unusual snuffbox collection.

LOUDOUN HOUSE
209 Castlewood Drive   254-7024

One of five remaining castellated Gothic villas designed by architect A.J. Davis in the United States, Loudoun House is currently home to the Lexington Art League. It was built in 1852.

Loudoun House features rotating exhibits and artist studio tours. It is open free to the public Tuesday-Friday, noon-4 PM, and Saturday-Sunday, 1-4 PM. To get there from downtown, go north on Broadway, turn east on Loudoun Avenue, left at the "V" in the road, and right on Castlewood Drive.

BOONE STATION
STATE HISTORIC SITE

Gentry Road in Athens   263-1073

This picturesque, 47-acre rural site where Daniel Boone and his family moved after Fort Boonesborough (located just south on the border of Clark and Madison counties) became too crowded offers a different look into the later, more domesticated years of one of America's greatest frontiersmen.

The site is open to the public April 1-October 31. Picnic tables and outdoor recreation areas are available. To get there, take exit 104 off I-75 to Ky. 418 to Cleveland Road to Gentry Road in Athens. It's worth the trip.

LEXINGTON CEMETERY

833 West Main Street   255-5522

The Lexington Cemetery, chartered in 1848, is perhaps most well known nationally as an arboretum. More than 200 varieties of trees grow in the cemetery, including the country's second-largest known linden tree. In addition to the many unusual memorials and the more than 60 pieces of statuary on family graves, the Lexington Cemetery is home to nearly 180 species of birds.

Among the famous people buried in its 173 acres are Henry Clay, General John Hunt Morgan, members of Mary Todd Lincoln's family, James Lane Allen, and basketball coach Adolph Rupp.

The Lexington Cemetery is open free to the public 8 AM-5 PM. Be sure to observe the time rules, since the gates are closed and locked at 5 PM, and it is easy to lose track of time in this beautiful location.

Inside
Arts

*F*or a relatively small city, Lexington has a huge arts community that is thriving and growing even in the midst of the economic slowdown following the boom years of the 1980s. From romance writing, poetry readings, and flamenco dance, to chamber music, painting, and live theater, any interest you may have in the way of the arts can usually be fulfilled by one of the arts groups in Lexington.

Arts events fill the calendar year, although many groups try to stage their performances during times in which the local universities are in session, roughly from January to May and September to December. There are a number of performance halls where various productions are staged. Many groups have their own performance space as well. Most of the concert halls, theaters and galleries are concentrated in the downtown area between the University of Kentucky to the north of the Main Street corridor, and Transylvania University to the south.

Major performance space includes the following: ArtsPlace, home to several arts groups, including the Lexington Arts & Cultural Council; the Lexington Opera House, on the corner of Short Street and Broadway; the Singletary Cen-

ter for the Arts, on the UK campus, which houses a concert hall, recital hall and the UK Art Museum; and the Mitchell Fine Arts Center, on the Transylvania University campus. Other smaller events are often held in the performance space at the Carnegie Center for Literacy and Learning, 251 West Second Street, and the Central Library Theatre on East Main Street.

The following list of arts organizations and performing groups is as inclusive as possible.

Organizations

LEXINGTON ARTS
& CULTURAL COUNCIL

ArtsPlace,
161 North Mill Street 233-1469, 255-2951

Created in 1986 by a merger of the Lexington Council for the Arts and the Lexington Fund for the Arts, the Lexington Arts and Cultural Council is a cultural planning organization that focuses its efforts on fund raising for and advocacy of the arts in the Lexington community. Housed in ArtsPlace, a 1904 Beaux Arts building downtown, the LACC raises about a half million dollars each year to fund local arts organizations and activities.

> Insiders like bringing the kids, the dog and a picnic to Woodland Park in July and August to enjoy productions of Shakespeare in the Park and the Renaissance carnival atmosphere.

THE KENTUCKY GUILD OF ARTISTS AND CRAFTSMEN

PO Box 291
Berea, KY 40403   *1-986-3192*

Since it began in 1961, the Kentucky Guild of Artists and Craftsmen has dedicated itself to educating the public and developing viable markets for members' work. One of the guild's original purposes was to help the economically depressed people of the state, particularly in the eastern region, which is rich with traditional art forms. The guild created an opportunity to raise the standard of living by allowing individuals to market baskets, quilts, carvings and other indigenous arts and crafts.

Through the ensuing years, the membership of the guild has expanded with the addition of professional artists and craftspeople and contemporary art and craft.

Each year, the guild sponsors a Fall and Spring Fair in Berea, featuring the works of more than 100 juried artists.

BLUEGRASS BLACK ARTS CONSORTIUM

216 East Main Street   *281-9080*

One of Lexington's youngest arts organizations is the Bluegrass Black Arts Consortium, formed in 1993 by area African-American artists. Founder Frank X Walker identifies one of the group's main purposes as serving as an umbrella group for the various African-American artists and arts organizations in Lexington.

The BBAC's goals include the promotion of African-based art forms and providing creative and financial support for area black artists. The group recently opened a downtown performance space and arts complex.

LEXINGTON ART LEAGUE

Loudoun House,
209 Castlewood Drive   *254-7024*

Started in 1957 by a group of friends united by the common bond of their love of art, the Lexington Art League was officially incorporated as a nonprofit organization in 1976. In 1984, the League moved into its present location — the historic Loudoun House, a restored Gothic villa built in 1852.

Now 450 members strong, the Lexington Art League is an active force in the local cultural arena, sponsoring numerous exhibits in public spaces around Lexington in addition to its own rotating Loudoun House exhibits. The league also offers workshops, programs and studios, and a small visual arts library. In addition, the league sponsors several community events, including the Woodland Arts Fair each summer and the Arts and Crafts Fair that is a part of Lexington's annual Fourth of July celebration.

Photo: Lexington Herald-Leader

Art can be found in every corner of Loudoun House.

Writers

THE WORKING CLASS KITCHEN
119 Westwood Drive   278-4107

The Working Class Kitchen was started by Lexington poet Laverne Zabielski in 1990 to provide a forum in which emerging writers in the region could have an opportunity to read their work in public.

Since that time, the organization has grown to encompass a variety of community poetry and prose readings, a series of small writing groups for emerging writers, and the publication of chapbooks of the works of local poets. The main series of readings is held the second Sunday of each month in the spring and fall at Alfalfa restaurant on Limestone Street from 6 to 8 PM. A $3 donation includes dessert. Call if you are interested in reading your work.

THE WRITER'S VOICE OF THE

YMCA OF CENTRAL KENTUCKY
251 West Second Street   233-4474

Started in 1991 as part of the National Writer's Voice Project of the YMCA of the USA, the Lexington Writer's Voice pursues a tri-fold mission of assisting emerging writers in their artistic and professional development, supporting accomplished writers, and providing public programs that challenge the traditional definition of the literary arts while enriching all sectors of the community.

Each season, the Writer's Voice offers writing workshops ranging from "Romancing the Novel" to "The Craft of Magazine Journalism," as well as programs of local community readings, children's programs through the YMCA of Central Kentucky, and programs for women incarcerated in the Federal Medical Facility for Women. The national readings series has included such famous writers as Allen Ginsberg, George Plimpton and Adrienne Rich. Although part of the YMCA of Central Kentucky, the program is housed in the Carnegie Center for Literacy and Learning.

AFFRILACHIAN POETS
216 East Main Street   281-9080

The Affrilachian Poets is made up of both emerging and established African-American poets in the Central Kentucky area. The group's name was coined to combine African with Appalachian to give member writers a distinct identity in a region that has typically excluded them from the literary mainstream society. The Affrilachian Poets meet Monday evenings at 216 East Main, where they hold critique and writing sessions. The group also does a lot of work with young people, holds workshops and performances both in Lexington and throughout the state, and strives to increase awareness of the numerous talented African-American writers in the area.

KENTUCKY ROMANCE WRITERS CHAPTER OF ROMANCE WRITERS OF AMERICA
873-6184

The Kentucky chapter of Romance Writers of America, based in Central Kentucky, was formed in 1990. The group is not large, but the members represent a variety of interests in sub-genres of romance fiction, from historical and suspense to futuristic and contemporary. Some members are also interested in children's literature. The group meets once a month for a series of programs that includes guest speakers, workshops

and critique sessions, and presentations by members. While about one-third of the group members are published, all levels of writers are accepted and welcomed at the meetings. There are dues to both the national and state organization that are required for membership.

BLUEGRASS SISTERS IN CRIME
272-6239 or 299-2503

As part of the national Sisters in Crime organization, the Bluegrass chapter's mission is to make the public more aware of the many talented women mystery writers in the region. The group, however, is not limited to women members; it is made up of both men and women writers, booksellers, librarians and other folks who enjoy a good mystery. Meetings are the first Thursday of the month except January. They are held in the evenings at various locations in the community. Call for meeting times and locations.

Music

SPOTLIGHT JAZZ SERIES
257-8427

A University of Kentucky project, the Spotlight Jazz series has featured some of the greatest jazz musicians in America over its 16 years of operation, including recent appearances by Joey Defrancesco. Concerts are held in auditoriums on the UK campus, and tickets usually run about $10-$15.

LEXINGTON PHILHARMONIC ORCHESTRA
161 North Mill Street   233-4226

Under the longtime direction of

Insiders like poetry readings by The Working Class Kitchen at Alfalfa Restaurant on Limestone Street.

George Zack, the Lexington Philharmonic Orchestra has pursued its mission of presenting high-quality orchestral and chamber music to Central Kentuckians. From its subscription series concerts to full-scale productions for school-age youngsters, the LPO strives to provide musical enrichment to all areas of the community. All concerts are at the UK Singletary Center for the Arts unless otherwise noted.

UNIVERSITY ARTIST SERIES
University of Kentucky College
of Fine Arts   257-4929

For the past 14 years, The University Artist series has been providing Lexingtonians with an outstanding series of distinguished classical music concerts. Past performers have included Isaac Stern, Leontyne Price and the Montreal Symphony Orchestra. Ticket prices vary. Season subscribers save up to 30 percent off individual ticket prices. All performances are at the Singletary Center for the Arts on the corner of Rose Street and Euclid Avenue.

SWEET ADELINES
848 Kingsway Drive, Versailles   873-2167

With about 30 women on its membership roster, the Lexington Chapter of Sweet Adelines International teaches and trains its members to sing in four-part harmony, barber-

shop style. The group's annual concerts are just good fun, as is membership in the chapter.

CENTRAL KENTUCKY YOUTH ORCHESTRAS
161 North Mill Street   254-0796

For more than 40 years, the Central Kentucky Youth Orchestras have been providing a training ground for serious young musicians in the Central Kentucky region. There are now two separate full orchestras with about 70 members in each: the Symphony Orchestra — high school age, and the Concert Orchestra — middle school age. The orchestras comprise 136 youngsters from 34 schools in 11 counties. They perform about 10 concerts each season. Membership is by audition each August.

CENTRAL KENTUCKY CONCERT BAND
                                   277-2539

For 17 years, this adult community band, whose members include lawyers, homemakers, teachers and factory workers, has provided Lexington with both the opportunity for amateur musicians to share their love of playing music, and for audiences to enjoy the efforts of their friends, neighbors and co-workers. The band gives three major concerts each year as well as performing for community events.

CENTER FOR OLD MUSIC IN THE NEW WORLD

P.O. Box 217, 40584   269-2908

Early music from the Medieval, Renaissance and Baroque periods is the primary area of interest for the Center for Old Music in the New World. The center's goals are to hear, share and present music from these eras that is both historical and beautiful. Founded in 1977, the Center's unique concerts, which have included such programs as "Six Centuries of Music by Women Composers" and "Old Music for the Amorous Season," have become popular additions to the Lexington cultural scene.

The center's programs are presented at Lexington locations including historic downtown churches and the campuses of both Transylvania University and the University of Kentucky. Member musicians offer lessons or can recommend teachers in historic instruments such as lute, recorder and harpsichord.

CHAMBER MUSIC SOCIETY OF CENTRAL KENTUCKY

257-8351

The Chamber Music Society of Central Kentucky brings nationally acclaimed small ensembles to perform in Lexington. All concerts are at 8 PM on scheduled Sunday nights at the UK Singletary Center for the Arts Recital Hall. Prices vary by program. Recent appearances include the Da Vinci Quartet and the Prague Wind Quintet.

LEXINGTON BACH ENSEMBLE

166 Market Street   254-4497

The Lexington Bach Ensemble, made up of about 15-20 musicians, most of whom are members of the Lexington Philharmonic Orchestra, performs several concerts each year highlighting Baroque and classical music. The ensemble is directed by Bruce Neswick, who is the organist/choirmaster at Christ Church Cathedral. The concerts are not limited to music by Bach, however. Recent programs have included

Photo: Lexington Herald-Leader

Loudoun House in Castlewood Park includes Lexington Art League offices and gallery space.

Handel organ concertos, and one of Lexington's favorite Christmas events — the performance of Handel's *Messiah* with the Christ Church Choir of Men and Boys. Performances are staged at Christ Church Cathedral, 166 Market Street, and tickets are $10 and up.

LEXINGTON COMMUNITY ORCHESTRA
858-0816

Formed to meet a need in the community for musicians who were not members of the Lexington Philharmonic Orchestra to have an opportunity to perform, the Lexington Community Orchestra held its first concert in April of 1990. Since then, the orchestra has performed a wide range of music for many local events and at locations throughout Lexington. All performances are free and open to the public.

LEXINGTON FEDERATED MUSIC CLUB
257-4929

A service organization dedicated to making music an integral part of "the spiritual, cultural, educational, civic and social life" of the local community, the Lexington Federated Music Club is active in a number of local projects. These include sponsoring the Young Musicians Club of Lexington and providing scholarships for young people to attend the Stephen Foster Music Camp of the UK Piano Institute. The group was organized in 1968 and is affiliated with both the national and state chapters of the Federation of Music Clubs. Monthly meetings usually include performances by area musicians. Tickets to performances are $5 with proceeds going toward scholarships.

LEXINGTON MEN'S CHORUS
272-3564

Now in its fourth season, the Lexington Men's Chorus, 40 members strong, has become one of Lexington's favorite performing arts organizations. A member of the International Gay and Lesbian Association of Choruses, the group usually performs two or three concerts a year at the UK Singletary Center for the Arts, with tickets priced at $10. There is no audition necessary to join this gay men's chorus, and a person does not have to be gay to become a member.

THE LEXINGTON CHAPTER OF THE SOCIETY FOR THE PRESERVATION AND ENCOURAGEMENT OF BARBERSHOP QUARTET SINGING IN AMERICA
505 Dover Road

The Lexington Chapter of the SPEBQSA's mission is incorporated in its name. The group typically performs more than 75 programs reaching 23,000 people at area events, hospitals, churches and nursing homes. Several large-scale performances are held each year at the Lexington Opera House, and tickets prices are $5, $8 and $10.

LEXINGTON SINGERS
P.O. Box 23002, 40523   278-6133

For 34 years, the Lexington Singers have offered Central Kentuckians both the opportunity to participate in the performance of and to enjoy the performance of good choral music. The Lexington Singers present several concerts a year at the Singletary Center for the Arts and Rupp Arena (for the Kentucky Christmas Chorus), including joining the Lexington Philharmonic Orchestra for performances of Handel's *Messiah*, and a spring concert of Brahms' *German Requiem*. Tickets are $8 for students and senior citizens and $10 for general admission, unless otherwise noted.

GUITAR SOCIETY OF LEXINGTON-CENTRAL KENTUCKY
258-5384

The Guitar Society of Lexington-Central Kentucky's three-concert season offers some of the finest guitar performances in the region. The season also includes lectures, meetings and workshops for guitar enthusiasts, as well as free concerts for local schools and civic groups.

Dance

LEXINGTON BALLET
161 North Mill Street   233-3925

Now in its 20th season, the Lexington Ballet continues to pursue its two-fold efforts to inspire interest in and appreciation for classical ballet. Through performances by its professional company of dancers and through its ballet school where students can begin as young as three years old, this established and noted dance company brings classical ballet into the lives of Lexingtonians throughout the year. The Ballet's presentation of *The Nutcracker* has become an annual Lexington tradition. Lexington Ballet performances are at the Opera House, and admission prices vary. The school is housed at ArtsPlace.

SYNCOPATED INC.
161 North Mill Street   252-6421

With its mission "to bring people of all cultures and ages together through the extraordinary phenomenon of dance," Syncopated Inc. was started in 1983. The group operates a school for children and adults, offering dance classes in everything from tap, modern jazz and African dance, to percussion and hip hop. Syncopated Inc. also presents performers and guest teachers of international stature, hosts a biennial outdoor festival of dance, and has a strong outreach program to underserved sectors of the community.

SCHOOL OF CLASSICAL BALLET

Clays Mill Center   223-8715, 253-3269

The School of Classical Ballet offers a wide variety of dance classes in ballet technique, variations, partnering, modern and flamenco.

FOLK AND TRADITIONAL DANCE ORGANIZATIONS

Folk and traditional dance groups are very popular in Lexington and the surrounding region. These groups are usually participatory more than presenting, although they do perform at many events and productions in the area throughout the year. Most of these groups are aimed at providing an opportunity for folks to get together and dance in a fun and relaxed environment. Beginners are almost always welcome, since those who practice these traditional dance forms are always glad to share them with others.

Listed below are some of the more established dance groups in the area:

Castlewood Morris	277-9493
International Folk Dancers	887-1250
(Focus on Eastern European and Mediterranean dances)	
Lexington Scottish Dance Society	277-7710
Lexington Vintage Dance Society	277-0422
Oh Contraire	1-986-2193
Traditional Dance Association of Lexington	269-2542
(Focus on English dance forms)	

Theater

BROADWAY LIVE AT THE OPERA HOUSE

401 West Short Street   233-4567

The Broadway Live at the Opera House series presents international touring professional theater performances to Central Kentucky audiences throughout the year. Recent productions include *Man of La Mancha, Porgy and Bess, Shirley Valentine, City of Angels* and the 50th anniversary celebration of *Oklahoma*. Ticket prices vary, and there are matinee shows.

ACTORS' GUILD OF LEXINGTON

139 West Short Street   233-7330

Now in its 10th season, Actors' Guild of Lexington has produced more than 80 plays since it started. The mission of the theater group is "to create and present compelling contemporary theatre for the region." The nonprofit group moved into its own space in 1992. Recent popular presentations have included *The Heidi Chronicles*, and *The Kathy and Mo Show: Parallel Lives.*

All actors are paid, and you can call the number listed above to read the scripts before auditions are held for upcoming parts. Actors' Guild also offers a variety of acting, directing and stage-building classes throughout the year. Tickets are $12, $8 for students and senior citizens.

PHOENIX GROUP THEATRE INC.
254-6268

Now in its third year, the Phoenix Group Theatre, which performs in the Lexington Public Library Theater, presents a diverse season of dramatic performances each year. Past performances have included *Les Liaisons Dangereuses*, *That Championship Season*, and *Look Back in Anger.* The group is made up of professional theater people who volunteer their time and talent.

STUDIO PLAYERS
Carriage House, Bell Court   253-2512

This all-volunteer theater group has been staging plays in Lexington for the past 40 years. Each season includes works by well-known and lesser-known playwrights in drama and comedy. Performances are at 2:30 PM and 8 PM on scheduled Sundays at the Carriage House, Bell Court. Prices vary.

WHODUNIT DINNER THEATRE
259-9045

For a night of mystery and romance, the Whodunit Dinner Theatre is your ticket to good food and entertainment. Performances are at the Coach House Restaurant, 855 South Broadway, on Friday and Saturday nights. Tickets, which include dinner, are $27.50, and reservations are required.

PARANOIX POOR PUPPET THEATRE
1-986-7570, 1-986-7356

This five-member troupe brings to life nearly 60 puppet characters based on traditional Greek puppetry with its strong Turkish, Indonesian and Chinese influences. Puppets are made of recycled materials, and the shows are produced on a homemade stage. The entire theater, including cast, crew, puppets and stage, fits into a small car. The group operates on donations, and usually a hat is passed at performances. The troupe performs throughout the area.

LEXINGTON CHILDREN'S THEATRE
161 North Mill Street   254-4546

The Lexington Children's Theatre has provided 55 years of professional theater and classes for young audiences. Each season, this professional acting company presents 200 performances reaching 85,000 young people in the area. Recent productions have included *The Legend of Sleepy Hollow*, *The Jungle Book* and *The Reluctant Dragon.*

KENTUCKY HORSE CENTER THEATRE FOR CHILDREN
3380 Paris Pike   293-1853

Performances are 10 AM Fridays for schools and groups, and 11 AM Saturdays for the general public at the Kentucky Horse Center. Admission is $3.75. Recent productions have included *Aladdin & His Magic Lamp; The Lion, the Witch & the Ward-*

The Shakespeare in the Park event features three plays each summer performed outdoors in Woodland Park.

robe; and *The Adventures of Peter Rabbit.*

LEXINGTON MUSICAL THEATRE
255-9488

For 21 years, Lexington Musical Theatre has been providing quality musical theater to Central Kentucky audiences. Performances are held scheduled Sundays at 2 PM and 8 PM at ArtsPlace unless otherwise noted. Tickets are $14. Productions for the 1993-'94 season included *Cabaret, Ain't Misbehavin',* and *Hello Dolly.*

Visual Arts

UNIVERSITY OF KENTUCKY ART MUSEUM
Singletary Center for the
Arts at Rose & Euclid   *257-5716*

One of the largest art museums in the area, the University of Kentucky Art Museum displays two or three special exhibits in addition to exhibits from its permanent collection. Recent special exhibits have included a collection of photographs by photojournalist Marvin Breckinridge and one of "Art of Africa, Southeast Asia, New Guinea and the Americas." The museum's permanent collection features many fine examples of European and American paintings, including Francisco Goya's "Portrait of a Bullfighter" and El Greco's "Boy Lighting a Candle." Hours are noon to 4:30 PM, Tuesday through Sunday.

LEXINGTON ART LEAGUE
209 Castlewood Drive   254-7024

The Lexington Art League sponsors a number of community art displays in various locations around town in addition to its main revolving shows at Loudoun House on Castlewood Drive (where the league's offices are located). The

Annual Nude Show is among the biggest and most interesting of these shows, and it takes place at the beginning of each new year.

Other Lexington locations where the Art League sponsors shows:

Blue Grass Airport Gallery, Versailles Road (open 24 hours a day).

Opera House Gallery, 401 West Short Street (open during Opera House events only).

ARTISTS' ATTIC
Victorian Square, 401 West Main   254-5501

This unusual studio offers Lexingtonians a chance to see local artists at work. About 15 artists have small studios in Victorian Square and spend at least 15 hours a week working there. Members of the public are invited to watch, browse and ask questions. Hours are 10 AM-6 PM, Monday through Wednesday and Saturday; 10 AM-9 PM Thursday and Friday; and 1-6 PM Sunday.

ARTSPLACE
161 North Mill Street   255-2951

A number of unusual exhibits by Kentucky's finest artists are on display in the ArtsPlace Gallery throughout the year, and are open free to the public. One of the more unique recent exhibits was "Beyond Sight," designed for the special needs of visually impaired audiences. Hours are 9 AM-4:30 PM, Monday through Friday, and 10 AM-2 PM, Saturday.

HEADLEY-WHITNEY MUSEUM
4435 Old Frankfort Pike   255-6653

A true treasure in the Lexington cultural milieu, the Headley-Whitney Museum houses an eclectic collection of some of the most beautiful and unusual fine art objects in Kentucky. For instance, the Jewel Room contains a stunning collection of bibelots (small objects of rarity or beauty). These bibelots are miniature plants, animals, gods and goddesses made of gold, ivory, coral, amber and lapis lazuli and studded with precious gemstones. This is the only contemporary collection of its kind open to the public.

Other parts of the museum include the Shell Grotto and the Oriental Gallery featuring Chinese robes embroidered with the "forbidden stitch," so named because the stitch was outlawed in the 19th century since many seamstresses went blind using it. Hours are 10 AM-5 PM, Tuesday through Friday, and noon-5 PM Saturday and Sunday. The museum is closed Mondays April through October, and Mondays and Tuesdays November through March.

KENTUCKY GALLERY OF FINE CRAFTS AND ART
139 West Short Street   281-1166

Contemporary art, functional crafts and folk art can all be found in this delightful downtown gallery. Featuring the work of Kentucky's finest artists and craftspeople, Kentucky Gallery offerings include paintings, photographs, pottery, jewelry, quilts, weavings, sculpture, furniture, blown glass and woodcuts. Hours are 10 AM-6 PM, Monday through Saturday and during Actors' Guild performances.

In addition to these galleries, rotating small exhibits by local and other artists are displayed in many Lexington businesses and public buildings. Exhibits range from art with an international theme by local elementary students to some of the works of the area's most promising up-and-coming young artists. Locations include the following:

CARNEGIE CENTER FOR LITERACY AND LEARNING
251 West Second Street   254-4175

Hours are 9 AM-7:30 PM, Monday through Thursday, 9 AM-5 PM Friday.

CENTRAL BANK GALLERIES
2nd and 3rd floors, Kincaid Tower,
300 West Vine St.   253-6135

Hours are 9 AM-4 PM, Monday through Friday.

CENTRAL LIBRARY GALLERY
140 East Main Street
231-5516

Hours are 9 AM-9 PM, Monday through Thursday; 9 AM-5 PM, Friday and Saturday; and 1-5 PM Sunday.

COMMON GROUNDS COFFEE HOUSE
343 East High Street   233-9761

Hours are 9 AM to midnight, Sunday through Thursday, and 9 AM-1 AM, Friday and Saturday.

ART ON MAIN, COMMUNITY BANK
155 East Main Street   254-3131

Hours are 9 AM-4 PM, Monday through Friday.

GALBREATH GALLERY
310 East Main Street   254-4579

Hours are 8 AM-6 PM, Monday through Friday, and 8 AM-1 PM, Saturday.

Outdoor Drama

Each summer in Central Kentucky brings many beautiful, sunny, warm (all right, sometimes HOT) evenings that are just perfect for the production of outdoor drama. The region's temperate climate and beautiful landscape, which is, for the most part, free from the noisy hustle and bustle of major metropolitan areas, combine to create ideal conditions for the staging of outdoor theater. Here is a listing of major annual outdoor events. However, many smaller productions come up during each season, so keep your eyes out for other opportunities to enjoy fine theater in the good old summertime in the great outdoors.

SHAKESPEARE IN THE PARK
Woodland Park, Lexington

For the past 11 summers, the Shakespeare Festival Commission and the Lexington parks department have combined forces to present one of Lexington's most popular and well-attended outdoor events. Staged in the centrally located and easily accessible Woodland Park (on the corner of Kentucky Avenue and High Street), Shakespeare in the Park draws thousands of audience members each July.

Usually three plays are presented, including one non-Shakespeare play. Most people bring dinner or snacks, pets and kids. Unless you want to sit on the grass, you should also bring lawn chairs or blankets. All performances are free, but donations (via a passed hat) are accepted.

While the shows don't start till 8:45 PM, pre-show entertainment gets in swing around 8:30 PM. Get there early to stake out your spot, since the plays usually attract huge audiences, especially on the not-too-hot evenings.

THE STEPHEN FOSTER STORY
My Old Kentucky Home State Park,
Bardstown   *(800) 626-1563*

For more than 35 years, *The Stephen Foster Story* has been delighting audiences of all ages with its grand, colorful depiction of one of America's most beloved songwriters. Staged on the grounds of My Old Kentucky Home (the antebellum mansion that inspired the song) in Bardstown, *The Stephen Foster Story* transports you more than 100 years in the past to the grace and hospitality of the old South. The show depicts a year in Foster's life and features dozens of his most famous songs, from "Oh! Susanna" to "Camptown Races."

The show runs from early June to early September, nightly except Mondays at 8:30 PM, with a Saturday matinee at 2 PM. Tickets are $10 for adults, $5 for kids 12 and younger.

THE LEGEND OF DANIEL BOONE
Old Fort Harrod State Park,
Harrodsburg   *(800) 85-BOONE*

Depicting the exciting adventures of one of America's most famous frontiersmen, *The Legend of Daniel Boone*, now in its 28th year, will take you back in time to the dangerous, energetic days when the American frontier (which included the area that would become Kentucky) was in its heyday.

The show is staged in the James Harrod Amphitheatre, which is built to resemble an old fort. Filled with comedy, drama and adventure for the whole family, this magnificent historical drama runs from early June to the end of August, with 8:30 PM shows Monday through Saturday. Tickets are $12 for adults, $6 for children 15 and younger.

JENNY WILEY THEATRE
Jenny Wiley State Resort Park,
Prestonsburg   *1-886-9274*

One of the oldest outdoor summer musical theaters in the country, Jenny Wiley Theatre has been providing a season of superb musical theater, apprentice program and arts workshops since 1965. It is one of the few rotating repertory theaters in existence. What is unusual about this is that when the season is in full swing, you can see as many as four Broadway musicals in as many days.

Over the past 29 years, Jenny Wiley has presented nearly 100 musicals to audiences totaling more than 400,000 by 1,000 actors, singers, dancers, musicians and technicians.

Staged June through August, evening performances begin at 8 PM, and matinees are at 12:30 PM Tuesday through Sunday. Tickets for performances are $11 for adults, $10 for senior citizens, and $6 for students. Some shows include a dinner buffet that starts at 6:45 PM. Call for information about when these dinner or luncheon packages are available.

SOMEDAY OUTDOOR DRAMA
Grayson   *1-286-4522*

This beautiful outdoor musical drama depicts a love story set in the hills of Eastern Kentucky during the

Civil War. Through the course of the drama, which has been performed for the past two summers, the characters explore many of the conflicts, especially in Kentucky as a border state, of that turbulent time in American history.

Shows are staged June through mid-July on weekends at 8:30 PM. Reserved tickets are $7 for adults, $4 for kids younger than 10. Tickets at the gate are $9 for adults, $5 for kids. For groups of 10 or more, the discount price is $5.50 per person. Call for specific show dates. Reservations are recommended.

PIONEER PLAYHOUSE

Danville   *1-236-2747*

With a list of alums that includes John Travolta, Lee Majors, and Jim Varney, Pioneer Playhouse has made its mark in show business history as a training ground for aspiring actors and theater technicians during its 45 seasons of operation. All in all, more than 3,000 up-and-coming actors have appeared in productions at the Pioneer Playhouse.

Shows are produced June through mid-August, Tuesdays through Saturdays. Dinner is served at 7:30 PM. Tickets are $14.95 for adults for the play and dinner, $8.50 for the play only, and $6.50 for the dinner and play for kids younger than 12, or $3.50 for the play only.

PINE KNOB OUTDOOR THEATRE

2250 Pine Knob Road,
Caneyville   *(502) 879-8190*

Each summer, Pine Knob Outdoor Theatre presents an exciting series of plays that centers on early life in the Pine Knob region. Filled with music, comedy and adventure, these grand-scale outdoor dramas are staged June through September on Friday and Saturday nights at 8:30 PM. Different plays are produced on different nights, so call for specific show information. Tickets are $8, and children younger than 6 are not admitted. There are no shows on the Labor Day weekend.

ents, and they were only allowed to have one glass of wine with a client.

At $5 a client, Brezing charged more than most other brothels, but "it was worth it," she said. She also hosted private dinner parties for the men. Often, during hunting season, the men would bring in half a veni-

Belle Brezing
"Bluegrass Bluebloods in the Red Light District"

Editor's Note: This story was written based on an interview with actress Nancy Sherburne, who portrays the famous Lexington madam in a one-woman dramatic presentation.

Nancy and her husband, author James Sherburne, put together the performance in 1991-92 as part of the Chautauqua performances of the lives of famous Kentuckians in commemoration of the state's bicentennial celebration. James wrote the dramatization of Belle Brezing's life, and Nancy performs it from the point of view of an older Belle reflecting on her tempestuous and colorful life.

The story has delighted audiences young and old around the state, and Nancy continues to perform Belle as part of the Kentucky Humanities Council Speakers Bureau program, as well as for school groups, civic organizations, and other events.

Nonprofit groups wishing to schedule a performance of Belle's life can contact the Kentucky Humanities Council at 257-5932. Other groups or individuals should contact the Sherburnes directly by calling (502) 839-4256.

Born in the Irishtown section of Lexington in 1860, Belle Brezing would rise from her humble and dysfunctional upbringing to become one of the most colorful and famous "madams" in the region.

Her house of ill repute was frequented by some of the most powerful men in Kentucky. She was choosy about her girls and her clients — only the best would do. And she was the heart of discretion when it came to who utilized her services. To this day, few records exist concerning her famous clientele.

Brezing is said to be the inspiration for the character of Belle Watling in Margaret Mitchell's novel *Gone With the Wind*. Mitchell was married to John Marsh, a Kentucky boy who worked at the *Lexington Herald* newspaper in the early 1900s.

Brezing was a great philanthropist, a smart business person, a kind friend, and a loyal mother. Misunderstood by the "decent folks," patronized by some of the most well-known politicians and businessmen in the state, and tolerated by just about everyone for nearly three decades, Brezing nevertheless carved out her own niche in Lexington history.

The road she followed to success, however, was a rocky one. And it had a rough start.

"When I was 1 year old, Mama married a German immigrant saloon keeper," she recalled. "It was a terrible marriage. They fought all the time, and he'd beat her. Mama used to go to the taverns and bring home other men."

From the time she was a very young child, Brezing's mother, Sarah, would dress her up like a doll in frilly dresses and jewelry, and the two would parade around the streets of Lexington.

"I remember thinking when we'd go walking after Mama had fitted me all out like this that all the men were staring at us, because we were just so beautiful — lovely mama Sarah, and lovely daughter Belle."

It was fun to pretend, but when Brezing entered grammar school at the age of five, she was ridiculed and snubbed by the other children, partly, she

Nancy Sherburne as Belle Brezing

says, because of her outlandish dress, and partly because the parents told their kids not to talk to her. "Anybody named Brezing was not fit company for decent folks" was the edict impressed upon the children.

Isolated and friendless, Brezing turned to books for companionship and soon became an avid reader. She also started spending more and more time with a kind next-door neighbor. By the time she was 12, the neighbor — married with several kids of his own — had seduced her. But Brezing remembers him as someone who cared about her and paid attention to her when no one else would.

"I was just so lonely, because the boys and girls didn't accept me, didn't speak to me. And he was very kind to me. He'd sit and talk to me about school and what I did every day."

It was at that time that Brezing became promiscuous, inviting local boys to the cemetery at night, hoping they would like her.

"Of course they never did," she said. "They would talk about me and laugh at me, and I knew it, and I would still go with them."

But she did fall in love with one boy — Johnny Cook. The 16-year-old boy loved her, too, she said. She became pregnant at the age of 14.

"My mother took care of things. Although she wasn't ever very good at managing her own life, she figured she could run mine without any problems. Johnny was too young and too poor for husband material, so she found a cigar maker named James Kenney, who had as much reason, after all, as anybody else to think he was responsible for my pregnancy. And she roped him into marrying me."

Naturally, the marriage soon fell apart. Kenney left her high and dry. Shortly after the baby was born, Brezing's mother died, leaving the 15-year-old girl alone to fend for herself and her new infant daughter.

"I did the only thing I knew how to do," she recalled. "For the next couple of years I was what was known as a kept woman."

A kindly neighbor woman took care of baby Daisy Mae while Brezing lived "with one man or another, trying to make enough money to pay her for taking care of Daisy Mae."

Things went OK for a while, but in the winter of 1879, Brezing found herself out on the street. So she went to a brothel on Main Street (the house had been home to Mary Todd Lincoln, wife of Abraham Lincoln, some 40 years before it was turned into a brothel, and is still open for public tours today). The madam of the brothel — Jenny Hill — took her in and taught her the business.

Always a fast learner, Brezing opened her own house at 194 North Upper Street two years later. Her daughter turned out to be retarded, and Brezing had to send her to a special home, which cost a great deal of money.

She started her first brothel with four girls and a maid. What Brezing hadn't thought about when she opened her "bawdy house" was that it was located just a few blocks from Transylvania's College of the Bible.

"There were those who did not like that very much. They told me, rather emphatically, that my establishment was 'inappropriately located,'" she recalled. But despite constant legal battles with those who opposed her, business boomed. Within a few years, Brezing said, she was no longer part of the "labor force."

In the mid-1880s, she opened her big house at 59 Megowan Street (now Eastern Avenue in the area around Thoroughbred Park).

"The thing that always set my Megowan Street house apart from the others in that same red-light community was the fact that I had very high standards for my girls and for my clientele, for that matter.

"You never saw my girls leaning out the window waving to people trying to get them to come in. They were never on the first floor of that house unless they were completely groomed and dressed in an evening gown. They were not allowed around in dishabille, in their robes and things. That just wasn't my style."

Brezing also made sure her girls didn't swear or smoke around clients, and they were only allowed to have one glass of wine with a client.

At $5 a client, Brezing charged more than most other brothels, but "it was worth it," she said. She also hosted private dinner parties for the men. Often, during hunting season, the men would bring in half a venison for Brezing to cook, and they would have a party for their friends — and, of course, several of the girls.

"I really made more money off the food and the liquor than I made off the girls," Brezing recalled. While most madams would charge their girls a percentage of all the money they made, Brezing charged her girls a flat weekly rate of $24 for room and board and laundry and maid service.

As her financial success and reputation for running a top-notch establishment increased, Brezing said, she faced less and less opposition from the Lexington community.

"The more money I made, the more tolerant the community got," she said with a laugh. "Never underestimate the power of money."

She added that she always felt "a quiet acceptance" from Lexington women.

"I think many of them knew that their husbands came to my establishment and were grateful," she said. "I probably kept many a marriage together."

However, Brezing was never accepted into the mainstream of Lexington society. One time, she recalled, in a gesture of goodwill, she bought a whole lot of new sheets and blankets to donate to a local hospital that had been severely damaged in a fire. When the hospital found out who had donated the bedding, they sent it back.

As World War I began and thousands of young men were drafted and brought into the city for basic training, a big campaign was mounted in Lexington to rid the city of all the brothels. Brezing's house was closed in 1917. However, by that time, she had made enough money to live comfortably until her death in 1940.

At her death, *Time* magazine ran an obituary commemorating Brezing as the "madam of the most orderly of disorderly houses."

Her belongings were auctioned off shortly after her death, and the famous brothel became a run-down hotel that was finally torn down in the 1970s.

Part of Brezing's legacy lives on today through a collection of books from her private library that she donated to the University of Kentucky. Many of these books are in the university's special collections.

Music: Past, Present and Future

One of these days, there will be a Kentucky Music Hall of Fame — and, oh, what a museum it will be!

Although we don't know of anyone who keeps statistics on such things, we'd venture that few states can lay claim to as many popular and influential music makers per capita as does Kentucky. Of course, singers, songwriters and musicians tend to flock to areas such as Nashville, Los Angeles and New York because that's where the action is. But an impressive number of them have either been born in the Bluegrass State or spent their formative years here.

It's not just country, either, although that's the kind of music most associated with the state, from the legendary Bill Monroe to "new country" heart throbs John Michael Montgomery and Billy Ray Cyrus. Jazz, blues and rock are also well represented.

A number of prominent musicians either hail from the Lexington area or have a significant Lexington connection. And when you include the musical products of the rest of the state, you realize that Kentucky is more than capable of putting a smile on your lips, a song in your heart and a tap in your toes.

Greater Lexington's Finest

One of the major country music success stories of the last couple of years has been that of John Michael Montgomery, a Nicholasville native who for more than five years led the house band at Lexington's Austin City Saloon. When it came time to shoot the video for his third single, "Beer and Bones," he did it at Austin City. Montgomery has made plenty of additional noise on the country charts with such hits as the Number 1 smash "I Love the Way You Love Me," "Life's A Dance" and "I Swear."

John Conlee, a Grand Ole Opry veteran who is probably best known for his 1978 hit "Rose Colored Glasses," was born and raised in nearby Versailles.

Noted country banjo picker J.D. Crowe, whose bands have included the likes of Doyle Lawson, Tony Rice, Jerry Douglas and fellow Kentucky native Ricky Skaggs, was born in Lexington and now lives in Jessamine County.

Well-known musicians from Central Kentucky include country singer John Michael Montgomery, bluegrass musician J.D. Crowe and jazz trumpeter Vince Di Martino.

Exile, a band whose 1978 single "Kiss You All Over" reached Number 1 on the Billboard pop charts, was formed by musicians from Lexington and Richmond. Since then, Exile has been a fairly consistent hit-producer on the country charts.

Red Foley, who was born near Berea and attended Georgetown College, in 1967 became the first Kentuckian elected to the Country Music Hall of Fame. His country and gospel hits included "Peace in the Valley" and "Chattanoogie Shoe Shine Boy."

Lexington is the hometown of acclaimed jazz musician Les McCann; Mike Wanchic, guitarist for rocker John Mellencamp's band; and bassist David Goldflies, an experienced jazz musician who has toured with The Allman Brothers Band and played on their 1979 album, *Enlightened Rogues.* Harlan Howard, for years a top writer of country hits including "Above and Beyond," "Why Not Me" and "Blame It on Your Heart," is also a Lexington native.

Vince Di Martino, a professor of music who in 1993 left the University of Kentucky to teach at Centre College in Danville, has played trumpet with some of the biggest names in jazz.

Remember the Hilltoppers, who had 21 Top 40 hits in the 1950s? The group was formed by Lexington's Don McGuire and three colleagues from Western Kentucky University.

Fans of the punk/new wave movement of the late '70s and early '80s are likely to recall a band called Richard Hell and the Voidoids, whose "Blank Generation" became an anthem of sorts for members of that generation. Strangely enough, although Hell made most of his noise in New York City, he grew up in Lexington (under another name).

The local music scene has been thriving for years. In fact, in 1988 or so, an ad that ran in some music trade publications suggested that perhaps Lexington was about to become the next Athens, Ga., which at that time was supposedly the nation's music mecca because it served as home base for R.E.M., the B-52's and a handful of other college favorites.

A Lexington band called Velvet Elvis made some noise with a self-titled national release on Enigma Records in 1988. At roughly the same time, Stealin Horses recorded an album, also eponymous, for Arista Records with a single that managed to crack the Top 40. In 1990, Shaking Family, whose members hailed from Lexington and Louisville, released *Dreaming in Detail* on Elektra Records.

Since then, the attention of music pundits has shifted to Seattle and other sites. But Lexington-area bands continue to make recordings and put on shows that are bound to capture the attention of movers and shakers outside the Bluegrass. Here are some musicians to keep an eye on:

• The Metro Blues All-Stars. This band has been around forever, but its songwriting and playing continue to get better and better. The Metros' 1992 release, *Devil Gets His Due,* was favorably reviewed in national blues publications. They have toured extensively and have truly paid their dues. (The Metros' blues soulmates, Louisville-based Curtis and the Kicks, a frequent attraction at Lexington bars, also are playing hotter than ever and could become a national force on the blues scene.)

• Paul K, a Detroit native who came to the University of Kentucky on a debate scholarship in the early '80s, was recently profiled in the "New Faces" section of *Rolling Stone* magazine. K, whose real last name is Kopasz, has self-released a number of albums on cassette and CD and has acquired quite a following overseas. With the help of this recent national exposure, he stands a strong chance of finding a larger market for his literate, streetwise folk and rock.

• 10-Foot Pole, a mind-bending band that fuses hard rock, funk and jazz influences into a consistently danceable style all its own, could greatly expand its fan base in the wake of success by bands like the Red Hot Chili Peppers. Also keep an eye on Candy Says, a pop-savvy band that frequently plays at Lynagh's and The Wrocklage.

• Still another candidate for the big time is Kelly Richey, onetime guitarist for Stealin Horses. Richey, a truly incendiary guitar player (she plays a mean slide, too, a la Bonnie Raitt) with a heavy blues influence,

Photo: Lexington Herald-Leader

Picnic with the Pops is an annual event starring the Lexington Philharmonic that draws thousands.

is known for her live performances, in which she takes well-worn rock classics by the likes of Led Zeppelin, Janis Joplin and Jimi Hendrix and somehow manages to make them her own. Recently she and her band have been working on some original tunes, which could increase her potential.

• The Mojo Filter Kings are a promising blues band with a repertoire that includes blues standards such as "Stormy Monday," bluesy rock songs by the likes of the Allman Brothers and Delbert McClinton, and originals.

• Folk rocker Michael Johnathan, who helped initiate the successful Kentucky Theatre concert series in 1993, has been featured on The Nashville Network with the video for his song "Miracle on Caney Creek," about the beginning of Alice Lloyd College in Pippa Passes.

Lexington jazz lovers, incidentally, should do themselves a favor and catch Duke Madison, a veteran saxophone player who frequently plays at clubs around town.

The Rest of the State

Some people are actually surprised when they come to Kentucky and discover that they can find jazz, rock, blues and even rap being played on local radio stations and in bars. They are under the mistaken impression that country music is all we listen to.

Their ignorance is understandable, though. After all, this state has produced some of the most enduring stars of country and bluegrass music past and present. This is "The Bluegrass State," and Bill Monroe, known as the "Father of Bluegrass," was born in Western Kentucky.

John Michael Montgomery is a new country star who hails from the Lexington area.

Even before Monroe came Bradley Kincaid, a Garrard County native who became popular nation-wide as a singer of moun-tain ballads on the "Na-tional Barn Dance" pro-gram on Chicago radio sta-tion WLS and, subse-quently, on other stations and the Grand Ole Opry.

Grandpa Jones (real name Louis Marshall Jones), a beloved longtime star of "Hee Haw" and the Opry, and fellow "Hee Haw" star David "Stringbean" Akeman were both born in Kentucky — Jones in Henderson County and Akeman in Jackson County.

Guitarist/singer/songwriter Merle Travis, born in Muhlenberg County, is revered for a number of accomplishments, including the development of a unique three-fingered guitar-playing style that became known as "Travis pick-ing." Travis, often mentioned in the same breath as his colleague Chet Atkins, also designed the first solid-body electric guitar and wrote the classic song "Sixteen Tons," which was made famous by Tennessee Ernie Ford.

For about 20 years, the funniest folks on the Opry were Lonzo and Oscar (real names John and Rollin Sullivan), two brothers from Edmonton, a town of about 1,400 in southcentral Kentucky. Lonzo and Oscar had a hit record in 1948 with the hilarious "I'm My Own Grandpa," about a series of marriages and the convoluted family relationships that resulted.

Western Kentucky's Phil and Don Everly, the Everly Brothers, are among the most influential groups in the history of either pop or country, having inspired such later stars as the Beatles and Simon and Garfunkel. Their signature harmonies were heard on such mammoth hits of the late '50s and early '60s as "Bye Bye Love," "Wake Up Little Susie" and "All I Have To Do Is Dream." Since 1988 the Everlys have returned annually to Central City, in Muhlenberg County, for the Everly Brothers Homecoming Festival, which features an impressive lineup of the state's musicians.

Dry Ridge native Skeeter Davis, whose biggest claims to fame were probably her 1962 crossover hit "The End of the World" and her ill-fated marriage to former "Nashville Now" host Ralph Emery, has appeared on the Opry off and on since the early '60s.

Loretta Lynn, widely recognized as the first lady of country music, was born and reared in Eastern Kentucky's Butcher Hollow, near Paintsville in Johnson County. Lynn, the singer and writer of hits including "Don't Come Home A-Drinkin' With Lovin' on Your Mind" and "You Ain't Woman Enough To Take My Man," was immortalized in the 1980 movie *Coal Miner's Daughter*, which starred Sissy Spacek and got its name from Lynn's best-known song. Her sister, Crystal Gayle, also became a star with a string of hits that included "Don't It Make My Brown Eyes Blue."

Tom T. Hall, from Olive Hill in Carter County, made it first as a songwriter and later as a singer of his own songs. His best-known compositions include "Harper Valley P.T.A.," a hit for Jeannie C. Riley in 1968, as well as "Old Dogs, Children and Watermelon Wine" and "The Year That Clayton Delaney Died."

Lawrence County's Ricky Skaggs, widely acclaimed as a bluegrass musician, has had numerous hits on the country charts, including "Don't Get Above Your Raisin' " and "Country Boy." Skaggs, a former child star whose instrumental mastery includes guitar, banjo, mandolin and fiddle, began his professional career with bluegrass legend Ralph Stanley's Clinch Mountain Boys and has played in bands with fellow Kentucky stars J.D. Crowe and Keith Whitley. He has received several awards over the years; in 1993, *Musician* magazine named Skaggs one of the top 100 guitar players of all time.

Keith Whitley, whose still-burgeoning career was cut short by his alcohol-related death in 1990, was an Elliott County native who early in his career played in bands with Ricky Skaggs. Whitley's country hits included "Miami, My Amy" and "I'm No Stranger to the Rain."

The 1980s and '90s have thus far been very good to Kentucky's country singers and musicians.

The most conspicuous — and controversial — success undoubtedly has been that of Billy Ray Cyrus, who rocketed to superstardom and sex-symbol status with his smash single "Achy Breaky Heart." Cyrus subsequently told anyone who would listen that he was just a "boy from Flatwoods, Kentucky" who had followed his dream.

The Judds, a mother-daughter duo from Ashland, dominated their categories at the Country Music Association and Grammy awards ceremonies in the mid- to late '80s and produced a string of hits that included "Mama, He's Crazy," "Grandpa (Tell Me 'Bout the Good Old Days)" and "Let Me Tell You About Love." After the mother, Naomi Judd, retired from her music career because of chronic hepatitis, daughter Wynonna began an instantly successful solo career in 1992, producing such huge hits as "I Saw the Light," "No One Else on Earth" and "Is It Over Yet."

Steve Wariner, from Russell Springs in Western Kentucky, has made a mark on country music with his guitar playing and hits that have included "The Weekend."

Dwight Yoakam, who grew up near Prestonsburg in the coal fields of Eastern Kentucky, found his initial success not in Nashville but in Los Angeles. His traditional country style, spiced with a touch of rock 'n' roll, has produced such hits as "Honky Tonk Man," a remake of Buck Owens' "Streets of Bakersfield," "Ain't That Lonely Yet" and "Fast as You."

One of the unlikeliest bunch of country stars in recent years has been the Kentucky HeadHunters, a rowdy and unkempt bunch from Edmonton whose musical influences ran more toward Led Zeppelin and Cream than traditional country. The HeadHunters burst onto the country charts in 1989, however, with a high-powered remake of Bill Monroe's "Walk Softly on My Heart of Mine," scored again with "Dumas Walker" and went on to win several awards. After a personnel change in 1993, the band began gravitating more toward bluesy rock and boogie and recorded a blues album with Johnnie Johnson, former piano player for Chuck Berry.

Patty Loveless, a Louisville native, and Marty Brown, from the tiny Western Kentucky community of Maceo, are also rising stars. Loveless has produced several hits, including "Timber I'm Falling in Love," "I'm That Kinda Girl" and "Blame It on Your Heart." Brown, whose influences range from Hank Williams Sr. to Buddy Holly, has found success with original songs including "Every Now and Then."

Paducah-born Boots Randolph, who has become known as Mr. "Yakety Sax" after his 1963 smash hit of the same name, has been one of Nashville's top session musicians. Honky-tonk legend Gary Stewart is also a Kentucky native.

Other past and present country stars from Kentucky include Bill Carlisle, the Coon Creek Girls, the Osborne Brothers and Molly O'Day.

But that's enough about country. Want some jazz? You got it. Vibraphonist Lionel Hampton was born in Louisville, as were singer

Helen Humes, who replaced Billie Holiday in Count Basie's band, guitarist Jimmy Raney and several others who attained popularity in the '20s and '30s.

How about blues? John Brim, who wrote the blues standard "Ice Cream Man" — given new life when it was featured on the 1978 debut album of the hard rock band Van Halen — was born in Hopkinsville.

Folk? Kentucky is the birthplace of Jean Ritchie, who is credited with popularizing the mountain dulcimer and helping spark the folk music revival of the '50s and '60s with her American Folk Song Festival. John Jacob Niles, a Louisville native, collected, wrote and performed thousands of folk ballads and other "songs of the common people"; his well-known compositions include the Christmas standard "I Wonder as I Wander." Jean Thomas, "The Traipsin' Woman" who collected mountain folklore and promoted folk music festivals from the 1930s through the early 1970s, was born and lived much of her life in Ashland.

Other types of music? Singer Rosemary Clooney, who became a star of movies and television in the '50s, is from Maysville, an Ohio River town in northeastern Kentucky.

Actress and singer Irene Dunne, a five-time Academy Award nominee for her roles in *I Remember Mama* and other movies of the '30s and '40s, was born in Louisville and spent the first 11 years of her life there.

Robert Todd Duncan, the baritone who originated the role of Porgy in George Gershwin's opera *Porgy and Bess* in 1935, was also a Kentucky native.

The Harlan Boys Choir, founded in 1966, has traveled overseas and earned international acclaim. The choir, made up of boys in grades five through 12, sang "This Is My Country" at George Bush's presidential inauguration in January 1989.

The time that John Prine spent with his relatives in Western Kentucky as a child inspired his song "Paradise," about the ravages of the strip mines, with its well-known refrain, "Daddy, won't you take me back to Muhlenberg County . . ."

Need still more proof of this state's musical prowess? Well, consider that, in 1893, Louisville kindergarten teacher Patty Smith Hill and her sister, Mildred J. Hill, wrote a little ditty called "Good Morning to You," and the melody of that song was later used for "Happy Birthday." And that, dear friend, is the most-played song ever written.

So there.

Photo: Lexington Herald-Leader

The Lexington Ballet company performs The Nutcracker *each Christmas season.*

Inside
Central Kentucky Annual Events and Festivals

NCAA basketball, thoroughbred horse racing, craft festivals, clogging competitions, and even a weekend festival celebrating a caterpillar — if you're looking for something fun and interesting to do in the Greater Lexington area, you won't be looking long.

Each year's calendar of events is chock-full of exhibits, festivals, shows and celebrations. Listed in this chapter you will read about many of these events that are held throughout the year. We hope this will entice you to go out and experience many of them for yourself!

January

"THE NUDE" EXHIBIT
Loudoun House,
209 Castlewood Drive   *254-7024*

This annual juried exhibit devoted to artistic depictions of the nude human figure has become the Lexington Art League's biggest show of the year. Now in its eighth year, "The Nude" draws the submission of work from about 100 artists annually from across the United States. The show is open to the public throughout most of the month.

LEXINGTON WINTER SCHOLASTIC CHESS TOURNAMENT
University of Kentucky
Student Center   *277-1733*

Sponsored by the Garden Springs Scholastic Chess Association, this tournament is open to young players in kindergarten through grade 12. There is an entry fee of about $20.

SWEET 16 ACADEMIC SHOWCASE AUCTION
Heritage Hall   *253-1124*

This huge auction, which is simultaneously televised on Lexington TV channels, is held each year to raise money for the scholarships given to area youngsters competing in the Sweet 16 Academic Competition in March. Viewers call in bids on everything from UK basketball tickets to cruises and cars.

February

ABRAHAM LINCOLN BIRTHDAY COMMEMORATION
Hodgenville   *(502) 358-3874*

This annual event commemorating the birth of President Abraham Lincoln is held at the Abraham Lincoln Birthplace National Historic Site.

March

SWEET 16 BOYS HIGH SCHOOL BASKETBALL CHAMPIONSHIP
299-5472

This is the highlight of the high school boys basketball competition each year. Sixteen of the best teams from across the state travel to the tournament, which alternates between Lexington and Louisville. It's a week of triumph and tears as teams are one by one eliminated.

SWEET 16 ACADEMIC SHOWCASE
Lexington   253-1124

The academic equivalent of the basketball tournament after which it was named, this statewide competition showcases the best and brightest Kentucky students in areas ranging from fine arts to mathematics. Competitions are held at locations throughout town.

ST. PATRICK'S DAY PARADE
Lexington   278-7349

Check the weather, don your green and get out early to enjoy the annual St. Patrick's Day parade that runs down Main Street about midmorning.

April

KEENELAND SPRING RACING
Lexington   254-3412, (800) 456-3412

The spring race meet at Keene-land, one of the most heralded events of the season, runs through the month with daily racing except on Monday. Reserved seats are $5, and post time is 1 PM.

ACTORS' GUILD PAUPERS' BALL
Lexington   233-0663

You can go all out at this exciting annual fund raiser for the Actors' Guild — the event's theme is Dance through the Decades. Each year, the ball raises $4,000-$6,000 for the theater group. Tickets are $20 per person in advance, $25 at the door.

ROLEX 3-DAY EVENT
Kentucky Horse Park   254-8123

This thrilling internationally recognized competition held each year at the Kentucky Horse Park showcases the best in equestrian competition and show, from the intricate schooling of dressage to the majestic athletic feats of stadium jumping. Admission is $20 for a pass to the entire event, or $5-$10 per day, depending on the events.

MOUNTAIN MUSHROOM FESTIVAL
Irvine   1-723-2554

For the fungally inclined, this unique annual festival includes everything from a street dance to a mushroom cook-off and the Fungus 5K race. Other events throughout the weekend include an antique car show, parade and gospel music festival.

Insiders' Tips

Insiders like to watch the lighting of the Christmas tree at Triangle Park.

CompuLEX

Central Kentucky Computer Society
1300 New Circle Road, Suite 105 255-2527

Each April, CompuLEX, one of the Midwest's largest computer shows, is held at Lexington Center's Heritage Hall. The show, sponsored by the Central Kentucky Computer Society Inc., features exhibits by international computer hardware manufacturers and software publishers as well as regional and local computer dealers selling from the floor. Admission to a large number of seminars put on by nationally known speakers is included in the ticket price.

May

KENTUCKY DERBY

Churchill Downs,
Louisville *(502) 636-4400*

This first and most prestigious leg of thoroughbred racing's Triple Crown competition is held the first Saturday in May. Post time is 11:30 AM. The race is for 3-year-olds and is 1 1/4 miles in length.

FRIENDS OF THE LIBRARY BOOK SALE
Lexington 231-5516

KENTUCKY MOUNTAIN LAUREL FESTIVAL
Pineville 1-337-6103

For 62 years, not a May has gone by without this festive weekend celebration that includes everything from the coronation of a festival queen to picnics, fireworks, parades, golf tournaments and hiking at Pine Mountain State Park. It is the second biggest annual event in Kentucky, just behind Louisville's Kentucky Derby Festival. Most events are open to the public free of charge.

MEMORIAL STAKES DAY
The Red Mile 255-0752

If you're looking for a fun way to celebrate your Memorial Day weekend, then come to The Red Mile for live entertainment, racing, music, and a to-die-for chili cook-off where you can eat all you can for $3, with proceeds benefiting the American Cancer Society. Admission to the

Photo: Lexington Herald-Leader

Festival of the Bluegrass draws thousands of bluegrass music fans to the Kentucky Horse Park each summer.

Memorial Stakes Day itself is $6.

KENTUCKY GUILD OF ARTISTS AND CRAFTSMEN SPRING FAIR

Indian Fort Theatre, Berea   1-986-2540

For 27 years, artists and craftspeople from across the commonwealth and surrounding region have brought the fruits of their labor to Berea's Indian Fort Theatre to showcase and sell. About 110 exhibitors attend this weekend event, including glass blowers, potters, weavers, silversmiths, photographers and basket makers. Friday and Sunday hours are 10 AM-5 PM, and the fair is open 10 AM-6 PM on Saturday. Admission is $3.50 for adults and $1 for kids 6-12.

THE WALK FOR LIFE

Lexington   254-AVOL

The annual Aids Volunteers of Lexington's Walk for Life is held each year the Sunday before the Kentucky Derby, which usually falls in May, but sometimes occurs the end of April. Last year, some 2,000 people participated in the 5K walk at UK's Commonwealth Stadium to raise money to help with the medical needs of HIV/AIDS patients in the area.

June

LEXINGTON LIONS BLUEGRASS FAIR

Masterson Station Park   266-8727

This is the big annual fund raising event for the Lexington Lions Club. It is a fun summer carnival featuring rides, food, games and entertainment. A small admission is charged (usually $2-$3). Tickets must be bought for the rides.

WOODLAND JUBILEE

Woodland Park   288-2930

This annual weekend event has become a favorite in Lexington. The weather at this time of year is nearly always pleasant, and the free performances of traditional Kentucky music and folk dancing by regional artists are always a treat for the whole family.

GAY PRIDE WEEK
Lexington
(and throughout state)   *255-5469, 269-5966*

GREAT AMERICAN BRASS BAND FESTIVAL AND BALLOON RACE
Centre College campus,
Danville   *1-236-7794*

Imagine the best brass bands from around the world all gathered together in one spot for a weekend musical festival. Then add a Friday night balloon race with 28 balloons, and about 30,000 people turning out for the festivities and you have one of the area's most exciting summer events. Bands have included Dallas Brass, Canadian Brass and the Salvation Army Band. Admission is free.

NATIONAL MOUNTAIN SQUARE DANCE AND CLOGGING FESTIVAL
Natural Bridge State Park   *(800) 325-1710*

For the past 27 years, this annual outdoor festival on Hoedown Island has drawn the best clogging teams from around the country to participate in this musical and dance extravaganza.

FESTIVAL OF THE BLUEGRASS
Kentucky Horse Park   *846-4995*

This annual Bluegrass and gospel extravaganza has become legendary in Lexington for presenting some of the very best bands and performers in the country. Ticket prices range from $7-$18 per day throughout the weekend, depending on the scheduled bands. Last year's roster included such greats as The Fairfield Four, Alison Krauss and Union Station, and J.D. Crowe and the New South.

ANNUAL EGYPTIAN EVENT
Kentucky Horse Park   *231-0771*

The Annual Egyptian Event highlights this rare breed that traces its pedigree back to the time of the pharaohs. Featured in this weekend event are show classes, demonstrations and sales, art exhibits, a film festival and a commercial bazaar.

ROCK AROUND THE POPS
The Red Mile

Take a few harness races, a picnic, the Lexington Philharmonic Orchestra and a great pop band like the Trendells, mix it with a balmy early summer evening, and you've got a surefire recipe for family fun. Tickets for this summer outdoor concert are $8-$10, and kids younger than 12 get in free.

SEEDTIME ON THE CUMBERLAND
Whitesburg   *1-633-0108*

Appalshop's annual festival of traditional mountain arts — Seedtime on the Cumberland — celebrates the exciting diversity of

Insiders like watching the Fourth of July fireworks set off at The Red Mile and at Masterson Station Park.

Insiders' Tips

Appalachian music. From old-time fiddle and banjo tunes to bluegrass, blues, gospel and labor songs, you'll find plenty to please any musical palate. This popular weekend event also features regional crafts, theater, and screenings of Appalshop films and videos. Tickets for evening concerts and theater presentations are $6 for adults, $5 for senior citizens, and $3 for students. Reservations are reccommended.

COUNTRY FAIR
St. Elizabeth Ann Seton Church
1750 Summerhill Drive   276-7103, 273-4260
A fun-for-the-whole-family summer event, the Country Fair runs Thursday through Saturday with a carnival, pony and elephant rides, games and entertainment.

July

JUNIOR LEAGUE HORSE SHOW
The Red Mile   252-1893
The world's largest outdoor American Saddlebred show, this event has been held in Lexington since 1937. Since it started, hundreds of thousands of visitors and competitors have come from across the United States and Canada to participate in this prestigious equestrian event.

SOULFEST
Lexington   255-5697
Sponsored by Micro-City Government, this soul, R&B, and jazz festival featuring national acts drew some 9,000 spectators in 1993. The pre-concert show on Friday night is held at Douglass Park and is free and open to the public. Saturday's festi-

val events are held at Masterson Station Park, and admission is $3.

KENTUCKY FAMILY REUNION
Kentucky Horse Park   (800) 678-8813
A lot of famous folks have ties to Kentucky, and each year some 64,000 transplanted Kentuckians from across the country and the state flock to the Kentucky Horse Park for good ol' down home fun. Lots of music and lots of fun for the whole family make this a special weekend for everyone involved. Last year's special musical guests included Ricky Skaggs, Patty Loveless, Exile, Steve Wariner and Bill Monroe. Bring a picnic and blankets and lawn chairs to this free event. Parking is $5.

BLUEGRASS STATE GAMES
Lexington   (800) 722-BGSG, 255-0336
See Parks and Recreation for more details on this major annual sporting event.

BEREA CRAFT FESTIVAL
Indian Fort Theatre   1-986-2540
Since 1896, Berea has hosted regional craft gatherings. The Berea Craft Festival has been held at Berea's Indian Fort Theatre since 1982. More than 100 exhibitors representing 20 states are featured each summer. Craft demonstrations, food and live entertainment round out the weekend event. Admission is $4.

BLUEGRASS 10,000
Lexington
For more information on this annual race that is part of the Lexington Fourth of July festivities, see Parks & Recreation.

Photo: Lexington Herald-Leader

Pineville's Mountain Laurel Festival, one of Eastern Kentucky's biggest festivals, draws thousands to its parade.

SHAKESPEARE IN THE PARK

Woodland Park

See Arts for more details on this outdoor theater event.

RAILWAY EXCURSION

Paris   1-293-0807

It may seem as if you're getting on a train for a nice trip through the countryside, but when you participate in this annual Railway Excursion, you're actually stepping back in time to the days of elegant train travel. These railway excursions run at different times throughout the summer between Paris and towns like Maysville and Carlisle. Ticket prices depend on the type of excursion and the destination.

OLD JOE CLARK
BLUEGRASS FESTIVAL

Renfro Valley   (800) 765-7464

This huge weekend event held at the Renfro Valley Country Music Center is for serious bluegrass, gospel and traditional music fans. Some of the best in the business can be seen on stage in this marathon musical event. Bring your family, food, lawn chairs, and be prepared to settle down and enjoy.

August

BATTLE OF RICHMOND
RE-ENACTMENT

Richmond   1-623-9178

BIG HILL MOUNTAIN
BLUEGRASS FESTIVAL

Big Hill   (800) 598-5263

Each year, bluegrass and gospel aficionados flock to Big Hill (just south of Berea) for this huge, bring-the-whole-family event. Headliners in the past have included John Cosby and the Bluegrass Drifters and Ralph Stanley and the Clinch Mountain Boys. A pig roast, band contest, arts and crafts exhibits and open stage jam sessions round out the action-packed weekend. Ticket prices range from $8 to $12 at the gate, children younger than 13 are admitted free with parents.

MIDSUMMER NIGHT'S RUN

Lexington   275-6665

One of Lexington's premier fitness events, the Midsummer Night's Run is actually a whole group of events that involves the entire family. Now in its 10th year, the Midsummer Night's Run (sponsored by Central Baptist Hospital) events include a one-mile family walk/run, the Baby Derby and Fastest Kid in Town race, and the 5K run through downtown.

KIDS FIRST EXPO

Lexington   299-0411

This huge expo is dedicated to kids, especially those ages 2-10 years old. Now four years old, the Kids First Expo is a showcase for products, ideas, services and activities for

Insiders' Tips

kids. About 12,000 people attend each year, and there is a small admission charge.

KENTUCKY HUNTER/JUMPER ASSOCIATION ANNUAL SHOW

Lexington   266-6937

LEXINGTON DREAM FACTORY'S ANNUAL IMPOSSIBLE DREAM AUCTION

Lexington   254-WISH

KENTUCKY STATE FAIR

Louisville   (502) 367-5002

The Kentucky State Fair is 10 days of some of the best summer fun and entertainment in the commonwealth. In addition to traditional state fair activities like livestock judging and baked goods competitions, the Kentucky State Fair is loaded with special events such as the World's Championship Horse Show and concerts by some of the biggest names in popular music. Bands and performers who have appeared at the fair in the past include Garth Brooks, Michael Bolton, Vince Gill, Kris Kross, Clint Black and Wynonna. General admission is $5 for adults, and $1 for kids 12 and younger and senior citizens. Concert admissions are extra and range from $13-$20, depending on the act.

WORLD'S LONGEST OUTDOOR SALE

U.S. 127   (800) 327-3945

It's called the "world's longest yard sale." Each August, vendors, businesses and other folks set up along a 450-mile stretch of U.S. 127 covering nine Kentucky counties down into Tennessee. Usually held the third weekend in August, the sale is open sunrise to sunset, Thursday through Sunday. About 80,000 people attend each year.

PICNIC WITH THE POPS

Kentucky Horse Park   233-3565

An evening under the stars with the heavenly music of the Lexington Philharmonic Orchestra, good food (that you bring), and good friends and neighbors make the annual Picnic with the Pops a favorite Lexington summertime event. General admission is $7.50, and you can also purchase table seats for you and a group of friends for $120-$160.

CENTRAL KENTUCKY STEAM & GAS ENGINE SHOW

Paris   1-987-4757

Held the first weekend in August, the Central Kentucky Steam & Gas Engine Show features working displays of antique farm and industrial machines. Admission cost is $3.

BALLET UNDER THE STARS

Woodland Park

Woodland Park is the site of many interesting summer arts events. Ballet Under the Stars is a festival of dance featuring excerpts from popular and well-known ballets performed by area dancers. It is usually held the first week and weekend in August and is free and open to the public.

ANNUAL GOLF FOR SIDS

The Champions Golf Club   1-987-2322
                              223-0596

About 30 foursomes compete in this annual golf tournament to raise money for SIDS (Sudden Infant Death Syndrome) research. The tournament was started about three years ago by the local SIDS Support Group.

September

CIVIL WAR DRAMA
AND TRAIN ROBBERY

Versailles   873-2476

If you're looking for an exciting way to experience Kentucky history while benefiting a good cause, the Civil War Drama and Train Robbery is one of the most fun. The train is actually "robbed" and donations made by passengers during the robbery benefit the Muscular Dystrophy Association. Admission is $6 for adults.

ROOTS & HERITAGE FESTIVAL

Rose Street

This annual event, which has grown to encompass a week of events culminating in a weekend street festival, celebrates African-American heritage and culture in Lexington and around the world. Theater, music, lectures, poetry readings and art exhibits are held during the week preceding the weekend festival. Weekend events include everything from vendors selling jewelry, T-shirts, music, arts & crafts and lots of food, to gymnastics exhibitions, live music, karate demonstrations, dance and fashion shows. The event is free and open to the public.

HISTORIC CONSTITUTION
SQUARE FESTIVAL

Danville   1-236-9690, 1-236-5089

Historical re-enactments, living history presentations, live entertainment, lots of food, arts & crafts from more than 80 artists and craftspeople, and museum tours round out the schedule of events that fill the weekend of this commemorative event celebrating Kentucky's statehood.

KENTUCKY ATHLETIC CLUB'S
CHARITY "BASH"

The Red Mile, Lexington

For the past 21 years, this annual charity ball at the Red Mile has generated thousands of dollars for local charities and kicks off the University of Kentucky's football season. Food, drink, and dancing to music by such popular bands as The Association and the Trendells make it an event to remember. Admission is $25-$30.

KENTUCKY BOURBON FESTIVAL

My Old Kentucky Home State Park,
Bardstown   (800) 638-4877

Perhaps the only bourbon festival in the world, this annual event features a variety of bourbon-related activities including bourbon tasting, a music festival, tours of local distilleries, a golf tournament and My Old Kentucky Dinner Train Bourbon Excursion.

WOODFORD COUNTY DAYS AND
HISTORIC MIDWAY FALL FESTIVAL

Midway   873-5122

This big outdoor festival celebrates the spirit of times gone by with a parade, flea market and exhibits by some 100 area craftspeople. The 5K Harvest Run is also part of the festivities.

WORLD CHICKEN FESTIVAL

London   (800) 348-0095

This "fowl" event is held each year in the home of the first Colonel

Harland Sanders (Kentucky Fried Chicken) restaurant the last weekend of each September. Carnival rides and games and live entertainment are some of the highlights.

MOUNTAIN HERITAGE FESTIVAL

Whitesburg   1-633-8034

The annual Mountain Heritage Festival celebrates the talents and pastimes of the past through such things as demonstrations of the making of moonshine and lye soap. The festival also includes a parade, arts and crafts exhibits and live music. It's free.

BANK ONE SENIOR GOLF CLASSIC

Lexington   259-1825

See Golf for more information on this prestigious golf tournament.

FESTIVAL OF THE HORSE

Georgetown   863-2547

See Horse Country for more information.

RENFRO VALLEY BLUEGRASS FESTIVAL

Renfro Valley   (800) 765-7464

This weekend-long bluegrass and gospel extravaganza is an intense presentation and performance by some the greatest bluegrass names in the country. It's the kind of event where you pack up the kids, the dog, lots of food and soft drinks, and head out for three days of good, old home music. Three-day admission passes are $31, two-day passes are $24, and single-day admission is $16.

POPS AT THE PARK

White Hall State Historic Site,
Richmond   1-623-1720

This concert is similar to the Picnic with the Pops in Lexington. It is held on the grounds of Cassius Marcellus Clay's stately Madison County mansion, with music provided by the Lexington Philharmonic Orchestra. Blanket seats are $8, and preferred and general tables are available, although they sell out quickly each year.

PICNIC WITH THE PUPS

Red Mile Paddock Park   272-7292, 266-5852

Entertainment, music, dancing, food and fun for the whole family, the annual Picnic with the Pups raises money for humane education and spay/neuter programs in Central Kentucky. There is a $5 donation for adult admission, and kids 12 and younger get in free.

ADMIRALS DAY PARADE

Fort Boonesborough   1-527-3131

A warm summer day, colorfully decorated boats, a wide, lazy river — these are the ingredients that make up the annual Admirals Day Parade on the Kentucky River. People bring lawn chairs, picnics and the kids to enjoy the live entertainment, boat rides and the parade of boats on the river. It's free.

October

KENTUCKY GUILD OF ARTISTS AND CRAFTSMEN FALL FAIR

Indian Fort Theatre, Berea   1-986-2540

This is the fall equivalent of the spring fair. See the previous entry for more details.

CELEBRATION OF TRADITIONAL MUSIC

Berea College   1-986-9341, ext. 5103

Some 800 people from across the country attend this annual event celebrating the best of old-time and folk art musical forms that predate bluegrass and country. Performances of ballads, duets, and string band music, workshops by participating artists, and nightly dances are some of the highlights of this exciting celebration.

EQUIFESTIVAL OF KENTUCKY

Lexington   255-4383, (800) 874-9508

This five-day horse extravaganza covers everything from harness racing at the Red Mile to horse farm tours, hayrides, and basketball. The festival celebrates just about everything having to do with horses, from a parade of breeds to equine art exhibits. Events are held at different locations around town, including the Kentucky Horse Park, The Red Mile, and Keeneland Race Course.

PERRYVILLE BATTLEFIELD COMMEMORATION AND RE-ENACTMENT

Perryville Battlefield   1-332-8631

Military drills and parades, a flea market, street dance, activities for kids and walking tours are all part of this historic weekend event commemorating a significant Civil War battle in Kentucky. See Inside Daytrips for more details on the actual re-enactment.

KEENELAND FALL RACING

Lexington   254-3412

WOOLLY WORM FESTIVAL

Beattyville   1-464-2888

Where can you rent a caterpillar to race for a quarter while you find out what the weather will be like for the next few months? At the annual Woolly Worm Festival, of course. Each October, the small town of Beattyville (population about 1,100) is crowded by the thousands of visitors who come to hear the weather predictions of Rosemary Kilduff from her annual Woolly Worm survey. It's not exactly scientific, but Rosemary's usually right.

WALK FOR HUNGER

UK's Commonwealth Stadium   252-2818

Each year, volunteers collect pledges from the community then walk a 5K or 10K course to raise money for God's Pantry, a Lexington food bank.

ALZHEIMER'S MEMORY WALK

Lexington   252-6282

ANNUAL GREASER'S CAR SHOW

*Fort Boonesborough
State Park   254-5701, Ext. 601*

Each year, 10,000 car enthusiasts from across the Commonwealth turn out for this event, which raises funds for Cardinal Hill Hospital. More than 800 cars and trucks, including antique, vintage and customized ve-hicles, are on display throughout the weekend. A small admission charge (usually $2) applies to adults and kids 12 and older.

COURT DAYS

Mount Sterling

It's big. Real big. About 2,000 vendors and tens of thousands of visitors crowd into downtown Mount Sterling each for Court Days festivities. You can buy everything from a "Barney" T-shirt to rifles, tools, crafts and Polish sausage.

KENTUCKY FALL
CLASSIC HORSE SHOW

Kentucky Horse Park   254-5701, Ext. 601

At this annual horse show, all different breeds, from American

Saddlebreds to hackney ponies, compete for $60,000 in prizes. The show benefits Cardinal Hill Hospital.

IROQUOIS HUNT CLUB
HORSE SHOW AND BARBEQUE
Athens-Boonesboro Road   *254-0501*

This annual, daylong event is held rain or shine. The fox hounds and jumping competition is complemented by some great Southern barbeque. There is no admission charge for the show, but lunch is $6.

November

BLUE GRASS TRUST ANTIQUE SHOW
Lexington   *253-0362*

Some three dozen antiques dealers from across the state participate in this annual show to raise money for the Blue Grass Trust for Historic Preservation. Proceeds from admission fees benefit the preservation group. Special events include appraisal of antique items brought in by the public and a silent auction that runs throughout the show.

CHRISTMAS TREE
LIGHTING CEREMONY
Triangle Park   *231-3000*

Gathering together with your friends and neighbors in beautiful Triangle Park downtown Lexington is always a special treat. The annual Christmas tree lighting makes it extra special. There is no admission charge.

KENTUCKY BOOK FAIR
Frankfort, Department of Libraries and Archives

Imagine dozens of your favorite authors all under one roof. Each year for the past 12 years, the Kentucky Book Fair in Frankfort has done just that — gather dozens of authors from across the state and the country to Kentucky to sell and sign their books. An added bonus is that profits from the book sales are given to public libraries and school libraries around the state to purchase books. In 1993, some 87 authors attended, including Wendell Berry, Ken Kesey, Carol Higgins Clark, Thomas D. Clark and Bobbie Ann Mason.

December

ANNUAL CHRISTMAS PARADE
Main Street, Lexington   *231-7335*

Usually held the first weekend in December in the early afternoon, Lexington's Annual Christmas Parade ushers in the holiday season with a colorful display of about 100-120 floats and entries that include some of the top Central Kentucky marching bands. The parade route typically runs down Main Street between Midland and Broadway.

CANDLELIGHT TOURS
Hunt-Morgan House and
Mary Todd Lincoln House   *253-0362*

These historic Lexington homes are decked out for the holidays, representing the periods in which they were in use by the former famous inhabitants. You can tour these gracious old homes and experience the excitement of Christmases past. A small admission is charged.

ANNUAL CHRISTMAS
CANDLELIGHT TOUR

Waveland State Historic Site   *272-3611*

Step back in time to Christmas in the old Bluegrass as you tour this historic mansion. Refreshments and live music complement the festive atmosphere. A small admission fee is charged.

KENTUCKY CHRISTMAS CHORUS

Rupp Arena   *258-3112*

This choral extravaganza features the singing talents of more than 80 choirs and choral groups. Some 7,000 people typically attend this festive evening yuletide event, which is free.

Inside
Daytrips

*I*f you spend any time at all in Lexington, you'll soon find out that one of the best things about it is its central location in the state. Just about anywhere you want to go in Kentucky is within a half-day's drive from Lexington.

Amusement parks, major metropolitan areas, spectacular state parks, ski resorts, fabulous fishing and boating areas, zoos, planetariums, art museums and national historic sites are all easily accessible from Lexington.

There are, at the very least, hundreds of possible daytrips from Lexington. In this section, however, we will take an in-depth look at a few of our favorites: Louisville, Cincinnati and Covington, Bardstown, Danville/Perryville, Renfro Valley, Shaker Village of Pleasant Hill, and Big South Fork National River and Recreation Area.

"Daytrip," in the cases of these listed above, is really a misnomer. While you could go and come back to Lexington within a day, once you get there, you're likely to find you want to stay at least overnight. The sections following list some of the high points and attractions of each daytrip destination. For more detailed information about lodging and restaurants, call the number listed at the beginning of the section.

This is by no means a complete listing of the wonderful daytrips from Lexington. All of the Kentucky State Parks make great trips for the whole family. For more information on specific parks, see The Great Outdoors and Campgrounds or call 1-(800) 225-TRIP.

Louisville

LOUISVILLE CONVENTION & VISITORS BUREAU
(800) 626-5646;
(Kentucky) (800) 633-3384

The annual "Run for the Roses," famous baseball bats, and one of the world's greatest heavyweight champions of all time are just a few of the things that have helped secure Louisville's place in American history.

Located on the banks of the Ohio River, Kentucky's largest city is a veritable cornucopia of great things to see, do and experience. If you think "veritable cornucopia" is hard to spit out, though, just wait till you try to pronounce the name of this river city as a native would. To prepare to get just the right accent, fill your mouth up with crackers or a big wad of bubble gum, then say it real fast. If it comes out something like "Looalvul," you're on the right track. If you can't pronounce it like a native, however, it's best to stick to the acceptable "Looeyville." But whatever you do, never say "Looisville."

Located about an hour and half west of Lexington on I-64, Louisville is a great mix of history and modern big-city activities. Thousands of visitors from around the world flock to Louisville each May for the annual Kentucky Derby. The 15-day Kentucky Derby Festival is the country's largest civic celebration.

The West Main Street Historic, Cultural and Arts District, between the 500 and 900 blocks downtown, features the largest collection of 19th-century cast-iron storefronts outside of Soho in New York City. Tour maps are available at the Preservation Alliance, (502) 583-8622.

A leisurely walk on the Belvedere along the Ohio River will give you a great view of the city as well as the world's tallest computerized floating fountain — Falls Fountain — in all its colorful splendor.

Heading across the river to Clarksville, Ind., will take you back in time some 350 million years as you walk out onto the Falls of the Ohio where the largest exposed fossil bed in the world is located.

Following are some of the great things to do during your daytrip to Louisville.

BELLE OF LOUISVILLE
Fourth Street and
River Road (502) 625-BELL

Built in 1914, the *Belle of Louisville* is a National Historic Landmark. It is the oldest operating steamboat on the Mississippi River system and one of the last authentic steamwheelers in the country.

Charter cruises are available April through October, and public cruises are offered Tuesdays through Saturdays from Memorial Day to Labor Day. Afternoon cruises run 2 to 4 PM EDT, boarding time 1 PM. Sunset cruises on Tuesdays and Thursdays board at 6 PM and run 7 to 9 PM with live entertainment. There is also an adult dance cruise Saturday nights from 8:30 to 11:30 PM, boarding time 7:30 PM.

Admission to the Saturday dance cruise is $12 per person. For all other public cruises, tickets are $7.50 for adults, $6.50 for senior citizens, $3.50 for kids, and children younger than 2 are admitted free.

CAVE HILL CEMETERY AND ARBORETUM
701 Baxter Avenue (502) 451-5630

According to one longtime Louisville resident, "everyone who's anyone is buried in Cave Hill Cemetery." That may be a bit of an overstatement, but there are some famous folks who have made this gorgeous cemetery and arboretum their final resting place, including General George Rogers Clark, who founded the city in 1778, and Colonel Harland Sanders of Kentucky Fried Chicken fame.

The cemetery is worth a trip just for the fantastic sculptures and monuments that adorn many of the graves. The "Temple of Love" is one of the most famous and most elaborate. Cave Hill Cemetery and Arboretum is open free to the public daily, 8 AM to 4:45 PM.

CHURCHILL DOWNS
700 Central Avenue (502) 636-4400

Made famous by the first leg of

Photo: Lexington Herald-Leader

My Old Kentucky Home in Bardstown features a musical performance complete with period costumes and a tour of the house that inspired Stephen Foster to write "My Old Kentucky Home."

thoroughbred racing's Triple Crown — the Kentucky Derby, run the first Saturday in May — Churchill Downs is also one of Louisville's historic landmarks. The Kentucky Derby has been run on this same course since 1875. Racing is scheduled here from the last week in April to the first week in July and from the end of October to the end of November.

The Kentucky Derby Museum, next door, is open daily 9 AM to 5 PM. Call (502) 637-1111 for more details.

KENTUCKY CENTER FOR THE ARTS
Main Street between
Fifth and Sixth streets   *(502) 562-0100*
    (800) 283-7777

Plays, music, dance — the Kentucky Center for the Arts has just about everything you'd want to experience in the arts. The center has three stages and a magnificent sculpture collection.

KENTUCKY KINGDOM AMUSEMENT PARK
Kentucky Fair and
Exposition Center   *(502) 366-7508*

The fourth largest wooden roller coaster in the world and the second largest wave pool in the country are only two of the more than 60 rides, games and attractions at this Kentucky amusement park. For more information see Kids Stuff.

LOUISVILLE SLUGGER TOUR/ HILLERICH & BRADSBY CO.
1525 Charleston-New Albany Road,
Jeffersonville, Indiana
    (502) 585-5229, Ext. 227

The name might say Kentucky, but the game is played in Indiana.

Yes, the Louisville Slugger has been manufactured across the river, in Jeffersonville, Ind., since 1974. Maybe its maker, Hillerich & Bradsby Co., should call its baseball bat the "Hoosier Hitter."

Guided tours of Hillerich & Bradsby's baseball bat and golf clubs manufacturing plant — the company also makes PowerBilt clubs — include a stop in a museum featuring a bat used by Babe Ruth and souvenir miniature bats.

The plant is open free to the public Monday through Friday with tours at 8 AM, 9 AM, 10 AM, 1 PM, and 2 PM. It is closed the last week in June, the first two weeks in July and Christmas week. To get there from Louisville, take I-65 north to Exit 4; stay in the middle lane at the bottom of the ramp, go straight through the stoplight, over the railroad tracks and it's the first entrance on the left.

Other places of interest you might want to check out while touring Louisville include the following.

AMERICAN PRINTING HOUSE FOR THE BLIND
1839 Frankfort Avenue   *(502) 895-2405*

This is the oldest national non-profit agency for the visually impaired in the United States. It is open, free of charge, Monday through Friday with tours at 10 AM and 2 PM.

COLONEL HARLAND SANDERS MUSEUM
1441 Gardiner Lane   *(502) 456-8352*

See the story behind the success of Kentucky Fried Chicken. Open free of charge Tuesday through Thursday, 8:30 AM to 4:30 PM.

FARMINGTON

3033 Bardstown Road   (502) 452-9920

Built by John and Lucy Speed in 1810, and designed by Thomas Jefferson, Farmington is a step back in history. Abraham Lincoln was among the famous visitors to the home. Open Monday through Saturday, 10 AM to 4:30 PM, and Sunday 1:30 until 4:30. Admission is $3 for adults, $1 for children younger than 16, and free for kids younger than 6.

FILSON CLUB

1310 South Third   (502) 635-5083

Filson Club is the museum of the historical society, named for Kentucky's first historian. There is an outstanding history and genealogy library on site. The museum is open free to the public Monday through Friday from 9 AM until 5 PM, and Saturday 9 AM to noon. There is a $2 admission charge to the library.

FORD KENTUCKY TRUCK PLANT

3001 Chamberlain Lane   (502) 429-2146

If trucks are your thing, plan to stop in here. It is the largest truck assembly plant in North America, producing everything from 18-wheelers to school buses. It's open free for tours by appointment.

HADLEY POTTERY

*1570 Story Avenue in historic
Butchertown   (502) 584-2171*

Hand-painted stoneware made using designs created by Mary Alice Hadley in the 1940s are the feature of Hadley Pottery. Free guided tours are given Monday through Friday at 2 PM if the temperature is not over 85 degrees. The pottery is open Monday through Friday from 8 AM until 4:30 PM, and Saturday from 9 AM until 12:30 PM.

J.B. SPEED ART MUSEUM

*2035 South Third, adjacent to the
University of Louisville   (502) 636-2893*

This museum is worth a visit, but it could take a while to go all the way through, because it contains more than 3,000 works of art. Hours are Tuesday through Saturday from 10 AM until 4 PM, and Sunday noon to 5 PM. There is no admission charge.

JOHN CONTI COFFEE MUSEUM

4023 Bardstown Road   (502) 499-8602

This is the only museum of its kind in the country, containing 1,500 coffee-related items. It's open free, Monday through Friday from 9 AM to 5 PM.

JOSEPH A. CALLAWAY ARCHEOLOGICAL MUSEUM

*Southern Baptist Seminary,
2825 Lexington Road   (502) 897-4141*

Take a step back in time and visit the Callaway Museum. It features a copy of the Rosetta Stone, a 2,700-year-old mummy, and other ancient Egyptian and Near Eastern artifacts. The public is admitted free, Mon-

Visitors can enjoy country and gospel music at Renfro Valley.

day through Friday from 8 AM until 5 PM.

KENTUCKY ART AND CRAFT GALLERY

609 West Main Street (502) 589-0102

You'll find many examples of the rich craft tradition in this region at this gallery. It is open free Monday through Saturday from 10 AM to 4 PM.

LOCUST GROVE

561 Blankenbaker Lane (502) 897-9845

Built in 1790, this beautiful Georgian home was the last residence of Louisville founder George Rogers Clark. Open Monday through Saturday from 10 AM to 4:30 PM, Sunday from 1:30 PM to 4:30 PM. Admission is $3, $2.50 for senior citizens.

LOUISVILLE STONEWARE

731 Brent Street (502) 582-1900

Home of the nationally famous handpainted dinnerware, free tours are offered Monday through Friday at 10:30 AM and 2:30 PM. The sales room is open Monday through Saturday from 8 AM to 4:30 PM.

THE STAR OF LOUISVILLE

Second Street and
River Road (800) 289-7245

Enjoy buffet dining, live entertainment and dancing while cruising the Ohio River on this 130-foot ship. Lunch, dinner and moonlight cruises are offered Monday through Thursday at noon and 7 PM, Friday and Saturday at noon, 7:30 PM and 11:30 PM, and Sunday at 1 PM and 7 PM. Prices range from $13.95 to $34.95.

WATER TOWER/LOUISVILLE VISUAL ART ASSOCIATION

River Road and
Zorn Avenue (502) 896-2146

Contemporary art is showcased in the oldest water tower in America. It's open free to the public Monday through Friday from 9 AM to 5 PM, Saturday 9 AM to 3 PM, and Sunday noon to 4 PM.

ZACHARY TAYLOR
NATIONAL CEMETERY

4701 Brownsboro Road   (502) 893-3852

This cemetery is the burial site of the 12th president of the United States and is open free daily from 8 AM to 4:30 PM.

Covington and
Northern Kentucky

NORTHERN KENTUCKY
CONVENTION AND VISITORS BUREAU
(800) 336-3535

A trip to the Covington area of northern Kentucky will most likely take more than a day since it also includes Cincinnati, one of Ohio's largest cities. However, since it is only about 70 miles from Lexington up I-75, you might want to plan to visit different areas on different daytrips.

Your daytrips to the area might coincide with a baseball or football game (Cincinnati is home to two major ball clubs, the Cincinnatti Bengals football and the Cincinnati Reds baseball) or a major concert — Riverbend hosts numerous national music acts, perhaps most famously to all you Parrotheads, Jimmy Buffett's annual late summer sell-out concerts.

You may want to plan a trip centered on the numerous beautiful and historic churches and cathedrals in Covington and Cincinnati, several of which are detailed below. You can go to the races at Turfway Park, or plan a whole day of shopping at Covington and Florence's many great malls and retail centers.

For the sake of brevity, only Covington area attractions are de-tailed here. However, to receive more information on Cincinnati activities and attractions, call (800) 344-3445.

MAINSTRASSE VILLAGE

Main Street   1-491-0458

This five-block-long restored 19th-century German village houses more than 40 unique shops, restaurants and businesses. The renovated buildings that make up the village are connected by cobblestone walkways, giving the area an old-world charm.

Two architectural highlights of the village are the Carroll Chimes Bell Tower — a German Gothic structure featuring a 43-bell carillon that plays hourly — and the Goose Girl Fountain, commissioned by the Northern Kentucky Convention and Visitors Bureau and constructed by noted Greek sculptor Eleftherios Karkadoulias.

MainStrasse Village is host to a number of festivals and special events throughout the year, including The World's Largest Outdoor Sale the third weekend in August, and Oktoberfest held on the weekend following Labor Day.

BEHRINGER-CRAWFORD MUSEUM

1600 Montague Avenue   1-491-4003

The Behringer-Crawford Museum features items illustrating the area's cultural and natural history. Displays cover a wide range of areas, from paleontology and wildlife to the arts. The museum is open Tuesday through Saturday, 10 AM to 5 PM, and Sunday 1 to 5 PM. To get there, take the Fifth Street exit off I-75 to Montague Avenue in Devou Park.

Fayette is one of three original Kentucky counties created in 1780, 12 years before Kentucky gained statehood.

COVINGTON LANDING

Madison Avenue   *1-291-9992*

One of the largest floating restaurant/entertainment centers on the nation's inland waterways, Covington Landing is an extravaganza of shopping, dining and recreation. It is located on the Ohio River next to the Roebling Suspension Bridge, the prototype for the Brooklyn Bridge in New York and one of the nation's first suspension bridges.

Covington Landing is open daily 10 AM to 2 AM Monday through Saturday; call for Sunday hours. To get there, take the Fifth Street exit off I-75.

MIMOSA HOUSE

412 East Second Street   *1-261-9000*

Historic Mimosa House, built in the mid-1850s, is the largest single-family home in the area. Its 22 rooms, with 14 fireplaces and the original gas lighting system, feature Rococo Revival furniture designed by Belter, Baudouine and Meeks. The house is open for tours Saturday and Sunday 1 to 6 PM, with Christmas tours December through mid-January on Saturdays and Sundays 1 to 8 PM. Admission is $3.

CATHEDRAL BASILICA OF THE ASSUMPTION

1140 Madison Avenue   *(606) 431-2060*

Modeled after the Notre Dame cathedral in Paris, France, Cathedral Basilica of the Assumption, completed in 1901, features a spectacular display of 82 stained glass windows, including the largest stained glass church window in the world.

The cathedral is open for self-guided tours Monday through Friday, 8 AM until 4:30 PM, and Saturday and Sunday, 8 AM to 6:30 PM, and guided tours at 2 PM on Sundays June through August.

MONTE CASINO

Turkeyfoot Road in
Crestview Hills   *1-341-5800*

Constructed of fieldstone from the area, this tiny chapel at Thomas More College is said to be the smallest house of worship in the world. It is open free to the public dawn to dusk every day. Take I-275 to Turkeyfoot Road south.

MOTHER OF GOD CHURCH

119 West Sixth Street   *1-291-2288*

Constructed around 1870, the Mother of God Church is an ecclesiastical art lover's dream come true. Among the treasures on display here are five large murals by Vatican artist Johann Schmitt, 200-foot twin Renaissance towers, stained glass and inlaid tile. It is open free to the public Monday through Saturday, 8 AM to 5 PM, and Sunday 8 AM to 3 PM.

Photo: Lexington Herald-Leader

Shaker craftsmanship, such as broommaking, is demonstrated at Shakertown.

Bardstown

BARDSTOWN-NELSON COUNTY TOURIST COMMISSION
(800) 638-4877

Known as the "Bourbon Capital of the World" and home of My Old Kentucky Home, which inspired the famous Stephen Foster song, Bardstown has a rich and colorful history.

Originally known as Salem, the area that is now Bardstown was formed by William Bard in the 1780s from a land grant of 1,000 acres issued by the Virginia General Assembly. Bardstown is the seat of Nelson County, formed in 1784 by the Virginia General Assembly as Kentucky's fourth county.

It is the site of the original Kentucky Court of Appeals, and it became a distillery center because of the abundance of lime in the water (a necessary ingredient for making bourbon). For more information on bourbon making in Kentucky, see Distilleries and Breweries.

Located about an hour's drive southwest of Lexington on the Bluegrass Parkway, Bardstown is home to many historic sites as well as the popular outdoor musical *The Stephen Foster Story*, featuring more than 50 songs of one of America's most beloved composers. The musical is presented June to Labor Day, Tuesday through Sunday at 8:30 PM, with an added 3 PM matinee on Saturday. Presented in My Old Kentucky Home State Park Amphitheater, admission to the play is $10 for adults and $5 for children 12 and younger. Call (800) 626-1563 for ticket information.

The drive to Bardstown is gorgeous. Some of its most famous attractions are listed below.

TALBOTT TAVERN

107 West Stephen Foster Avenue   *(502) 348-3494*

America's oldest stagecoach stop and inn, Talbott Tavern has hosted some of the nation's most colorful historical figures, including Daniel Boone, Andrew Jackson, Jesse James, Abraham Lincoln, and General George Patton.

Talbott Tavern is open daily 11 AM to 3 PM and 5 to 9 PM, Saturday until 10 PM, and Sunday 11:30 AM to 9 PM. You can also plan to enjoy lunch or dinner in this historic inn.

ST. JOSEPH PROTO-CATHEDRAL

310 West Stephen Foster Avenue   *(502) 348-3126*

Completed in 1816, St. Joseph's was the first Catholic cathedral west of the Alleghenies. It now contains a valuable collection of 17th-century European paintings. Guided tours are offered Monday through Friday from 9 AM until 5 PM, Saturday 9 AM to 3 PM, and Sunday 1 to 5 PM.

MY OLD KENTUCKY HOME STATE PARK

U.S. 150   *(502) 348-3502*

Made famous throughout the country by the Stephen Foster song immortalizing it, My Old Kentucky Home is a beautiful park surrounding the southern mansion Federal Hill, which was the inspiration for the song. Federal Hill is open June through Labor Day daily from 8:30 AM until 6:30 PM; May, September and October daily from 8:30 AM to

5 PM; and 9 AM to 5 PM daily the rest of the year. It is closed Mondays in January and February.

Admission to the house is $3.50 for adults, $1 for kids, and $3 per person for groups and senior citizens.

WICKLAND
U.S. 62, 1/2 mile east of
Court Square   *(502) 348-5428*

Built in 1817, the Smithsonian called this historic home the most perfect example of Georgian architecture in the country.

It is open for tours April through October, Monday through Saturday, 9 AM to 7 PM, Sunday 1 to 7 PM. Admission is $3.50 for adults, $1 for kids, and $2 per person for groups.

MY OLD KENTUCKY DINNER TRAIN
602 North Third Street   (502) 348-7300

This unique dinner excursion allows you to enjoy an elegant four-course meal during a two-hour roundtrip run from Bardstown to Limestone Springs. The dinner train is made up of 1940s vintage railroad cars.

Excursions are available daily April through October at 11 AM, 5:15 PM and 8:15 PM, and November through March by reservation.

AMERICA'S MINIATURE SOLDIER MUSEUM
804 North Third Street   (502) 348-4879

This unusual museum displays more than 10,000 toy soldiers from around the world. Open May through December, Tuesday through Saturday, 10 AM to 5 PM. Admission to the museum is $2 for adults, $1 for kids, and $1 per person for groups.

THE DOLL COTTAGE MUSEUM
213 East Stephen
Foster Avenue   (502) 348-8210

More than 700 dolls, from Barbie and G.I. Joe to Shirley Temple, are on display at the Doll Cottage. The museum is open daily in the spring and fall 11 AM to 5 PM, and in the summer 10 AM to 5 PM. Admission is $1.50 for adults, $1 for kids 12 and younger.

Danville and Perryville

DANVILLE-BOYLE COUNTY TOURIST COMMISSION
1-236-7794

The site of one of the most desperate battles of the Civil War, the location of the filming of the epic motion picture *Raintree County*, starring Elizabeth Taylor, and the home of the Great American Brass Band Festival, the Danville/Perryville area offers a wide variety of activities to enjoy on your daytrip to the area.

About 45 minutes southwest of Lexington (take U.S. 27 to Ky. 34) your daytrip to Danville and Perryville should definitely include a visit to historic Centre College, established in 1819, whose famous alums include U.S. vice presidents Adlai Stevenson and John Breckinridge and U.S. Supreme Court justices John Marshall Harlan and Fred M. Vinson. The college is on West Walnut Street.

Other areas of interest include the Perryville battle site, a 500-acre wildlife refuge, the Kentucky School for the Deaf, and Pioneer Playhouse outdoor dinner theater (for more information about Pioneer Playhouse, please see the Arts section).

Danville is the site of the framing of Kentucky's first constitution in 1792 and the site of the first post office west of the Alleghenies, which still stands today in Constitution Square. In fact, Constitution Square is probably a good spot to start your tour of the Danville/Perryville area. All attractions detailed below are in Danville unless otherwise noted.

CONSITUTION SQUARE STATE HISTORIC SITE

105 East Walnut Street   1-236-5089

Called the birthplace of Kentucky's statehood, 10 constitutional conventions took place here before the final Kentucky Constitution was finally drafted. Today, this historic site features the original oldest post office west of the Alleghenies, and replicas of the meetinghouse, jail and courthouse that were around at the time of Kentucky's statehood. A park, gift shop and picnic areas are open year round, and a museum and art gallery are open April through October. These attractions are free and open daily 9 AM to 5PM.

McDOWELL HOUSE & APOTHECARY SHOP

125 South Second Street   1-236-2804

Visit this turn of the 19th century Georgian-style home of Dr. Ephraim McDowell, the Kentucky surgeon who performed the first successful removal of an ovarian tumor in 1809. Open Monday through Saturday, 10 AM to noon and 1 to 3:30 PM, and Sunday 2 to 3:30 PM (closed Mondays November through February), admission to the McDowell House is $3 adults, $2 ages 13-21, 50 cents for

12 and younger, and $2 for ages 62 and older. Group rates are available for groups of 10 or more.

JACOBS HALL

South Second Street   1-236-5132

This 1855 Italianate building is home to the offices of the Kentucky School for the Deaf, the first state-supported school for the deaf in the U.S., founded in 1823. Open free Monday through Friday, 8 AM until 4:30 PM, the museum has artifacts and photos of the school's history as well as period furnishings on display.

PERRYVILLE BATTLEFIELD STATE HISTORIC SITE

Off U.S. 68 & U.S. 150,
10 miles west of Danville   1-332-8631

On October 8, 1862, Kentucky's greatest Civil War battle was waged at Perryville. It was the South's last serious attempt to gain control of Kentucky. Today, this battle is re-enacted annually on the weekend closest to the actual battle date. It is unique among many such re-enactments because it is staged on the actual site of the battle. This 100-acre park also features a Civil War museum open April through October, picnic shelter, playground and gift shop. It is open free throughout the year.

WILLIAM WHITLEY HOUSE STATE HISTORIC SITE

U.S. 150 between Stanford and
Crab Orchard   1-355-2881

Aside from its historic value as a 1780s home used as a refuge by Kentucky frontiersmen, the William Whitley House is perhaps best known

Visitors touring Shakertown can see Centre Family House, furnished with original Shaker furniture and textiles.

for its significance to American horse racing.

In 1785, Colonel Whitley laid the country's first circular horse racing track here, and to defy the British, he raced his horses counterclockwise around the track, setting a precedent for all future American racetracks.

The house is open March through November, Tuesday through Sunday, 9 AM to 5 PM, and daily June through August. A $1 admission fee is charged.

Renfro Valley

(800) 765-SING

A visit to "The Valley Where Time Stands Still" is indeed a trip back in time. Renfro Valley is home of the nationally famous Saturday Night

Barn Dance, started by John Lair in 1939. Featuring such famous country musicians as Red Foley and Lily May Ledford and the Coon Creek Girls, the Barn Dance was broadcast on WGN from Chicago for many years. The "Sunday Morning Gatherin'," still being broadcast today, is the second oldest radio broadcast in America. You can attend the "Gatherin'" Sunday mornings at 8:30.

Renfro Valley is about an hour south of Lexington on I-75, near Mount Vernon (Exit 62). This is more of a late day and evening trip, because you'll want to be sure to take in one of the great country-western music variety shows offered several evenings a week — the Barn Dance, the Gospel Jubilee, and the Jamboree. These shows feature some of the region's best performers, from singers and a left-handed fiddler, to cloggers and comedians — "Bun" Wilson is a longtime Renfro Valley favorite. The shows run about 1 1/2 hours, and they're worth every cent of the $8 admission for adults.

In March, shows are staged Saturday nights at 7 PM. In April, November and December, there are shows Friday nights at 7 PM and Saturdays at 3 PM and 7 PM. May through October, there are shows Thursdays at 7 PM, Fridays at 7 and 9 PM, and Saturdays at 3, 7 and 9 PM.

The shows staged in the Old Barn are a unique treat—when the crowd really gets into the music, the wood plank floor vibrates with the stomping of hundreds of feet, and you feel like you truly are in an old-fashioned barn dance. The New Barn, however, is a grand auditorium with a state-of-the-art sound system. Shows in both barns are perfect for the entire family. The casual, down-home atmosphere, with lots of folks joining in singing, tapping their feet and clapping with the music, is oblivious to fidgety kids and frequent needs to use the restroom.

You'll probably want to start your trip to Renfro Valley in the afternoon so you can visit Renfro Village, a replica of an old-time small Southern town. It features gift and candy shops, and craft stores displaying and selling the fine handiwork of many local artists and craftspeople.

There are several motels in the area, as well as a large KOA campground next door. Call the Rockcastle Tourist Commission for more information on lodging at (800) 252-6685.

Shaker Village of Pleasant Hill

I-734-5411

Comprising 33 19th-century buildings on 2,700 acres of Bluegrass farmland, Pleasant Hill is the largest of all restored Shaker Villages. This quaint settlement, 7 miles east of Harrodsburg and 25 miles southwest of Lexington on U.S. 60, was established in 1805 by a group of the United Society of Believers in Christ's Second Coming. This religious sect was better known by the name "Shakers" because of the energetic dances that played a big role in their religious ceremonies.

The Shakers were the largest and most well-known of the communal societies in 19th-century America. The Pleasant Hill settlement was an attempt of sorts to established a utopic community whose residents could pursue their religious beliefs and simple lifestyle in peace. An interesting aspect of Shaker life was that they believed in celibacy. Men and women worked, worshipped and slept in segregated quarters, and the only way they added to the population of the village was by adopting children into the community.

Practical and innovative, the Shakers are still known today for their economy, beauty and simplicity of style. They invented many time-saving devices, including the flat broom. The Shakers believed in equality of race and sex and freedom from prejudice.

By the middle of the 1800s, the Pleasant Hill community had grown to some 500 residents and 4,000 acres. Nationally, there were some 6,000 Shakers in the eastern United States, from Maine to Kentucky.

The society, however, dwindled during the last part of the 19th century, and the village at Pleasant Hill closed in 1910. The village sat unused for 50 years until restoration efforts began in 1961.

Today the Pleasant Hill community is open for tours throughout the year. While it takes about two hours to complete your self-guided tour of the village, to take in the whole village, from the working furniture, weaving, candlemaking and broom-making studios, to the riverboat excursion on the sternwheeler *Dixie Belle*, you should set aside the better part of a day for your exploration of Shaker Village at Pleasant Hill.

Shaker Village at Pleasant Hill is open year-round, except Christmas Eve and Christmas Day, 9:30 AM to 5 PM every day. While the village is open throughout the rest of the year, some of the exhibition buildings are closed November through March. Admission to the village is $8.50 for adults, $4 for ages 12-17, $2 for ages 6-11. Families are admitted for $22. For the combination riverboat excursion and village admission, the cost is $11.50 for adults, $6 for youth and $3 kids. Families pay $30. Kids younger than 6 are always admitted for free.

Below you'll find some detailed information about your stay at this beautiful and interesting piece of Kentucky and national history.

GROUP RESERVATIONS

With reservations, groups of 20 or more receive a special rate for entrance to the village. For group reservation information call 1-734-5411 Monday through Friday, 9 AM to 5 PM.

RIVERBOAT EXCURSIONS

A picturesque and relaxing addition to your visit to Pleasant Hill is a one-hour Kentucky River excursion on the sternwheeler *Dixie Belle*. Excursions leave from Shaker Landing on the Kentucky River at 10:30 AM, noon, 1:30 PM, 3 PM, 4:30 PM, and 6 PM April 19 through October 31. Special cruises are offered in the spring and fall, and the *Dixie Belle* is also available for charters.

All departure times are subject to weather conditions, special cruises and previous charters. Rates for the cruise only (excluding admission to the village) are $5.50 for adults, $3.50 for ages 12-17, and $2 for kids 6-11.

Dining

Traditional Kentucky country cuisine is served daily in the Trustee's Office at Pleasant Hill. Reservations are required, and there is a no-tipping policy.

The country buffet breakfast costs $7.50 per person, and there are seatings at 7:30, 8:30 and 9:30 AM.

For lunch, which ranges in price from $6.50 to $9.50, seatings are available at 11:30 AM, 1 and 2:30 PM.

Seatings for dinner, ranging in price from $13.25 to $17.75, are available daily at 5:30 and 7:30 PM, and on Sunday at noon, 1:45, 3:15, and 5:30 PM.

A children's menu is available. All first seatings are prompt, others are approximate. Call 1-734-5411 for reservations.

Lodging

Lodging on the grounds of Pleasant Hill is available in 15 restored buildings. For reservations, call 1-734-5411 Monday through Friday, 8 AM to 6 PM, and Saturday 8 AM to 4 PM.

Rates are $44-$90 single, $54-$100 double, and kids younger than 17 are free when staying with parents. MasterCard and Visa are accepted.

Winter Activities

Shaker Village offers several special activities and packages during the winter months (November to spring). Winter Teas are offered Monday through Friday. Call the general information number for reservations.

Winter Weekend Packages include lodging Friday and Saturday night, five meals, in-depth guided tours, seminars and special music presentations.

Winter Weekday Packages are available Sunday through Thursday nights and include one night's lodging, dinner and breakfast.

Big South Fork

(615) 879-3625
Big South Fork Recreation Area and National Park Service covers a big chunk of southeast Kentucky and northcentral Tennessee. The recreation area traces the waters of Big South Fork for more than 80 miles and covers some 125,000 acres of protected wild lands on the Cumberland Plateau.

With an area this immense, you could spend weeks here enjoying the dozens of outdoor recreational activities available, from swimming, canoeing and whitewater rafting, to hunting, hiking and horseback riding.

This author's suggestion is to decide on one or two activities you'd most enjoy, then pick the most favorable spots to do them. The Kentucky areas of Big South Fork Recreation Area are mostly within two to three hours' drive from Lexington. The Tennessee portions of the park can be a six- to seven-hour drive, depending on where you're headed.

Several activities you might enjoy are listed below.

Big South Fork Scenic Railway
Stearns   *(800) 462-5664*
Hopping on the Big South Fork Scenic Railway will give you an exciting trip to another time and another

culture as you "ride the rails" to the Blue Heron Outdoor Historical Museum of coal mining and logging life in the isolated regions of the Big South Fork River basin.

This unique museum includes frame structures you can visit and hear taped oral histories of families who lived in the immediate area where the museum now sits. Other displays include men working in underground coal mines and other aspects of mountain life.

The train ride itself is a beautiful three-hour trip through some of eastern Kentucky's lushest forests and mountain areas, so you'll want to be sure to bring your camera. The museum has a gift shop and snack bar. A "Coal Miner's Lunch," served in a souvenir red bandana and consisting of half a ham sandwich, half a turkey sandwich, cole slaw, fruit, dessert, and choice of drink, is available for $6 with advanced reservations.

Train fare is $8.95 for adults, $4.95 for kids younger than 12, and kids 3 and younger are admitted free. The scenic railway operates April through October with two daily trips on Saturdays and Sundays, and one trip on weekdays. Call for more detailed departure information.

HIKING

Big South Fork contains more than 150 miles of marked hiking trails, ranging in length from one mile to 50 miles, suitable for day hikes or backpack trips.

HUNTING AND FISHING

Both hunting and fishing are allowed within the recreation area and are subject to all state and federal regulations and licensing procedures. Because the recreation area covers parts of two states, make sure you hold valid licenses for each state in which you want to hunt or fish.

CAMPING

Primitive camping is allowed throughout most of the backcountry, except within marked safety zones, directly on the trail, or within 200 feet of paved roads and developed areas.

The Blue Heron Campground in Kentucky has 50 improved sites with water and a restroom/shower house.

WATER SPORTS

If you are interested in rafting (including for beginners and the entire family), beginner and family canoe trips, or whitewater raft or canoe trips in the Big South Fork area, call Sheltowee Trace Outfitters at (800) 541-RAFT. Rates for these trips range from $20 to $65 per person. Reservations are strongly suggested.

Inside
Neighbors Helping Neighbors

One of the nicest things about Lexington is that it has a lot of the characteristics of a big city—a strong cultural element, public transportation, major universities, and even, unfortunately, traffic — but it still maintains the feeling of a small town. Folks know their neighbors and their neighbors' granddaddies, and everyone went to school with everyone else, and played football and/or basketball together. There is a strong sense of community, and because of that, there is an equally strong sense of responsibility for the common good of the community.

Which is a really roundabout way of saying that people in Lexington like to get involved in their community, whether it's sitting on a school council, selling hotdogs at a soccer game, teaching someone how to read, or donating blood. There are hundreds of clubs, groups and organizations that represent thousands of opportunities for Lexingtonians to get involved and volunteer their time and expertise for the betterment of the community.

There is a strong commitment here to the idea of neighbors helping neighbors. And the evidence of this commitment can be seen everyday and in virtually every circumstance.

Folks getting together, for instance, to build creative playgrounds at city parks for local youngsters. Or a couple dozen people turning up early on a cold Saturday morning to construct a home for Habitat for Humanity. Or members of the local 4-Wheelers Club transporting medical and emergency personnel to work in the midst of a winter storm.

If you're trying to figure out how to get involved, there are a couple of questions you might ask yourself. What needs do I see in my immediate neighborhood, my kids' school, my church? What do I enjoy doing? What skills do I have to offer? How much free time do I have?

Once you identify a need you are interested in helping to fill and you have determined what skills, time and other resources you have or have access to that will help you fill that need, you're well on your way to Community Involvement. It is at this point, however, that you'll probably come up against a barrier. How do you go about doing what you see needs to be done?

One of the main answers to this question is that there is likely to be a group in Lexington that is either addressing the need in some other area or some other way, or is interested in doing so and is just waiting

Photo: Lexington Herald-Leader

Volunteers from the Ashmoor neighborhood assemble a new playground set in the Hickman Creek Ribbon Park.

for someone like you to come along with the extra excitement and energy to make the project fly.

So how do you get in touch with these groups?

We suggest starting with a couple of larger "umbrella" agencies, such as the United Way of the Bluegrass, the Volunteer Center of the Bluegrass, your local school council, or the American Red Cross' "Ask Us" hot line.

This chapter will detail some of the information and referral services offered by these umbrella groups as well as giving some specific information on a cross-section of groups and volunteer opportunities in the area. It is by no means a comprehensive listing. Rather, the listing is designed to give newcomers to the area an idea of the variety of projects and activities in which they can get involved.

UNITED WAY OF THE BLUEGRASS

227 North Upper Street   *233-4460*

The United Way of the Bluegrass serves a vital need in the Greater Lexington area: raising money to allocate to area service agencies for their operation. The list of agencies The United Way of the Bluegrass helps finance in its eight-county service area runs the gamut from literacy training and education to programs for kids and services for the homeless.

Last year, United Way of the Bluegrass raised about $6 million to support 200 member agencies in Anderson, Bourbon, Clark, Fayette, Jessamine, Madison, Montgomery and Scott counties.

AMERICAN RED CROSS "ASK US"
255-2374

This program of the American Red Cross provides an invaluable service to Central Kentuckians in its role as an information and referral clearinghouse for hundreds of community groups. This hot line is open Monday through Friday, 9 AM-7 PM, and it links 22,000 callers to social and community services each year.

The program was started in 1972 as part of the Suburban Woman's Club to help fill the big need in the community to link people with the services they need. "Ask Us" also publishes a comprehensive *Community Services Directory* every few years that is an invaluable resource for people dealing with social and community service organizations.

VOLUNTEER CENTER OF THE BLUEGRASS

2029 Bellefonte Drive   278-6258

The Volunteer Center of the Bluegrass is the heart of Lexington's volunteerism connection and referral efforts. The center keeps files on the volunteer needs of hundreds of area agencies and organizations. People who are looking for ways to become volunteers call the center, and staff members there work to match up the volunteer's skills and interests with the needs it has on file.

Special volunteer placement programs include the Retired Senior Volunteer Program and the University of Kentucky Student Volunteer Center. The Volunteer Center of the Bluegrass also provides training sessions and sponsors annual awards for volunteer efforts in the community.

There is no reasonable way to present or even attempt a comprehensive list of community organizations in which you might want to become involved, but described be-

low is a sampling of some the Lexington organizations you may want to join. Not all are community service organizations — some are social, some are trade, and some are just for fun. But what they all have in common is that they provide the space in which Lexingtonians from diverse backgrounds and experiences can join together with their neighbors and experience the true spirit of "community."

OPERATION READ INC.

251 West Second Street   254-9964

Giving someone the gift of literacy is one of the most rewarding and exciting examples of neighbors helping neighbors. This nonprofit organization, headquartered in the Carnegie Center for Literacy and Learning, was started by a group of concerned citizens in 1979 as an outgrowth of the Lexington Public Library.

The services provided by Operation Read serve a great need both locally and across the state. Some 400,000 Kentuckians cannot read a newspaper, job application, or even the warning label on an aspirin bottle. In Lexington alone, there are an estimated 22,000 adults who cannot read above a sixth-grade level. The mission of Operation Read is to help those 22,000 neighbors achieve a level of functional literacy that is the first step toward an enriched life.

Operation Read has a number of volunteer needs that range from serving as a reading tutor to helping with fund raising and publicity or donating money for operating costs. Last year, Operation Read served

269 students, trained 160 tutors, and recorded 20,574 volunteer hours.

LEXINGTON CREATIVE CAMERA CLUB
278-2591

Whether you're really into photography or you're just looking for a creative and interesting hobby the whole family can enjoy, the Lexington Creative Camera Club might be what you've been waiting for. The group began about 13 years ago, and today has close to 75 members. Meetings are held the third Thursday of the month at the Kentucky Tech campus on Leestown Road from 7 PM to 10 PM. Meetings include a presentation on a specific area of photography, such as portraiture, weddings or commercial work.

Additionally, the club sponsors competitions throughout the year, and members display their work at the club's annual print show, usually held at the University of Kentucky Student Center in November. Weekend workshops provide hands-on work with a variety of subjects, and are usually held at various outdoor locations in the region.

Membership in the club costs $22 a year for individuals, and $28 a year for families.

AIDS VOLUNTEERS OF LEXINGTON
P.O. Box 431   254-2865

As the number of people affected by HIV and AIDS continues to grow in our country and in our community, so does the need for caring, concerned neighbors to volunteer a few hours of their week to help people cope with this disease.

AIDS Volunteers of Lexington, AVOL, was started in 1987 to serve the needs of people in Lexington and Central and Eastern Kentucky. AVOL offers a wide range of services, from education about the disease to emotional support. Some of the confidential support groups AVOL offers include HIV+ Individuals, Partners of HIV+ Individuals, Caregivers of AIDS Patients, and Family and Friends Support Group.

If you have a few spare hours a week, you can help AVOL provide these vital services to the community. Volunteer hours are flexible, and training and support are provided. Volunteer opportunities include providing office, telephone and clerical support, assisting with transportation of clients, serving as Buddies for HIV/AIDS clients, presenting community education programs, and offering telephone assurance and help with hospital visits.

LA LECHE LEAGUE
266-8789, 223-3389, (800) LA LECHE

The La Leche League of Lexington is part of an international organization that offers information and encouragement to women who want to breastfeed their babies. The organization was founded in 1956 by seven women who wanted to make breastfeeding easier and more rewarding for both mother and child.

Locally, the organization offers women help with breastfeeding problems, answers questions mothers have about nursing their babies, and provides mother-to-mother support for adjusting to the new role of being a parent.

The La Leche League of Lexington has monthly informal meetings where mothers and their babies gather to meet other mothers and keep up-to-date on current information about breastfeeding and parenting. There is an evening group that meets the second Friday of every month at 7:30 PM, and a morning group that meets the third Thursday of the month at 10 AM.

LEXINGTON RAPE CRISIS CENTER

P.O. Box 1603, 40592   253-2615
Crisis hot line   253-2511

Providing emotional, legal and medical support for victims of sexual assault and their families, the Lexington Rape Crisis Center has a number of volunteer needs that range from staffing a 24-hour crisis hot line to counseling victims of sexual abuse and assault.

The center holds volunteer training sessions throughout the year, and needs people to volunteer for a number of areas, including accompanying people to court or meeting victims at hospitals, and providing follow-up services and referrals to other agencies.

Among the services provided by the Lexington Rape Crisis Center are crisis intervention counseling, support groups for women recovering from rape and child sexual abuse, advocacy services for victims of abuse, and a therapy and individual counseling program.

HABITAT FOR HUMANITY

219 East Short Street   252-2224

What more basic need can you help provide than a clean, new, affordable place to live? The Lexington chapter of Habitat for Humanity does just that — helping families build modest homes with volunteer labor and donated construction materials from the community.

Many area churches and service organizations have a continuing commitment to the work of Habitat for Humanity, but there is always a need for more volunteers. If you can heft a hammer, wire a house, or tote two-by-fours, Habitat for Humanity can use you. Check local media announcements for house building projects or call the office for more information.

LIONS CLUB

809 Glendover Road   266-8727

Started in 1921, the Lexington Lions Club (175 members strong) is the city's original Lions Club. Today, however, there are a total of five clubs in town. To find out the meeting times of the club that best suits your schedule, call Jim Alcorn at the number listed above. Lexington Lions and Lionesses are involved with numerous fund-raising events to generate money to support a wide range of charities, from the eyesight conservation program (to date the club has purchased more than 700 pairs of eyeglasses for people who need them but can't afford them), to youth camps for blind children and kids with diabetes.

The Lexington Lions Club's primary fund-raising event of the year is the Lions Bluegrass Fair, held each June at Masterson Station Park.

GAY AND LESBIAN
SERVICES ORGANIZATION

P.O. Box 11471   231-0335

From funding, planning and sponsoring events during Gay Pride Week each year to offering programs that educate the public about issues related to gay and lesbian people, the Gay and Lesbian Services Organization is dedicated to providing educational, emotional support and referral services to Lexingtonians.

Started in 1977, GLSO is the oldest continually operating gay and lesbian services organization in Kentucky. There are many ways to get involved, whether you're looking for ways to volunteer in the community or to participate in social and recreational activities. Membership is $10 for individuals and $15 for couples.

Inside
Activities and Services for Older Adults

As the number of people in the "55 and older" category grows daily, Lexington is working hard to meet the needs and wishes of this expanding segment of our population. New challenges, new opportunities, and an entirely new perspective on life and community are some of the efforts to keep older adults a viable part of the Lexington community.

As one elderly Lexingtonian said of the retirement community he lives in, "It's fascinating to observe the entirely new social structure that is developing where large groups of retired and older people are living, working and socializing together."

Lexington is responding to this relatively new population through a variety of activities, work and volunteer programs, health-care services and social-service programs targeted specifically at Lexingtonians older than age 55. Education and special interest classes and workshops are offered through the Elderhostel Program and the Donovan Scholars Program at the University of Kentucky. Recreational activities, trips, classes and volunteer opportunities are provided by a number of agencies and organizations, ranging from the Lexington Senior Citizens Center to the American Red Cross.

There are programs that encourage local businesses to hire retired and older people, advocacy programs, and nutritional and health assistance programs.

But Lexington programs are not limited to services provided to or for older adults. This is by no means a segment of the Lexington community that needs to be "taken care of." Retirement does not mean an end to one's effectual contribution to society. Many Lexington organizations and programs focus on what older adults can do for Lexington. The Service Corps of Retired Executives (SCORE), for instance, works through the Small Business Administration to use the expertise of retired business people to help local people starting or operating small businesses.

What is listed in this chapter is as comprehensive an overview of services and programs for older and retired Lexingtonians as is possible. Areas of focus include programs and organizations of and for older adults, services (medical/nutritional, advocacy, and government assistance), and residences (retirement communities, nursing homes, and apartments). You will also find a section dealing with education, job placement and volunteer opportunities.

Programs and Organizations

BELL HOUSE SENIOR CITIZENS CENTER

Sayre Avenue   223-0986

The Division of Parks and Recreation operates this senior citizens activity center in Bell Mansion. The wide range of cultural, recreational and social activities offers something for everyone. Activities include ceramics, oil painting, crafts, aerobics, bowling, square dancing, bingo, and day and overnight trips.

The center, located near a bus line, is open 9 AM-5 PM and is handicapped accessible. Programs are open to anyone 60 years old or older, and a lifetime membership costs only $2!

You can get more information on two other senior citizen activities centers through the Bell House. These are:

LAFAYETTE CENTER

Lafayette Christian Church, 1836 Clays Mill Road

CONNIE GRIFFITH MANOR AND BALLARD PLACE

540 West Second Street

Both of these centers offer activities and trips.

LEXINGTON SENIOR CITIZENS CENTER

1530 Nicholasville Road   278-6072

The Lexington Senior Citizens Center serves as a clearinghouse for information on services for older adults. Among the services offered are information, referral, recreational, social and some health services to any Fayette Countian 60 and older. The center operates Monday-Friday, 8 AM-5 PM. Senior groups can schedule meeting space during the day, and the center is available in the evenings and on weekends for rental.

The Division of Parks and Recreation runs a recreation and education program at the center, which includes activities such as exercise, day trips, arts and crafts, square dancing, bridge and area history classes.

Among the programs in the center (but not necessarily part of the center) are the following:

• **Center for Creative Living**, which offers medical care, supervision, counseling, social activities and therapy for about 30 people each day. To be eligible for this program, a person must be a Fayette County resident age 60 or older and must have a need for mental, physical or social health care during the day in order to remain at home (as opposed to entering a long-term care facility). There is a sliding scale cost based on income.

• **Bluegrass Community Services**, also known as the Elder Nutrition Program, provides daily noon meals and nutritional education for older people, as well as transportation to and from the Nutrition Center and limited essential trips, such as grocery shopping. Family-style meals are served Monday-Friday at four Lexington locations — the Senior Citizens Center, Black and Williams Cultural Center (498 Georgetown Street), Dunbar Center (545 North Upper Street), and the Carver Center (522 Patterson Street). Call 277-6141 for more information.

• **Bluegrass Long-term Care Ombudsman Program**, 278-6072, Ext. 322, can answer questions con-

Seniors 65 and over can further their education through the University of Kentucky's free Donovan Scholars Program.

cerning the quality of care and information about nursing homes as well as working to solve problems through ombudsmen in local nursing homes.

• **Retired Senior Volunteer Program** (RSVP), 278-6072, Ext. 324, is for people 60 and older who want to volunteer their time and abilities to help other Central Kentuckians. Volunteers are transported to and from the location they are offering their services upon request.

• **Meals on Wheels** provides a hot noon meal, breakfast cereal, milk, juice and a supper snack to homebound people in Fayette County. Meals are delivered from 11:30 AM to 12:30 PM Monday-Friday. Alternative meals are available for those on special diets. There is a weekly sliding scale cost for the meals, and the maximum cost per week is $18 or $21.25 for special diets. Call 278-6072, Ext. 307 Monday-Friday, 8:30 AM-12:30 PM for more information.

MANCHESTER CENTER
1026 Manchester Street   255-1047
The center's activities are open to those 55 and older at no cost. There are fees, however, for trips and ceramics. The center operates Tuesday-Friday, 10 AM-2 PM, and transportation is available for folks living in Davistown, Woodward Heights,

Speigle Heights, and on Thompson Road and Bennett Avenue.

CENTRAL ADULT DAY CENTER
219 East Short Street   254-5300
For people 60 and older who need assistance with daily living activities, Central Adult Day Center provides mentally and physically stimulating activities and a hot lunch Monday-Friday, 7:30 AM-5:30 PM. This program is specifically designed for those people who cannot function independently but do not require rehabilitative or nursing home care. People of any age who have memory disorders are also accepted into this program. There is a sliding scale fee charged based on income.

AMERICAN ASSOCIATION OF RETIRED PERSONS (AARP)
1513 Port Royal   277-5365
The Lexington AARP chapter meets once a month at the Bell House (see address above). Nationally, AARP is a lobbying organization to influence legislation dealing with issues of specific concern to retired people and senior citizens. Anyone older than 50 can join, and annual dues are $5 national and $2 local.

BLUEGRASS RETIRED OFFICERS ASSOCIATION
3220 Pepperhill Drive   266-8710
This local chapter of The Retired

Officers Association (TROA) meets monthly to conduct a short business session and then to enjoy a dinner and guest speaker. Membership is open to active, retired and former officers and warrant officers in any of the U.S. uniformed services. Surviving spouses of officers can join the organization as auxiliary members. Annual dues are $20 national and $10 local.

BLUEGRASS RETIRED
TEACHERS ASSOCIATION
c/o Bell House, Sayre Avenue   233-0986

This is part of a state and national organization of retired educators. Members meet monthly and participate in group activities. Members are also eligible for such benefits as insurance, pharmaceutical, travel and educational programs. Local dues are $5/year, state dues are $15/year, and national dues are $5/year.

ELDERCRAFTSMEN
Black and Williams Center
498 Georgetown Street   252-1288

Open 10 AM-2 PM Monday-Thursday, the Eldercraftsmen program schedules a variety of activities for seniors, from crafts and ceramics to special interest courses. Anyone age 55 or older is eligible to join, and there is a $6 annual membership fee, plus fees to cover the cost of materials for special projects.

GOLDEN K KIWANIS CLUBS
4794 Hartland Parkway   273-4005
732 Providence   269-1751

There are two local chapters of this national community service organization, which is open to people of retirement age. Anyone is eligible to join, and there are annual and program dues, depending on the club.

SERVICE CORPS OF RETIRED
EXECUTIVES (SCORE)
1460 Newtown Pike, Suite A   231-9902

Members of this organization volunteer their time and expertise in the business field by advising and helping people running or starting a small business in the area. Sponsored by the Small Business Administration, SCORE is open to any retired executive. There is no cost to join, and the office is open Monday-Friday, 9 AM-noon.

Lexington's older adults are also eligible for a number of special discount programs to everything from programs by local school kids to taxi and bus rides. Following are some of the discounted and free programs available. In addition to these, most local attractions and arts organizations offer senior discounts of 10 percent-50 percent off regular admission.

GOLD CARDS FOR SENIORS

This card entitles those 65 and older to free admission to programs of the Fayette County Public Schools. Call 281-0108 for more information.

OLDER KENTUCKIANS
DISCOUNT CARD

If you are a Kentucky resident age 60 or older, or disabled, you are eligible for this card, which entitles you to special discounts from participating merchants and other organizations. To get your card, contact the Outreach Worker at the

Lexington Senior Citizens Center, 278-6072.

LexTran (public bus system)

If you are 65 or older, you can get a special ID card from the Lexington Transit Authority that entitles you to 50 percent-60 percent discount off bus and trolley rides. There are also special transportation options available for seniors and those with permanent disabilities. See Getting Around for more detailed information on these services, or call LexTran at 252-4936.

Taxis

United Transportation Inc. (which operates the Lexington taxi services) offers coupon booklets for 20 percent discounts off taxi rides for senior citizens. Call 233-4890 for more information.

Services

Bluegrass Area Agency on Aging

South Park
3220 Nicholasville Road   272-6656

Part of a national network of area agencies on aging who plan, coordinate and advocate for older people, the Bluegrass chapter works to develop local systems of social, nutritional and in-home services to assist the elderly.

Kentucky Medical Assistance Program (KMAP)

1179 Winburn Drive   253-1500

Based on financial need (determined by state and federal guidelines), you may be eligible for KMAP's services, which include medical assistance to the elderly, blind or disabled. This office is also responsible for Medicaid.

Social Security Administration

1460 Newtown Pike   (800) 772-1213

This office administers several monthly income programs including Social Security Retirement Benefits, Supplemental Security Income, and Medicare. There are specific age, income and status requirements for these programs, so call the office for more detailed information.

Central Kentucky Hearing Aid Bank

P.O. Box 24384   278-2810

Based on your financial need, you may be eligible for this nonprofit organization's service, which is to provide hearing aids for those who cannot afford them. There is a $20 administrative cost for this service.

Eyeglasses

Lexington-Fayette County
Health Department
650 Newtown Pike   252-2371, Ext. 314

For those who are medically indigent, the Health Department works with the Lions Club to provide free eye exams and glasses. Applications are available at the Health Department.

Elderly Health Maintenance Clinics

Health Department
650 Newtown Pike   252-2371, Ext. 319

Fayette County residents 60 and older are eligible to participate in these nurse-conducted health clinics held 12 times a month throughout the community. Check the news-

Photo: Lexington Herald-Leader

Walkers can find many exercise opportunities around Lexington.

paper for specific times and locations, which change monthly. Medical services provided include blood pressure monitoring, evaluation, help with diet and prescriptions, and referrals to physicians and other health services. There is no charge for the clinic, but contributions are welcome.

GERIATRIC CLINIC (UNIVERSITY OF KENTUCKY MEDICAL CENTER)

D233 Medical Plaza,
800 Rose Street   233-5365
For new patient appointments   233-5550

This interdisciplinary geriatric team approach clinic includes evaluations by a geriatrician, social worker, pharmacist and nurse specialist. Services are available to those 65 and older who would benefit from care by such an interdisciplinary team. The evaluation clinic is held Wednesday mornings, and the continuing care clinic is on Monday mornings. The cost of the program varies according to the types of services provided. Medicare and Medicaid are accepted. For more information and for new patient appointments, contact the Sanders-Brown Center on Aging at 233-5550.

The Sanders-Brown Center on Aging also houses the the Alzheimer's Disease Research Center, which is one of 28 programs federally funded and designated by the National Institute on Aging. In addition to the center's primary focus on Alzheimer's research, it also provides a range of services to the Central Kentucky community, including information and referral, respite care, support groups and a Memory Disorders Clinic. Call Barbara Helm at 233-6040 for more information.

GERIATRIC SUPPORT SERVICES

Sanders-Brown Center on Aging
915 South Limestone   233-6422

This interdisciplinary geriatric team represents dentistry, medicine, pharmacy and social work. Services are provided to patients and their caregivers both in the home and at the University of Kentucky Geriatric Clinic. The team does not offer home health care, but team members visit patients' homes to assess and monitor safety, medications and other needs. The program is open to anyone 65 or older who would benefit from such a program. Fees vary according to what is provided.

There are times when you may feel an injustice has been done to you, whether it was discrimination on the job or being unfairly treated by someone with whom you were doing business. Listed here are several agencies that can help you deal with problems such as these.

Insiders like leisurely drives on roads that have "Mill" in their names.

BETTER BUSINESS BUREAU OF CENTRAL & EASTERN KENTUCKY

311 West Short Street   259-1008
                              (800) 866-6668

If you're looking for information on the reliability of local and national businesses or other consumer topics, the Better Business Bureau is the place to turn. Office hours are 8:30 AM-4:30 PM and phone hours are 9:30 AM-3:30 PM, Monday-Friday.

DEPARTMENT FOR SOCIAL SERVICES

710 West High Street   253-0656

This agency investigates reports of abuse, neglect or exploitation. It also offers information about and referral help with nursing home placement.

LEXINGTON-FAYETTE URBAN COUNTY HUMAN RIGHTS COMMISSION

162 East Main Street, Suite 226   252-4931

If you are between the ages of 40 and 70, you are covered by the age discrimination law of Kentucky, as well as that of the federal government. This agency deals with cases of discrimination because of age in employment, housing and public accommodation.

Residences

There are a number of housing options for people of retirement age and the elderly in Lexington. Listed in this section you will find apartment complexes, retirement complexes and nursing homes. There is also information about services available to those older adults who live in their own homes but need assistance

from time to time.

The following rent-subsidized apartment complexes are open to people older than 50 who are able to live independently, as well as to disabled people. There is a sliding scale cost according to income. The apartment units are unfurnished, but each kitchen is equipped with a stove and refrigerator. Each complex has programs and activities for its residents. Most of the complexes have waiting lists for admission, so those wanting to apply for residence are encouraged to do so as soon as possible.

Briarwood Apartments, 1349 Centre Parkway, 272-3421

Christ Church Apartments, 137 Rose Street, 254-7762

Christian Towers Apartments, 1511 Versailles Road, 253-3625

Emerson Center, 2050 Garden Springs Road, 278-0526

Malabu Manor Apartments, 145 Malabu Drive, 278-5111

Ballard Place, 635 Ballard Place, 281-5060, 281-5054 hearing impaired

Connie Griffith Manor, 540 West Second Street, 281-5060, 281-5054 hearing impaired

Sayre Christian Village, 3816 Camelot Drive, 273-1845

Main Street Baptist Church Manor, 428 Darby Creek Road, 263-5153

Central Christian Church Apartments, 249 East Short Street, 252-3671

Lexington also has several community living options for people who want to and are able to live independently but want the comfort and socialization of living in a small community setting.

These retirement communities are quite luxurious, and in many cases, quite costly. However, they offer all the creature comforts and conveniences of a small, self-contained community, offering everything from hair salons and medical care stations to full-service, white tablecloth restaurants, golf, craft and art studios, libraries and exercise rooms.

LAFAYETTE RETIREMENT COMMUNITY
690 Mason Headley Road   259-1331

Lafayette Retirement Community, opened in 1985, is made up of three types of living arrangements for senior citizens and retirees. The independent living section is designed for those people who do not need assistance, but who want to live in a secure and friendly community setting. The Ambassador Club members receive some assistance in the performance of daily living activities, but they are still able to live independently for the most part in their own apartments. The health care facility has 111 skilled nursing beds, and it is designed for those people who need supervised health care and are unable to live independently.

The retirement community has 100 apartments available. Monthly rents are $1,425 for one-bedroom units, and $1,700 for two-bedroom units. Included in this monthly rate are all utilities (except cable TV and telephone), two meals per day, transportation anywhere within Fayette County, weekly housekeeping and linen service.

Lafayette plans a variety of programs, parties, trips and entertainment for residents throughout the year. Other amenities include 24-hour security, an exercise room and 10 free days in the health center per year.

RICHMOND PLACE
3051 Rio Dosa Road   269-6308

Located in southern Lexington far enough away from the "main drag" to be serene and picturesque, yet close enough to be convenient, Richmond Place offers its residents full-scale retirement living including a comprehensive health-care plan.

Apartment options range from studios (480 square feet) to two-bedrooms (1,064 square feet), and these are priced from $1,100-$1,835 per month. The monthly rent price includes one meal per day, weekly housekeeping, utilities, maintenance, security, and use of the fitness center, heated pool, library, putting green, tennis court, walking and jogging paths, and woodworking shop.

The on-site wellness program offers a range of health-care services from optical and podiatry care to pharmaceutical and emotional well-being services. There is also a convenience store and beauty salon/barber shop at the facility.

MAYFAIR VILLAGE
3310 Tates Creek Road   266-2129

Conveniently located just across the street from a branch of the public library, restaurants, banks, doctor and dental offices, specialty shops and boutiques, Mayfair Village offers many of the amenities you'd look for in a retirement community. From 24-hour security and weekly housekeeping to delicious and nutritious meals, a full calendar of planned activities and transportation, Mayfair Village has a lot to offer its residents.

Mayfair Village offers 10 floor plans, ranging from a studio to a luxurious penthouse. Independent living apartments include all utilities, maintenance and upkeep, transportation, weekly housekeeping, and a meal allowance. Monthly rates range from $1,236 for a single studio apartment to $2,546 for a double occupancy penthouse. Personal care unit prices range from $36 to $120 per day. Apartments come equipped with a solarium or terrace, individually governed heat and air conditioning and kitchen appliances.

ASHLAND TERRACE RETIREMENT HOME
475 South Ashland Avenue   266-2581

For women 65 and older who are ambulatory and able to take care of themselves, Ashland Terrace offers a homey community living option. The $600/month rent includes three meals a day, planned activities, and weekly linen and housekeeping services. There are 21 units in this nonprofit facility.

FRIENDSHIP TOWERS
580 Greenfield Drive   271-9000

Part of the Sayre Christian Village Complex, Friendship Towers offers moderately priced apartment units equipped with electric heat, air conditioners, carpet, curtains, electric range, refrigerator and cable TV hook-up. To be eligible, you must be 55 or older and able to live independently. There are no income requirements.

Lexington has more than two dozen nursing homes and facilities that offer assisted living at several levels. According to licensing guidelines, nursing homes are divided into three categories: family care homes, personal care homes, and nursing facilities.

Family care homes are private homes that provide rooms, meals and some personal assistance for two or three people. Residents must be able to live independently. Medicare and Medicaid do not pay for family care homes. A complete list of family care homes in the area is available from the Department of Social Services or the Long-term Care Ombudsmen Program (addresses and phone numbers are listed at the end of this section).

Personal care homes are designed for those who can basically care for themselves but need to live in a protected environment. These facilities offer meals, rooms and some personal assistance, but there are usually no professional nurses on duty. Medicare and Medicaid do not cover these services, but there is money available from the state to cover some situations. Again, call one of the help numbers at the end of this section for specific questions. Among Lexington's personal care homes are the following:

The Clairmont, 1121 Tanbark Road, 273-7377

Richmond Place, 3051 Rio Dosa Drive, 269-6308

Homestead Nursing Home, 1608 Versailles Road, 252-0871

Hayden's Personal Care Home, 553 East Third Street, 233-1944

Glen Arvin, 444 Glen Arvin, 255-4606

Arnett Pritchett Home of the YMCA. 319 Duke Road, 266-6031

Nursing facilities offer intermediate or skilled nursing care. A person must have a doctor's orders and must require daily nursing intervention to be eligible for admission. Medicare and Medicaid may pay for some nursing services in these facilities. The following are among Lexington's nursing facilities:

Heartland Health Care Center, 1537 North Limestone, 252-6673

Good Samaritan Hospital, 310 South Limestone, 252-6612

Lexington Country Place, 700 Mason Headley Road, 259-3486

Lexington Manor Health Care Facility, 353 Waller Avenue, 252-3558

Mayfair Manor, 3300 Tates Creek Road, 266-2126

Christian Health Center, 1500 Trent Boulevard, 272-2273

Darby Square, 2770 Palumbo Drive, 263-2410

Rose Manor Intermediate Health Care Facility, 3057 Cleveland Road, 299-4117

Sayre Christian Village Nursing Home, 3840 Camelot Drive, 272-1845

Tanbark, 1121 Tanbark Road, 273-7337

The following are both personal care homes and nursing facilities:

Meadowbrook, 2020 Cambridge Drive, 252-6747

Tates Creek Health Care Center, 3576 Pimlico Parkway, 272-0608

For help in choosing a nursing home or to report complaints about the quality of care provided by such facilities, contact one of the following agencies:

Kentucky Association of Health Care Facilities, 9403 Mill Brook Road, Louisville, (502) 425-5000

Bluegrass Long-term Care Ombudsman, 1530 Nicholasville Road, 278-6072, Ext. 322

Department for Social Services, 710 West High Street, 253-0656

Office of Inspector General, 627 West Fourth Street, 255-4414

If you choose to stay in your own home, but sometimes feel the need for a little added security or perhaps medical assistance, Lexington has several programs that offer everything from home health care to someone to talk to if you're feeling lonely or concerned or just want to pass the time of day. Some of these programs are described below.

Insiders like running in the Bluegrass 10,000
on July 4.

HELPING HANDS

801 South Limestone, Suite E   252-6282

This is basically a day-care center for people diagnosed with Alzheimer's Disease or other non-treatable memory disorders. The local Alzheimer's Association operates the center Monday through Saturday at the Second Presbyterian Church, and there is a sliding-scale fee for the program. An in-home respite program is also available.

AMERICAN RED CROSS

1450 Newtown Pike   253-1331

The Bluegrass Area Chapter of the American Red Cross offers several programs for older adults that are free. The Carrier Alert program, coordinated through the U.S. Postal Service, arranges for your postal carrier to alert the Red Cross if you are not picking up your mail. This service is available to people living alone. The Hello Daily Line, for the elderly and disabled who are homebound, arranges for someone who shares your interests to call you at scheduled times throughout the week to chat. This is a good volunteer opportunity as well. Additionally, because the calls are scheduled, if you do not answer the phone at the agreed-upon time, the Hello Daily volunteer will alert the Red Cross.

KELLY ASSISTED LIVING SERVICES

333 Waller Avenue, Suite 100   255-2297

This service offers in-home help with such things as meal preparation, light housekeeping, laundry, transportation, personal care and companionship. Services are available 24 hours a day, seven days a week at a per-service cost.

SENIOR COMPANION PROGRAM

3445A Versailles Road,
Frankfort   (800) 456-6571

This program is great both for those folks who need a companion and helper for daily living activities and for those who want to spend some time each week helping the homebound elderly. To be eligible to get a companion, you must be older than 60 and live alone. To be a companion (for which you are paid a small hourly stipend for about 20 hours a week), you must be over 60 and have a limited income. Companions provide such services as personal care, meal preparation, errand running and escorting services. There is no charge for this program.

Another service that might be helpful for those living alone is emergency signaling devices that operate through your telephone to alert a monitoring station when you are in trouble at home. The devices, which can be worn or carried with you, are available for rent for $15-$50/month.

There are three basic local systems available: Life Line of Central Baptist Hospital, 275-6100; Link to Life of Grogans Healthcare Supply, 254-6661; and Perfect Companion of the Humana Seniors Program (you must be a member of the program to rent this system), 268-3753.

Finally, there are about a dozen local agencies that offer services to homebound people ranging from nursing care to speech therapy. Some of these agencies also provide live-in companions and homemaker services. Most accept Medicare and Medicaid as payment. Following is a list of those agencies.

American Nursing Care and Home Health Providers, 851 Corporate Drive, Suite 100, 224-1979

Bluegrass Home Health Agency, 650 Newtown Pike, 288-2331

Caretenders of the Bluegrass, Bob-O-Link Drive, Suite 100, 276-5369

Central Baptist Hospital Home Health Services, 270 Southland Drive, 275-6569

Medical Personnel Pool, 1051 Red Mile Road, 231-7222

Nurses Registry and Home Health, 607 South Broadway, 255-4411

Olsten Healthcare, 900 North Broadway, 252-1032

Spectra Care of Lexington, 274 Southland Drive, 276-1417

University of Kentucky Homecare, 357 Waller Avenue, 233-5196

Volunteer, Education, and Other Activities

From updating your driving skills to starting a new career, Lexington has quite a few opportunities for older adults to go to college, volunteer their time and skills or just get together and have fun doing something they enjoy. In this section, a few of these opportunities are described.

CAREERS AFTER SIXTY
Lexington Senior Citizens Center
1530 Nicholasville Road 278-6072, Ext. 320
If you are older than 60 and would like help finding a full- or part-time job, call the Careers After Sixty office between 9 AM and noon on weekdays.

HIRE OLDER WORKERS
1530 Nicholasville Road 278-6072, Ext. 323
To be eligible for this program, you must be a Fayette County resident 55 or older with a limited income (specific guidelines apply). This program offers job referral and placement, workshops, occupational training, assessment and testing.

Book Buddies

Lexington Public Library
140 East Main Street   *231-5592*

This program pairs up volunteers and homebound people older than 50 who have chronic disabilities. Homebound participants receive two visits a month from their Book Buddies, who bring books, records or tapes from the public library. Volunteers must go through a training program and submit to a police check.

Donovan Scholars Program

Ligon House
University of Kentucky   *257-2656*

The Donovan Scholars Program is a great way for folks older than 65 to go to college. The program provides tuition-free education at the University of Kentucky for people older than 65. Other special noncredit course are offered, including the Forum on Tuesday and Thursday afternoons, Great Discussions book groups, writing workshops and a radio drama group. The only expenses that might be incurred are those associated with textbooks, special materials for classes, and travel.

Kentucky Elderhostel

110 Maxwelton Court   *257-5234*

For people 60 and older or whose participating spouse or companion is 60 or older, Kentucky Elderhostel offers a broad range of exciting and interesting classes and programs throughout the state in cooperation with universities, community colleges, education agencies, state resort parks and environmental centers. These weeklong residential education programs cost an average of $275 per week, which includes the course, lodging, recreations and food. Scholarships are available.

Inside
Hospitals and Medical Care

*I*t may sound rather morbid, but Lexington is a good place to get sick.

With seven general hospitals and four special service hospitals prepared to deal with everything from broken legs and newborn babies to major heart surgery and drug addiction, Lexington is fortunate to have a wide variety of health care options available.

Places Rated Almanac — which surveys some 300 major American metropolitan areas — has listed Lexington among the Top Ten in the nation in terms of health care availability. Some 1,400 physicians — representing each specialty recognized by the American Board of Medical Specialties — and more than 260 dentists place Lexington well above the national doctor to number of residents ratio average.

Lexington is the site of many pioneering medical efforts in the state, nation and the world. The state's only bone-marrow transplant program can be found at the University of Kentucky's Chandler Medical Center (part of the University of Kentucky Hospital), as can the first non-prototype Magnetic Resonance Imaging diagnostic system in the world. Lexington's Shriners Hospital for Crippled Children is one of only 19 Shriners orthopedic hospitals in the world. Fayette County was the first county in the state to offer HIV antibody testing and anonymous testing for HIV infection.

In terms of general medical assistance, a couple of phone numbers that may help include 911 for emergency service and Saint Joseph Hospital's Ask-A-Nurse 24-hour free and confidential information and referral hotline, 278-3444.

Also, for minor emergency and no-appointment doctor visits, you might try one of Lexington's Urgent Treatment Centers. There are three locations: North Park — 1498 Boardwalk, 254-5520, open 8 AM-8 PM Monday through Friday, 8 AM-6 PM Saturday; Lansdowne — 1055 Dove Run Road, 269-4668, open 8 AM-10 PM every day; and Park Hills — 3174 Custer Drive, 272-4882, open 8 AM-8 PM Monday through Friday, 8 AM-6 PM Saturday.

The listings in this chapter detail some of the services offered by local hospitals as well as by the Fayette County Health Department. For more information on individual physicians by specialty, check the Yellow Pages of the phone book.

LEXINGTON-FAYETTE COUNTY HEALTH DEPARTMENT

650 Newtown Pike   *252-2371*

Governed by the Board of Health, which meets monthly, the Lexington-Fayette County Health Department provides a wide array of health services to Lexingtonians, including general outpatient clinical care, dentistry, X-ray, social services, school health and health and nutritional education and counseling. Additionally, the department is responsible for restaurant and hotel regulations and inspections.

The Health Department's Primary Care Center, licensed in 1980, combines traditional health services with nontraditional comprehensive health care service such as home health, health education, and adult day care. And the center combines preventive health care with the diagnosis and treatment of acute and chronic diseases. You can get more information about any of these programs by calling 288-2446, unless otherwise listed.

Payment for services is on a sliding-scale basis, but no one is refused services because they can't pay. Clinics are open Monday through Friday (except Wednesday) 8 AM-4:30 PM and Wednesday 12:30-7 PM. Appointments are necessary for all services and can be made by calling 288-2307.

Among services available in the Primary Care Center is the General Medical Clinic offering preventive and maintenance care for adults 18 and older, including physical examinations, diagnoses and treatment of acute and chronic health problems. The Child Health Program offers health care services to children up the age of 17, including vision and hearing testing, physical exams, developmental testing and counseling, and sickle cell and tuberculosis skin tests.

Other Primary Care programs and services include the Childhood Lead Poisoning Prevention Program (288-2431), the Family Planning Program for women ages 20-44 who are at or below 150 percent poverty level, a maternity program offering both medical and educational services (288-2436), breast and cervical cancer screening and education program (288-2436), a health care program for the homeless, and the Bluegrass District Commission for Handicapped Children Program (276-5563).

In addition, the Primary Care Center has a Communicable Disease Clinic that tests for, treats and monitors a variety of diseases including tuberculosis, sexually transmitted diseases (288-2461), and AIDS/HIV (288-AIDS).

The Health Department's Division of Community Nursing (288-2319) encompasses a broad range of home- and school-based health care programs as well as field testing programs for such things as tuberculosis and communicable diseases. Also, this division is responsible for many of the department's services to the elderly including the Center for Creative Living Adult Day Health Care Center (for more information, see Activities and Services for Older Adults) and the Elderly Health Maintenance clinics held monthly at different locations in the community for people 60 and older.

The Division of Nutrition and Health Education is responsible for many of the educational services offered by the Health Department. Among the programs in this division are the Diabetes Control Program (288-2310), the Fluoride Mouthrinse Program for elementary school children (288-2333), the Child Car Seat Program (288-2333) which loans car seats (required by law) to Lexingtonians, and the Teen Initiative Center, an after-school drop-in center for youngsters in the Bluegrass-Aspendale Housing District.

And if you have problems with anything from unsanitary public restrooms or pest infestations to sewage back-up, the Division of Environmental Health (231-9791) is the place to turn. Also covered under this division are such things as vending company licenses and mobile homes, public and private swimming pools, hotels, motels, restaurants and school inspections for code violations.

CENTRAL BAPTIST HOSPITAL
1740 Nicholasville Road   275-6100

Since opening in 1954, Central Baptist Hospital has remained dedicated to the tenets of its "Vision Statement" which emphasize the hospital's role as a provider of health-care services "through a Christ-centered, not-for-profit health-care system undergirded by a commitment to quality" to meet the changing needs of patients and health-care providers in the region.

As one of four acute-care hospitals in the Baptist Healthcare System, Central Baptist Hospital provides a wide variety of health and educational services, ranging from state-of-the-art radiology services to one of the finest obstetric and pediatric departments in the region. More Lexington babies are born at Central Baptist than at any other local hospital.

The 383-bed hospital has grown a great deal over the past 40 years. The most recent addition to the hospital complex is a six-story office building and expanded parking garage to accommodate more than 50 physicians' offices.

In addition to the "regular" services provided by a hospital — features include a 12-bed surgical intensive care unit with 14 surgical suites where more than 9,000 operations are performed each year, outpatient surgery facilities, emergency and rehabilitative services — Central Baptist also operates many special programs, such as home health services, community outreach programs and continuing education programs for doctors and nurses as well as community education programs.

Additionally, outpatient care is available in the areas of surgery, radiology, physical therapy, cardiovascular testing and respiratory care.

One of the best-known Central Baptist programs is its services for women and children, which include a 16-bed neonatal intensive care unit, a car seat loaner program, a lactation center to help new mothers learn more about breast-feeding, and the WomanCare Plaza, which covers gynecology and reproductive testing, counseling and management.

A guide to all services offered by Central Baptist is available from the hospital in the form of a handy, colorful brochure. Call for more information.

GOOD SAMARITAN HOSPITAL

310 South Limestone   *252-6612*

In 1940, it established Kentucky's first cancer clinic. In 1972, it established Kentucky's first hospital-based outpatient surgery service. In 1976, it installed Kentucky's first Total Body CT Scanner. And then there was the 1983 birth of a test tube baby, the first in the state.

It seems an appropriate list of accomplishments for one of Lexington's oldest hospitals, started in the late 19th century by a group of local church women who took the responsibilities and obligations of their Christian faith very seriously.

It all started in 1888 when Mary Eliza Harrison, a member of the Woman's Guild of Christ Church (Episcopal) began talking to other women in the guild about her dream of establishing a hospital. That dream was supported by the other women, and despite the seemingly insurmountable obstacles that stood between the announcement of Miss Harrison's dream and its realization, Mrs. Louisa Bruce got the project started by contributing a $5 bill to the hospital fund. That started an exhausting schedule of fundraising activities staged by the guild.

Their efforts paid off with the opening of the Protestant Infirmary in the Gratz home on East Short Street, a project made possible by community contributions of everything from butter and strawberries to linen, furniture and even a smoking jacket.

In 1892, the 80-bed Infirmary was incorporated, and in addition to offering medical care, the Good Samaritan School of Nursing began offering medical education to Lexington women, an effort that continued until the school closed in 1971.

In 1898, the Infirmary became Good Samaritan Hospital, and in 1907, it moved to a new 137-room facility on South Limestone.

During World War I, Dr. David Barrow recruited 233 enlisted personnel, 100 nurses (many from Good Samaritan) and 48 medical officers to go to England to help fight an influenza epidemic as well as helping those wounded in the war. Community contributions to that project so far exceeded the need that when the unit returned to Lexington, it used the leftover money to purchase Lexington's first X-ray equipment, which was used jointly by Good Samaritan and Saint Joseph Hospital.

Good Samaritan has continued to expand throughout the 20th century to its present 336-bed capacity. Among the hallmarks of the hospital today are its unique management team made up of physicians and administrators and its state-of-the-art medical treatment, which includes lesion lasers used to remove port wine stain birthmarks, age spots, freckles and tattoos. The hospital also features the Center for Behavioral Health (specialized inpatient and outpatient mental health services), BirthPlace (which includes a special care nursery), and in-house nursing home, the Kentucky Spine Institute, coronary and cancer care units, and occupational and physical therapy.

Where do I park?

When can I see my physician?

How many LDR rooms are there at the UK Birthing Center?

Do I need to check in early?

Questions?

How do I make an

Is my physician board certified?

kind medical specialist need?

Answers.

Whether you need a routine physical exam or highly specialized health care, one telephone call to UK Health Connection will open the door to an array of health care professionals and resources. UK Health Connection is a free service for help with physician referrals, clinic appointments, and information on health care services at the University of Kentucky Chandler Medical Center.

257-1000

Kentucky Clinic
University of Kentucky Hospital

UK HEALTH CONNECTION

HUMANA HOSPITAL LEXINGTON
150 North Eagle Creek Drive   268-4800

During the past two evaluation periods, a national accreditation commission has ranked Humana Hospital Lexington among the top 5 percent of hospitals nationwide in terms of the level of quality patient care. Now in its 11th year in Lexington, Humana Hospital has recently expanded several of its departments in its continuing effort to keep pace with what Lexington needs in terms of state-of-the-art health-care facilities.

The expanded emergency room is a prime example of this effort. With one of the most respected physician staffs in the area, Humana's emergency room is prepared to meet with nearly any kind of emergency. It is the only Lexington hospital fully equipped to deal with a chemical spill.

A recently expanded intensive care unit and cardiac care unit add to the services Humana offers. The hospital has 176 licensed patient beds. However, with the rising costs of health care, many people opt for outpatient treatment through Humana's day surgery program.

One of the most highly acclaimed programs at Humana is the Center for Urological Wellness, a program that deals with such conditions as impotency, urinary problems and sexual dysfunction. The Center for Urological Wellness uses laser surgery to perform many operations formerly done by conventional surgery methods.

SAINT JOSEPH HOSPITAL
Corner of Harrodsburg Road
and Waller Avenue   278-2436

The largest private not-for-profit hospital in Central and Eastern Kentucky, Saint Joseph Hospital traces its roots back to 1877 when the Sisters of Charity of Nazareth established it as Lexington's first hospital.

In 1959, the first open heart surgery in Central Kentucky was performed at Saint Joseph, and the Saint Joseph Heart Institute remains one of the cornerstones of the hospital's service areas. Since that first open heart surgery, the Heart Institute has treated more cardiac patients than all other Lexington hospitals combined. More than 100 specially equipped patient rooms, three operating rooms dedicated exclusively to cardiac surgery patients, and a cardiothoracic intensive care area provide care of the highest quality for the more than 3,000 patients who undergo cardiac catheterization and angioplasty procedures at Saint Joseph.

Other special programs at Saint Joseph include the Cancer Center, which addresses a wide range of needs of cancer patients and their families, from the latest in diagnostic services to psychological and spiritual support. The Sleep Disorders Center, Central Kentucky's first nationally accredited full-service sleep center, provides diagnosis and treatment of sleep disorders including insomnia and sleep apnea.

Other programs include the Chemical Recovery Center and the HealthNet IV aeromedical service, which provides helicopter transport services to patients throughout Eastern Kentucky.

UNIVERSITY OF KENTUCKY HOSPITAL (A.B. CHANDLER MEDICAL CENTER)
800 Rose Street   233-5000

A new $6 million Birthing Center opened in early 1993 is one of the hallmarks of the University of Kentucky Hospital, located on the UK campus. UK Hospital is second only to Central Baptist in the number of babies born each year, and the new high-tech Birthing Center makes the birth experience safer and more pleasant for both mother and newborn. UK Hospital has the only high-level neonatal intensive care unit in Central and Eastern Kentucky.

The hospital opened in 1962 and has been on the cutting edge of medical technology for nearly four decades. In 1964, UK Hospital's urology department was one of the first in the nation to begin kidney transplants. More recently, the hospital opened a $38 million critical care center housing the emergency room, operating rooms and a 32-bed intensive care unit. Its Level I Trauma Center is one of the top-ranked such centers in Kentucky.

Part of the UK Hospital system is the A.B. Chandler Medical Center, which has gained a national reputation for its state-of-the-art medical services. The only bone-marrow transplant program in Kentucky is housed here, as is the first non-prototype Magnetic Resonance Imaging diagnostic system in the world. The Medical Center has also been involved in the development of PASAR, which is a new kind of pacemaker used to treat severe cardiac arrhythmias.

MARKEY CANCER CENTER
800 Rose Street   257-4500

Opened January 1986, the Markey Cancer Center is a comprehensive center whose national reputation continues to grow as a result of its research, patient care, community outreach and education.

Markey Cancer Center patient care facilities include 56 beds, a bone marrow transplant unit, and a 7,000-square-foot outpatient care division, all integrated with the major services of the University of Kentucky Medical Center. The cancer center treats approximately 1,000 new cancer cases per year, offering about 150 treatment options, a number of which are the result of research conducted by physicians and researchers associated with the cancer center.

Markey Cancer Center Director, Dr. Kenneth Foon, is a national leader in research on the development of vaccines to treat different types of cancer.

CARDINAL HILL

2050 Versailles Road   *254-5701*

For more than half a century, Lexington's Cardinal Hill Hospital has been providing specialized rehabilitation services for kids and adults in Kentucky and the surrounding region. The program is the largest physical rehabilitation center in Kentucky.

The not-for-profit hospital has made a name for itself by providing, as its mission statement says, "the finest rehabilitative treatment for adults and children with physical disabilities from Kentucky and surrounding states."

An interdisciplinary team of nurses, occupational and physical therapists, physicians, speech and language pathologists and social workers addresses the wide range of needs of people dealing with orthopedic and neurological problems. Cardinal Hill provides rehabilitative services to amputees, people who suffer from debilitating arthritis, victims of head and spinal cord injuries, stroke victims and people needing neuromuscular rehabilitation as a result of diseases such as multiple sclerosis and Parkinson's disease.

To be admitted to Cardinal Hill, a person must be diagnosed as needing an intensive rehabilitation program and must have an identified source of funding and a support system of family or friends to help with the rehabilitation process and the transition back into an independent living situation.

CHARTER RIDGE HOSPITAL

3050 Rio Dosa Drive   *269-2325*

As the only freestanding Central Kentucky facility specializing in the treatment of psychiatric illnesses and addictive disease, Charter Ridge Hospital has been offering psychiatric and medical care to Central Kentuckians since 1982.

A variety of inpatient, partial hospitalization and outpatient services is designed to deal with emotional and behavioral difficulties ranging from addiction to drugs and/or alcohol to childhood and adolescent behavioral or emotional disorders.

Free confidential screening is available to help people determine what level of care would best suit them or the person about whom they are concerned. Call 268-6400 or 800-753-HOPE, ext. 400 for more information about the screening program.

The Steps to Recovery Program is a six-week-long intensive outpatient chemical dependency program that includes mandatory weeknight and Saturday morning sessions designed to help people recover from an addictive disease.

Partial hospitalization programs include the Young Champions program for emotionally troubled teens and the Voyages program for adults. These programs, scheduled for weekdays 8 AM-4 PM, provide intensive structured activities and therapy sessions as a more inexpensive alternative to inpatient services.

Another unique Charter Ridge program is Wings, that ministers to the spirit, soul and body using the spiritual resources of the Christian faith in conjunction with medical and psychiatric services.

EASTERN STATE HOSPITAL

627 West Fourth Street   *255-1431*

The second-oldest state psychiat-

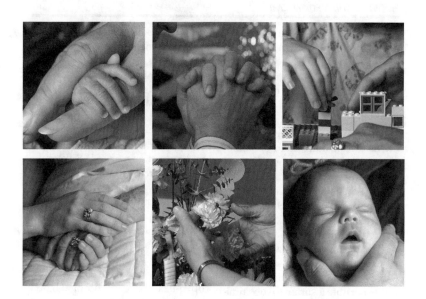

40 Years of Helping Hands

Need a Physician?
Let us help you find one.
Please call 606 - 278 - 9265 or
Statewide, 1 - 800 - 354 - 1212

CENTRAL **BAPTIST** HOSPITAL

1740 Nicholasville Road
Lexington, KY 40503
606 - 275 - 6100

ric hospital in the country, Eastern State Hospital opened in Lexington on May 1, 1824. The hospital provides psychiatric and medical services to adults from 74 counties in Central and Eastern Kentucky.

People dealing with emotional problems are usually referred to Eastern State from other state or community agencies, private physicians, individuals and families. Many patients are first evaluated by local Comprehensive Care centers (see listing for Bluegrass East Comprehensive Care Center later in this chapter).

The hospital provides treatment regardless of an individual's ability to pay for services. If Medicare, Medicaid or private insurance is not available to pay for hospitalization, fees are charged on a sliding scale.

Eastern State Hospital's services are concentrated in three main treatment programs. The Intensive Treatment Service emphasizes very focused short-term therapy with a quick return to the community — usually in about 30 days. For longer-term stays, patients may be placed in the Psychiatric Rehabilitation Service, which uses such therapy techniques as milieu therapy, group therapy and community involvement. Finally, the Medical and Extended Care Service is designed for those patients — typically geriatric patients — who require close supervision and medical attention while being hospitalized for psychiatric illness.

About 60 percent of those people discharged from Eastern State are able to live in their own homes or the home of a family member. Others are placed in halfway houses or other institutions. Eastern State employs about 500 full- and part-time staff members.

VETERANS ADMINISTRATION MEDICAL CENTER

2250 Leestown Road
Cooper Drive   *233-4511*

The Veterans Administration Medical Center provides inpatient and outpatient care to U.S. veterans from the area. This modern tertiary care facility comprises two divisions — the Leestown Road and Cooper Drive complexes — with a total of 730 hospital beds. The medical center also has a 100-bed nursing home.

Special patient care programs include substance abuse treatment, open-heart surgery, hospital-based home care, geriatric evaluation and rehabilitation, prosthetics, kidney dialysis, audio and speech pathology and nuclear medicine.

The more than 1,800 employees of the medical center are dedicated to providing quality health care to 140,000 outpatient visitors and 8,500 inpatients each year. The medical center serves the needs of veterans in Central and Eastern Kentucky as well as portions of Ohio, West Virginia and Tennessee.

Research is an integral part of medical center activities. An annual budget of $3.5 million supports 155 medical research projects, allowing the VA Medical Center to recruit and retain some of the region's most outstanding physicians and medical personnel.

SHRINERS HOSPITAL FOR CRIPPLED CHILDREN

1900 Richmond Road   *266-2101*

One of 19 such orthopedic hospitals operated by the Shriners (an

In Less Than a Month, Our Patients See Signs of Progress.

Getting people home is what Hillhaven's Steps Ahead program is all about. In fact, the majority of our patients get there within a month. The average stay in our subacute medical and rehabilitation facilities is less than 30 days. And compared to other settings, our payers save between 30 and 60 percent. That's progress. For more information on Steps Ahead or referrals to our network of 311 facilities nationwide, call 1-800-526-5782.

HILLHAVEN

international fraternity) worldwide, the Lexington Shriners Hospital for Crippled Children provides treatment for a variety of orthopedic problems free of charge to children up to the age of 18.

Some of the types of orthopedic problems the hospital works with include scoliosis (curvature of the spine), orthopedic complications of cerebral palsy, limb deficiencies and growth problems, spina bifida with myelodysplasia (paralysis of arms and legs caused by congenital misdevelopment of the spine and spinal nerves), club foot and dislocated hip, rickets and leg length discrepancies. The hospital also treats children with orthopedic problems that are the result of scarring and deformity from severe burns.

The Shriners Hospital emphasizes a family-centered treatment approach that focuses on both the healing of the body through medicine and the healing of the mind and spirit.

BLUEGRASS EAST
COMPREHENSIVE CARE CENTER
201 Mechanic Street   *233-0444*

As the only full-service mental health center in Lexington, Comprehensive Care serves people of all ages and income levels with a wide range of mental health problems.

Mental health services offered by Comprehensive Care include prevention and education programs, outpatient counseling and residential treatment programs. The center operates Monday through Friday 8 AM-5 PM and evenings by appointment. Appointments are necessary for those seeking service from the center. Comprehensive Care's staff of trained professionals includes psychologists, psychiatrists and physicians, social workers and nurses.

Individual, family and group counseling is available, as are psychiatric evaluation services, specialized programs for teens and support groups.

Comprehensive Care also operates a 24-hour-a-day crisis intervention hot line — 233-0444, 800-928-8000 outside the Lexington service area. More than 28,000 callers use this service each year.

Comprehensive Care facilitates and works with a number of other special programs in Lexington, ranging from drug and alcohol programs to intensive programs for children with long-term serious emotional problems. Call for a brochure detailing the services available. Treatment fees may be adjusted according to family size and income level.

HOSPICE OF THE BLUEGRASS
2312 Alexandria Drive   *276-5344*

Providing compassionate care for terminally ill patients and their families and providing a way for people to die at home with dignity, love and care is the heart of the mission of Hospice of the Bluegrass. In-home care for terminally ill people is provided through a multidisciplinary team of volunteers, physicians, nurses, social workers, home care aides and clergy members who attend to the spiritual, emotional and physical needs of patients. The service has been active for over 15 years. A number of support groups for family members and caregivers complement Hospice's efforts to offer services to the whole family.

Inside
Places of Worship

You probably couldn't tell it from the grand old churches that highlight many of Lexington's streets and neighborhoods, but the early years of Christianity in the area were far from grandiose. Many of what are today large and prominent congregations in Lexington began in the 1700s in log cabins, makeshift buildings, and even people's homes.

Lexington was part of the western frontier, and pioneer life was never a bed of roses. In fact, Kentucky's first sermon was preached by an Episcopal priest under an elm tree at Fort Boonesborough (just south of Lexington) in 1775.

Even when groups of people from the various denominations did begin to gather, they often found themselves without a "real" minister. The few preachers and priests in the region often served numerous small congregations on their "circuits." But despite the hardships, fledgling congregations under the leadership of such men of vision as Lewis Craig, Adam Rankin, Bishop Francis Asbury, James Moore, and Peter "Old Captain" Duerett clung to their beliefs and their mission to establish the churches of the future.

To this day, religion plays a big role in the lives of Lexingtonians, who live in the "Bible Belt" of the South. There are more than 240 churches and synagogues in Fayette County, representing some 50 denominations and religious groups, from Southern Baptist, Catholic and Methodist to Baha'i, Mennonite and Mormon.

This chapter cannot begin to highlight all the Lexington churches or even all the historic Lexington churches. So we have decided to focus on six of Lexington's oldest congregations: Christ Church Cathedral (Episcopal), First Baptist, First Presbyterian, Central Christian, Pleasant Green, and First United Methodist, as well as several other area churches and synagogues.

To find out more about specific churches and denominations, look in the phone book or contact the Chamber of Commerce at 254-4447.

CHRIST CHURCH CATHEDRAL
166 Market Street   *254-4497*

In 1796, a small group of Episcopalians began holding services in a makeshift frame building on the corner of what is now Market and Church streets. The services were led by James Moore, a Virginia native who had come to Lexington to become a Presbyterian minister. While pursuing his plans to enter the clergy, Moore accepted a teaching position at Transylvania Seminary (now Transylvania University).

It was during this time that Moore came in contact with the Episcopalian Society of Lexington. He found the tenets of the denomination to be much in line with his own doctrine, and he soon returned to Virginia to be ordained an Episcopal priest. Back in Lexington, he took on the position of rector of the small congregation until he went back into teaching full time at the Presbyterian Kentucky Academy. When the academy merged with Transylvania Seminary in 1799 to become Transylvania University, Moore became the university's first president.

The Market Street church continued to grow, and in 1808, the congregation built a brick house on the site of the old frame building. Money for the construction was generated in part through a lottery, a common way to raise money from the community in those days. A larger brick building was erected in the 1820s, and on March 17, 1847, the cornerstone for the present church building was laid. The church was enlarged to its present size during the Civil War.

Over the years, Christ Church has had many famous people worship beneath its grand vaulted ceiling. American statesman Henry Clay (a prominent Lexington lawyer) was among the most famous. He worshipped in the present church from 1847 to 1852, and was finally baptized there at the age of 70.

Today, Christ Church has 1,600 members under the leadership of the Right Rev. Don Adger Wimberly,

Bishop of Lexington, and the Very Rev. James L. Burns, Dean and Rector. It is well known throughout the region for its fine Choir of Men and Boys and the Girls' Choir, which perform various concerts and religious observances throughout the year. For 30 years, the church has maintained its choir program in the English tradition in affiliation with the Royal School of Church Music. The program has a strong emphasis on training children's voices, and boys 8-12 and girls 8-17 are encouraged to join, regardless of their musical background or training. Parents should contact Organist/Choirmaster Bruce Neswick for more information.

FIRST BAPTIST CHURCH OF LEXINGTON

548 West Short Street　　　*252-4808*

A fiery Baptist preacher from Virginia organized one of the earliest Baptist congregations in the Bluegrass on South Elkhorn Creek in the early 1780s. Elder Lewis Craig came to Kentucky with a group of Spotsylvania County Baptists in 1783 in search of religious freedom.

The South Elkhorn location, however, was a little too far from town for most Lexingtonians, so many of the area's earliest Baptists met in small groups in their cabins until the end of the 1780s. In 1787, a chaplain in the Continental Army during the Revolutionary War — Elder John Gano — came to Lexington. Two years later, along with Edward Payne and other Lexingtonians, he erected a church on Main Street, the site of the present church.

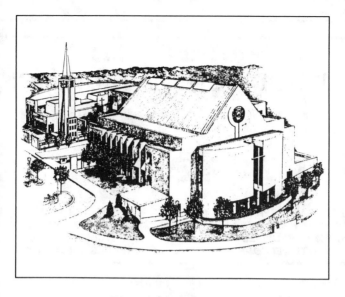

Centenary

A United Methodist Congregation

2800 Tates Creek Road   Lexington, KY 40502-2806

8:30, 9:50 & 11:00am Worship
9:45am Sunday School
Sunday & Wednesday Evening Activities
•Youth   •College   •Seniors   •Singles Activities
Christian Living Center Activities

269-2800

Dr. Al Gwinn, Senior Pastor

SOUTHERN HILLS UNITED METHODIST CHURCH

**SUNDAY CHURCH SCHOOL & WORSHIP 9:30 AM & 11:00 AM
YOUTH ACTIVITIES 5 PM**

277-6176

**SENIOR MINISTER
DONALD R. HERREN
NURSERY PROVIDED
"VISITORS WELCOME"**

**MONTESSORI & PRE-SCHOOL & DAY CARE
2356 HARRODSBURG RD. LEXINGTON
TURFLAND MALL AREA
ACTIVITIES BUILDING 277-8557**

FIRST PRESBYTERIAN CHURCH
174 North Mill Street   252-1919

In 1784, another Virginian — Adam Rankin — answered a call from Lexington Presbyterians to come to Kentucky. The congregation built a small log church on Rankin's land on the outskirts of town. The site of Mt. Zion Presbyterian Church is now covered by the University of Kentucky Agricultural Experiment Station on Limestone Street between Virginia and Washington avenues.

Within a decade, ideological differences split the church, and the group who opposed Rankin's views moved to a new location in what is now the heart of downtown Lexington on North Mill Street near Short Street. They built a church in 1790, and the congregation met there until 1805. These Mill Street Presbyterians would eventually grow into what is today First Presbyterian Church.

During the ensuing six decades, this congregation moved several times and built a number of church structures, including two major buildings at Broadway and Second. During the Civil War, as with many churches in the border states, the congregation was split into northern and southern segments.

In 1872, the congregation built what is now the nucleus of the First Presbyterian Church complex. One of the members of the congregation at that time just happened to be Cincinnatus Shyrock, younger brother of Gideon Shyrock who was the architect who brought Greek Revival architecture to western America. Cincinnatus designed the new church, which became the crowning achievement of his architectural career.

The church was dedicated on May 5, 1872. The church had cost $50,000 and was fully paid for at the time of the dedication.

Since that time, First Presbyterian has added a number of new structures to that first church, including two educational buildings in 1929 and 1959. The congregation today, under the leadership of Jeb Magruder, who went to prison for his role as a key figure in the 1972 Watergate scandal, numbers some 1,200 members.

First Presbyterian is active in a number of community service efforts, including Habitat for Humanity and the HOPE Center (homeless shelter). The church also runs the Learning Center, which is a child care facility for inner city kids.

A strong adult education program and a superb choir and musical program are among the many programs church members get involved in.

First Presbyterian is currently in the process of building a chapel addition to the main church. The sanctuary, which features a 100-year-old organ, was recently refurbished, maintaining its historical integrity.

CENTRAL CHRISTIAN CHURCH (DISCIPLES OF CHRIST)

205 East Short Street   *233-1551*

It was on the American frontier that the Disciples of Christ denomination began in Kentucky, Pennsylvania, West Virginia and Ohio in the early 19th century.

Central Christian is a direct descendent of the Cane Ridge Church founded by Robert Finley in 1790. Cane Ridge was the site of an explosive revival in 1801 that brought in thousands of people from throughout the region. This revival was part of the greater spirit of revival that was sweeping the region at that time and that would result in an erasure of denominational lines and the

emergence of the Christian Church and Disciples of Christ from Presbyterian, Methodist and Baptist roots. You can still visit the Cane Ridge meetinghouse in Paris (see "Inside Lexington's Neighbors").

Barton Stone was one of the leaders of this movement. He succeeded Finley in the leadership of the Cane Ridge church in the 1790s. During the next decade of preaching, Stone began to question the established doctrine of the older denominations. He and his followers, along with other leaders of this movement (Thomas and Alexander Campbell and James McGready), immersed themselves and their congregations in New Testament teachings, leading to the great western revival around the turn of the century.

The Cane Ridge Revival in 1801 was a sort of culmination of this revival. A week of intense preaching — often six or seven men preached at once in various locations — drew in crowds of 10,000-20,000 people.

During the following three decades, these ardent followers of Stone and Campbell aligned themselves in two camps — the Stone movement, known as the Christian Church, and the Campbell movement, known as the Disciples of Christ.

Lexington played a key role in the unification of these two groups into what is now the Christian Church (Disciples of Christ). In the early 1800s, the Disciples and the Christians were meeting in small groups in people's homes or in other makeshift worship areas. However in 1831, the Christian Church erected a church on Hill Street (now High Street), and it was in this church

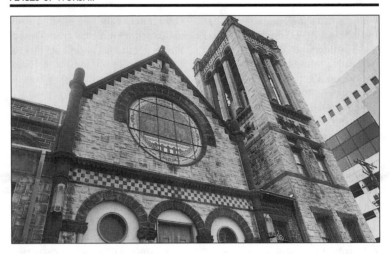

Central Christian Church, on East Short Street, is one of Lexington's oldest churches and one of the most active in the community.

that the Disciples and Christians finally united in 1832.

John Smith, a representative of the Disciples, exhorted the believers gathered on that historic occasion to join together: "Let us then, my brethren, be no longer Campbellites or Stoneites, New Lights or Old Lights, or any other kind of lights, but let us all come to the Bible, and the Bible alone, as the only book in the world that can give us all the Light we need," (from *Life of John Smith* by John Augustus Williams).

The Hill Street Church grew quickly, so quickly that by 1842 a large new building was constructed on Main Street, becoming the Main Street Christian Church.

Main Street Christian moved once again, again changing its name toward the end of the 19th century. The present-day Richardsonian Romanesque church was erected in 1894 on the site of the old Grand

Masonic Hall on the corner of Short and Walnut streets.

Today, under the leadership of senior minister M. Glynn Burke, Central Christian has some 2,000 members and is an active force in the Lexington community. Central Christian is a very community-oriented church, sponsoring a variety of service programs including the Central Church Apartments, a child care center and an adult day care center for senior citizens who need assistance in everyday living.

The Habitat for Humanity offices are housed in the Central Christian church complex, and the church is actively involved in that organization. It is also involved in plans to start a single resident occupancy complex which would offer affordable housing to Lexingtonians.

Beyond social and community

service efforts, Central Christian is also host to several musical groups throughout the year. The Lexington Philharmonic Orchestra performs chamber concerts there, and Musick's Company practices and performs at the church as well.

PLEASANT GREEN MISSIONARY BAPTIST CHURCH

540 West Maxwell Street   254-7387

The fourth oldest Black Baptist church in America, Pleasant Green Missionary Baptist Church traces its roots back more than 200 years to the remarkable efforts of a man with a mission and the drive to accomplish it. Peter Duerett, a slave known as "Old Captain" or "Captain," moved to Kentucky with his owners in the 1780s. In 1785, Captain organized a small Separate Baptist Church at the "head of Boone's Creek" (what is now Richmond Road just outside of town).

A few years later he hired himself and his wife out from their owner and moved into Lexington. In 1790, Lexingtonian John Maxwell allowed Captain some space on his land to build a cabin, and it was here, on the corner of Lexington and Euclid avenues, that Captain established the first Black Baptist Church west of the Alleghenies — called African Baptist Church (which was to become Pleasant Green).

The African Baptist Church met at that location until about 1812 when Captain began holding services at the old cotton factory lot on the corner of High and Limestone streets. He preached there and at various locations around town for the next decade

or so, his dedicated congregation following him.

In 1819, the church purchased land on the corner of Maxwell and Limestone. In 1822, they exchanged that land for a lot across the street (on the corner of Maxwell and Patterson streets) which had a building on it that could be used for worship. This is the site of the present Pleasant Green church.

Before his death at the age of 90 in 1823, the membership of Captain's church reached 300.

The name of the church was changed to Pleasant Green in 1829 after the hill on which it was located. The name was changed so that slaves wishing to attend services there would know where the church was located.

Today, Pleasant Green is an active part of the Lexington community. In addition to its own programs for all age levels, the church is involved in community service through its work and financial contributions to Habitat for Humanity, Black Achievers, Community Action and the Black Coalition. Its congregation of 1,900 members is pastored by Rev. T.H. Peoples, Jr. along with a ministerial staff of 11.

The offices of the Consolidated District, which includes 52 churches in Central and Northern Kentucky, are located at Pleasant Green. Rev. Peoples is the national president of the Progressive National Baptist Congress, an international organization serving churches in the United States, England, Africa and the Bahamas.

Pleasant Green is currently establishing a Christian Life Center to

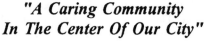

"A Caring Community In The Center Of Our City"

Calvary Baptist Church

150 East High Street - Lexington, KY 40507

Dr. Robert G. Baker, Pastor
Sunday School 9:45 a.m.
Worship 11:00 a.m.

house its many programs for church members as well as the community at large. In addition, the church recently purchased an entire city block on Pine and Patterson streets, and plans are in the works to build a five-story senior citizens home on the lot.

FIRST UNITED METHODIST
214 West High Street   233-0545

The denomination's opposition to slavery was a factor in the relatively slow start Methodism had in Kentucky in the late 1700s and early 1800s. However, Bishop Francis Asbury was a strong voice in frontier Kentucky, and in the spring of 1790 he came to Lexington to attend a two-day conference in the Methodist meeting house built by Richard and Sarah Masterson on their Fayette County property (now Leestown Road).

Frontier Methodists were served by the famed circuit preachers of the early years of American history. These mobile men of God rode thou-

sands of miles through rugged and isolated countryside from cabin to cabin and settlement to settlement ministering to small groups of believers.

While this was a boon to people in remote areas, the continued assignment of a circuit preacher to Lexington delayed the establishment of a permanent Methodist church here until the later part of the 18th century.

In 1789, local Methodists purchased a small cabin on the corner of Short and Back (now Dewees) streets. However, regular services were not held until 1819 when the Lexington Methodist congregation moved into its new two-story brick building on the north side of Church Street between Limestone and Upper streets.

The congregation moved to First United Methodist's present site in 1841.

The church today has 1,750 members under the leadership of James C. Stratton. An active presence in the Lexington community, First Methodist, along with Calvary Baptist Church, has sponsored the High Street Neighborhood Day Care Center for the past 22 years. The center offers child care to low income families on a sliding payment schedule.

The church is also a big supporter of Nathaniel Mission, located between Lexington and Versailles. In addition to worship opportunities, the mission has a medical and dental clinic, veterinary clinic and clothing bank for people who need these types of services but are unable to get them elsewhere.

Additionally, First Methodist works with Habitat for Humanity and the annual Lexington Clergy Campaign for the Homeless.

As far as services for members, First Methodist offers a number of unique ministry and Bible study opportunities, including a 32-week intensive Disciple Bible Study program and excellent music, youth and senior citizens programs and activities.

St. Peter Claver Catholic Church

410 Jefferson Street   254-0030

The only African-American Catholic Church in Lexington, St. Peter Claver has been serving the local parish for more than a century. There are about 150 families in the St. Peter Claver parish.

St. Peter Claver, under the leadership of Father Carl Johnson, offers parishioners a wide variety of programs in which they can get involved. For the men of the church, there is the St. Peter Claver chapter of the Knights of Columbus. The

Women's Auxiliary and the Progressive Adult Leaders (a Bible study and leadership group for people in their 20s) are also popular church groups.

St. Peter Claver has a Commission on African-American Catholic concerns, affiliated with the National Commission on African-American Catholic concerns, which provides a forum for the examination and discussion of issues relating to African-American Catholics in the area.

The church emphasizes a strong tie to cultural heritage along with the adherence to Catholic tenets. As a result, St. Peter Claver Church uses African art and decorations in the church, and the traditional Catholic mass features gospel music alongside traditional liturgical music.

Southland Christian Church

5001 Harrodsburg Road   224-1600

Although Southland Christian is actually located in Nicholasville, it is just across the county line from Lexington, and a big part of the 4,000-member congregation is composed of Lexingtonians.

Southland Christian is one of the largest and most active churches in Central Kentucky — evidenced in part by the attendance at the three Sunday morning services, which averages 3,300 people. The church is under the leadership of Senior Minister Wayne B. Smith, who has been with Southland since it began in 1957.

Southland's music ministry has become legendary in the area, and the church's two main special annual musical events — the Easter musical drama and the Living Christmas Tree — draw standing room only crowds. In fact, there are 11 performances of each of these events, and more than 2,000 people attend each performance.

Southland has a wide range of classes and groups for members and others in the community, ranging from weekly aerobics classes to the Divorce Support/ Divorce Recovery group that meets each Thursday night. Some 170 people in the 18-34 age group attend the Wednesday night Young Adult Bible class. There are also choirs for kids, youth and adults, as well as a Family Life Center with a gym where basketball programs for all ages are held.

TEMPLE ADATH ISRAEL

124 North Ashland Avenue   *269-2979*

As the oldest Jewish synagogue in Lexington, Temple Adath Israel has been an active part of the local community since it was established in 1903.

Affiliated with the liberal branch of Judaism, Adath Israel focuses on social justice as a central part of its mission. Along this line, participation in the local community is an important part of the lives of the close to 350 families and individuals who form the membership of the synagogue, which is under the leadership of Rabbi Jon Adland.

Adath Israel is actively involved in Habitat for Humanity, the Hope Center and the Lexington Clergy's Campaign for the Homeless each year. Additionally, congregation members hold a significant nonper-

ishable foods drive each fall, collecting some 2,300 pounds of food each year. An active women's group does many community service projects, including a Mitzvah Crib (a project to collect clothing and other items for area infants and children), and the selling of "house pins," unique accessories made by former homeless people on the East Coast. Profits from the sale of the pins are donated to local service agencies and organizations.

Temple Adath Israel also has a community preschool. Services are held Friday evenings at 8 PM (6 PM in July and August). There is also a Torah study two Saturday mornings a month, and a Sunday religious school that studies Judaism as a way of life.

CALVARY BAPTIST CHURCH

150 East High Street   *254-3491*

"A Caring Community of Faith in the Center of Our City" is how Calvary Baptist Church likes to identify itself. Indeed, the church and its 2,300 members and seven ministers hold as a primary mission the commitment to being a strong spiritual presence in downtown Lexington.

The Southern Baptist church has been serving Lexington for more than a century since its establishment in January 1875.

Today, under the leadership of senior minister Dr. Robert G. Baker, Calvary Baptist focuses on a wide range of ministries and services both for its members and the community at large. Since 1977, a strong emphasis has been placed on the church's singles ministry. Part of this ministry is an eight-week divorce recovery seminar that is held several times during the year. Since it started, 3,500 people have participated in the seminar.

Calvary Baptist's location near both major Lexington universities — Transylvania and UK — as well as its proximity to Georgetown College makes it an ideal place for a strong college ministry. It is one of the few Southern Baptist churches in the region that has a full-time college minister.

Community involvement also plays a big part in the church's programs. Calvary Baptist is currently working to establish a Christian counseling center that will be available for use by the community as well as church members. In cooperation with First United Methodist Church, Calvary also runs the High Street Neighborhood Center, a daycare program primarily for inner-city children.

Calvary Baptist is well known for its music program. The Sanctuary Choir has gained regional recognition throughout the South, and the graded choirs for children are a popular activity.

SOUTHERN HILLS UNITED METHODIST CHURCH

2356 Harrodsburg Road   277-6176

Celebrating its 35th anniversary this year, Southern Hills United Methodist Church has a distinct physical appearance. The church's unique architecture incorporates a large semicircular sanctuary that seats some 800 people. Southern Hills also has a large gymnasium complex where it houses many activities for church members and people in the community. In fact, the University of Kentucky basketball team has used the gym for practice in years past.

Southern Hills' 3,000-plus membership is under the leadership of senior minister Donald R. Herren. Of the many programs the church offers, the choir programs, led by Music Director Dick Kerr, are among the most popular. The handbell choirs are particularly unique.

As with other Lexington churches, Southern Hills is actively involved in community service. Each year the church facilitates one-third of a Habitat for Humanity house and participates in supporting Nathaniel Mission and God's Pantry. Church members collect clothing and toys for Appalachian youngsters, and they "adopt" families at Christmas.

Southern Hills also runs a large day-care center (licensed for 130 kids), as well as a Montessori school and Early Learning Lab for very young children.

CENTENARY UNITED METHODIST CHURCH

2800 Tates Creek Road   269-2800

Centenary United Methodist Church traces its Lexington roots back to the mid-1800s. Today, the church (which is growing so rapidly it has recently added a third Sunday morning service) is dedicated to a Christian ideal best explained by its mission statement: "The primary task of Centenary United Methodist Church is to help persons become disciples of Jesus Christ. We seek to be persons who are rooted in the Word, renewed through worship, and reaching into the world."

Centenary has a membership of about 1,800 under the leadership of senior minister Dr. Al Gwinn. However, there actually are approximately 3,000 folks who are associated with and participate in church programs. One of the most notable programs Centenary offers is the Wednesday night activities, which include family time and a supper followed by "electives," which are activities and classes for all ages. Centenary also has a fine choir program.

Community service plays a big role at the church, and members are involved with such projects as Habitat for Humanity and local, national and international missions. Centenary also has day-care and pre-school programs.

Inside
Media

Lexington's history as a communications leader dates to 1787, when John Bradford began publishing the weekly *Kentucke Gazette,* recognized as the first newspaper west of the Alleghenies. Although Bradford's background was in land surveying and he had no printing experience, he was nonetheless awarded the task of keeping the region's frontier dwellers informed as they made plans to separate from Virginia and form a new state. Ultimately the Kentuckians were successful, of course, and so was the *Gazette,* which soon learned how to spell Kentucky correctly. It continued to publish through the end of 1848.

The pioneer tradition continued with radio and television. The University of Kentucky, in conjunction with Louisville radio station WHAS, received national attention in 1929 when it began educational broadcasts from the Lexington campus to remote areas of the state. In 1940, UK started WBKY (now WUKY), the oldest university-owned, non-commercial FM station in the country. And the Lexington-based Kentucky Educational Television network, nationally recognized for its excellence, began broadcasting in 1968.

Newspapers

LEXINGTON HERALD-LEADER
100 Midland Avenue   231-3100

The *Herald-Leader,* which got its start in 1870 as the *Lexington Daily Press,* is the second-largest newspaper in Kentucky, covering most of the state, with a daily circulation of 127,000 and a Sunday circulation of 169,000. It has been Lexington's only daily newspaper since 1983, when the morning *Herald* merged with the afternoon *Leader.*

Although there have been periodic rumblings about starting a rival newspaper — usually following such perceived slights as an unsatisfactory report about the beloved UK Wildcats or an inflammatory Joel Pett editorial cartoon, or because of the paper's "liberal" editorial policy in general — none has materialized.

Before the merger, the Democratic *Herald* and the Republican *Leader* had been owned by the same company since 1937. Since 1973 the *Herald-Leader* has been owned by Miami-based Knight-Ridder Inc., whose other papers include *The Philadelphia Inquirer,* the *Detroit Free Press* and *The Miami Herald.*

The *Herald-Leader,* which has regional bureaus throughout Central

The Lexington Herald-Leader has been the city's only daily newspaper since 1983. The paper has bureaus throughout Central and Eastern Kentucky.

and Eastern Kentucky as well as a Washington bureau, has won two Pulitzer Prizes in recent years. In 1985 it earned one in investigative reporting — along with the wrath of thousands of Kentucky Wildcat basketball fans — with its series detailing improper payments to UK players. Editorial writer Maria Henson received another Pulitzer in 1992 for her series of editorials on battered women. Popular columnists include Merlene Davis and Don Edwards.

An extensive revamping of the newspaper's format and appearance was completed in 1993, making the *Herald-Leader* more reader-friendly and giving it a special tabloid section for each day of the week. Sunday brings "Sunday Business"; Monday covers "Your Money"; Tuesday rotates topics, including health, seniors and kids; Wednesday is "Community" day, with features on what your neighbors in Fayette and surrounding counties are doing; Thursday has "YOU," devoted to a variety of women's issues; Friday gives you the information you need to prepare for the blessed days off with "Weekender;" and Saturday provides "At Home," which addresses such Saturday-type subjects as gardening and fixing up your home.

THE KENTUCKY KERNEL
University of Kentucky
Journalism Building   257-2871

The Kernel is the student-run newspaper of the University of Kentucky. Free copies are available in racks around campus and in selected businesses nearby. *The Kernel,* which has seen a number of its alumni go on to distinguished journalism careers, is published Monday through Friday during the regular school year and on Thursdays during the summer.

THE RICHMOND REGISTER
380 Big Hill Avenue, Richmond   1-623-1669
The Register, published Monday through Friday afternoons and Saturday mornings, covers Madison County. It also includes some state, national and international news.

THE WOODFORD SUN
184 South Main Street, Versailles   873-4131
Established in 1869, this weekly can claim the distinction of being the oldest newspaper still being published in the Lexington metropolitan area. The paper, which covers Versailles, Midway, and the rest of Woodford County, is published every Thursday. Former Gov. A.B. "Happy" Chandler is a former president of the *Sun,* which continues to be published by the Chandler family.

THE JESSAMINE JOURNAL
507 North Main Street, Nicholasville   885-5381
This newspaper covers Jessamine County, including Nicholasville and Wilmore, and is published every Thursday.

THE BEREA CITIZEN
711 Chestnut Street, Berea   1-986-0959
This weekly paper, published every Thursday, features news of Berea and other parts of Madison County.

THE GEORGETOWN NEWS GRAPHIC
P.O. Box 461, Georgetown 40324   863-1111
This twice-weekly (Wednesday and Saturday) newspaper is the result of the recent merger of two weeklies. It focuses on Scott County, including Georgetown, Sadieville and Stamping Ground.

THE BOURBON COUNTY CITIZEN-ADVOCATE
123 West 8th Street, Paris   1-987-1870
We actually have two newspapers here: the *Citizen,* published on Wednesday, and the *Advertiser,* published on Monday.

THE WINCHESTER SUN
20 Wall Street, Winchester   1-744-3123
This source for Winchester-Clark County news is published Monday through Saturday.

Other Publications

ACE MAGAZINE
111 South Ashland Avenue   266-4441
"ACE" is an acronym for "Arts, Commentary and Entertainment," and that's what this monthly newsprint tabloid covers, with style and wit. Jennie Leavell, publisher and editor, has assembled a group of local contributing writers as well as syndicated features that take a sometimes irreverent, sometimes serious look at life in the Bluegrass and elsewhere. You can pick *ACE Magazine* up for free at numerous locations around town.

THE BLOOD-HORSE

1736 Alexandria Drive   *278-2361*

Published weekly by the Thoroughbred Owners and Breeders Association, *The Blood-Horse* is a slick magazine offering news, features, statistics and commentary on thoroughbred breeding and racing.

THE CATS' PAUSE

2691 Regency Road   *278-3474*

For the die-hard University of Kentucky sports fan, *The Cats' Pause* offers game recaps, recruiting news, analyses, statistics and opinions regarding UK and the Southeastern Conference. Publisher Oscar Combs puts out 35 tabloid issues a year: weekly from September through April and monthly from May through August.

HORSEMAN & FAIR WORLD

535 West Second Street   *254-4026*

This weekly publication is devoted to the sport of harness racing.

THE KENTUCKY MANUFACTURER
THE OHIO MANUFACTURER

2363 Chauvin Drive   *266-3303*

These two sister tabloids, published monthly by Industrial Marketing Inc., profile successful manufacturing operations in the two states, offer informative articles written by industry insiders, and provide news of plant openings and expansions.

THE LANE REPORT

269 West Main Street   *254-6600*

The Lane Report, a monthly publication subtitled "The Business & Economic News Magazine for Central Kentucky," offers analyses of relevant issues, interviews with business and political leaders, business updates, financial advice and profiles of area companies, entrepreneurs and women in business.

THE THOROUGHBRED TIMES

801 Corporate Drive   *223-9800*

The Thoroughbred Times, like *The Blood-Horse,* is a weekly publication for thoroughbred owners and breeders. As such, it has plenty of statistics on stakes races, sires and the like.

Television

WLEX-TV (Channel 18), an NBC affiliate

WKYT-TV (Channel 27), a CBS affiliate

WTVQ-TV (Channel 36), an ABC affiliate

WDKY-TV (Channel 56), a Fox affiliate

WKLE (Channel 46), Kentucky Educational Television/Public Broadcasting System.

In addition to these stations, cable subscribers receive such "basic" channels as CNN and CNN Headline News, ESPN sports programming, C-SPAN, MTV, WTBS (Atlanta), WGN (Chicago), American Movie Classics, The Nashville Network, The Learning Channel, The Discovery Channel, Nickelodeon and Comedy Central.

"Premium" cable channels, available for an additional fee, include Home Box Office, Showtime, Cinemax, The Movie Channel and The Disney Channel. TeleCable, the local cable provider, also offers a selection of pay-per-view programs.

A note about channel designations: Cable subscribers will notice that the cable numbers assigned to channels usually do not match the channel numbers. For example, WLEX is Channel 18, but it's number 8 on cable.

Radio

In most cases, radio station phone numbers listed are for request lines. Please note that radio formats do change from time to time.

FM STATIONS

WRFL 88.1
257-9735

The signal for Radio Free Lexington, a student-operated, commercial-free 250-watt station on the University of Kentucky campus, doesn't carry far beyond Fayette County. But what it lacks in broadcasting range it makes up in musical range. Mislabeled by some as strictly a "college" or "alternative" rock station, WRFL actually offers a smorgasbord of programs catering to tastes that include blues, jazz, rap, rockabilly, folk, Celtic, reggae, world beat, metal, women's and Christian. Pick up a program schedule at assorted on-campus sites or at Cut Corner Records at the edge of campus.

You probably won't care for all the programming on WRFL, but you may find yourself planning your schedule around the programs you do like. The disc jockeys aren't professional — after all, they're volunteers — but it's the music that matters. And much of this music you're simply not going to hear on a commercial radio station.

WVLK 92.9
280-9393

K-93 is the market's leading country station, and it's the station for those who keep up with "American Country Countdown." As with most modern country stations, the emphasis is more on Garth, Billy Ray and Mary-Chapin than George, Waylon and Loretta. For a little fun with your music, catch Andrea Sayre and Sam Stephens in the morning or Kathy Stamps at night, especially during her hilarious "Lovin', Leavin' or Lookin'" call-in request show.

WKQQ 98.1
280-7625

Double Q sticks primarily to classic '70s and '80s rock, with a sprinkling of today's rock hits thrown in for good measure. Kruser's morning show mixes rock with weird news and general irreverence. You can thank WKQQ for sponsoring the Decent Exposure battle-of-the-bands contest and Memorial Stakes Day at The Red Mile, both annual Lexington traditions.

WUKY 91.3
257-3221

This National Public Radio affiliate, broadcast from the University of Kentucky's McVey Hall, puts its musical emphasis on jazz and blues. You can also catch news and information programs like NPR's award-winning "All Things Considered" (host Noah Adams is a Kentucky native whose public radio career began in Lexington) and "Morning Edition," as well as Garrison Keillor.

Insiders listen to
"The Hot Burrito Show" from 9 AM to noon Sundays on
WRFL.

WEKU 88.9
1-623-1655

This National Public Radio affiliate, broadcast from the Eastern Kentucky University campus in Richmond, emphasizes classical music.

WWYC 100.1
280-9100

Since switching from a Top 40 format to "young country" last year, this station, formerly known as WLFX, has been making inroads into K-93 territory. As with its country competitor WVLK-FM, you're far more likely to hear Hank Williams, Jr., than his daddy.

WGKS 96.9
280-5477

KISS 96.9 specializes in "lite rock with less talk."

WMXL 94.5
280-9450

MIX 94.5 plays adult contemporary music.

WCKU 102
280-9258

U102 is the choice for urban contemporary music.

WTKT 103
299-1103

Oldies 103 boasts "all oldies all the time."

WJMM 106
873-8096

WJMM plays adult contemporary Christian music.

AM RADIO STATIONS

WVLK 590
280-9590

Lexington listeners rely on WVLK-AM for broadcasts of Wildcat basketball and football, high school sports and thoroughbred racing. This is the station to catch the coaches' call-in shows and other sports commentary as well. You'll also hear Paul Harvey, Bruce Williams, news, traffic reports, plus advice on such topics as the law, health, finance, gardening and travel. WVLK-AM also plays adult contemporary music, and Jack Pattie is one of the market's top morning hosts.

WLXG 1300
280-5477

Talk Radio 1300 features plenty of talk about news, business and sports, including Rush Limbaugh's controversial three-hour daily talk show as well as "The Original Sportsline" call-in show with Pete Kules and Scott Pierce.

WLAP 630
280-9527

WLAP features Business Radio

WRFL-FM (88.1) is a student-operated, commercial-free station on the University of Kentucky campus that plays a wide range of music.

Network programming 24 hours a day, with the exception of religious broadcasts on Sunday mornings.

WBBE 1580

299-1103

WBBE, which calls itself Stardust, spotlights Big Band music.

WCGW 770

887-4182

WCGW plays country gospel music.

WNVL 1250

885-6031

WNVL plays country throughout the week and gospel on Sunday.

Inside
Service Directory

Whether you're new to the Lexington area or just visiting, this service directory will point you in the right direction to obtain many of the services you will need. Included in this section is information on utilities, US Post Office locations, Lexington-Fayette Urban County Government services, licensing, voter registration, the public library system, support groups, 12-step programs and hotlines, and a listing of help numbers.

For more detailed information on such things as parks and recreation activities, senior citizens, schools, and various groups where you can volunteer your time or donate goods, services or money, check the specific chapters dealing with those areas.

Utilities

KENTUCKY UTILITIES
Quality Street   255-0394

BLUEGRASS RURAL ELECTRIC COOPERATIVE
1201 Lexington Road,
Nicholasville   885-4191

The Bluegrass RECC office that serves Fayette County is just across the county line in Jessamine County (Nicholasville). The road that connects the two cities is called Nicholasville Road in Lexington and Lexington Road in Nicholasville.

COLUMBIA GAS
166 N. Martin Luther King Blvd.   255-3612

GTE (TELEPHONE)
318 E. Main Street   223-9422

KENTUCKY-AMERICAN WATER CO.
2300 Richmond Road   269-2386

TELECABLE OF LEXINGTON
Palumbo Drive   268-1134

CELLULAR ONE
112 Mt. Tabor Road   268-2355

US Postal Service

MAIN OFFICE
1088 Nandino Blvd.   231-6700

BARR STREET STATION (DOWNTOWN)
101 Barr Street   231-6726

BLUEGRASS STATION
3525 Lansdowne Drive   231-6740

GARDENSIDE STATION
1729 Alexandria Drive   231-6731

HENRY CLAY STATION
365 Duke Road   231-6742

LIBERTY ROAD STATION
2041 Creative Drive   231-6778

Photo: Lexington Herald-Leader

A Kentucky Utilities worker prepares to reorient the crossarms on a utility pole.

Lexington-Fayette Urban County Government Services

From garbage pick-up and pothole repair to literacy training, carpooling and sewer usage, many of the services you will need in Lexington are provided through the Lexington-Fayette Urban County Government. Offices are in the government center at 200 E. Main Street, unless otherwise noted. For general information and referral, call the Public Information Office at 258-3010. The government center switchboard number is 258-3000.

The following list will provide you with detailed information about services provided by various departments of the Lexington-Fayette Urban County Government.

MAYOR'S CAREER RESOURCE AND TRAINING CENTER
258 Clark Street   258-3140

The Mayor's Career Resource and Training Center administers the federal Jobs Training Partnership Act, or JTPA. The center also offers a variety of job training, literacy and career counseling services.

OFFICE OF ECONOMIC DEVELOPMENT
258-3131

Planning and developing public and private partnerships, working with local businesses and industries as well as those thinking about relocating to Lexington, and developing programs to assist and foster the growth of area small businesses are among the many functions of the Office of Economic Development.

CARNEGIE CENTER FOR LITERACY AND LEARNING
251 West Second Street   245-4175

Housed in the beautifully restored old public library on picturesque Gratz Park, the Carnegie Center for Literacy and Learning addresses a wide range of needs of the community, from basic literacy skills to advanced writing. The center has many media resources, including personal computers, VCRs and laser disc players that are available for public use in the center at no charge. The center also offers classes in various levels of writing and computer skills, and hosts readings by local writers throughout the year. Operation Read (literacy program), The Writer's Voice (literary program), and the Bluegrass Writing Project are all housed in the Carnegie Center.

KENTUCKY WORLD TRADE CENTER
410 West Vine Street   258-3139

Promoting growth in the business world as well as in the local and regional job market is one of the primary missions of this non-profit corporation. The Kentucky World Trade Center offers business and trade counseling and education, helps local business people establish contacts around Kentucky and the world, and hosts trade missions and trade fairs.

DIVISION OF TAX COLLECTION
258-3340

When you have to pay anything from parking tickets to property taxes, this is the department to contact. The Division of Tax Collection receives all money and fees owed to

SOME OF THE LOWEST ELECTRIC RATES IN THE NATION AREN'T ALL WE HAVE TO OFFER.

IF YOU'RE MOVING TO LEXINGTON FROM ANOTHER PART OF THE COUNTRY, WE THINK YOU'RE IN FOR A PLEASANT SURPRISE. NOT ONLY ARE OUR RESIDENTIAL RATES AMONG THE LOWEST, BUT OUR SERVICE IS JUST AS CONSUMER-FRIENDLY.

WE PRIDE OURSELVES ON BEING PROMPT AND RELIABLE, AND OFFER CONVENIENT PROGRAMS LIKE BUDGET BILLING AND AUTOMATIC PAYMENT. WE ALSO HAVE CUSTOMER SERVICE CENTERS AT THREE HANDY LEXINGTON LOCATIONS. AND, AS KENTUCKY'S "ENERGY COUNSELER," WE CAN SHOW YOU WAYS TO SAVE BOTH ENERGY AND MONEY.

LIKE TO KNOW MORE? CALL US AT (606) 255-2100, OR WRITE TO KENTUCKY UTILITIES CUSTOMER SERVICE, ONE QUALITY STREET, LEXINGTON, KY 40507.

KENTUCKY UTILITIES COMPANY

WE HAVE THE ENERGY TO SERVE YOU

the Urban County Government, including occupational license fees, sewer user fees, ambulance billings, payroll taxes, parking tickets and property taxes.

DIVISION OF SANITATION

2181 Old Frankfort Pike   258-3470

When you move to Lexington, the Urban County Government's sanitation department is who you should call first to try to get your garbage pick-up arranged. The Division of Sanitation is responsible for garbage pick-up in the urban services area which includes most of the Lexington metropolitan area. The Division of Sanitation also oversees dumpster service, dead animal pick-up, special pick-ups for large refuse items, the "Rosie" recycling pick-up program, and repairs to "Herbie the Curbie" and "Rosie" home trash receptacles. "Herbie the Curbie" and "Rosie" are the plastic trash cans (with wheels!) provided by the city. There are very specific regulations concerning the use of these city-owned receptacles, and the sanitation department can provide you with a handy brochure outlining everything you need to know and do to make sure your trash is properly picked up.

If you do not fall within the urban services area, the Division of Sanitation will tell you which private companies pick up trash in your area.

DIVISION OF STREETS AND ROADS

1555 Old Frankfort Pike   258-3450

The Division of Streets and Roads becomes one of Lexington's most vital services during periods of bad weather, such as winter snows and summer wind and thunder storms. This department is responsible for servicing all city and county roads, except those in the state and federal highway system. Services such as pothole repair, snow removal, street cleaning, handicap ramp installation on sidewalks, and dead or hazardous tree removal (in specific areas) all fall within the jurisdiction of this department.

DEPARTMENT OF PUBLIC SAFETY

121 N. Martin Luther King Blvd.   258-3796

The Urban County Government's Department of Public Safety employs more people than any other government department. This department has six divisions and oversees the Detention Center and the Humane Society as well:

• **Division of Building Inspection**, 200 East Main Street, 258-3770

• **Division of Communications**, 121 North Martin Luther King Blvd., 258-3103

• **Division of Environmental and Emergency Management**, 121 North Martin Luther King Blvd., 258-3784

• **Division of Fire and Emergency Services**, 219 East Third Street 254-1120, Emergency 911

Kids can let their imaginations soar in an F-16 familiarization cockpit at The Lexington Children's Museum.

• **Division of Police**, 150 East Main Street, 258-3600, Emergency 911

• **Division of Alcoholic Beverage Control**, 121 North Martin Luther King Blvd., 258-3796

DEPARTMENT OF SOCIAL SERVICES
200 East Main Street   258-3800

Many government services that concern the well being and functioning of individuals fall under the umbrella of the Department of Social Services. These include services to senior citizens, victims of neglect and abuse, and even educational services. There are three main divisions in this department:

DIVISION OF ADULT SERVICES
258-3810

For Lexingtonians 18 and older, the Division of Adult Services provides help to adults who have been abused, neglected or exploited; offers assistance with the payment of rent, utilities and cremations to those in crisis situations (eligibility requirements must be met); collects and disburses child-support payments; and operates the Lexington Senior Citizens Center (for more on this center and other such programs, see our chapter on Retirement and Senior Citizens Services).

DIVISION OF FAMILY SERVICES
Family Care Center,
1135 Red Mile Place   288-4040

With programming targeted at parents ages 17-21 years old and their children, Family Services provides child care, education, health and social services in an integrated environment designed to help families become self-sufficient. The services offered by this department are not limited to parents in that age group, however. Other families can receive help at the Family Care Center.

DIVISION OF YOUTH SERVICES
115 Cisco Road   253-1581

Merged from two other city departments in 1991, the Division of Youth Services is a multi-service agency providing assistance to local youth and their families in a campus setting. Services provided by this division include such things as educational training, social work services to neglected, dependent, wayward, status offender and pre-delinquent youth, and probation and court services.

DIVISION OF PARKS & RECREATION
545 North Upper Street   288-2900

Part of the Urban County Government's Department of General Services, the Division of Parks & Recreation is responsible for the maintenance and development of more than 3,000 acres of public parks, playgrounds, swimming pools and golf course in Lexington. For more information on specific services offered by this division, see "Inside Kids' Stuff" and "Inside Parks & Recreation."

DEPARTMENT OF HOUSING
200 East Main Street   258-3260

The Department of Housing was formed in 1988 to meet the housing needs of Lexingtonians through services offered by its various departments:

DIVISION OF HOUSING AND COMMUNITY DEVELOPMENT
258-3070

This division manages all state and federal grants to fund community development and other public projects, and the housing rehabilitation and relocation programs. It also provides financial assistance to property owners to help them make necessary home repairs.

DIVISION OF HOUSING MAINTENANCE
258-3270

This division is responsible for building inspections and issuing notices for repairs, condemnation or demolition of large structures.

HISTORIC PRESERVATION OFFICE
258-3265

The Historic Preservation Office surveys and designates historic Lexington resources. It also works toward firmly establishing and implementing a preservation plan for Lexington, and addressing preservation issues as part of the city's comprehensive planning process.

TENANT SERVICES AND HOUSING COUNSELING
258-3960

This division addresses special housing needs in the community, including providing counseling and guidance to lower-income individuals and families with housing and related economic and legal concerns. These services include mediation in tenant/landlord conflicts and home ownership counseling.

Recycling

As concern over environmental issues has grown in Lexington over the past decade or so, the increased efforts to help all citizens participate in recycling programs on some level have produced many valuable environmental protection programs. Some of those programs are listed below:

HOUSEHOLD ITEM RECYCLING

If your garbage is picked up by the Urban County Government, you can participate in the Rosie recycling program, which provides free weekly curbside pick-up of such household items as glass, newspapers, plastics, mixed paper and cans.

VEHICLE OIL RECYCLING

Through the city's Protect the Environment Through Recycling Oil, or PETRO, program, you can take your used oil to the fire station at 2234 Richmond Road where it is collected in special pods. Other recycling sites include the Lexington Recycling Center at 845 Angliana Avenue, and many local service stations. You can find out the closest oil recycling center by calling 258-3784.

CHRISTMAS TREE RECYCLING

The Urban County Government's Division of Streets and Roads picks up Christmas trees immediately following the holiday. The trees are chipped into mulch for public use. Call 258-3450 for more information.

GRASS CLIPPING RECYCLING

Grass clippings, leaves and yard waste unnecessarily clog our landfills. By leaving clippings on your lawn when you mow, reusing them as mulch for your garden and composting them with other yard waste, you can help with the landfill overcrowding problem. The city provides free wooden pallets for compost bins, and they are available by calling 258-3470. The Fayette County Extension Office, 257-5582, can also provide you with information about yard waste recycling.

Other Lexington recycling centers include Baker Iron & Metal, 255-5676; Commonwealth Aluminum Recycling, 252-1237, and the Lexington Recycling Center, 231-7770. Call the Urban County Government Recycling Coordinator at

258-3470 for more help and information.

Licenses

VEHICLE LICENSE PLATES
County Clerk's Office,
162 East Main Street   253-3344

People relocating to Kentucky from another state or country need to get a Kentucky license plate for their vehicles within 15 days after establishing their Kentucky residency. Information on various aspects of licensing, including handicap and motorcycle classifications, is available Monday-Friday, 8:30 AM-4 PM, in Room 108 of the County Clerk's Office.

MARRIAGE LICENSES
162 East Main Street   253-3344

The cash fee for a marriage license is $22. Checks are not accepted. There is no waiting period, physical or blood test required for obtaining a marriage license. The office is open Monday-Friday, 8:30 AM-4 PM.

HUNTING AND FISHING LICENSES
162 East Main Street

Licenses expire December 31 of each year. They are available in Room 107 of the County Clerk's Office, Monday-Friday, 8:30 AM-4 PM, and at various locations around town, such as convenience stores.

DRIVER'S AND BOAT LICENSES
162 East Main Street,
Circuit Court Clerk's Office   254-9861
2519 Regency Road   278-2315

If you have a valid out-of-state license, you must pass a written test and eye test (a road test is also required in some cases) to obtain a Kentucky driver's license. If you don't have a valid license, you must apply for one, pass a written test and eye test to obtain a learner's permit, which costs $2. After one month, you must then pass a road test to obtain your license. Licenses cost $8 and are good for four years. Combination driver's and motorcycle licenses cost $14 per year.

Downtown hours are 8:30 AM-6 PM Monday, and 8:30 AM-4:30 PM Tuesday-Friday, with testing hours 8:30 AM-3:30 PM.

Regency Road hours are Monday and Wednesday-Friday, 9 AM-5 PM, and Tuesday 9 AM-7 PM. Tests for permits and out-of-state drivers are given on Tuesday and Thursday only from 9-11:20 AM and 1-4:20 PM.

Boat licenses are available at the same places and hours.

PET LICENSES
Humane Society,
1600 Old Frankfort Pike   252-1771

State and local regulations require Lexington pet owners to purchase and maintain the proper licenses for their pets. Dog licenses are good from July 1 till June 30 of the following year and cost $1.50 per year for spayed and neutered dogs, and $8.50/year for unaltered dogs. Cat licenses (required only in the Lexington urban services area — most developed areas in the city fall within this jurisdiction) are $3 for spayed and neutered cats, $10 for unaltered cats. They are available from the Lexington Humane Society or most area pet stores.

Voter Registration

COUNTY CLERK OFFICE

162 East Main Street 255-7563 or 253-3344

To register to vote, you must be a U.S. citizen 18 or older, you must have been in residence in the state and precinct in which you are registering by the date of the next election, and you must be properly registered within the county in which you plan to vote.

To register by mail, send your name, address and proper state registration form to the County Clerk, 162 East Main Street, Lexington. You can also come to the office in person 8:30 AM-4 PM Monday-Friday. Registration books close ten days prior to special elections and 30 days prior to general elections.

Lexington Public Library

Lexington has an excellent public library system that encompasses four branches in addition to the main Central Library location downtown on Main Street. Library locations and hours of operation are listed below. Anyone living or working in Lexington is eligible for a library card. Overdue fines are 10 cents per day.

CENTRAL LIBRARY

140 East Main Street	231-5530
Monday-Thursday	9 AM-9 PM
Friday-Saturday	9 AM-5 PM
Sunday	1-5 PM

EAGLE CREEK BRANCH

101 North Eagle Creek Drive	231-5560

LANSDOWNE-EMRATH BRANCH

3317 Tates Creek Road	231-5580

NORTHSIDE BRANCH

1737 Russell Cave Road	231-5590

SOUTHSIDE BRANCH

3340 Holwyn Road	231-5570

All branch hours:	
Monday-Thursday	9:30 AM-9 PM
Friday-Saturday	9:30 AM-5 PM
Sunday	1-5 PM

Support Groups and Hot Lines

Abuse Hotline	(800) 752-6200
Abuse Victims Support	858-4181
Adult Children of Alcoholics	255-2374
AIDS Info-Kentucky AIDS	
Education Program	(502) 564-6539
AVOL (AIDS Volunteers of Lexington)	254-2865
Al-Anon	277-1877
Al-Ateen	277-1877
Alcoholics Anonymous	276-2917
Alzheimer's Association Support Group	252-6282
American Cancer Society Hospital	
Visitation Groups	276-3223
American Red Cross	
"Get to Know Us"	253-1331
Anxiety and Panic Attack	
Support Group	269-2325
Arthritis Foundation Caring	
Together Support Group (ACT)	255-6841
Association for Children for the	
Enforcement of Child Support	268-1485
Attention Deficit Disorder	
Support Group	272-2166
Beginning to Understand	
Downs (BUD)	273-9094
Bereaved Spouse Support	276-5344
Blind Buddies	254-6795
Bluegrass Council of the Blind	259-1834
Bluegrass Mothers of Twins	
and Triplets	263-3680
Bluegrass Alliance for the	
Mentally Ill	266-3448, 271-5520
Bone Marrow Transplant	
Support Group	233-5521

Caregivers Support Group 276-5344
Central Kentucky Depressive and
    Manic Depressive Asso. 277-4909, 268-4775
Central Kentucky Independent
    Living Association 277-8500
Child Protection Hotline (800) 752-6200
Chronic Fatigue Immune Dysfunction
    Syndrome Support Group 887-2171
Chronic Pain Support Group 254-5701
Cocaine Hotline (800) COCAINE
Co-Dependents Anonymous 269-2325
Compassionate Friends 873-8853
Diabetes Support Group 288-2473
Divorce Support Group 254-3491
ElderCare Locator (800) 677-1116
Expressive Therapy Kids Group
    (children served by Hospice) 276-5344
Families Anonymous 269-2325
Fresh Start of the American
    Cancer Society 276-3223
Gamblers Anonymous 277-8236
Gay and Lesbian Services Organization 231-0335
Hallerman-Strieff Syndrome
    Support Group 273-6928
Head Injury Support Group 272-4519
    254-5701, ext. 506
Healing Hearts 281-8339
Help Smokers Quit
    (American Cancer Society) 276-3223
Hospice of the Bluegrass 276-5344
Incest Survivors 253-2511
Kentucky AIDS Hotline (800) 654-AIDS
KIPWAC Support Group
    (for people with HIV/AIDS) 281-2100
Kidney Foundation 277-8259
La Leche League 266-6392
Laryngectomee Visitation 276-3223
Learning to Live Through Grief 276-5344
Look Good...Feel Better 252-6612 ext. 8185
Lost Chord Club of the American
    Cancer Society 276-3223
Lupus Support Group 233-6700, 233-5038
Multiple Sclerosis
    Support Group (800) 873-6367
Narcotics Anonymous 253-4673
National AIDS Hotline (800) 342-AIDS
Nurses Assisting Nurses 257-1587
Overeaters Anonymous 271-4655
Parents Anonymous (800) 432-9251
Parents Without Partners 272-1165

Parents Support Group for Severely
    Emotionally Disturbed Children 254-3106
Parkinson Support Group 299-0804, 278-5957
Physicians Referral Service (800) 633-8100
Pregnancy Help Center 278-8469
Reach to Recovery of the
    American Cancer Society 276-3223
Recovery Inc. 266-3376 after 5 PM
Runaway Hotline 254-2501
Safe Place 254-2501
Sandwich Generation Support Group 277-7511
Scleroderma Support Group (800) 722-4673
Spina Bifida Support Group 269-5707
Spinal Cord Injury Support Group 254-5701
Stroke Support Group 254-5701 ext. 348
Spouse Abuse
    Crisis Line 255-9808, (800) 544-2022
Survivors of Suicide 271-6819
Talk About Cancer
    (TAC) 257-4447, (800) 4-CANCER
Thursday Group (women who have and have
    had breast cancer) 269-4836, 224-1096
Time Out: Lexington (cancer patients and
    their families) 272-3732, 278-3436
Tourette Syndrome Association-
    Kentucky Chapter 277-1145
United Ostomy Association 276-3223
Us Too (Prostate Cancer
    Support Group) 276-3223
Women Reaching Out (women who have
    or have had gynecologic cancer) 276-3223

Other Help Numbers

Animal Control 252-7733
Better Business Bureau 259-1008
Birth/Death Certificates (502) 564-4212
Children's Advocacy Centers
    of the Bluegrass 252-3571
Coroner 272-3354
CPR Training 233-6613
Crime Stoppers 253-2020
Crisis Intervention 233-0444
Dream Factory 254-9474
Fayette County Health Department 288-2395
FBI 254-4038, (800) 752-6000
Food Stamps 253-1500

At Your Service

Nutrition
Juice Plus +
309 Irvine Road
(606) 269-9099

Kentucky State Police	(800) 222-5555
League of Women Voters	272-5322
Lexington Child Abuse Council	259-1974
Lexington Hearing and Speech Center	268-4545
Planned Parenthood	252-8494

Poison Control	278-3411, (800) 722-5725
Rape Crisis Center	253-2511
Salvation Army	252-7706
US Secret Service	(502) 582-5171
Women's Center of Central Kentucky	254-9319

Index of Advertisers

Inside
Index